ARCHAEOLOGY AT CERROS, BELIZE, CENTRAL AMERICA

David A. Freidel
Series Editor

ARCHAEOLOGY AT CERROS, BELIZE, CENTRAL AMERICA

Volume III
The Settlement System in a Late Preclassic Maya Community

by

Vernon L. Scarborough

SOUTHERN METHODIST UNIVERSITY PRESS · 1991

ARCHAEOLOGY AT CERROS, BELIZE, CENTRAL AMERICA
VOLUME III, THE SETTLEMENT SYSTEM IN A LATE PRECLASSIC MAYA COMMUNITY

Copyright © 1991 by Southern Methodist University Press
Box 415
Dallas, Texas 75275
Printed in the United States of America

The paper in this book meets the standards for permanence and durability
established by the Committee on Production Guidelines for Book Longevity
of the Council on Library Resources.

Library of Congress Cataloging in Publication Data

(Revised for volume 3)

Archaeology at Cerros, Belize, Central America.

     Includes bibliographical references.
     Contents: v. 1. An interim report / volume editors,
Robin A. Robertson, David A. Freidel ; contributors,
Helen Sorayya Carr . . . [et al.] — v. 2. The artifacts /
by James F. Garber — v. 3. The settlement system in a
late preclassic Maya community / by Vernon L. Scarborough.
     1. Cerros site (Belize)   2. Mayas—Antiquities.
3. Indians of Central America—Belize—Antiquities.
4. Belize—Antiquities.   I. Freidel, David A.
F1435.1.C43A73   1986   972.82'1   86-3843
ISBN 0-87074-214-0   (v. 1 : alk. paper)
ISBN 0-87074-285-X   (v. 2 : alk. paper)
ISBN 0-87074-307-4   (v. 3 : alk. paper)

COVER ILLUSTRATION:

Initial field map of the Cerros settlement following the 1978 field season. Additional
survey and excavation allowed greater accuracy in the location and form of structures,
as well as the expansion of the survey perimeter (see Figs. 2.1 and 2.2).

To my parents
Jim and Lucille Scarborough

CONTENTS

ACKNOWLEDGMENTS

Many people have helped shape the form and direction of this monograph. While I was at Southern Methodist University, David Freidel offered me the opportunity to do dissertation research at Cerros. He has influenced my theoretical orientation and encouraged my diverse interests from the outset of my graduate training. Further, Garth Sampson and Anthony Marks provided methodological rigor to my work during my entire stay at Southern Methodist University. Both cultivated the ecological perspective of the present piece. Wyllys Andrews V of the Middle American Research Institute also encouraged my research and furnished me with advance information regarding the Preclassic community of Komchen. Richard E. W. Adams has been supportive of the Cerros Survey Project and provided me with the side-looking airborne radar imagery I use in the text.

The archaeological commissioner of Belize has supported the Cerros Project from the beginning, and the merchants and laborers of Corozal have repeatedly helped with logistics. However, special mention must be made of the kind and diligent people from the villages of Chunox and Copperbank. They have provided the major work force for the Cerros Project and have become close friends of many of the staff. The six seasons the Cerros Survey Project has been in the field (initiated in 1975) not only have produced a force of trained archaeological technicians in these villages, but have promoted a better understanding of Maya heritage and perhaps village identity. I am grateful for the opportunity to have worked in Belize.

The senior staff members of the Cerros Project have been very supportive. Our work at Cerros must be considered a team effort, with each person contributing valuable input to the overall success of the project. I have benefited from and enjoyed countless discussions with Sorayya Carr, Cathy Crane, Maynard Cliff, Jim Garber, Susan Lewenstein, Beverly Mitchum, and Robin Robertson. Robin has spent long hours preparing ceramic identification and correlation charts to allow the chronological placement of the many excavated lots from the settlement. Beverly provided supervisory control over many of the test unit exposures and, with Sorayya, oversaw the horizontal excavation exposures on the two ball courts. Susan carried out survey and excavation in the settlement. Her experience with the Río Hondo Project proved very helpful in the identification of raised-field agricultural plots. The botanical identifications were markedly strengthened by Cathy's expertise.

The Cerros Survey Project has been fortunate to have recruited a number of qualified volunteers. Tom Babcock, Tom Guderjan, Eleanor King, Marge Morin, Truett Roberts, Karim Sadr, Denise Seymour, Karin Smith, and Fred Valdez, Jr., have been instrumental in the success of the settlement program. James Webb was responsible for the survey data collected during the 1974 and 1975 field seasons.

Drafting of plans and profiles was done by Karim Sadr, Eleanor Powers, Laurie Evans, and Chris Vallender. Robin Robertson produced the final draft of the site map. Karim Sadr provided the final draft of the environmental site map. Typing of the final manuscript was done by Wilma George of the University of Texas at El Paso and Sandi Cannell of the University of Cincinnati. Suzanne Comer and Freddie Goff of Southern Methodist University Press and Barry Isaac of the University of Cincinnati provided strong editorial guidance for the completion of this book.

In addition to the major National Science Foundation funding to David Freidel and Southern Methodist University, I was privileged to receive an NSF dissertation improvement grant during the 1979 field season. This grant, coupled with a seed grant from the Institute for the Study of Earth and Man at Southern Methodist University, permitted the completion of the site maps for Cerros. Additional manuscript preparation support was given by the Office of the Dean for Arts and Sciences as well as the University Research Council at the University of Cincinnati. The Charles Phelps Taft Memorial Fund at the University of Cincinnati provided partial subvention support for this volume.

I would also like to extend my gratitude to those other professionals who have encouraged this research. Both in the field and at national meetings, ideas and orientations have been exchanged. I thank Anthony

Andrews, Diane Chase, Arlen Chase, T. Patrick Culbert, William Denevan, Jack Eaton, Norman Hammond, Peter Harrison, Thomas Hester, Grant Jones, Edward Kurjack, Thomas Lee, Richard Mac-Neish, David Pendergast, Mary Pohl, Alfred Siemens, and B. L. Turner.

Portions of this manuscript have appeared in previously published articles. Permission to reprint excerpts from these articles was generously granted by the editors of these journals. The selected excerpts represent my own senior authorship, although sometimes they come from co-authored pieces. Excerpts, sometimes lengthy, were extracted from the following articles:

Scarborough, V. L.
1983 "A Preclassic Maya Water System." *American Antiquity* 48:720–744.
1985 "Late Preclassic Northern Belize: Context and Interpretation." In *Status, Structure and Stratification,* edited by M. Thompson, M. T. García and F. J. Kense, pp. 331–344. Chacmool Conference Proceedings, Calgary.

Scarborough, V.; B. Mitchum; S. Carr; and D. Freidel
1982 "Two Late Preclassic Ballcourts at the Lowland Maya Center at Cerros, Northern Belize." *Journal of Field Archaeology* 9(1):21–34.

Scarborough, V. L., and R. A. Robertson
1986 "Civic and Residential Settlement at a Late Preclassic Maya Center." *Journal of Field Archaeology* 13(2):155–175.

Freidel, D. A. and V. L. Scarborough
1982 "Subsistence, Trade and Development of the Coastal Maya." In *Maya Subsistence: Studies in Memory of Dennis E. Puleston,* edited by K. V. Flannery, pp. 131–151. Academic Press, New York.

Although heavily edited and much expanded, chapters 4 and 6 initially appeared in R. A. Robertson and D. A. Freidel, *Archaeology at Cerros Belize, Central America, Volume I: An Interim Report.*

The present volume brings together the entirety of the Cerros Survey Project results. As noted, some of this material has appeared previously; however, the following presentation is designed to unify earlier discussions as well as to present new data and interpretations to allow a synthesis of Cerros materials.

1. INTRODUCTION

The present study examines the settlement system at Cerros, a Late Preclassic Lowland Maya center situated on the northern leeward shore of Lowry's Bight, Northern Belize (latitude 18°12′08″N., longitude 88°21′10″W.) (Figs. 1.1 and 1.2). The Cerros Survey Project was designed to investigate the Maya settlement and environment surrounding the small central precinct (Fig. 1.3). The near absence of later construction at Cerros makes it unique in the archaeology of the Southern Maya Lowlands and has allowed the study of Late Preclassic settlement patterns undisturbed by later site modifications or mixing of deposits.

PREVIOUS RESEARCH

The Late Preclassic Period in the Maya Lowlands (300 B.C.–A.D. 150) has been recognized as a time of coalescence that culminated in the technological and sociological achievements of the Classic Maya (Adams 1977; Freidel 1979, 1981). As a result of extensive investigations, it has become clear that the majority of large Classic centers had their origins in the Late Preclassic Period (Adams 1977; Coe 1965a, 1965b). A key question for the rise of Maya civilization has been the process by which the settlement system (see Winters 1969), as a reflection of social organization, developed from Late Preclassic antecedents toward the stratified "state" level of complexity manifest in Late Classic times (ca. A.D. 600–900).

Population density in the lowlands was not great during the Early and Middle Preclassic periods (ca. 2000–300 B.C.). Prior to the Late Preclassic Period, the Maya Lowlands contained a scattered distribution of small autonomous villages adapted to riverine, lacustrine, and coastal environments (Ball 1977a, 1977b, 1977c; Puleston and Puleston 1971; Rice 1976; Rice and Puleston 1981; Willey 1977:137). Social control and social differentiation were less well defined and developed than in later periods. The Early Classic Period, as will be shown, demonstrates a strong tendency toward social as well as spatial centralization, with the advent of widespread public architecture, an overall population increase, and a more elaborate settlement organization than found in previous periods. Greater stratification and social control are suggested by the planning, construction, and maintenance of large "organizational centers" (Webster 1977).

Settlement pattern analysis in the Maya Lowlands has been critically reviewed by Haviland (1963, 1966), Fry (1969), Kurjack (1974), Puleston (1973), Rice and Puleston (1981), and Ashmore (1981). However, a brief discussion is warranted concerning those sites and areas known to contain Late Preclassic manifestations.

Two primary schools of thought have existed. The first argued that the settlement data indicate a loosely dispersed distribution of domestic mounded features (house mounds) throughout the lowlands. To these authors this suggested an unstratified, egalitarian social organization (Sanders 1962, 1963; Willey 1956). Concentrations or clusters of mounded features were thought to be linked socially with "minor ceremonial centers" (Bullard 1960; Willey and Bullard 1965). Even a system of rotating *cargos,* analogous to that described by Cancian (1965) for present-day Zinacantan, Chiapas, was suggested as a mechanism for integrating ancient Maya communities (Vogt 1961). The proponents of this interpretation suggested that the Maya were organized around vacant towns or ceremonial centers, perhaps similar to the concourse village described by de Borhegyi (1956), in which highly scheduled marketing activities were conducted. These arguments appear to have developed from the notion that swidden agriculturalists were compelled to distribute themselves some distance from the ceremonial centers (Willey 1956). It should be noted that these authors based their interpretations on data derived from Uaxactun (Ricketson and Ricketson 1937), the Chontalpa region of Tabasco (Sanders 1963), and the Belize Valley (Willey et al. 1965). Little current thinking now supports this school of thought.

In the last quarter century, a second interpretation has received support and increased popularity. It suggests that the ceremonial center might be better understood as an organizational or administrative center in which the sustaining population was less dispersed and

1

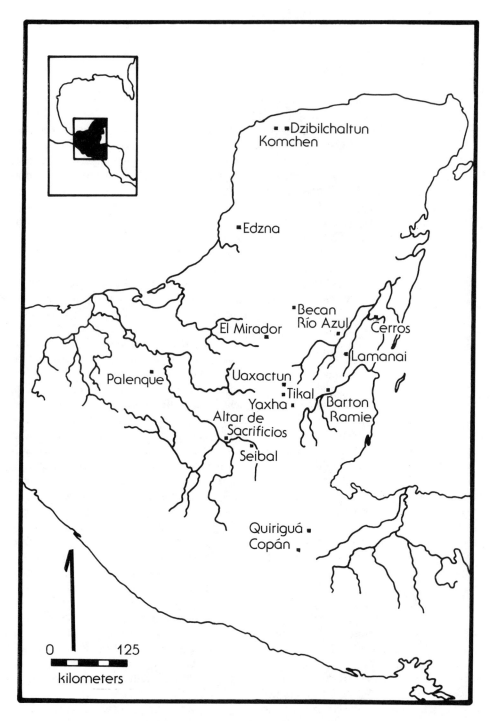

Figure 1.1.   Map of the Maya lowlands.

Figure 1.2. Aerial view of core area and periphery at Cerros. The main canal is apparent in the lower center of the photograph. The central precinct projects into Corozal Bay and the floodplain of the New River lies in the right background.

Figure 1.3. The central precinct at Cerros.

was defined by an "extended town pattern" (Miles 1957). Shook and Proskouriakoff (1956) appear to have been the first to argue this approach. They suggested that the Maya Lowlands may have been substantially more densely populated than previously considered.

More recent investigations in the settlement zone at Tikal have argued for truly urban dimensions to some Late Classic Maya sites (Willey and Shimkin 1973). A revised population estimate for Tikal has been set at 49,000 during the Late Classic Period, indicating a "nucleation tendency" (Haviland 1969, 1970). A program of survey and test excavations by the Tikal Sustaining Area Project has further strengthened this argument (Puleston 1973; 1983). Puleston's data suggest that there is a salient decrease in mounded features 6 to 7 kilometers from the site's epicenter (Puleston 1974; Rice and Puleston 1981). Seibal (Tourtellot 1970, 1976; Willey et al. 1975) has been interpreted in a similar light (Puleston commenting on Tourtellot's map). In addition, earthworks have been defined at Tikal to the north and southeast of the epicenter (Puleston and Callender 1967), corresponding to the drop-off in mound density during the Late Classic Period (Puleston 1974). This suggests that the periphery of the site was consciously defined by the residents of Tikal. Puleston (1973) has proposed a figure closer to 80,000 people within this perimeter. It should be noted that the earthworks appear to have been constructed by the Early Classic Period (Fry 1969; Puleston 1973; Puleston and Callender 1967).

Unfortunately, not all settlement pattern data can be neatly catalogued under one or another of these interpretations. Becán, in southeastern Campeche, is a fortified community with massive earthworks initially constructed by A.D. 100 (Ball and Andrews V 1978; Webster 1976). However, there appears to be little discernible decrease in mounded features outside the fortification (Thomas 1974, 1981). In contrast, at Altar de Sacrificios, the settlement appears to be sparsely occupied immediately outside the central precinct (Smith 1972).

Kurjack's work (1974, 1976) at Dzibilchaltún suggests increased compaction of the elite resident population through time. Early Period elite structures are believed to be more scattered than in subsequent periods. Through an examination of the distribution of vaulted features, Kurjack suggests that wealth and energy investments were concentrated in a core zone of the site through time. Additionally, he suggests that there are concentrations of domestic

structures surrounding larger mounded features. Similarly, Puleston states that *plazuela* groups at Tikal are represented by "a simple compaction of a basic pattern involving one or two groups and a surrounding vacant area" (1977a:16).

Although a great deal of variability exists, a "dispersed-compact" pattern of settlement organization can generally be argued for the Maya Lowlands. This settlement design has received additional support in the literature relating to intensive agriculture as early as the Preclassic Period (Freidel and Scarborough 1982; Matheny 1976; Puleston 1977b; Scarborough 1983a and b, 1985a and b; Turner and Harrison 1981). This evidence suggests that large population aggregates could have been supported in the lowlands by employing these techniques. Ridged fields have been documented in the Candelaria Basin of Southern Campeche (Siemens and Puleston 1972) and raised fields identified along the Río Hondo of Northern Belize (Belisle et al. 1977; Bloom et al. 1983, 1985; Hammond et al. 1987; Seimens 1982). Moreover, raised fields have been reported in Quintana Roo (Harrison 1977, 1978, 1982; Turner and Harrison 1978), along the Belize River of Central Belize (Kirke 1980) and along the New River of Northern Belize (Harrison and Turner 1983; Turner and Harrison 1981). Terraced fields have been reported in the Río Bec region and in adjacent Quintana Roo (Eaton 1975; Thomas 1981; Turner 1974; Turner and Harrison 1978), as well as in the Cayo District of Central Belize (Healy et al. 1980, 1984; Lundell 1940; Thompson 1931). Further, advances in aerial remote-sensing techniques have revealed extensive tracts of canal network believed associated with raised-field agriculture (Adams 1980, 1983; Adams et al. 1981; Scarborough 1983b; however, see Pope and Dahlin 1989 for counter view). Such technical advances reduce the significance of elaborate slash-and-burn subsistence equations for arriving at the carrying capacity of pre-Columbian populations.

The community organization and settlement system incorporated at each site and site area must be seen in terms of specific economic and political conditions. Each community represents an adaptation made to a unique social and physical environment, although various regional traditions were clearly fostered and reemphasized through time. Outside or intersite influences were accepted and manifested only if the community could tolerate their demands. The specialized adaptation made by one Late Preclassic settlement is the subject of this monograph.

CERROS IN PERSPECTIVE

The settlement data from Cerros permit a specific statement about one type of prestate community development. Residential population aggregates initially colonized Lowry's Bight, prior to the extensive land modification and civic construction completed by the end of the Late Preclassic Period. The residential population has been found to have remained dense and to have increased through time, even though civic architectural activity severely modified the landscape and forced a different residential adaptation to the site environment.

The growth of the community documents the transition from local resource dependency during its initial occupation to regional interaction of goods and services during its final major occupation. The community developed from a principally residential locus to a well-planned central place composed of civic monuments and residential space. The site reflects "synchorism" (Crumley 1976), the character of a center to manifest both civic attraction and residential aggregation, by the Tulix phase (50 B.C.–A.D. 150).

The adaptation of a community to a compacted settlement design with substantial civic construction by the Late Preclassic Period has evolutionary implications. Previous research in the Maya Lowlands suggests that the dispersed-compact settlement adaptation was a recurrent one made by later Classic Period centers. The question then becomes: Why did the Maya continue this settlement design for some fifteen hundred years, given the complexity of their institutions and our knowledge of state development and social control from other areas? (See Krader 1968 and Service 1975; also see Sanders et al. 1979, and Flannery and Marcus 1983 for the most comprehensive theses addressing state formation using empirical data.)

Although Maya centers attained sizable population aggregates and performed various "urban" functions, they seldom developed into cities in the manner of the nucleated residential and civic centers found in Highland Mexico. This is not to say that the Maya were incapable of creating such communities, as evidenced by Mayapán (Pollock et al. 1962) and Chunchucmil (Vlcek et al. 1978). Agricultural constraints were no more severe in the lowlands than in the highlands, as indicated by the extensive raised-field systems identified throughout the lowlands. Clearly, the Maya were aware of nucleated urban organization and the advantages of population centralization for social control, but opted to maintain a more dispersed settlement design. Surely the environmental and organizational resources were available for greater settlement nucleation among the Maya.

Given the elements of state formation in the Maya Lowlands, the Maya developed a dispersed-compact settlement pattern which allowed the control and regulation of these institutions. The dynamics of this system will be analyzed further in the final chapter of this monograph (see Scarborough and Robertson 1986).

2. INTRODUCTION TO THE SURVEY

One of the principal tasks of the Cerros Survey Project was the detailed mapping of the ruins. When complemented by the excavation operations in the settlement, structure variability within groups and between groups was revealed. The following review of survey methods, techniques, and problems provides a guide for future survey in the region as well as an assessment of the reliability of our data.

THE MAPS

The Cerros base map or structure rectification map was rendered to allow comparisons with other sites in the Maya Lowlands. Even though standing architecture has not been defined in the settlement zone, form and orientation data have been derived from contour maps and excavation plans (Fig. 2.1). The scale adopted for the published maps is identical to that of the Tikal and Dzibilchaltún site maps (Carr and Hazard 1961; Stuart et al. 1979), two of the most ambitious and extensive mapping projects undertaken in the lowlands. The 1:2000 scale has been reduced from a series of 151 square hectare quadrat maps drafted at a 1:200 scale. Finished copies of these maps are not available at the present time, but the originals drafted on millimeter grid graph paper are on file at Southern Methodist University. These latter maps are contour maps of all mounded features encountered in the settlement, although depressions understood as being the result of land modification during the pre-Hispanic and early historic occupation of the site were also plotted. In addition, a selective range of environmental data were retrieved and plotted.

The rectification of the mounded features at Cerros conforms with the general practice at other Maya sites. Although landscape topography has been mapped, a general contour map superimposed over the rectification was decided against for two reasons: to prevent clutter and distraction in reading the spatial disposition of structures; and to convey the exaggerated degree of flatness at Cerros when compared to other Maya settlements. It is believed that the relief

manifest across the core area as defined by the main canal at Cerros can best be attributed to human land modification. This type of relief will be referred to as cultural relief in the body of this monograph, as opposed to the natural relief described outside the confines of the core area. The second map, the environmental map of Cerros, includes all contour relief.

The environmental map was rendered at the same scale as the rectification for comparability (Fig. 2.2). In producing the rectification map, certain interpretations were made as a result of not encountering any standing masonry. For this reason, it was decided that the structures for the environmental map should be presented as they were alidade and plane table mapped in the field. To reduce confusion, only the basal contours of the structures have been provided, although the absolute elevation of the mounds relative to their bases is noted elsewhere (Appendix A). The mounded features can be seen as truncated pyramids, or as elongated variations of truncated pyramids in the case of rangelike structures. It should be noted that in a few cases time and energy have permitted the lateral exposure of selected structures. In these cases, we have reconstructed the form of the rectified structure from excavation exposure. This will become clear in the chapters dealing with excavation, but on the rectification map it is most apparent on those structures which provide a degree of detail unlike adjacent mounds. Unless other reliable information has been available, the structures have been oriented to the north.

The environmental map has presented the general site contour at an interval of 0.5 meter. This interval was chosen to convey the subtleties in the hydrology at Cerros. The cultural relief at Cerros is perhaps even more pronounced than depicted in this environmental reconstruction, but the horizontal survey interval between points throughout the settlement was routinely 50 meters unless visually apparent troughs or ridges were encountered. As a consequence of the thick vegetation cover, some environmental features may have been overlooked. Nevertheless, the contour map represents a very close approximation of the present-day setting at Cerros. In addition to the elevational

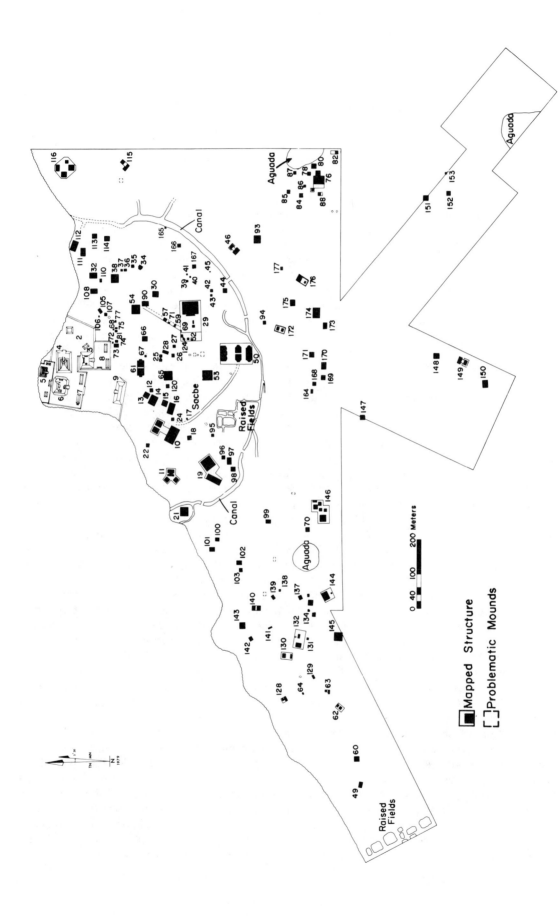

Figure 2.1. Map of Cerros. (See large-scale map in pocket at back of book.)

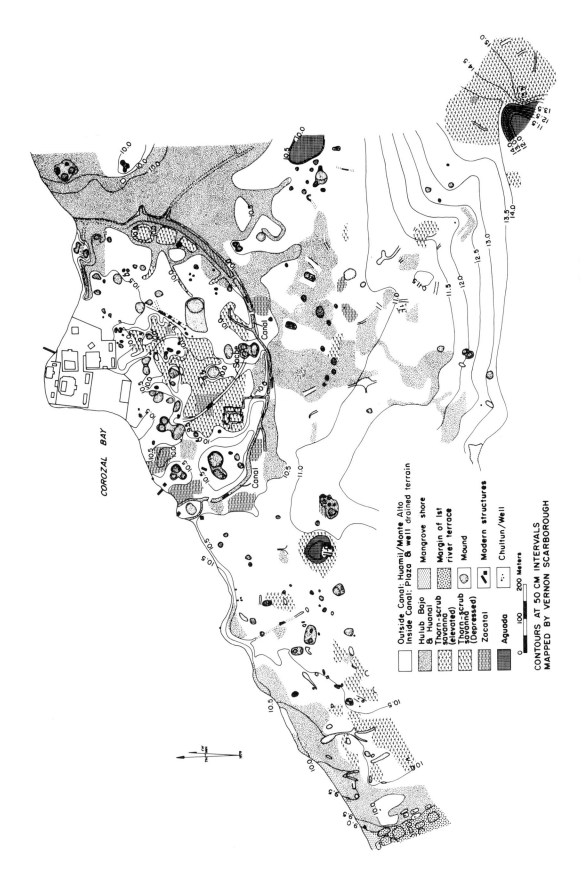

CORONZAL BAY

Outside Canal: Huamil/Monte Alto
Inside Canal: Plaza & well drained terrain

	Hulub Bajo & Huanal		Mangrove shore
	Thorn-scrub savanna (elevated)		Margin of 1st river terrace
	Thorn-scrub savanna (Depressed)		Mound
	Zacatal		Modern structures
	Aguada		Chultun/Well

0   100   200 Meters

CONTOURS AT 50 CM INTERVALS
MAPPED BY VERNON SCARBOROUGH

Figure 2.2.   Map of Cerros environs. (See large-scale map in pocket at back of book.)

readings recorded in centimeters, the collection of vegetational cover types and the use of aerial photographs (both 1:10000 and 1:1500 scales) have aided in the completion of the environmental map.

Although the contour map might be assessed best in terms of hydrology and gradient cues, it is also one of the variables necessary in the microenvironmental typology established from the survey data. The environmental zones defined on the environmental map have been given vegetational cover labels, but they reflect soils, elevational differences, and drainage patterns, as well as microclimatic differences (Wilken 1972).

The vegetation covering Lowry's Bight can be considered secondary or tertiary regrowth. Systematic transect and alidade survey as well as reconnaissance methods have demonstrated the presence of past hardwood logging operations throughout the peninsula. Slash-and-burn agriculture is still practiced in the interior of the bight along the flanks of the gentle slope of the low limestone crest, a kilometer or more from the central precinct of Cerros. Within the core zone as defined by the canal, as well as within limited areas outside the canal, extensive bush-cutting operations twenty years ago allowed the reestablishment of tertiary growth. This thick understory made survey operations doubly difficult because of poor visibility and accessibility. Nonetheless, an advantage to this seemingly inhospitable environment (an environment commented on by most researchers in Northern Belize: Belisle et al. 1977; R. E. W. Adams, personal communication) may be its reflection of the types of regrowth the original occupants were forced to contend with at Cerros (Scarborough 1985b).

The location of points on either map can be obtained readily by using the alpha-numeric grid coordinate system drawn on the rectification map. Because the scales of both the rectification map and the environmental map are identical and because the maps are designed to be used in concert, it was deemed unnecessary to add the alpha-numeric grid coordinates to the latter map. To avoid cluttering the illustration, grid lines were not superimposed over the rectification

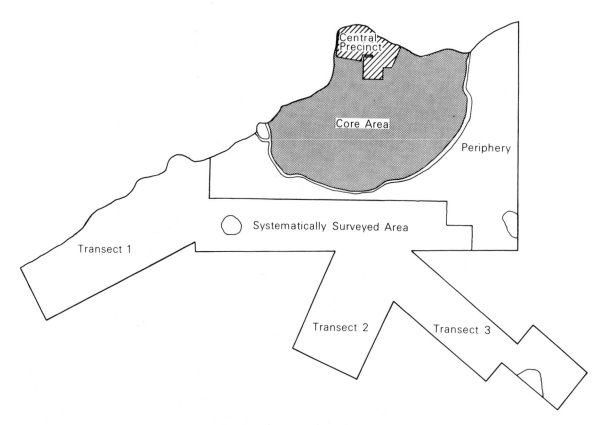

Figure 2.3.   Map of site zonation.

map, but tick marks are provided along the margins for reference. Separate alpha-numeric grid coordinates have been provided for the three transects that radiate from the main site quadrat block. These transects have been sequentially labeled: 1 represents the west-southwestern coastal transect; 2, the south-southwestern interior transect; and 3, the southeastern *aguada* transect (Fig. 2.3). It should be noted that point locations for features in the transects must be referenced to the orientation of the transect and not to true north.

In addition to point locations, each feature has been arbitrarily assigned a feature (structure) number, which has been incorporated into all excavation provenience labels. These feature numbers appear on the rectification map. Operation (OP) numbers, or the identification of excavation loci, have not been added to the maps. This information is readily available from the text.

A HISTORY OF METHODS

The survey methods employed for the Cerros settlement represent a historical compromise between explicit theoretical propositions and pragmatic changes in the funding base. This is not to say that the data collected at the initiation of the survey are incomparable to those retrieved at a later date; to the contrary, we have retraced our steps when information appeared lacking or incomparable in any way. The sketch that follows is provided to quell any doubts in regard to our systematic recovery of data.

As a consequence of the shoestring nature of financial support at the outset of the project, we were allowed to control only for the monumental architecture in the central precinct and what few ancillary structures might appear in a standard traverse closure, with the corner of our main camp house defined as principal datum. The northwestern corner of the cement foundation is located S 46m E 10m in Quadrat 4E and arbitrarily defined at an elevation of 10.00 meters. Although the precise relationship of this datum to sea level has not been calculated, its proximity to the present Corozal Bay (14 meters south) suggests that it is approximately 2 meters above sea level.

Our initial A-traverse encompassed a 9-hectare unit with twenty permanent transit stations. From this traverse, two additional closed traverses were initiated. The D-traverse permitted the transit mapping of all monumental architecture on the main plaza, while the B-traverse allowed the inclusion of the then-isolated pyramid Structure 29 on our preliminary map. A third line was established on the eastern side of the central precinct to better assess the mound density in this quarter of the settlement, but it was not properly closed.

In the formative seasons, the settlement was arbitrarily defined by employing unsystematic reconnaissance procedures to assess the spatial disposition of features. *Brechas,* or bush trails, were cut as lines of sight, but little systematic survey was undertaken. Only structures encountered on the *brechas* were cleared and transit mapped in their entirety. On the other hand, the central precinct resting on the main plaza at Cerros was cleared and systematically surveyed and mapped. As a matter of priority, it was deemed necessary to have an accurate map of the main plaza should funding disappear. Although the rest of the site was eventually remapped, the central precinct as depicted on the 1:2000 scale maps has not been significantly altered from this original mapping event.

Upon evaluation of the initial excavation program taken from within arbitrarily selected features in the settlement and the central precinct, we developed general theoretical statements as to the form and function of the site. The testing program demonstrated a formidable Late Preclassic component, with an ephemeral Early Classic and Late Postclassic occupation. Only minor constructional modifications could be assigned to these later periods, a proposition that is maintained to date. On grounds of sophistication and size, as well as artifactual inventory, Freidel (1978, 1979) posited a long-distance trading adaptation for the site.

In an attempt to test the implications of the model further, we initiated a systematic survey of the ruins at Cerros. In order to rationalize the obvious need for additional survey, a testable hypothesis was presented (Scarborough 1978). If a trading adaptation was the primary focus of the site and the service community, then a tightly integrated support population would be anticipated. This would be manifested by a compacted residential population and reflected in terms of structure density. The alternative to this pattern would be a dispersed settlement less well coordinated by a centralized trading economy. This pattern would be the result of social and economic constraints. Agricultural land use has been suggested as a key element in producing a dispersed residential pattern (Netting 1974, 1977; Sanders 1963).

The systematic transit and alidade survey was initiated from the main plaza and tied to the original A-traverse. A block of 72 hectares was surveyed to the immediate southwest, south, and east of the central precinct. Upon subsequently stratifying the mounded features and test excavating a 20% or better sample, a clear Late Preclassic construction and occupation date was established for the settlement. A service population, as defined by small mounded structures, appeared to be concentrated to the immediate east and south of the central precinct, although a greater area surrounding the site had to be surveyed before the spatial disposition of the service community could be assessed adequately. In addition, a 1,200-meter-long canal segment was isolated and found to circumscribe the major architecture in the settlement. This feature was believed to have defined the "emic" limits of a settlement core zone. Further, it provided a meaningful spatial division for examining the geographic integrity of the settlement, both inside and outside this core zone.

To better confirm or disconfirm the settlement compaction hypothesis, three transect blocks were established into the interior of the peninsula. Two of the transects radiated from a point at the south-central edge of the main site quadrat block and a third ran along the southwestern edge of the shoreline. The overall effect of these survey transects was to ascertain the amount of settlement compaction or dispersion as measured by mound density when compared to the organizational center (i.e., the settlement core zone). However, each transect line provided additional types of ancillary information. Although these additional 79 hectares of transit and alidade survey have not been test excavated, we have assumed a proportionate number of Late Preclassic features (in keeping with the percentage of known Late Formative mounded features identified outside the core area) for purposes of testing the compaction hypothesis (see chapter 7).

TECHNIQUES

The techniques employed in the transit and alidade survey were derived from the pioneer work conducted by the Tikal Project (Carr and Hazard 1961; Puleston 1973). However, some revisions were made to accommodate the dense understory found at Cerros. A 100-square-meter grid system oriented to true north was established at the outset. Each hectare quadrat was defined by a 1- to 2-meter-wide *brecha* cut as a line of sight for the transit survey. At the beginning, we tried to close each hectare unit one at a time to assure accuracy, but as we gained confidence in the survey procedure, this technique was altered in favor of a more rapid technique. This revised technique involved the cutting of over four times as many *brechas* as allowed by the old method (Figs. 2.4, 2.5). Although closure occurred somewhat less periodically, it always did eventually result. Nevertheless, the faster technique required more labor and greater concentration skills on the part of the surveyor and crew. Where two men were sufficient in the initial technique, six were now necessary for maximum speed and efficiency.

The technique now called for the cutting of three lines simultaneously in the cardinal directions issuing from the transit station. Although the technique required the rapid reshooting of each line as the workmen chopped so as to maintain the proper bearing, it permitted a recurrent check equivalent to a back angle for each pair of lines. At every 50-meter interval, we staked and labeled the location for future ties. A point elevation was also taken. At every 100-meter interval, that is, every transit station, we recorded the foregoing information and also staked the location with a 12-inch section of concrete reinforcing rod. Staking with these rebar pins was found to be an absolute necessity, given the deterioration of wooden stakes after just one season. This permanent grid layout can be incorporated by future researchers as well. All distances were chained using a 50-meter metal tape.

Upon closure of a few hectare units, the next phase of the survey was promptly deployed. This entailed the most difficult aspect of the survey because of the rapidity at which it was necessarily conducted. Depending on the density of vegetation, four to five workmen were placed 10 to 15 meters apart between the transit station and a 50-meter stake. Each man then walked through the vegetation in a line parallel to the sides of the quadrat unit. Upon emerging on the opposite side of the quadrat, a report was made as to the approximate location of any mounded features, as well as related environmental data. The crew was then redirected through the other half of the hectare unit in a similar manner and received at the other side.

At the initiation of this program, a man near the center of the survey crew was provided with a Brunton compass to maintain a proper bearing for himself and the others. However, this was not always necessary, as

Figure 2.4.   Transit station at the convergence of three *brecha* lines. Informants Teodoro Martinez (left) and Roberto Pott (center) pose with the author.

Figure 2.5.   *Brecha* clearing.

the men were made to maintain their distance from one another by shouting and whistling. Visibility was usually obscured. If the workmen were found to gravitate toward one another by the time they exited from the bush onto the opposite *brecha,* they were asked to reenter the quadrat and search that ground believed to be insufficiently examined.

Once a crew was trained to conduct this type of reconnaissance, all data recovery proceeded smoothly. In an attempt to control the quality of data recovered, the coverage of two previously surveyed, arbitrarily selected hectare units was reexamined whenever a new crew was hired. This exercise was deemed necessary due to the periodic rotation of our work force. This check confirmed the efficiency of the technique, as no additional mounded features were located on previously foot-surveyed hectare units. In addition, to reduce the severity of "boundary effects" at the margin of our systematic survey area (Hodder and Orton 1976:41), we always examined the zone immediately around a mound for a distance of 30 meters from its summit.

The final phase of the survey involved the accurate location of the mounded structures and associated features as well as a complete alidade and plane table map of mound dimensions. In the case of small mounds, two workmen were sent out to clear the entire platform, which was mapped at a scale of 1:10. Larger mounds entailed the cutting of radiating *brechas* issuing from the alidade station, which was always the summit of the mound. A minimum of four lines of sight from one summit station were cut along the maximum length and width of the mound. In the case of large-range structures or complicated acropolises, it was necessary to establish as many as four summit stations. All large structures in the settlement were mapped at a 1:50 scale. Upon completion of the alidade contour map, each mound was tied back to the nearest grid *brecha* stake by again cutting a line of sight to the trail. Once the grid *brecha* was intersected, it became an easy matter to measure the distance from the intercept back to the original transit survey stake.

The mound summit station for the alidade and plane table was also permanently staked for future excavation unit ties. All measurements were chained, as a number of instruments were used during the course of the survey and stadia distance is always a less satisfactory procedure, given the variability in telescope optics. Elevations were taken using a hardwood stadia rod calibrated to the nearest centimeter. All mounds were

contour mapped in the field at 10-centimeter intervals, but remapped on the 1:200 composite hectare grid maps in 0.5-meter contours.

TECHNICAL PROBLEMS

The Cerros Survey Program has striven for accuracy in the retrieval of the locational and dimensional data for the various features noted in the settlement. However, certain deranging factors were periodically isolated during the course of the project. The precision of our survey was constantly challenged by the restricted visibility afforded by the dense semitropical forest setting. Large windfalls and standing hardwood trees repeatedly blocked sightings, to say nothing about the vines and thornbush entanglements. However, we found that by raising or lowering the instrument height, a curve or notch in an obstruction usually allowed a clear line of sight for the necessary 100 meters between stations. This manipulation usually permitted fewer stations and less chance for mechanical error.

Another problem attributable to the undergrowth was in the chaining of distances. Initially, we cut 2-meter-wide *brechas,* but the utility of these swaths was less for a clear line of sight than for mobility along the *brechas.* As a consequence, we attempted to reduce the *brechas'* width, but the metal 50-meter chain became more difficult to wield. Stumps and branches seemed to attract the taut chain and some of the time saved by cutting narrower trails was offset by clearing them again. Perhaps the most difficult situations arose from attempting to close or check quadrats bordering hectare survey units mapped during a previous season. Old lines could be identified immediately even without a compass bearing due to the thicker tertiary growth defining the original *brechas.* We did not reopen all of the lines defining a hectare unit in these cases, although we did check some of them.

Another factor attributable to the setting was the soft, organically rich topsoil floor into which the transit and tripod were anchored. The typical splayed root system of the tropics did not always form a secure foundation for a tripod. Besides the obvious problems associated with the steel chain and machetes affecting the orientation of the magnetic compass needle, the necessity of threading our only chain between the extended legs of the transit tripod forced additional frequent checks on closure throughout the settlement survey.

Perhaps the most difficult factor in controlling the accuracy of the transit survey involved the significance of error inherent in the instrument. This coupled with human error produced a 5-meter horizontal discrepancy in the southwest corner of the main quadrat block during the final field season. The source of the error was not precisely determined, but it appears to be a result of comparing one season's survey work against another's. It is believed to be a discrepancy in the setting of the magnetic declination between the two years involved. However, if, as it appears, our only error is this 5-meter difference across the 26 kilometers that have been grid line cut, then our precision has been astonishingly good. It should be noted that the amount of *brecha* length cut during the Cerros Survey Project surpassed that cut by the Tikal Sustaining Area Project (Puleston 1973).

The necessity to identify and map environmental indicators and cultural remains accurately within the dense secondary regrowth at Cerros forced our survey crews to examine closely microenvironmental differences and relationships seldom recorded for the Maya area. This scrutiny is the subject of the next chapter.

THE DEFINITION OF A MOUNDED FEATURE AND THE ROLE OF TOPOGRAPHY

The function of mounded features has received considerable attention over the years, particularly since the early 1970s (Haviland 1963; Kurjack 1974; Puleston 1973; Thompson 1971; Scarborough and Robertson 1986). However, the simple identification of a mounded feature has received considerably less attention. A number of naturally occurring features resembling mounds have been located throughout the settlement at Cerros, causing some confusion as to what constitutes an aboriginal activity platform. Those disturbances which could be identified as natural in origin received little more attention, but fourteen mounds whose origin cannot be determined without test excavations have been plotted on the settlement map. In all cases, these problematic mounded features are 30 centimeters or less in elevation and usually isolated from well-defined structure groups.

The factors responsible for naturally occurring mounds at Cerros may certainly affect other sites in the subtropics. Some trees tend to mound soil through root and trunk growth. This upheaval is particularly difficult to distinguish from culturally prepared mounds

if the tree or stump has disappeared. Another natural agent responsible for mounded features is insect activity. A number of ant species have the unsettling behavior of constructing large colonies using clay and sand-sized particles. Active colonies are all too easy to detect, but abandoned mounds are more difficult: "Amongst geological agents mention should be made of the 'wee-wee' ant that lives in colonies and forms mounds often 20 yards in diameter and several feet high. There is much earth excavation in making their homes and even soft rock is brought to the surface, but their main service is to allow surface water to penetrate lower" (Ower 1929:7).

The last factor to produce natural mounding is erosional agents, which attack the soft limestone caprock and poorly secured vegetation during the *bajo* inundation and drainage flow of the rainy season. The effect of this erosion can produce a series of interconnected depressions, or "potato holes" (Wright et al. 1959), with the associated high ground preserved by means of well-anchored vegetation. The very slight natural relief at Cerros relative to other sites has prevented deeply incised arroyos and apparently permitted the shallow meandering pattern of depressions so marked along the western transect. The end result of this erosion has sometimes confused our interpretation of a mounded feature.

One mounded feature which deserves comment is indicated by the ridge running parallel to the coast in selected locations. It is most apparent immediately east of the central precinct and again to the southwest outside the canal perimeter. This feature is the result of high winds and severe wave action during hurricane conditions (Simmons 1957). Although no excavation was carried out, the obvious mixed particle size would suggest such an origin for the feature. The curious trough immediately behind the ridge is thought to be a runoff channel associated with the turbid high water trapped behind the ridge during the event. Although the eastern end of the canal seems to be connected into the canal course, it is understood to be a coincidental occurrence.

Some of the shallow pits and runnels identified in the settlement are attributable to the foregoing degradational processes, but most sizable depressions within the core zone are assumed to have been intentionally excavated. The absence of a clear quarry site at Cerros coupled with the thinness of the caprock formation suggests that much of the shallow relief is a result of extensive and deliberate directed caprock removal.

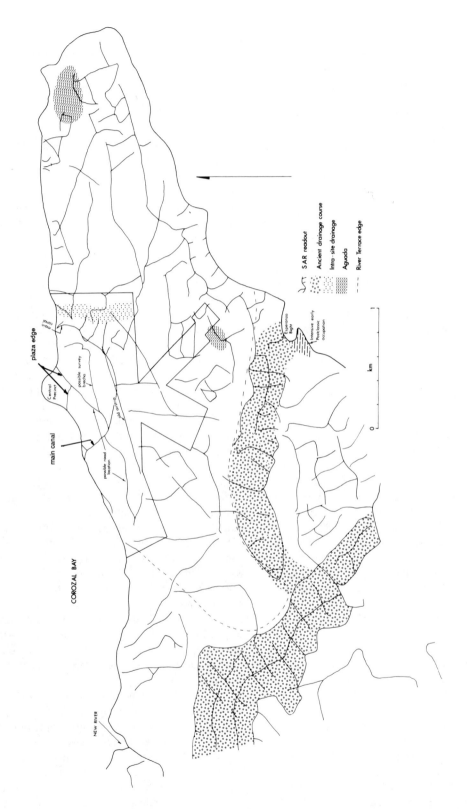

Figure 2.6.   Map of Lowry's Bight with SAR readout.

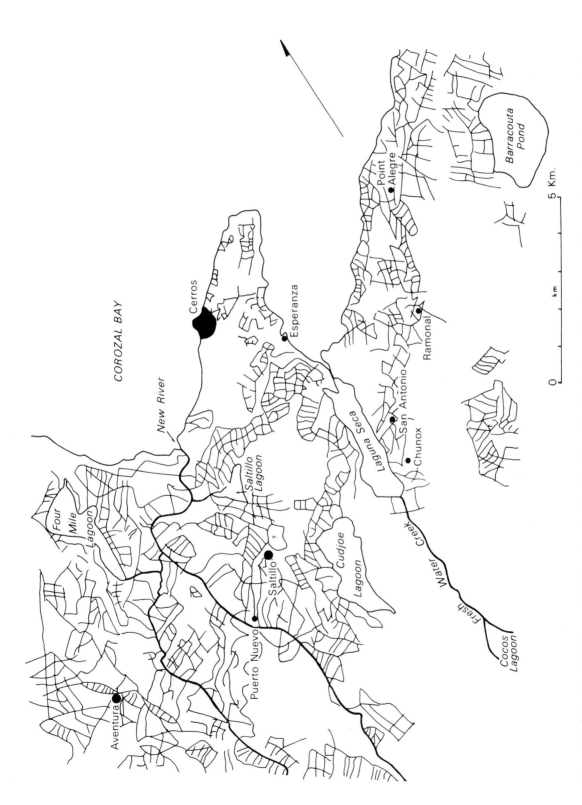

Figure 2.7. Map of areal relations with SAR readout (subjectively filtered for right lattice and dentritic patterns). Survey data collected by reconnaissance methods.

The relief within the core zone of the site is a consequence of this selective quarrying. The spatial organization of the community suggests that the removal of the caprock and the position of the resultant depressions is as important as the location of the mounded complement. Outside the canal perimeter this relief is less patterned.

Clearly, natural processes are responsible for some of the contour relief at Cerros. However, most of the landscape modification can be directly attributable to the deliberate removal of the caprock, with subsequent erosional agents sometimes masking the actual origins of these human-made features. This argument is predicated on the absence of similar relief outside a kilometer or better radius from the main plaza, or as defined by the elevated ground located above the 11.5-meter contour line. All things being equal, the slightly more elevated area of greater slope to the south of the site near the crest of the low ridge defining the spine of the peninsula would be expected to have been etched as severely as the lower ground surrounding the site. However, systematic survey and reconnaissance indicate this area to be very little affected by pits and scars of any kind.

Any discussion of mounded features at Cerros must include the effects of recent historic land-use modifications. Particularly evident are the scraper blade piles deposited by bulldozer action. Informants have indicated that heavy equipment has had an impact on the western quarter of the contiguous block defining the major site universe. In addition to two roads leading into the camp area, a small airstrip and a sizable reexcavated aboriginal rainwater reservoir

have been identified. All of these features lay abandoned and reclaimed by the vegetation at the outset of the project. The precise extent of damage could not be assessed, as the contractor responsible for the land modification would not reply to my inquiries. However, only in two instances did it become difficult to discern what was formerly a mound, what remained a mound, and what was a back dirt pile. In both cases, a problematic mound designation was assigned.

Before leaving the discussion of contour relief outside the canal perimeter, it should be noted that a preliminary side-looking airborne radar (SAR) readout of the environment surrounding Cerros has been made available to me by Richard E. W. Adams (Figs. 2.6, 2.7). These data indicate a system of interconnecting depressions sometimes forming a lattice or dendritic network outside the canal perimeter. This same network is apparent throughout the lower reaches of the New River and may be indicative of raised-field intensive agriculture. The gilgae argument (Puleston 1973, 1978) can be reasonably dismissed in most of these settings due to the high year-round water table (see Antoine et al. 1982; Darch 1983). Although no direct evidence for raised fields could be identified from those low-lying areas immediately outside the canal periphery, subsequent siltation of these tracts may have buried former fields. The identification of the main canal as well as the probable detection of the plaza edge for the central precinct at Cerros suggests the utility of SAR (Scarborough 1983b). Elsewhere, Adams et al. (1981) indicate that 20% of the lineaments depicted represent ancient canals of uncertain date.

3. PHYSICAL ENVIRONMENT

The physical environment has been defined as a system of interacting natural phenomena producing stable settings at various points in time. At Cerros, a setting was principally identified as a community of plants, associated soils, and drainage conditions scrutinized at a microenvironmental level and found distinct from other adjacent settings. The major components of the physical environment were geological, climatological, biological, and cultural, with major subcomponents comprising each of these divisions. Because subsequent monographs will examine the physical environment in different detail, this presentation will devote considerable attention to the geological and climatological components, with an important treatment of the floral subcomponent of the biological aspect.

GEOLOGY

The geological formation of the Maya Lowlands is a relatively recent event. The Department of Petén, Guatemala, manifests folded and faulted Cretaceous rock underlying marine clastics and limestone of Tertiary age (Maldonado-Koerdell 1964; West 1964). The predominant east-west orientation of this relief is associated with Miocene events which are in part responsible for the north-south down-faulting of the Cayman Trough between the eastern Yucatán coast and Cuba. Although the Cayman, or Bartlett, Trough may share antecedents with the Old Antilla Trough (West 1964:38), the north-northeast/south-southwest trending fold and fault zone of Northern Belize is understood to be a consequence of this same Miocene activity (Hazelden 1973; McDonald 1979). The Hondo River, New River, and Freshwater Creek define the course of this structural zone through Northern Belize. The Maya Mountains of Central and Southern Belize, as well as the hill ranges of the southern Petén, are the most pronounced result of this orogeny.

The greater Yucatán peninsula is associated with similar Tertiary events. The Yucatán platform is argued to have slowly risen from south to north, emerging from a shallow Pliocene sea (Maldonado-Koerdell

1964:2). Additional faulting separated it from Cuba early in time. Schuchert (1935) argued that the platform tilted northward and westward during the Pleistocene. The mechanisms associated with this tilting action are not believed to be orogenic in nature, and more recent interpretations suggest a southern tilt to portions of the plate: "In the Peninsula of Yucatán geologists of Petróleos Mexicanos have added further evidence of geotectonic influences through the discovery of an intrusive body in the subsurface of its northern coast, under calcareous rocks of younger age" (Maldonado-Koerdell 1964:24). This appears to be an intrusive replacement of the Old Antillan Foreland geosyncline of the region.

Wright et al. (1959) indicate that Northern Belize was a shallow sea during the Cretaceous Period, with siliceous sands eroding into it from the newly created Maya Mountain massif. Uplift in the Tertiary exposed the underlying calcium carbonate–rich sea floor sediments, with the overlying denuded sands rapidly eroding away. However, two ancient shoal-like areas emerged north of the Belize River in what is North-Central Belize. These "islands" are apparent on soil-formation parent material maps (Wright et al. 1959) and represent remnant quartz sands redeposited from the Maya Mountains.

Ower (1929) indicates that the bulk of the uplifted, dense, white limestone platform dates to the Oligocene, but Wright et al. maintain that these chalks are Cretaceous or Eocene in origin. Flores (1952) and Hazelden (1973), on the other hand, see much of the limestone deposit in the New River and Freshwater Creek area as Mio-Pliocene in date. Regardless, this limestone has become indurated at its surface but has remained relatively unconsolidated at lower depths.

Shoreline conditions in the North were similar to those found on the offshore Cays today. On the Cays there is a surface crust of indurated white limestone containing corals and occasional mollusc shells. Below this is a scarcely consolidated cream coloured coral sand; this horizon is unconsolidated, and at Corozal, the final emergence brought to light a very similar strip of unconsolidated rubbly chalk. Even today it is only slightly to moderately consolidated. (Wright et al. 1959:25)

The indurated white limestone to which both Ower and Wright et al. make reference is locally referred to as caprock and has its origin in caliche development (see Quiñones and Allende 1974). Although various particle sizes can be involved, "a thick, permeable, carbonate-rich sand will allow independent formation of a thick caliche if the climatic regimen fluctuates from humid to semi-arid and if the sand does not become plugged near the surface" (Reeves 1970:354).

The faulting or folding associated with the Tertiary appears to have produced the limestone tongues, or bights, of Northern Belize. This fracturing resulted in a series of near-parallel ridges and troughs running the length of Northern Belize. (See McDonald 1979 for a discussion of the dynamics of this structural zone.) These fault lines are defined by a low scarp along the eastern edge of the ridges and a gentle slope to the west. "The limestone tongues were almost certainly produced by faulting of the coastal shelf and associated with a gentle dip slope to the west. In the troughs that formed between the parallel tongues, silt, clay and typical lagoon sediments accumulated. These give rise to heavy grey clays—yet another type of soil parent material" (Wright et al. 1959:25).

On Lowry's Bight, the main canal exposure revealed the nature of the caprock, or indurated white limestone. Because the site rests on the western, or gentle, slope of the ridge, it is argued that the underlying unconsolidated limestone is not as rich in coral fragments as the eastern scarp location. Excavations in the canal, as well as a large extant *sascabera,* or lime quarry, exposed near the village of Chunox on the western side of the next eastern fault line, indicate that the matrices are a fine calcareous clay fraction intruded by few coral sands or gravels. This is explicable in terms of the location at which corals would indeed be most likely to grow, that is, along the most elevated ridge areas. This process has been described on the present-day cays.

The crests of these submarine ridges nowhere break the surface and their geological composition is unknown. The islands along the course of submarine ridges are being formed by gradual accumulation of coral fragments. These are bound together on the leeward side by a cementing action which appears to be associated with movement of waves to and fro over the slowly accumulating strand of limestone sand and coral fragments. (Wright et al. 1959:28)

The resulting "cementing action" at this location is thought to account for the apparent graded grain size. The finer clay fraction would be expected downslope and west of the wave-damaged sands and gravels defining the reef margins. This would also explain the apparent grain size differences reported between Corozal, located at the summit of one of these eastern crests associated with a fault line, and our site, lying only 3 kilometers to the southeast.

It should be noted that volcanic ash has been incorporated into the Pliocene chalks of Corozal and in the Cretaceous/Eocene limestones of Hillbank (a village in the northwestern portion of the country, not the ruin immediately south of Cerros on Freshwater Creek) (Wright et al. 1959:27). This subaqueous lensing represents reworked tuff deposited by ancient drainages and should not be confused with more recent events in the Guatemalan and Salvadoran Highlands, such as the violent eruption of Ilopango (Sharer 1974; Sheets 1979).

Siemens (1978:143) has suggested that the land reclamation associated with the emerging Yucatán platform indicates a similar recent phenomenon for Northern Belize. However, a number of independent sources now suggest that this is probably not the case. The upward tilting action of the Yucatán platform found most evident in the northwest portion of the peninsula may have the unsettling tendency of submerging the southeastern and eastern portions of the platform.

Evidence for land subsidence or sea level rise on the Belizean coast comes from four archaeological sources. Work on Moho Cay (located less than 1 kilometer north of Belize City) indicates Classic Period workshop debris lying approximately 1 meter below the present sea level (Buhler personal communication; McKillop 1984). Ower (1929) suggested that the mouth of the Belize River, which issues immediately north of Belize City, had been recently submerged, producing its truncated appearance.

A second source of information comes from two control pits excavated on what were formerly understood to be raised-field platforms on Albion Island in Northern Belize. Unlike Moho Cay, Albion Island rests in the path of the Hondo River, well inland on the

Mexican border. Antoine, Skarie, and Bloom (1982) indicate that the water table has risen as a consequence of the retreat of the Pleistocene glaciation but do state that the process was slowed about twenty-five hundred years ago (after High 1975). Their argument denying the presence of raised fields in their test area rests on the existence of a rising water table into the Classic, and probably Historic, periods. More recently, work on Albion Island confirms the presence of prehistoric drained-field agriculture but further supports a rising water table since the Late Preclassic Period (Bloom et al. 1983, 1985).

At the nearby site area of Pulltrouser Swamp, one of the most important ecological studies treating raised-field intensive agriculture in the Maya Lowlands has been completed (Harrison and Turner 1983; Turner and Harrison 1981). Although the researchers do not directly identify fluctuations in the water table at Pulltrouser Swamp, their data suggest a water level at least 1 meter lower than today. One raised-field site area revealed a buried paleosol at 2.5–3.0 meters Below Surface Datum (BSD). Bloom et al. (1983) indicate a peatlike matrix occurring in a similar context on Albion Island and note that it is a natural deposit resulting from a less-elevated water table during the recent Holocene. Harrison and Turner (1983) suggest that this paleosol had been routinely removed from most fields prior to construction and subsequently returned to the surface of a field upon construction. Because the paleosol lies 1 meter below the present water table and because the earliest evidence for agricultural intensification in the swamp dates to the Late Preclassic Period, it is suggested that the water table has risen in the area at least a meter beginning as early as the Late Formative Period.

The argument for sea level rise and/or land subsidence in Northern Belize can be supported further by our work at Cerros (Freidel and Scarborough 1982; Scarborough 1983a). We suggest that the mouth of the New River regressed up its channel, which formerly emptied into a low-energy lagoon environment. The proximity of the river to the site and the rapid erosional rate recorded along the Corozal Bay shoreline (10 to 20 inches a year; Belize Lands Department personal communication) suggest that the main canal at Cerros may have even tapped into the former course of the New River (see chapter 6). The shallowness of the bay may indicate a recent localized isostatic subsidence. Although the precise sediment load carried by the New River is unknown, the mouth of the channel

has been periodically dredged to accommodate river barge traffic (Belize Sugar Industries, Ltd. personal communication). In addition, numerous tests within the central precinct of the site have isolated *in situ* cultural material well below the present water table. (A similar argument is presented for the submerged ridged and raised fields of the San Jorge floodplain, Colombia [Parsons and Bowen 1966:327].)

Additional suggestive evidence for sea level rise and/or land subsidence at Cerros comes again from SAR. Adams et al. (1981) illustrate the appearance of several gridded lineaments extending immediately offshore into the shallow water near the ancient site of Sarteneja. This site lies 20 kilometers from Cerros along the same shared coastline. Although the lineaments have not been inspected on the ground, they have the same appearance as those identified elsewhere as canals. If constructed during a pre-Hispanic occupation of the area, they reveal an inundation of the shoreline at an uncertain date.

The dense midden concentration associated with dark lacustrine clays and high frequencies of an associated shallow-water, estuarine-adapted snail (*Melongena melongena,* identified by Anthony Andrews) suggest that the environmental setting at Cerros was considerably different from that of today. Judging from the present proximity of the numerous lagoons and salt marshes along the New River and Freshwater Creek, it is likely that Corozal Bay was formerly a constricted-mouth lagoon.

It should be noted that it is difficult to attribute the rise in the water table at Moho Cay, Albion Island, Pulltrouser Swamp, or Cerros solely to sea level transgression without further evidence. Given the geological history for tectonic disturbance in Northern Belize, an alternative explanation for the depositional dynamics may be land subsidence.

Nevertheless, eustatic changes in global sea levels over the last four thousand years have produced small, but significant, oscillations (Bloom 1971; Emery 1969). Block (1963) indicates an important rise in sea level beginning shortly before the Christian Era and not ending until the seventh or eighth century, during which sea level rose approximately 2.5 meters. Butzer (1976:36) suggests that by 300 B.C. sea level along the northern Delta region of Lower Egypt was 2 meters lower than today. For the Bahamas, Lind (1969) suggests a similar oscillation near the end of the first millennium B.C. Further, Parsons and Denevan (1967:95) indicate that the construction of ridged fields in swamp settings of

Surinam was made possible by the encroachment of the sea at circa A.D. 700.

In regard to present-day regional drainage patterns in Northern Belize, Siemens (1976, 1978) indicates that the karstic nature of the Hondo River setting has allowed a "reservoir effect" in which seasonal precipitation fluctuations have not severely affected the water level of the drainage. Apparently, the karstic terrain permits a slow-release discharge during both dry and wet seasons, allowing a discharge rate more even and continuous than that found in most other river systems of Mesoamerica. This takes on significance when examining the disposition of adjacent raised-field complexes.

The soils of the Maya Lowlands have only recently received the attention they deserve. The Petén soils are a complex array of leached zonal soils with calcimorphic and hydromorphic intrazonal groups represented (Sanders 1977; Simmons et al. 1959; Stevens 1964). These soils can be deep and well developed but tend to be viscous and acidic. The Yucatán platform is characterized by thin soils, which are undergoing laterization, although those soils between Northern Yucatán and the Petén are more typically rendzina soils. Rendzina soils, having experienced less leaching than soil farther to the north, cover much of Northern Belize. Rendzina soils contain a superabundance of calcium carbonate and, with the process of gleization, represent the general soil character of Quintana Roo, Mexico, and Northern Belize.

The preceding geologic sketch has been presented to aid in understanding the origins and processes responsible for the topography and parent materials affecting Lowry's Bight and the adjacent area. This background material will be referred to frequently in the course of the monograph. Before treating another major component of the environmental system, a further detailed examination of a subcomponent of the geology—the soils—will be discussed. Soil development is inextricably tied to the other major components in the physical environmental system, but geologic processes are extremely influential in their final characterization.

Soils

The soils of the Maya Lowlands are heterogeneous (Wiseman 1978), reflecting a diversity in microenvironmental settings. Although Meggers (1954) and

Sanders (1977) suggest the inadequacy of the soils in the region, this is no longer a reasonable assertion (Altschuler 1958; Ferdon 1959; Sánchez and Buol 1975; Stevens 1964). It is true that some settings are less productive than others, but the implementation of sufficient drainage control and the selection of appropriate flora can permit an increased "agricultural potential" (Ferdon 1959; Denevan 1982; Turner 1983) far beyond the unaltered endemic conditions.

Lowland Maya soils include all three types of intrazonal classes, as well as leached zonal soils (following the U.S. Department of Agriculture 1962). (It should be noted that I have opted to maintain this older soils nomenclature, as much of the pioneer research examining the ecology of the lowlands uses it. This is done with the knowledge that a more precise taxonomic system is currently used by most soils scientists [USDA 1975].) On the Yucatán peninsula, the thin zonal soils are lateritic in some locations (Stevens 1964), but the severity of the condition is not as great as once believed (Sanchez and Buol 1975). The effects of laterization in the Maya Lowlands is extensive, with some types of yellowish and reddish soils (*tierra rosa*) occurring as a consequence of iron sesquioxides (Fe_2O_3) precipitating during the leaching process. Podzolization, unlike lateritic conditions, affects only the loose matrix overlying the parent material and appears to be a widespread process in the lowlands. This zonal process is significant in that in highly acidic humus horizons, this leaching will remove most metallic minerals, while silica (SiO_2) will precipitate out. This factor should be assessed in areas such as the Petén, where acidity is high. (See Deevey et al. 1979 and Rice et al. 1985 for the significance of silica in assessing prehistoric land use patterns.) At Cerros, the amount of silica precipitate is not great because of the basic condition of the soils.

One of the most naturally productive intrazonal soils is the calcimorphic rendzina soil ("mollisols" in the most recent literature). Stevens (1964) describes its distribution across the southern portion of the Yucatán peninsula and into the Petén and Northern Belize. Wright et al. (1959) also indicate its wide distribution throughout Northern Belize. Rendzina soils are superabundant in calcium due to the limestone parent material from which they are derived. This abundance permits the calcification process to take place in this relatively humid climate. These soils are rich in minerals (except perhaps phosphates) and alkaline in chemistry, allowing for the rigors of slash-and-burn agriculture.

Hydromorphic soils also appear throughout the lowlands. They are characterized by high accumulations of organic matter with acidic conditions sometimes leading to podzolization. "The largest area of hydromorphic soils in Middle America lies in the swamp and marsh land region of Tabasco, extending in an irregular pattern into the inundatable part of the Petén" (Stevens 1964:287).

One of the more common processes affecting these soils is gleization, in which a bluish-gray to yellowish-gray mottling occurs in the subsoil as a consequence of "the partial oxidation and reduction of iron caused by intermittent water-logging" (Jacks 1954:196). This process has affected the low-lying soils of Northern Belize and is responsible for some of the post-depositional processes at work at Cerros. Specific reference can be made to the mottled gray clays within the canal system that contain small percentages of limonite.

The third type of intrazonal soil is the halomorphic type. It is usually considered to be restricted to arid locations, where insufficient rainfall and drainage prevent the periodic flushing of salts. Stagnant water coupled with high evaporation rates results in high salt concentrations. This situation can develop in littoral locations where salt air and laterally migrating groundwater can produce a higher-than-normal salt content. These factors and infrequent hurricane inundation may explain the high salt content at Cerros. This is believed to be a postabandonment phenomenon, as canalization would have allowed a much more efficient drainage network than is currently available. The mangrove swamp area at Cerros and elsewhere has been most affected by halomorphic and hydromorphic soil processes.

The Cerros soils are more alkaline than those reported for similarly depressed settings in the Petén (Lundell 1937; Puleston 1973) and as close by as Albion Island (Olson 1977) (approximately 50 kilometers south-southwest of Cerros). Although the attendant effects of saline seawater on Lowry's Bight following high winds or hurricane damage are a partial explanation, the elevated limestone caprock exposure at some locations near Cerros suggests the presence of a calcium carbonate–rich reservoir affecting these readings.

The soil survey conducted by Wright et al. (1959) in Belize has provided the best single source of data on the soils of Northern Belize. Only that material which

directly influences the soil profiles on and around Lowry's Bight will be reviewed here. The soils on which Cerros rests are termed "Remate" soils. These soils overlie the limestone caprock and are considered better drained than those of adjacent areas. They consist of red-brown clays which fix phosphates, making them insoluble for plant consumption. "In alkaline soils it [phosphate] is likely to be combined with calcium as a nearly insoluble compound. . . . Finally it may absorb on the surface of clay particles or become complexed with the clay minerals" (Cook and Heizer 1965:12).

The Xaibe clays appear similar in this phosphate deficiency, but both the Xaibe and the Remate soils have adequate amounts of nitrogen and potassium. The darker Louisville soils which lie adjacent to Lowry's Bight are perhaps the best agricultural soils in the Corozal District, containing adequate phosphate for continuous corn production without fertilizer. The Pucte series is mentioned because in isolated locations on Lowry's Bight the soils resemble gray waterlogged matrices undergoing gleization, although Wright et al. do not define their distribution on the Bight.

Soil crazing or cracking does not appear to be the problem here that it is for the Petén (Lundell 1934; Puleston 1973, 1978) due to the elevated water table. Further, the clay types in Northern Belize may also lessen gilgae formation. (See Antoine et al. 1982 for discussion of the 2:1 clays of Albion Island.)

Soil textures in proximity to Cerros are a consequence of differential weathering processes. Beach sands have affected grain size at locations immediately adjacent to the shoreline, while silts and clays define points farther inland along ancient river courses. Free-draining sandy soils can be defined in areas of *cocal* (*Cocos nucifera*) growth, as this tree crop requires well-drained matrices. Most quantifiable textural analysis of the sediments from Northern Belize requires thin sectioning and particle counts because of the high percentage of calcium carbonate in the soil. Wet sieving cannot be performed without first removing the calcium carbonate, which constitutes by weight the greatest particle fraction. Soil scientists have provided wet sieve grain-size separation data (Antoine et al. 1982), but it must be considered skewed.

Wright et al. (1959) appear to concur with Morley (1956) and the Carnegie Institution Experiment Station (Steggerda 1941) in viewing the soils of the lowlands as adequate in nutrients for continuous slash-and-burn agriculture. It is the effects of weed invasion that are ultimately responsible for the necessary fallow period. This conclusion, however, is far from a general consensus and is at best a minority opinion (Cowgill 1962; Cowgill and Hutchinson 1963; Hester 1954; Nye and Greenland 1960). Although most of the soils on Lowry's Bight are deficient in phosphates, mulching the crops will allow a slow release of phosphates, thus ensuring an adequate harvest (Wright et al. 1959:222).

CLIMATOLOGY

Many researchers have suggested that climate is the most telling component in producing the ecology of a region (Tosi 1964). The following sketch, however, will present only that information which directly pertains to the physical environment at Cerros. In the Koeppen system, Northern Belize is classified as Amw', having a tropical rainy climate characterized by a dry period from February through April and a concentration of rain from June through September. The dry season is more predictable than the wet season (see Wright et al. 1959:21). It should be noted that the "Little Dry," or August *canicula* drought (Hester 1954:23) in Northern Yucatán, can seriously disrupt crop growth, even though August is considered a wet month.

Northern Belize is generally much drier than the rest of the country. Rainfall is less than 1,500 millimeters annually and, as is typical of tropical settings, the rainfall may fluctuate radically from year to year. The semitropical climate accommodates a mean annual humidity of approximately 80%, an average winter temperature of 23.9°C (75°F), and an average summer temperature of 27.2°C (81°F) (Hammond 1973:2). Annual temperatures do drop as low as 10°C (50°F) and rise above 37.8°C (100°F).

Precipitation is in part directed by the southeasterly trade winds, although severe storms, termed "northers," or *nortes,* bring cool, wet weather from a southward extension of the North American anticyclone system. Reflecting the course of the southeasterlies are the nutrient-enriched sea currents, with origins in the Venezuelan and Colombian basins (Collier 1964). The upwelling of these currents off the Belizean coast increases the nitrogen and phosphorous content of the coastal waters. Their effect on the fishing industry is significant.

Hurricane activity is not unusual off the Belizean coast and appears to have affected the flat, low-lying relief of Lowry's Bight. Hurricanes are most likely to hit during August or September.

The climate of the region is greatly influenced by the hurricanes in the fall and the northers in the winter. . . . The hurricanes which sweep inland are direly destructive to the vegetation. Large areas are mutilated as, for instance in September 1931, when a strip of the forest in British Honduras was destroyed from Belize inland to Cocquericot, a distance of about 45 miles. In such wide-spread destruction, the climax forest is destroyed and complex successional stages take its place. In some areas not a single large tree remains after the hurricane has passed. (Lundell 1934:216)

BIOLOGY

The biological or organic environment exerts the most immediate effect on the cultural component. Food, shelter, and clothing in the tropical lowlands are derived directly from the organic world and play a fundamental role in cultural development. The fauna of the Maya Lowlands and Northern Belize will not be systematically examined in this study, as this subcomponent does not appear greatly to influence the other components in the environmental system as defined at Cerros. This is not to say that animals were not an important food resource and instrumental in the dispersion of plants or that they did not play a key role in socioreligious belief systems (Carr 1985, 1986). Rather, other components in the physical environment appear to have had a significantly greater impact on the cultural landscape. However, some attention will focus on the less-mobile molluscan remains and microfossils from Cerros in an attempt to reconstruct the various microenvironmental settings.

Flora

The vegetation of Northern Belize is more akin to the semitropical rain forest formations found in the Petén than to the dry evergreen formations suggested for the northern Yucatán peninsula. The vegetation of the Petén and Northern Belize is best characterized by Holdridge's classification of Tropical Dry Forest (1967) or Beard's Deciduous Seasonal Forest (1944, 1955). Northern Belize does not possess a true tropical rain forest: "British Honduras lies somewhere between 'tropical and subtropical' categories" (Wright et al. 1959:29). Lundell refers to the Petén and, by extension, Northern Belize, as a "quasi-rain forest" (1937). This fits Wagner's characterization of a tropical rain forest, because the Petén and Northern Belize have more seasonal climatic regimes: "The tropical rainforest grows in a hot, moist climate, with annual mean temperatures over 20°C and precipitation in excess of 1200 mm annually. The true tropical rain forest does not grow where rainfall is less than 50 mm in any one month, except where the annual total is above 2000 mm. This formation occupies deep, well-drained soils; it is less well developed where the soil is thin or subject to frequent inundation" (Wagner 1964:224).

The vegetation along the coast of Northern Belize is also subject to seasonal swamp formations. The brackish water mangrove swamps (*Rhizophora mangle*) along the southwest survey *brecha* on Lowry's Bight are especially illustrative of this vegetation pattern. The extreme effects of salt air and brackish water inundation have complicated the vegetation cover of Lowry's Bight.

Two levels of plant succession are at work on much of the vegetation of the lowlands (Lundell 1934, 1937). The long-term primary succession which Charter (1941) and Wright (1959:31) outline suggests a slow development from broadleaf forest to savanna grasslands, as a consequence of progressive soil deterioration. This process may be accelerated when rapid and extensive modification of the vegetation occurs, exposing soils to excessive erosional damage. The more widely accepted successional series is grounded in a shorter-term equilibrium state in which primary climax associations result in broadleaf dominants (Lundell 1934, 1937; Wagner 1964).

The second, more rapid, plant successional process is associated with the return of subclimax vegetation, or that soil and drainage condition permitting the most developed plant community following the extensive disruption of the primary vegetation. Secondary succession occurs on any abandoned field throughout the lowlands characterized by *acahual* or *huamil,* consisting of dense brush or thickets (see Appendix D):

> The succession [secondary] varies considerably from one area to another, depending on the manner of disturbance and on the climatic and

edaphic situation. In general, in the early stages the assemblage of plants in old clearings tends to include mostly species capable of wide dispersal and of rapid growth in open sunlight. Many of these are plants that also grow normally in stream beds, where natural disturbance is frequent. A great many are spread by animals. The progression in time is from low herb cover, approximating the weeds of cultivated fields, through a dense brush to thickets, often composed of a single species, with the slow accession of the usual forest trees to dominance if the site remains thereafter undisturbed. (Wagner 1964:232)

These two successional trends have interacted to produce the present vegetation cover of the lowlands. However, Northern Belize is more strongly influenced than the Petén by the secondary successions due to the extensive land use modification it has undergone since the Conquest. When Cerros was constructed and occupied during the Late Preclassic Period, the degree of soil deterioration had not accelerated to the degree currently apparent. However, *huamil* growth during and following construction of the site certainly demanded periodic clearing. It is likely that the setting was selectively culled of less useful vegetation to foster the growth and conservation of utilizable wild and feral tree crops (Lundell 1937:10; Puleston 1973; Wiseman 1978). Such pollard trees provide shade from direct sunlight and shelter from rainfall. Even so, repeated encroachment of the jungle growth would have had a significant effect on spatial boundaries (Scarborough 1985b; Scarborough and Robertson 1986).

THE ENVIRONMENTAL INTERACTION AT CERROS

The environmental settings defined for Lowry's Bight and Cerros are derived from the systematic survey of approximately 16% of the peninsula, as well as from numerous reconnaissance ventures carried out around and through the bight. Soils data were obtained from twenty contexts across the site and subjected to chemical analysis. The high percentage of calcium carbonate prohibited physical analysis, except for "the field 'touch' test" (see Appendix B). Additional soil samples were compared to this control sample in terms of color, texture, structure, and environmental setting in a less systematic manner. The definition of our environmental settings permitted comparisons with the soils maps of Wright et al. (1959).

The vegetation at Cerros was also studied to better discern the soil types found on the bight, because extensive and detailed soils analysis was not possible. Expectably, the defined microenvironments reflect the vegetation cover more closely than do the actual soil types. The present microenvironments at Cerros, however, do reflect the varying degrees of soil degradation. Precise identification of the broad range of plant species within each microenvironment was not possible, but an extensive representation of the dominant and subdominant species was made.

Crane (1986) has made a systematic and detailed inventory of plant species from Cerros. Her plant community associations generally complement the microenvironments established by the Cerros Survey Project. Discrepancies between the two classificatory systems do exist, but are attributable to the different methods each project attempts to use and goals each attempts to address. The microenvironments defined below are based on soil and drainage conditions. Plant associations are drawn upon to understand these conditions better. Crane's work focuses specifically on the vegetation.

The ultimate identifications for the species list (Appendix D) were done by Roberto Pott and Teodoro Martínez of Chunox village. For those who have worked in the lowlands, the concern and awareness of Maya cultivators for their environment and particularly for the vegetation is unquestioned, and I developed identification skills through working with them. Years of experience and tradition have taught them to use the various vegetation and soil zones efficiently, given the shortcomings of slash-and-burn agriculture. The duration of the project has allowed me to learn some of the complexities associated with the tropical forest. As Wright et al. (1959:286) state, "the process of familiarization with the component parts of the tropical forest is something that cannot be hurried; the information soaks in slowly and powers of observation develop slowly."

Both Bartlett (1936) and Lundell (1934, 1937) acknowledge the importance of the Maya informant, but both also stress the need to collect plants and ascribe proper species names. The Cerros Survey Project was unable initially to collect and directly identify plants according to the Linnean classification (though subsequent botanical research has been undertaken; Crane

personal communication), but by using the works of Barrera et al. (1976), Bartlett (1936), Lundell (1934, 1937, 1938), Standley and Record (1936), and Wright et al. (1959), I was able to correlate the Maya or Spanish field name identification with the Linnean classification (Appendix D provides this information). If the reader harbors doubts about this technique of identification, I provide the accompanying quote from Cyrus L. Lundell (1934:267), perhaps the foremost authority on the botany of the Maya Lowlands:

> The writer fully agrees with Bartlett. Since 1928 ecological studies have been carried out, using the folk knowledge as a basis. The folk classification and nomenclature take into consideration (1) the physiographical areas, (2) the successional types of vegetation, and (3) the dominant species characterizing the associations. . . .
>
> As an opening wedge in an unfamiliar region, no better method could be followed than to become acquainted with such folk nomenclature and classifications. And further, as Bartlett points out, much of this folk knowledge can be taken over and systematically formulated in an ecological study.

Before defining the microenvironments, the drainage patterns on Lowry's Bight should be mentioned. The bight is positioned within 15 kilometers of the mouths of the three principal external drainages for Northern Belize. The New River and Freshwater Creek drainage avenues flank the peninsula and probably defined it in the past. The mouth of the Hondo River lies to the north. The absence of significant natural relief on the bight has been a major factor in determining the present appearance of the site. Some precipitation drains and percolates into the groundwater system, with the low-lying savanna and *bajo* localities of the site area holding significant amounts of standing water. Groundwater levels fluctuate as much as 2 meters between seasons, as revealed by our canal exposures. Although some surface current movement is predictable, the major volume of water evaporates during the dry season. Severe erosion as a consequence of runoff is not a major problem on Lowry's Bight due to the flatness of the topography. However, slow infilling of depressed features is apparent throughout the settlement, eroding from the immediate high ground that defines these depressions as well as from the slight gradient from south/

southeast (upslope) to north/northwest (downslope) across the bight.

Five microenvironments within the 1.51-square-kilometer area systematically surveyed have been defined on Lowry's Bight. Detailed coverage for the remainder of the bight has not been collected, although aerial photographic coverage and reconnaissance surveys have permitted a less systematic identification of these settings. Two *bajo* settings should be mentioned outside the systematic survey area (Fig. 2.6). The first lies on the northeastern tip of the peninsula and appears to be a shallow doline closed off from Corozal Bay by mangrove reclamation and a possible hurricane ridge. This depression contains brackish water during most of the year. Although the north shore depression is natural, it is quite shallow, and informants suggest that it is recent in origin, perhaps as a consequence of localized land subsidence.

The second *bajo* area outside the systematic survey area is an ancient river channel or course of the New River. It appears formerly to have emptied into the shallow embayment immediately south of the intrasite area on the southeast side of Lowry's Bight. A concentration of Early Postclassic midden debris (labeled Esperanza on Fig. 2.7) was located on the south levee at the mouth of this old drainage. This channel is readily traceable back to the New River terrace (on aerial photographs) at the northeast margin of the river's mouth. The presence of this drainage is peculiar in that it crosses the ridge defining the longitudinal axis of the bight and the crest of the earlier mentioned north/northeast–south/southwest structural formation. Reconnaissance into this area indicates a possible shallow, vertical thrust block fault uplifted on the southwest side of the ancient channel. Such a geological event would have permitted the New River to meander in the manner described.

The most extensive microenvironment covering the systematic survey area is the *monte alto* and *huamil* setting. Wright et al. (1959) have defined this vegetation on Lowry's Bight as deciduous, seasonal, broadleaf forest, rich in lime-loving species, and having a maximum canopy height of 50 to 70 feet (Fig. 3.1). This setting is characterized by dark, slightly basic, well-drained, friable loamy soils. These soils are thin and overlie the caprock formation. They occupy slightly elevated settings and occur on or near plaza or mound space, with the greatest frequency in the core area of the site. These soils can best be summarized as rendzina soils (mollisols) and are Remate-types in the Wright et al. (1959) classification. Although the term *"huamil"*

Figure 3.1. *Monte alto.*

usually refers to secondary growth within most any setting, Lowry's Bight has not accommodated large village aggregates in recent history. For this reason, the few cultivators using the peninsula have been permitted to use the best, most fertile land without troubling to clear the less-desirable, poorly drained areas. For Lowry's Bight, *huamil* can be considered synonymous with *monte alto* (Fig. 3.2).

The next most extensive microenvironment is the *hulub bajo* setting characterized by yaxom soils. It is nearly uninterrupted in its distribution along the eastern portion of the site. This setting is the most depressed in the settlement, excepting the *aguadas* and portions of the low-lying *zacatal*, which contain 30 to 40 centimeters of viscous, organically rich clay overlying a viscous, compacted, mottled gray clay. Only our excavations in the main canal (OP116) have

Figure 3.2.   Recently cleared house mound in *huamil* setting.

been taken down below the dry season water table in this setting. The basal, sterile, clean, white *sascab* (white marl) was located approximately 2 meters below the surface.

These soils are not highly acidic because of a superabundance of $CaCO_3$ and do not appear to suffer from cracking, in part as a result of the high water table at Cerros. They have undergone severe gleization and appear to have their closest affinity to the Pucte series, as defined by Wright et al. (1959). Further, these soils have very high percentages of NaCl. It should be noted that the gastropod *Pomacea flagellata* has been collected in abundance from this setting, suggesting the poorly drained condition of these soils (Covich 1983; Feldman 1979). The dominant vegetation is *hulub* (*Bravaisia tubiflora*), which is a subtype of the *tembladeral* in Bartlett's 1936 classification (Fig. 3.3). "This [tembladeral] is the wettest part of the *bajo,* and is avoided at all seasons since mules are likely to be mired in it and lost" (p. 23). Although this may be a slight overstatement of the Cerros soils, it certainly captures the spirit and condition of this microenvironment.

A slightly better-drained location was lumped in with the typical *hulub bajo* setting at Cerros (after Beard 1944:130). This was done because of the difficulty resulting from attempting to separate the two settings by vegetation type. This latter setting has been defined at the *bajo* fringe and is perhaps most similar to an intermediate association leading to a broadleaf climax forest. The dominant vegetation is *huano (Sabal mayarum)* and the location can be referred to as *huanal.* This location has much in common with the *escobal* defined throughout the Peten by Lundell (1934, 1937) and more recently by Puleston (1973) and Siemens (1978).

In a very limited portion of the site, grassland savanna or *zacatal* has been identified. The origin of this setting is unclear. In the early 1960s, a portion of the survey area was converted to pasture, or *potrero.* It is possible that the *zacatal,* which represents some of the most depressed and poorly drained land on the peninsula and is seasonally inundated by a meter or more of water, was affected (Fig. 3.4). Although the vegetation cover is significantly different from that in other areas,

Figure 3.3.   Transit station in *hulubol*.

the soils are similar to those defined in the *hulub bajo* setting. The thickness of the viscous, compacted, humic clay horizon ranges from 10 to 30 centimeters and is underlain by a viscous, compacted, mottled gray clay. The grasses, as well as the elevated water table, prevent soil cracking. These soils have a basic pH and undergo severe seasonal waterlogging. The NaCl content is extremely high. These glei soils have a superabundance of $CaCO_3$ and a balanced proportion of other minerals except for a phosphate deficiency. *Pomacea flagellata* pervade the setting and have severely disrupted the stratigraphy (see OP115, OP116, OP153, OP154, OP156).

A slightly more extensive microenvironment than that defined by the *zacatal* is the thorn-scrub savanna (after Wiseman 1978) (Fig. 3.5). At the margins of the *zacatal* are the slightly better drained soils associated with this setting. Most of the known canalization at

Cerros is located in this microenvironment. The vegetation cover is dominated by *muk (Dalbergia glabra),* a most disagreeable bush. The soils are similar to those in the *zacatal,* although they have undergone less gleization. A thin A-horizon of loamy clay is underlain by viscous, compacted, mottled gray clays. The soils are charged with $CaCO_3$, have a high pH, and, except for the phosphates, a suitable mineral matrix for most crops (OP151, OP152). *Pomacea flagellata* occur in this setting, but in lesser numbers. The NaCl content is again very high. This setting usually flanks *monte alto/huamil* and is the most depressed setting in the settlement. It can be considered a transitional zone in terms of both vegetation and elevation.

A variation of the thorn-scrub savanna setting occurs in a spotty distribution along the southwestern coastal *brechas* and most extensively surrounding the large Aguada 2. These areas appear to be better drained and higher in elevation than the low-lying thorn-scrub savanna settings, although the associated soils have not been closely examined. However, these soils are understood to be quite thin, because of the exposure of the limestone caprock at some locations. "Potato holes," or diminutive solution channels, have been noted in this setting. *Katsim (Mimosa hemiendyta)* is the dominant thorn bush.

The final microenvironment at Cerros is the mangrove shoreline. This setting can best be understood as a river mouth association almost entirely defined by mangrove (*Rhizophora mangle*). The soil is typically entrapped beach sand. In the area surveyed it occupies a sporadic distribution along the southwestern *brecha,* but our reconnaissance by boat along the south side of the bight indicates a more continuous distribution. As is the case with most of the distributional settings defined at Cerros, it is recent in origin, although it was certainly in proximity to the site prehistorically. This is suggested in part by the rich molluscan life of the mangrove swamps, which was likely exploited during the late Preclassic Period (see Carr 1986). Our core zone midden exposures have yet to produce the brackish water oyster which makes its home in the stilt-root entanglement of the mangroves, but it is found in association with the Early Postclassic midden area on Esperanza Bight (on the south side of Lowry's Bight). The water table in the mangrove setting is subject to tidal fluctuations, which allow access to many estuarine species (Fig. 3.6).

To summarize, an attempt has been made to correlate the known vegetation and drainage conditions

Figure 3.4.   Aguada 2 at onset of dry season.

Figure 3.5.   Clearing operations associated with low-lying thorn-scrub and *zacatel*.

Figure 3.6.   Margins of First River terrace from shoreline.

within the survey area with the soils. This has emphasized the dynamic interplay between the various components in the physical environment today, but it will also permit a reconstruction of the past "cultural" environmental component. Three of the five microenvironments have undergone controlled soil analysis. The other two settings are controlled by past studies carried out by Wright et al. (1959) on Lowry's Bight.

AN ENVIRONMENTAL RECONSTRUCTION

The foregoing has been provided as background for the first of three settlement reconstructions to be developed for the Cerros Survey Project. The microenvironments presented will not be argued to be the same as those existing two thousand years ago at the Late Preclassic climax of Cerros' development. Moreover, it is suggested that regional climatic conditions have triggered some of the changes which do occur on Lowry's Bight (see Raikes 1984:108). The present physical environment is understood to be a

consequence of sea level rise/localized subsidence as well as cultural abandonment.

Cerros is argued to have been colonized initially by fisherfolk who rapidly adapted to an intensive commercial exchange system. The primal environment is argued to have been a lagoon-estuarine setting (Freidel and Scarborough 1982; Scarborough 1983a). The site environment at that time is posited to have been more similar to the well-drained *monte alto* setting defined throughout the survey area than to the depressed, poorly drained environments. The vegetation would have been closer to climax than the present settings. This hypothesis is suggested on grounds that the initial residents at Cerros would have selected a well-drained site for supplemental agricultural pursuits and the broad-spectrum exploitation of mammals and tree resources made available in this setting. The evidence for a lower relative sea level would further indicate a well-drained setting in the past. The nucleated village midden debris associated with the earliest occupations at Cerros (the early facet of the Late Preclassic Period at Cerros is the Ixtabai phase, ca. 300–200 B.C.; table 1)

TABLE 1

Chronological Chart

LATE POSTCLASSIC
(Lobil)

1250 -

EARLY POSTCLASSIC
(New Town)

950 -

LATE CLASSIC
(Tepeu)

550 -

EARLY CLASSIC
(Tzakol)

200 -

Floral Park
- - - - - - - - - - - - - - -

AD
- - - - - -   0   Tulix (Phase 3)
BC   50 - - - - - - - - - - - -   LATE PRECLASSIC
                                             (Chicanel)

C'oh (Phase 2)

200 - - - - - - - - - - - - -

Ixtabai (Phase 1)

300 -

MIDDLE PRECLASSIC
(Mamom)

600

appears to support this hypothesis (Cliff 1986). The well-drained nature of this village is further supported by the presence of only ground-level structures and the absence of any identified *Pomacea flagellata* from the midden.

Exploitation of and adaptation to the forest resources is further suggested by the presence of an Ixtabai component at or near the large Aguada 2 located 1.5 kilometers south-southeast of the early nucleated village. A surface collection taken from the flanks of the *aguada* indicates the extensive use of the northern half of the basin. All identifiable sherds collected have been assigned to the Ixtabai phase (Robertson personal communication). If the freshwater lagoon-estuary reconstruction for the site is correct, then a freshwater supply from this *aguada* for the shoreline nucleated village would have been unnecessary.

The amount and distribution of pottery collected from the rim of this *aguada* may suggest the presence of another Ixtabai community. It is suggested that these two communities would not have differed significantly in their formative adaptations to the environment. Only later would the geographic position of the lagoon-

shoreline nucleated village have permitted the pre-adaptation necessary for extended maritime relationships. It should be noted that not one mound has been discovered within 100 meters of the edge of this *aguada*, suggesting a further similarity to the ground-level structures of the estuarine shoreline village.

During the next phase of construction and occupation at Cerros (the middle facet of the Late Preclassic Period is the C'oh phase, ca. 200–50 B.C.), the settlement data suggest that the community underwent a residential transition (see Fig. 3.7). This pattern was an extension of the well-drained ground-level compacted village arrangement defined in the earlier Ixtabai phase. These structures rest on a steely-blue alluvial clay and cluster around the central precinct. It will be shown that these C'oh phase residents best reflect an infield/outfield agricultural settlement system. The environment during this period is hypothesized to have been similar to that defined for Ixtabai times but with kitchen gardens and the creation of an artificial rain forest (Geertz 1963; Lundell 1937:11; Wiseman 1978) within the confines of the site. The soils and the vegetation characterized a well-drained setting. This is supported partially by the absence of *Pomacea flagellata* from any archaeological context associated with this or any other phase within the Late Preclassic Period at Cerros. Considering the frequency of this gastropod at a similar time at other sites in Northern Belize (Feldman 1979) and the apparent relish for this species by Late Preclassic Maya (e.g., at Cuello; see Donaghey et al. 1979:26), its total absence at Cerros is peculiar (note that *P. flagellata* occurs in relatively high frequencies at Cerros, but only in post-abandonment contexts). From this, I would suggest that the site was well-drained until its Late Preclassic abandonment.

Late in the C'oh phase there was a further change in the settlement pattern and agricultural base. It is at this time that the main canal was excavated around the site and the concentration of mounded features constructed. Structure 76 at the margin of Aguada 1 was erected, as were additional structures clustered around and overlying the earlier ground-level C'oh phase residences. The canal and *aguada* fill appear to have been used in the construction of these structures. With the initiation of canal construction, the Cerros community experienced its most significant environmental transition. However, as will be demonstrated below, the main canal was not solely a drainage device. Most of the monumental architecture had not yet been erected and little extensive quarrying had been initiated.

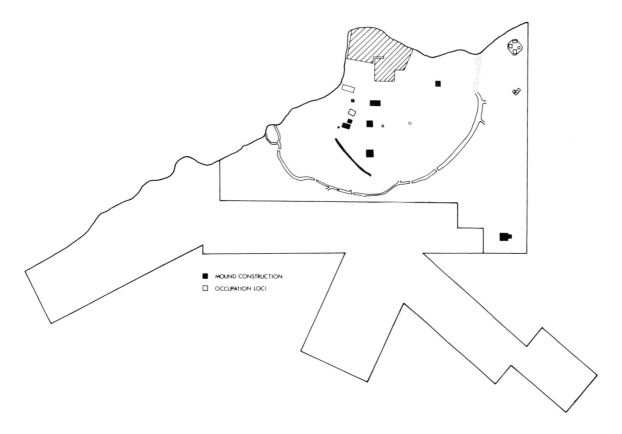

Figure 3.7.   Map of C'oh phase occupation (200–50 B.C.).

During the Tulix phase (or the late facet of the Late Preclassic at Cerros, ca. 50 B.C.–A.D. 150), the previous well-drained setting was significantly altered (see Fig. 3.8). The major construction in the central precinct occurred, as well as the construction or reuse of over 90% of the plaza and structure space defined on the present settlement map, including Structure 29 and the two ball courts (Structure Groups 61 and 50). Raised plaza space occurred throughout the settlement, capping earlier C'oh phase structures. Complementing this construction of monumental architecture was the system of depressions resulting from the necessary quarrying activities. This is readily apparent from the environmental map (see Fig. 2.2).

The environs at this time were not those of a seasonally drained setting, but a perennial watershed controlled by a system of sills, or dikes, and canalization. The existence of formal irrigation, short of pot irrigation, cannot be supported at the present time. Further, our speculative arguments in favor of controlled irrigation

(Freidel and Scarborough 1982) have been challenged by more recent survey and excavation at Cerros (Scarborough 1983a). Although the main canal could have tapped into the regressing channel of the New River, a less-complicated explanation can be reconstructed. Given present evidence, the involved cultural relief at Cerros represented in part a drainage system directed into the main canal but capable of holding runoff in reservoirs or "canal basins" for use during the dry season. The contour map of the site supports this latter thesis, as do our most recent excavations.

The soils and vegetation during the Tulix phase were well drained. Most of the setting was artificially altered to produce a true cultural relief having tremendous agricultural potential. The poor condition of the present soils is in no way a reflection of their original fertility.

Since my 1982 paper (Freidel and Scarborough 1982), few researchers have quibbled with the formal definition of raised fields and canalization at Cerros. In

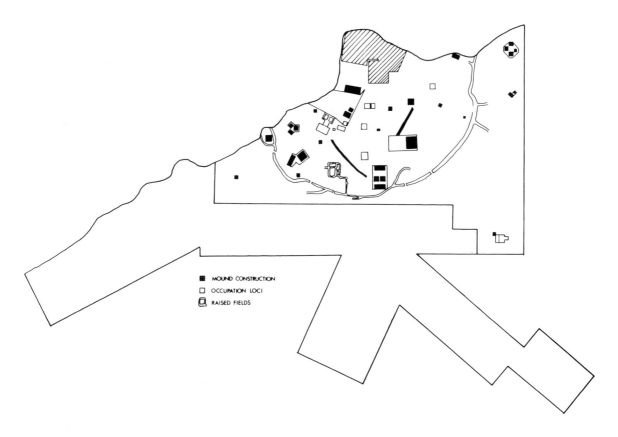

Figure 3.8.   Map of Tulix phase occupation (50 B.C.–A.D. 150).

that article, I stated that the fields were most likely drained seasonally to accommodate wet season intensive agriculture. However, the main canal itself could not have contained the anticipated runoff from the intrasite area alone. The known dimensions of the canal are 2 meters in depth, 6 meters in width, and 1,200 meters in length, which would have provided a 14,400-cubic-meter catchment volume for draining the site area. There are 37 hectares, or 370,000 square meters, within the confines of the site as defined by the main canal perimeter. If only this area were drained by the canal (and our contour map would indicate a much more extensive drainage system), it would take fewer than 5 centimeters of runoff across this area to fill and overflow the canal immediately. Wright et al. (1959:17) state, "Falls of rain are often of an intense kind; 5 inches in 24 hours is experienced not infrequently." The exposed impermeable clays underlying the quarried caprock as well as the exposed and more dense caprock allow little absorption of precipitation. Cowgill and Hutchinson (1963:20) indicate that only 20% of the

runoff into the Bajo de Santa Fe is absorbed by the soil. However, the large depression near the center of the core zone as well as the known and hypothesized feeder canals across the site would have held a large amount of water. The severity of flooding at Cerros was most clearly appreciated in July of 1976, when stagnant chest-high water levels were negotiated while traversing the 9.5-meter contour interval through the settlement. Only a well-managed system of hydraulic control could have reduced the damage to soils, to say nothing of household disruptions, as a consequence of this high water.

In addition, the Tulix phase settlement was constructed from a preconceived general plan. Together the great arc of the main canal (Freidel and Scarborough 1982; Scarborough 1983a), the central precinct, the position of the ball courts along a north/south axis of the site, and their relationship to Structure 29 (Scarborough et al. 1982) suggest a sophisticated degree of symmetry (see Fig. 3.9). This plan had been initiated by the end of the C'oh phase but was not completed until the end

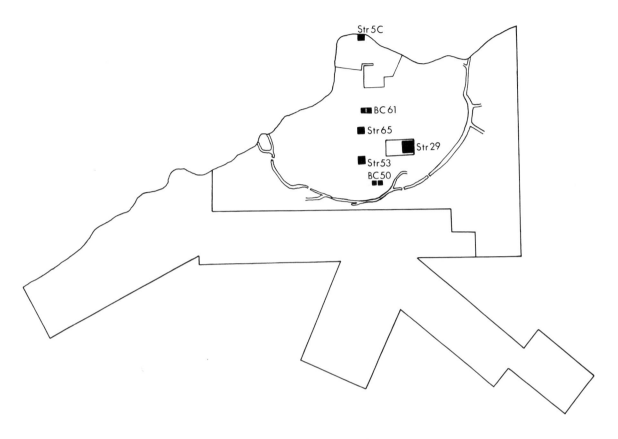

Figure 3.9.   Map of ball court spatial relationships.

of the Tulix phase. Judging from the patterned arrangement of features generally, it is suggested that the location of and control over quarrying activities were carefully regulated to permit the subsequent use of these depressions for water manipulation projects.

The amount of fill necessary to construct the limestone rubble core supporting the bulk of the structures at Cerros has been calculated to be 226,395 cubic meters (see Appendix A). This fill could have been obtained locally if most of the 2-meter-thick caprock were removed back to the 10.5-meter contour surrounding the site. This contour break corresponds to the approximate location at which the pocked and pitted caprock defining the impacted site area changes to a more level and flat topography. After reviewing the geology of Northern Belize, Hazelden (1973:85) states:

> The Maya seem to have used only very local stone for building, perhaps quarried on the site itself. Evidence of this is seen 100 meters east of Plaza C at San Estevan. No great lengths were

gone to in obtaining building stone, even if the effort involved in carrying better quality stone from a short distance would have been very small. The emphasis seems to have been on obtaining the stone from as close to the site of building as was feasible.

Although the caprock at Cerros may have undulated slightly across the settlement and its thickness may have varied slightly, our exposure of its thickness in the main canal profiles will be used as an approximate figure for its proportions across the settlement. Reeves (1970:358) has indicated that "fine bedded lacustrine clays tend to impart bedding to the caliche and to restrict infiltration; thus bedding, an absence of carbonate nodules, and rapid formation of an upper laminated zone are characteristic of caliche formed on clays or shales."

The fine particle fraction and clay-sized cement underlying the caprock permitted a continuous bedding plane for the caprock on Lowry's Bight. Further support for the homogeneous bedding of the caprock is suggested by the absence of carbonate nodules in the matrix. Reeves continues (1970:358–359):

> There are undoubtedly several different types of structures found in thick caliche profiles, some formed by expansion or contraction due to various reasons, some formed by solution and settling, some even being structures which antedate formation of the caliche. *However, large caliche structures are not typical of caliche profiles and represent very local effects* . . . the type of structures that form in caliche is the combined result of the parent sediments, amount of carbonate, the vegetation, the climatic environment, and the time or extent of caliche formation. (Emphasis added)

It is submitted that all of these factors were relatively the same across the bight and that the caliche or caprock deposit can be considered homogeneous except where quarried.

It should be noted that the fill for monumental architecture was not taken from under raised plaza and structure space prior to its construction. This has been demonstrated repeatedly in the civic and residential architecture testing program and further suggests the planned nature of the settlement. In determining the amount of quarry fill made available at the site, those low-lying areas containing architectural remains capping an unquarried matrix below have been subtracted from the overall quarry volume total (see Appendix A).

As indicated earlier, Ixtabai and C'oh phase residential structures cluster around the main plaza and precinct center, with most dwellings resting on alluvial clays. Excavated exposures indicate that these clays in turn rest on sterile, yellowish, granular *sascab*. It is not believed that the caprock was removed from these locations, but rather, that it has been resorbed by the rising water table associated with subsidence and sea level rise. That the alluvial clays were deposited by the New River before the site was occupied is indicated by the absence of any cultural debris associated with them. The restricted shoreline distribution of these alluvial sediments reveals the northern course of the river and indicates that the New River had been regressing up its mouth sometime before the site was colonized. Again, this area was not considered in arriving at the total quarry area.

The major source of error in determining the fill volume for the site comes from the eroded shoreline. The eastern portion of the site appears to have weathered less than the western portion. Cliff (1986) argues for the presence of a docking facility immediately east of the central precinct, suggesting reduced erosional loss at the margins of the monumental architecture. However, the western shoreline of the site is littered with eroded cultural debris and plagued with shallow-lying limestone chunks trailing 100 meters into the bay. Although beach rock formations (see Russell 1967) do occur along this coast, it is suggested that the lateral extent of this limestone is a better reflection of the inundation of small structures than it is the result of natural agents. The extent of the fill error is in part balanced by the incalculable mass of these small structures.

Because of the ubiquitous and apparently continuous distribution of caprock outside the culturally impacted area, it is suggested that the residents of Tulix phase Cerros systematically quarried away more than 190,651 cubic meters of caprock within the core area of the site as defined by the main canal. This figure compares favorably with the 210,986 cubic meters of structure fill recorded in the core area. A significant portion of the area within and defined by the 10.5-meter contour line was also quarried away, but it is apparent from our volumetric comparisons that a portion of the present eastern *hulub bajo* was depressed prior to extensive quarrying operations. This area may represent the remanants of an interior drainage locality receiving the runoff from the canals and reservoirs when they overflowed.

In most areas of the settlement, the caprock was not completely excavated down to the underlying sterile, white *sascab* level, apparently to define and maintain the course of channels and canals. Initially, it was hypothesized that, given the basal surface contours reported in this area (Scarborough 1983a:740), the low-lying *zacatal* in the center of the core area had been excavated through the caprock. It was assumed that if the amount and rate of sedimentation identified by our excavations in the main canal (principally OP116) were the same as in the *zacatal*, then the fact that the surface contours indicated the *zacatal* to have been 1 meter lower than the silted-in main canal suggested that the *zacatal* would have been excavated through the 2-meter-thick caprock. However, this hypothesis has been subsequently tested by digging into the *zacatal* "reservoir," only to find a half meter of sediment above the resorbing caprock. Clearly, sedimentation rates across the site differed. More important, the apparent depth of aboriginal excavation in the core area was determined by the thickness of the caprock and an attempt by the residents of Cerros to use the rigidity and impervious nature of this stone for containing water. It should be noted that by not breaking the caprock, possible saline-rich groundwater *below* the caprock would have been prevented from readily contaminating freshwater stores.

As already indicated, the site environment was unlike its present appearance. However, the present setting can tell us something about the past environs. The extensive presence of *yaxom* or *bajo* soils and accompanying vegetation indicates considerable sedimentation from adjacent high ground despite our inability to determine the precise amount of infilling from setting to setting. Generally speaking, the *zacatal* setting appears to have undergone the most silting in the settlement. The bulk of these denuded blocky clays are thought to have eroded from a small, well-defined raised-field complex, which would have collapsed into the more depressed locations within the site. There is little dispute that *bajo* settings throughout the lowlands have undergone substantial infilling from the mass wasting of adjacent well-drained rendzina soils (mollisols) (Cowgill and Hutchinson 1963:274; Lundell 1937:89; Ricketson 1937:11). In the case of Cerros, some of the fill has found its way in from the adjacent crest running through Lowry's Bight, even though the relief from the spine of this ridge to the edge of Corozal Bay is less than 6 meters over a distance of 1.5 kilometers. This sedimentation has affected the perimeter of the site outside the canal much more than it has the core area, as revealed by the presence of numerous depressions which are only partially infilled. For this reason, the bulk of the sediments within the core area defined by the main canal are wasting from plaza margins and the more friable field platforms. The depth of these sediments can be assessed in our canal and reservoir exposures, which indicate a 0.5-meter-to more than a 1.5-meter-deep deposit of clay and silt.

The six microenvironments defined on the peninsula can be lumped into three major soil and drainage groups that reflect the original drainage of Tulix phase Cerros: the low-lying *hulub bajo* and *zacatal* reveal the quarrying locations and canal system; the elevated, well-drained *monte alto/huamil* (as well as the elevated thorn-scrub savanna) defines the original caprock surface, or raised "cultural relief"; the depressed thorn-scrub savanna and the *huanal* (a less well defined subdivision of the *hulub bajo* resting at the *bajo* fringe) mark the transition zone between high and low ground. In general, in computing the area

effectively quarried, only the *hulub bajo* and the *zacatal* settings have been considered. Although caprock removal has had an impact on some of the thorn-scrub savanna setting (OP152, OP159, OP161), similar settings have been less affected. At any rate, some of this error has been compensated for by the inclusion of the *huanal* or *bajo* fringe in the quarry area figure.

Quarrying the caprock for mound fill and channeling water for agricultural purposes were not the only benefits obtainable from this landscape modification. Lime-rich *sascab*, clays would have been periodically exposed (a *sascabera*, or lime quarry, appears to have been identified near Structure 38) and perhaps mixed with the more loamy rendzinas or the more distant beach sands to produce the foundations for the raised-field platforms (after Hester 1954:82; see Serpenti 1965:41 for ethnographic analogy). For corn production some experiments indicate that phosphate requirements are reduced significantly when lime has been added to phosphate-deficient soils (Soils Science Department 1978:130). (Urrutia, however, indicates that liming phosphate-deficient soils is only effective if the soils have an acidic nature [1967:26].) Harrison and Turner (1983) have suggested the presence of such an intensive reworking of the soils by Late Preclassic times in the Pulltrouser Swamp area located approximately 30 kilometers south of Cerros.

LAND USE POTENTIAL

Judging from the planned spatial organization of the settlement at Cerros, it is argued that the site was selected carefully for environmental as well as geographical considerations during the Tulix phase. The trading posture of the community has been outlined by Freidel (1977, 1978) and discussed by me (1978). However, the agricultural potential of the site warrants greater attention. The conversion of the site from natural topographic relief to the complicated cultural landscape during the Tulix phase must be considered in socioeconomic terms. Simple drainage of the natural setting can hardly be seen as a cause for the extensive quarrying, given the postulated well-drained setting at the outset of occupation. Monument construction was a major force behind quarrying the site, but the excavation of the main canal appears to antedate the major monuments by at least one hundred years (Robertson personal communication; Scarborough and Robertson 1986). The initial construction of the main canal would appear to have been for reasons other than drainage or monument fill.

Irrigation or the control of a year-round water flow system cannot be argued easily. The extremely high salt content throughout the site and especially in the fields (see Jacobson and Adams 1958), coupled with the very poorly drained clays occupying the eastern quarter of the site in the location most likely to receive the fine particle fraction in west to east irrigation flow (after Gibson 1974:10), might suggest a worn-out prehistoric irrigation system. However, a carefully landscaped localized gradient could have produced a similar appearance. The molluscan data can be viewed as only equivocal (see Appendix C), and the soils analysis must be refined. Still, the downslope west-to-east gradient of the main canal is argued to be a restricted drainage feature designed with a system of sills to produce a rather elaborate catchment reservoir servicing the entire site (see Hauck 1973). Although the initial canal excavation cannot be demonstrated empirically to have functioned as an irrigation canal, it must have facilitated communications across the site regardless of its other uses. Canoe traffic has been demonstrated elsewhere from the Late Preclassic Period (Connor 1975) and strongly stated for Cerros (Freidel 1978).

The exact nature of the transition from C'oh phase to Tulix phase is unclear, but it is argued that the core site area was partially covered at this later time by a controlled water level. Whether it was a permanent, well-flushed system regulated by the stable water level of the New River (see pp. 33, 152–53) or a seasonal runoff system, perhaps internally drained within the core area as defined by the main canal perimeter, communication and intrasite exchange are suggested to have been facilitated by an elaborate, though poorly understood, system of waterways (see Fig. 2.2). If the artificial seasonal watershed argument is made (a proposition believed more convincing), then a system of sills would have been necessary to control the flow of wet season as well as dry season reservoirs. The impermeable clays and basal caprock at the lower reaches of the canals would retain most of the water, preventing the vertical percolation of moisture. Evaporation-retarding plants (after Freidel and Scarborough 1982; Matheny 1978; Puleston 1977; Stephens 1843) may have further conserved water levels, although the humidity would always have been quite high.

The subsidence on Lowry's Bight has had an accelerating effect on the infilling of the system. Although the poorly drained internal catchment defining the core site area at Cerros may collect a meter and a half of standing water today, it would have been much different if the entire site were raised a meter and a half and allowed to drain into the postulated lagoon. Even then, dry season catchment basins would have been maintained in the seasonal watershed system.

Although raised fields, or earthen platforms, have been defined within the core site area, their elaborate form and orientation as well as the presence of cultural debris and high phosphate concentrations more than 60 meters from the nearest mounded feature may suggest ground-level residential loci. The prospect that the fields were fertilized and mulched using household trash from other locations within the settlement has been postulated elsewhere (Freidel and Scarborough 1982), but the large size of the sherds may suggest primary deposition on well-drained kitchen gardens. The ground-level occupation characterized by the Ixtabai and C'oh phases coupled with the squarish shape of the Tulix phase raised-field loci identified inside the main canal may argue for a residential function for these features.

In addition to the elaborate form of some of these earthen platforms (mounded *sascab* and stone-buttressed platform sides), the squarish shape of the features is somewhat unusual when compared to raised, ridged, and ditched fields elsewhere in the world. Nevertheless, the variability of form registered in the Cerros examples would permit their inclusion in any of these settings (see Denevan 1966, 1970, 1982; Denevan and Turner 1974; Parsons and Denevan 1967; Serpenti 1965). The length-to-width ratio of our features approaches one, suggesting that simple pot irrigation and the dredging of organic matter for fertilizer are not the whole story. The narrower the field, the easier it is to tend a crop dependent on canal supplies. By widening the platform, one increases the distance one must carry water to the interior of the plot. If this is considered a less efficient agricultural adjustment, then at least one other cultural component enters the description. I suggest that a household would have such an effect. The area of our largest field plot is sufficient to accommodate one family and adjacent garden space, if we use an analogy to the space requirements of a family in the nearby village of Chunox (Mitchum 1978).

I am in no way suggesting that every raised field defined in the Maya Lowlands was a household locus. However, I will assert that some of them were used for household residences (see Calnek 1972 for a

Tenochtitlán example). Such a system may have allowed the efficient rotation of the household over a restricted field plot area. This would have permitted kitchen midden debris to enrich an abandoned house site, while the new residence could be relocated to an exhausted fallow plot. The life expectancy of a present-day thatched house is thirty years (Wauchope 1938), at which time the house is overrun by insect pests and wood rot.

Adhering to Freidel's model of trade, it is posited that commercial as well as social interaction rested on maritime exchange. At the intrasite level of analysis, the site is thought to have been a floating garden city during the wet season and during at least a portion of the dry season. If the settlement dried out from February through May, a system of high ground would have connected all public and private space. This is best illustrated by the 210-meter-long Sacbe 1 extending from the large *plazuela* Structure 10 Group to the ball court Structure 50 Group, which traverses the most depressed *zacatal* terrain in the settlement.

During the wet season and perhaps during a portion of the dry season, the main canal is believed to have made maritime traffic possible to many points in the settlement. The greater depth of the main canal would allow larger canoes access to interior locations and shallow-draft dugouts may have been able to venture around the site even during the dry season. I have suggested elsewhere (Freidel and Scarborough 1982) that some of the causeways or check dam–like features bridging the main canal were utilized by the Late Preclassic occupants of the site, but I would revise that hypothesis and suggest that they are Early Classic or later in origin. Our single cross section through one of these features (OP116) indicates that it is later in time, following the abandonment of the Late Preclassic occupation at Cerros. The kind of drainage system envisioned at Cerros is perhaps hinted at by Denevan (1966:18, 73) in his discussion of the chiefdoms of Mojos in Northern Bolivia:

> For all forms of life the most significant changes in the landscape are not the semipermanent and unusual ones, but rather the regular seasonal changes. During the wet summer, rainfall is plentiful and the vegetation is verdant; but as the season progresses the pampas are converted into vast marshes dotted with scattered islands and sinuous bands of gallery forest. Great flocks of bright-colored birds fly overhead and fish come

> out of the rivers and swarm over the flooded llanos. Terrestrial life, including man, seeks the high ground but also of necessity becomes amphibious. . . .

> During the dry season everything changes. The marshes first become muddy and are filled with stagnant pools, rotting dead fish, and rank grasses; and then they dry out completely. Rains are infrequent, many trees lose their leaves, the grasses turn brown, and the clay soils crack. The serial view is one of tall pampa grasses, scattered scrub trees and palms, and forest patches. The bajios and small rivers dry up, but the shallow, rectangular lakes persist. The trails become dusty, and grass fires fill the sky with smoke. The aspect is one of bleak grayness and aridity. . . . For the traveler who has seen the llanos during flooding it is disconcerting to return in August and find water being brought many miles by oxcart to be sold in town and to see canoes tied up to the hitching post of a ranch house with the nearest body of water many miles away. . . .

> While causeways facilitated foot travel during periods of flooding, they did not have the utility of watercraft for transporting food, belongings, and fuel. When flood waters rose to a height of several feet on the pampas, canoes could travel unhindered cross-country over vast seas of water.

The major challenge to this description for the Cerros setting is the resultant reservoirs of stagnant water throughout the settlement. This factor would have allowed the growth of insect pests unless the system were periodically flushed or predatory fish were made to occupy such ponds (Cooke 1931). The latter possibility would also have provided a welcome source of protein (see Puleston 1977; Thompson 1974).

The size of the mounded structures and the elevated plaza space at Cerros relative to other well-documented Preclassic communities (e.g., Komchen, see chapter 8; also see Andrews 1981; Andrews et al. 1981) may suggest, in part, the annual high water levels to which the settlement was exposed. Although mounded space reflected permanent social space, it may have been exaggerated at Cerros as a consequence of the seasonal water levels. A pattern which has emerged from the settlement testing program is the presence of a "preparatory surface" or ground-level house floor underlying most of the larger and more complicated structures. Many of these underlying floors are associated with C'oh phase debris and may reflect the changing water control at Cerros.

Except for the fields along the first river terrace at the southwest end of our shoreline traverse, most of the agricultural activity on the bight is speculated to have been located immediately outside the canal within the 10.0-meter contour. Unfortunately, the vegetation and sedimentation in the *hulub bajo* area in the eastern portion of the site have severely impaired the definition of these postulated features. This area is believed to have received much of the runoff drainage from the main canal. It should be noted that the SAR readout may indicate that this area was affected by canalization (see Fig. 2.6). However, the lineaments identified do not present a clear dendritic or lattice patterning. Such a pattern does occur throughout the first river terrace of both the New River and Freshwater Creek drainages (Fig. 2.7) and closely resembles the embanked and irregular field design of Lake Titicaca (Smith et al. 1968:358).

The evidence to date does not support extensive agricultural production inside the core site area. It suggests that intensive agriculture was not carried out within this area except for kitchen gardens. The very depressed elevations found in the centrally located core site *zacatal* indicate that the necessary raised-field platform fill was not made available. There is not enough wasted sediment in the depression to argue for adjacent raised fields if the elevation of the four raised features already defined is a reflection of the water levels involved. The elite and their retainers are argued to have occupied the core site area, while the bulk of the population resided around a poorly defined raised-field complex outside the main canal.

As Denevan (1966) has indicated for the savanna settings of Northern Bolivia, the main reasons given for not cropping the present depressions are low fertility, poor drainage, clay pans, and grass competition. Except for clay pans, these conditions pervade the Cerros setting of today. Whether the fields at Cerros were irrigated by a perennial high flowing water table or subject to seasonal drainage, the field construction would have been adaptable to either system.

4. SETTLEMENT EXCAVATIONS

From a methodological point of view, the focus of the survey has been on spatial variability within and between mound groups. To deal with this variability, a working morphological typology of mounded features using form, size, and groupings was devised for the settlement zone. Tables 2 and 3 present this preliminary classification, which was developed, in part,

TABLE 2

Structure Types in the Systematically Surveyed and Excavated Settlement Area

Type	Description	Frequency
1	4 or more building platforms on a shared substructure	2
2	3 building platforms on a shared substructure	4
3	2 building platforms on a shared substructure	4
4	Substructure greater than 150 m^2 and more than 1 m high	18
5	Substructure greater than 150 m^2 and less than or equal to 1 m high	28
6	Substructure less than 150 m^2 and less than or equal to 1 m high	34

TABLE 3

Structure Type Frequency and Exposure in Systematically Surveyed and Excavated Settlement Area

Type	Frequency	No. Tested	% Tested	Total Exposure/ Stratum
1	2	2	100	451 m^2
2	4	4	100	269 m^2
3	4	3	75	101 m^2
4	18	13	72	80 m^2*
5	28	6	21	74 m^2
6	34	7	21	45 m^2

*Excludes extensive exposure on Structure 29B.

because of the absence of standing masonry architecture in the settlement. The typology was drawn from the mound population identified within the area systematically surveyed and excavated at Cerros. This included the core zone of the site and a peripheral zone outside the canal, the latter being an equivalent area to that defined by the core zone (Fig. 2.3). The remainder of the systematically surveyed area, including the transect legs, was unsampled except for occasional surface collections.

The typology was used to stratify the known sample of mounds around the central precinct and to provide the basis for selecting particular mounds for excavation in order to investigate social organization. It was hypothesized that the size of these mounds would be correlated with the status of the occupants. Even if the residents were not directly responsible for the initial construction of the mound, their ability to elevate themselves above others in terms of occupying a larger or more complicated mound grouping would indicate their rank in the community. Intrasite distance relationships were also expected to reflect elements of social organization related to the clustering of mound groups (see Andrews et al. 1981; Folan et al. 1983; Kurjack 1974, 1976).

Underlying this typology was the implicit assumption that the majority of mounds served a residential function. Recent information, however, suggests that this assumption must be reevaluated. Most of the large and formally complex mounds within the area defined by the main canal zone are considered to be civic monuments. Although the functional justification for stratifying the mound excavation sample must be reassessed, the typology still stands on formal grounds and may prove functionally appropriate for other sites. The strength of the typology was that it allowed the stratification of our basic unit of analysis: mounded features.

IDENTIFICATION OF STRUCTURES

The Cerros settlement data have been used to treat that most elusive and recurrent problem in settlement pattern analysis: the identification of a house. Our problem is perhaps more extreme than in other studies because of the absence of dependable ethnohistorical continuities and poor preservation of the ruins. These factors are a consequence of the amount of time that has elapsed since major construction and occupation occurred at the site. Most settlement studies which have accurately approached the problem of household detection and population density have dealt with Late Classic and Postclassic populations. The Cerros mound population has been beset by the ravages of at least twice that much time. Still, the Cerros data base has been used to identify house mounds, given the morphological variability at the site.

House mounds have been defined at Cerros through various independent checks. Size, complexity, and abundance have generally been the bases for identification, given the absence of dense domestic trash deposits and such household features as hearths and burials (after Haviland 1963, 1970). However, a high number of utilitarian or domestic objects (i.e., probable digging stick weights, fishing net weights, spindle whorls, and so on) have been screen collected from the settlement in association with structures dating to the Tulix and C'oh phases. These artifacts are generally interpreted as indicating the location of a household. In addition, there is some reason to believe that ritual objects (i.e., jade fragments or painted stucco) are expectably less frequent in house mound locations than on civic monuments. Domestic objects and other small finds from the settlement are currently under study (Garber 1981, 1983, 1986).

Another means used to assess the function of a mound has been the ceramic inventory. Robertson [-Freidel] (1980, 1983) has analyzed the Cerros ceramic assemblage and, in addition to establishing the chronology for the site, has made a functional assessment of pottery forms. In an article examining Late Preclassic residential and civic architecture at Cerros (Scarborough and Robertson 1986), she distinguishes ceramic assemblages associated with public structures from those associated with residential occupation. Moreover, within residential structures it is possible to differentiate between elite as opposed to nonelite occupants from the ceramic inventory, given adequate sample size. This analysis has been correlated with the formal field identification of structures to assess the "goodness of fit." The correspondence is extremely good, with the ceramic identifications in most cases providing a greater degree of interpretive depth than otherwise allowed (table 4).

The following discussion of the mounded features from Cerros is taken from Scarborough and Robertson (1986: 166–169). It provides a concise summary of the excavated settlement data from Cerros and represents a useful introduction to the individual structure excavation material.

In the settlement, most small mounds isolated or in groups of two or three have been defined as house mounds. Of the twenty-one excavated structures that were assigned a residence function, approximately 81% (seventeen mounds) fit in the Type 4, Type 5, or Type 6 category. These structures are simple in form and make up 74% of the mounds in the 75 hectares defining the systematic survey and excavation area.

More than half (seven) of the excavated Type 4 mounds were residences, as indicated by both the ceramic and the field criteria. The ceramic inventory also revealed that only two of these Type 4 mounds were civic facilities. Excavations on Structure 53 suggested that during the Late C'oh phase it functioned as an elite residence but during the Tulix phase, it took on a civic function. This was confirmed by both the formal field data and the ceramic evaluations. Although clear architectural indications were lacking, the location of Structures 53 and 65, equidistant from the westward-facing Tulix phase Structure 29 and the two ball courts, suggests an intentional civic plan (Scarborough et al. 1982).

The excavated Type 5 mounds were assigned a residence function on the basis of the field and ceramic criteria just outlined, though small lots precluded a clear ceramic identification for approximately 50% of these mounds. Such criteria, however, did indicate that the other half of the mounds sampled were elite residences. The horizontal exposure of Structure 34 also revealed a small Tulix midden deposit off the eastern corner of the structure, confirming a residential function for the structure.

The excavated Type 6 structures included five residences and two outbuildings. Except for the ground-level elite residence Structure 33, all of the structures assessed as residences produced nonelite domestic pottery. Structures 165 and 22 were horizontally stripped to test their residential function, but unfortunately neither produced distinctive household features. Structure 165 was a ground-level residential structure near the main canal. The outbuildings (Structures 24 and

TABLE 4

Functional Interpretation of Structures Excavated in the Settlement

Structure or Structure Group No.	Formal Field Identification	Ceramic Assessment	Initial Construction Period
9	Civic facility	Civic/ritual	Tulix
10	Civic facility	Indeterminate	EC
11	Elite residence	Elite residence	Tulix
13	Residence	Nonelite residence	Tulix
14	Civic facility	Indeterminate*	Tulix
15	Residence	Elite residence	L. C'oh
16	Residence	Elite residence	L. C'oh
18	Residence	Elite residence	Tulix
19	Civic storage platform[†]	Civic/ritual	Tulix
21	Civic facility	Indeterminate*	Tulix
22	Residence	Nonelite residence	Tulix
24	Outbuilding	Nonelite residence	L. C'oh
26	Residence	Nonelite residence	Tulix
29	Civic facility	Civic/ritual	Tulix
33	Ground-level residence	Elite residence	L. C'oh
34	Residence	Elite residence	L. Tulix
38	Residence	Nonelite residence	L. C'oh
46	Elite residence	Indeterminate	EC
50	Ball court	Civic/ritual	Tulix
53 (1st)	Residence	Elite residence	L. C'oh
53 (2nd)	Civic facility	Civic/ritual	Tulix
54	Civic facility	Indeterminate*	Tulix
57	Outbuilding	Nonelite residence	Tulix
61	Ball court	Civic/ritual	L. C'oh
65	Residence	Indeterminate*	L. C'oh
66	Residence	Elite residence	Tulix
76	Civic facility	Civic/ritual	Tulix
77	Residence	Indeterminate	LPC
84	Residence	Indeterminate	EC
94	Residence	Indeterminate	LPC
98	Residence	Elite residence	Tulix
102	Residence	Indeterminate*	L. Tulix
112	Docking facility	Civic/ritual	Tulix
115	Residence	Elite residence	Tulix
116	Residence	Indeterminate*	Tulix
165	Ground-level residence	Indeterminate*	Tulix

*Prohibitive sample size.
[†]Structure summit area is 1,280 m^2.

57) were identified as such by their small size and close proximity to other mounds or features in the settlement. The pottery recovered in both cases was typical of a nonelite residence.

More elaborate structures belonging to Types 1, 2, and 3 were also assigned a residential function. These raised plaza groups have from two to four additional structures on top of their plazas. In all cases within the systematically surveyed area, one of the summit structures is larger and more prominent than the others, an arrangement also present at Mayapán (Smith 1962:218), Tikal (Haviland 1966:31), and other sites in the lowlands. Their form may be related to the elevated status of a household head and his nuclear

family. Presumably, members of the associated extended family would have occupied some of the remaining structures. The ceramic inventories from
these more elaborate structures are characteristic of
elite residences. The exception, Structure 116, did not
produce enough sherds for an evaluation.

As an example of this *plazuela* association, the Structure 11 Group was horizontally stripped. Although little midden debris was located, the presence of painted
stucco facading within an exterior wall niche coupled
with the overall architectural design of the structure
suggests that it was an elite dwelling.

The ceramic assessments permitted a further test of
the functional significance of the mound typology. A
comparison of mound volumes with ceramically identified elite and nonelite residences did not prove to
be useful, but a clear correlation was evident when
the summit surface area or presumed floor space of a
residence (derived from 1:50 or larger-scale contour
maps) was compared with the functional ceramic inventory. Consequently, summit surface area must be
considered a better index of "eliteness" than are gross
earth-moving expenditures of energy. (See Flannery
and Marcus [1983:80] for discussion of floor space as
an indicator of complex community development during Monte Albán II times, ca. 200 B.C.–A.D. 100.) Table
5 indicates that a structure summit area of approximately 50 square meters or more is associated with
elite residence. The only exception occurs on Structure
38. The recovery of nonceramic ritual objects from this
locus (Garber 1981), however, may provide an explanation for this reversal of the norm.

Civic architecture is the other class of structure
recognized at Cerros, defined as special-function
buildings which do not incorporate the range of domestic activities carried out on house mounds. They
were identified by their imposing size, unusual plan,
elaborate masonry, and/or facades (the latter seldom
preserved *in situ*), and, in the Tulix phase, by their
spatial relationships to Structure 29 (see Fig. 3.9).
Similarly, the ceramic inventory is distinctive and
domestic objects are present in significantly lower
percentages than in domiciles (Garber personal communication).

Civic architecture has a greater variability in form
than do the house mounds. Given the activity-
specific function of many civic structures and the
number of social and economic tasks performed at a
Maya center, greater variability would be anticipated. This variability in form has been clarified by

TABLE 5

Late Preclassic Residential Function Assessed

Structure No.	Summit Area in m^2	Ceramic Assessment
98	160	Elite residence
11B*	130	Elite residence
116B*	120	Indeterminate
115B*	100	Elite residence
38	100	Nonelite residence
15	96	Elite residence
18	80	Elite residence
66	80	Elite residence
53	72	Elite residence
16	48	Elite residence
33	8†	Elite residence
34	36	Indeterminate
102	36	Indeterminate
13	25	Nonelite residence
26	24	Nonelite residence
57	16	Nonelite residence
24	16	Nonelite residence
165	16	Indeterminate
22	9	Nonelite residence

*Largest structure in *plazuela* group.
†Limited flat test exposure.

testing and by lateral exposures on representative
mounds from the four mound types that arguably
represent civic architecture.

In the Tulix phase, six excavated Type 4 structures
have been interpreted as civic architecture. The
amount of labor required to construct these simple but
more imposing mounds would have been considerably
greater than for the largest structures in Types 5 and
6. The 21,460 cubic meters of fill in Structure 29
and its supporting plaza, for example, represent the
largest construction investment in the core zone, and
extensive lateral exposure has revealed architectural
details associated with a civic function in this case
(Freidel 1986a,b).

Of the three Type 3 structure groups that were
tested, the two Late Preclassic groups were assigned a
civic function. Group 61 was unequivocally identified
as a ball court and Group 19 appears to be a storage
platform. The Early Classic Group 46, on the other
hand, appears to be a rural elite residence.

Within the four tested Type 2 structures, Groups
76 and 10 were assigned a civic function. They date to

TABLE 6

Civic and Residential Construction and Occupation Frequencies through Time
(Excavated Sample)

	C'oh	% of Total	Tulix	% of Total	Early Classic	% of Total	Late Postclassic	% of Total
Mound Count*								
Total mound construction (52)	11	21	33	63	6	12	2	4
Total occupation† (52)	11	21	13	25	19	37	8	15
Total number of mounds utilized at one time (52)	22	42	46	88	25	48	10	19
Civic mound construction (20)	4	20	13	65	3	15	0	0
Civic mound modification (20)	0	0	4	20	0	0	0	0
Civic construction inside canal (17)	2	12	12	71	3	18	0	0
Civic construction outside canal (3)	2	67	1	33	0	0		
Residence construction inside canal (20)	7	35	12	60	0	0	1	5
Residence construction outside canal (12)	0	0	8	67	3	25	1	8
Total residence occupation inside canal# (37/71%)	11	30	19	51	12	32	8	22
Total residence occupation outside canal# (15/29%)	7	47	8	53	10	67	2	13
Area Count*								
Total mound construction (35)	9	26	21	63	3	9	2	6
Total occupation† (35)	6	17	8	23	9	26	6	17
Total number of mounds utilized at one time (35)	15	43	29	86	12	34	8	23
Civic mound construction (11)	2	18	8	73	1	9	0	0
Civic mound modification (11)	0	0	3	27	0	0	0	0
Civic construction inside canal (10)	1	10	8	80	1	10	0	0
Civic construction outside canal (1)	1	100	0	0	0	0	0	0
Residence construction inside canal (18)	7	39	10	56	0	0	1	6
Residence construction outside canal (6)	0	0	3	50	2	33	1	17
Total residence occupation inside canal# (28/80%)	11	39	15	54	6	21	6	21
Total residence occupation outside canal# (7/20%)	2	29	3	43	5	71	2	29

*Occupation percentages need not add up to 100 due to the reoccupation of mounds through time.

†Excludes coeval mound construction and indicates initial (buried) occupation or reoccupation of earlier structures.

#Excludes utilized civic structures.

Numbers in parentheses indicate total mounds possible within each category.

the Tulix phase of the Late Preclassic and to the Early Classic, respectively.

Both of the Type 1 structures were excavated. Group 50 is clearly a Tulix phase ball court, whereas Group 116 has a residential function. Group 116 is outside the core zone and is located within the *bajo,* or internally drained swamp, suggesting that its residents may have played a managerial role in the raised-field agriculture practiced at the site. If so, the residential function of this group would have had civic components that may account for its greater complexity.

PROBLEMS IN INTERPRETATION

Changes in the residential- and civic-structure populations through time are important indices for comparative purposes. In order to extract these data, two units of occupation and construction analysis were designed. Single-mound populations were estimated by counting all the mounded features individually. A *plazuela* group and all mounds in it were assigned a date on the basis of a single test unit, unless additional tests indicated that not all the mounds were contemporaneous. Although such inferential dating is common practice in the Maya Lowlands, it may give an inflated idea of the actual number of mounds constructed or occupied at any one time. For this reason, an area-count assessment has been calculated (tables 6, 7).

The area count simply evaluates discrete occupation loci by weighting an entire *plazuela* as if it were a single mound. This figure is perhaps most meaningful when discussing reoccupation of a mound group. In these cases, residence on each mound was probably unnecessary to create the observable distribution of ceramics and related litter. In both methods, plaza-type features have been excluded from the counts. Although these must be considered major construction expenditures, they only directly affect percentages of civic construction. In postulating the number and density of civic and residential structures in the systematic survey and excavation area (tables 7, 8), the functional identification of excavated structures was necessary. This was effected by comparing the individual structures with the sample of identified structures and was possible only after the excavation data had been collected.

A major problem with the Cerros data base is the presence of ground-level structures throughout the settlement. Although the issue has been an elusive one, many researchers have devoted a great deal of attention

to it (Haviland 1963; Puleston 1973; Sanders 1960; Willey et al. 1965). Puleston indicates that "hidden" dwellings at Tikal are most evident during the Early Classic Period. Although they may continue through the entire occupational history of the site, Cerros ground-level dwellings are most significant during the Late Preclassic phases.

Cliff (1986), for example, has demonstrated the presence of ground-level structures along the coastline that date to all phases of the Late Preclassic Period at Cerros. Moreover, because mound construction within the perimeter created by the canal apparently was restricted to the Late C'oh and Tulix phases, it seems that during the Early and Middle C'oh phase much, if not all, of the occupation of the dispersed settlement was at ground level. Actual human population estimates during the Late C'oh and Tulix phases for the site must be considered conservative until Cliff has analyzed the data. The structural density figures, however, are comparable to those at other Maya sites (see Chapter 8).

EXCAVATED STRUCTURES

The excavation program involved a series of 4-square-meter test excavations dispersed throughout the 75 hectares immediately surrounding the center. Moreover, in order to place the formal typology on a strong interpretive footing, extensive lateral exposure was carried out on at least one structure from each of the six structure types in the settlement. Excavation and recovery techniques included the screening of natural and architectural strata.

The subdatum for each of the excavated units was the highest corner of the exposure. All test units were oriented to magnetic north unless otherwise indicated. Excavations in the central precinct were generally oriented to true north. All four walls of each excavation unit were profiled, although only two have been redrafted for this presentation. The depth of the various natural lenses is generally not provided because of their undulation through the unit as well as the position of the test units on the sloping margins of the mound. The profiles can be consulted for precise measurements, and all significant features are described in the text. The test unit excavations are described from top to bottom in keeping with the frequent sequential references to our lot and level system. Horizontal exposures are described from bottom to top because of the

TABLE 7

Civic and Residential Density Figures through Time
(Extrapolated from Excavation Sample to Visible Mound Population)

	C'oh		Tulix		Early Classic		Late Postclassic	
	No.	Density*	No.	Density*	No.	Density*	No.	Density*
Mound Count								
Total mound construction (108)	23	0.33	68	0.99	13	0.19	4	0.06
Total occupation† (108)	23	0.33	27	0.39	40	0.58	16	0.23
Total number of mounds utilized at one time (108)	46	0.65	95	1.38	53	0.75	20	0.30
Civic mounds & plaza construction (25)	5		16		4		0	
Civic mounds & plaza modification (25)	0		5		0		0	
Civic construction inside canal (22)	3		16		4		0	
Civic construction outside canal (3)	2		1		0		0	
Residence construction inside canal (59)	21	0.62	35	1.03	0		3	0.09
Residence construction outside canal (24)	0		16	0.46	6	0.17	2	0.06
Total residence occupation inside canal* (81)	24	0.71	41	1.21	26	0.76	18	0.53
Total residence occupation outside canal* (27)	13	0.37	14	0.40	18	0.51	4	0.11
Area Count								
Total mound construction (93)	23	0.33	57	0.83	8	0.12	5	0.07
Total occupation† (90)	15	0.22	21	0.30	23	0.33	15	0.22
Total number of mounds utilized at one time (90)	38	0.57	78	1.12	31	0.45	20	0.30
Civic mounds & plaza construction (16)	3		12		1		0	
Civic mounds & plaza modification (16)	0		4		0		0	
Civic construction inside canal (15)	1.5		12		1.5		0	
Civic construction outside canal (1)	1		0		0		0	
Residence construction inside canal (56)	22	0.65	31	0.91	0		3	0.09
Residence construction outside canal (18)	0		9	0.26	6	0.17	3	0.09
Total residence occupation inside canal* (71)	28	0.82	38	1.12	15	0.44	15	0.44
Total residence occupation outside canal* (19)	6	0.17	8	0.23	13	0.37	6	0.17

*Density = count/ha.
†Excludes coeval construction loci.
*Excludes utilized civic structures.
Numbers in parentheses indicate total possible within each category.

TABLE 8

Areas and Mounds Excavated and Surveyed in the Settlement,
Inside and Outside the Core Area

| | Inside | | Outside | | |
	Civic	Residential	Civic	Residential	Total
Areas excavated	10	18	1	6	35
Mounds excavated	17	20	3	12	52
Areas visible	15*	56†	1*	18†	90
Mounds visible	22*	59†	3*	24†	108
Total surface area in hectares (excluding center)		34		35	69

*Presumed civic.
†Presumed residential.

developmental nature of the data and the ease of relating various feature modifications through time. The two Late Preclassic ball courts (Structure Groups 50 and 61) as well as the canal and drained-field excavations will be presented in separate chapters because of the special character of these data.

Mound groups were selected for test excavation from a stratified judgmental sample (Redman 1978). At minimum, a 20% sample was taken from each of the typological divisions in the mound typology (table 3). The typological divisions with fewer mounds, however, were sampled more extensively. Specific mound selection within each type was determined by the desire to maintain a dispersed geographical representation of mounds and by fortuitous trash exposures revealed by natural agents (tree falls, erosional shoreline profiles, and so on). The judgmental sample was developed to take advantage of known surface indicators in order to achieve maximum data retrieval for minimum labor costs. Although the sample was not rigidly controlled geographically, every environmental and spatial sector of the community was tested. It should be noted that the decision to test a large percentage of Type 4 structures was a pragmatic one. Because preservation was generally good in this mound type and poor in Types 5 and 6, a greater number of Type 4 mounds were excavated in an attempt to refine our architectural typology further.

The purpose of the test excavation program in the settlement was threefold. First, it was to establish chronological control, primarily by penetrating and examining the contents of the mound. A sealed dating context was defined as primary material capped by an impenetrable layer of flooring or thick plaster melt. Unfortunately, few burial or cache offerings were found. Primary trash was identified as such by the presence of large (long axis greater than 10 centimeters), uneroded sherds from a single time period.

Although such material would generally be classified as midden or habitation debris at other sites, this assumption was not made at Cerros because bone, charcoal, and other domestic debris such as *manos, metates,* and other stone tools or debitage were sometimes absent from the deposits. Moreover, in some instances, the ceramics were deposited as part of a termination ritual marking the abandonment of civic structures (Garber 1983; Robertson 1983) and actually represented offerings rather than habitation debris. Because Late Preclassic pottery is easily broken into small bits (long axis of sherd less than 2 centimeters) and eroded when exposed, trampled, or transported and redeposited, sherd size and erosion could be used to detect these processes. In these situations, chronological homogeneity of the excavated sherds, while always utilized, became a critical factor in determining whether the deposit was primary. Although deposits subjected to extended exposure prior to burial were not used to date mound construction directly, some deposits containing "freshly" redeposited sherds were. In all cases, the redeposited material postdated the C'oh phase, the *terminus post quem* of interest to this study (after Robertson 1983).

The second intent of the testing program was to expose any architectural features that would aid in describing the structures from the perspective of a refined settlement typology. Exposure of well-preserved architecture in the settlement was also designed to aid in the identification of those mounded types deserving significant lateral excavation exposure. Unfortunately, the quality and quantity of architecture revealed in the limited exposures did not produce the correlations with the morphology of the mounds prior to excavation necessary to modify the typology itself.

The third focus of the testing program was to determine the function of structures. It was anticipated that certain kinds of information would be culled from our limited exposures which could be compared with the quality and quantity of information collected from our lateral stripping operations. In meeting this goal, the ceramics recovered proved to be most useful.

The Absence of Burials

The practice of burying human remains in "nonceremonial" contexts in mounded features has been generally regarded as one indicator of household occupation (Haviland 1970; Thompson 1971). The absence of burials in the settlement at Cerros is quite peculiar when compared to other Late Preclassic sites in the Maya Lowlands. At Altar de Sacrificios, 9 of the 15 Plancha phase burials were taken from the settlement (Smith 1972: table 5). A total of five burials were recovered from Barton Ramie during the Mount Hope and Floral Park phases (Willey et al. 1965:531). At Tikal during the combined Chuen and Cauac phases ten ritually interred burials were apparent in the North Acropolis alone (Coe 1965a), and Haviland (1963, 1967) reports at least two in the sustaining area during the Late Preclassic Period. The frequency of Late Preclassic burials in house mounds at other sites is considerably greater than that found in the Cerros settlement. Considering both the extent of our excavation program and the small amount of construction dating after the Late Preclassic Period, it is puzzling that we have not located more Late Preclassic interments. It should be noted that thirty-one Late Preclassic burials have been excavated at Cerros from the shoreline setting associated with a dense ground-level occupation immediately underlying and east of the central precinct (Cliff 1982). This area is currently under investigation (Cliff 1986).

The lack of interments in the Cerros settlement results from any one of four factors: (1) the site was not occupied long enough for significant numbers of people to have died; (2) the excavated sample has not been extensive enough to define burials; (3) the settlement population at Cerros interred the dead within the dense ground-level occupation located near the central precinct; or (4) the high seasonal water table coupled with the stone construction fill of the mounds have promoted the rapid decomposition of bone and other organic substances.

The first explanation has been disconfirmed by the ceramic analysis (Robertson 1980, 1986) as well as the radiocarbon dates (Cliff 1982:199; Freidel 1986a:12; Freidel and Scarborough 1982:151). Robertson indicates that the combined C'oh and Tulix phases lasted for 350 years, or fourteen generations. The second suggestion, too, can be dismissed because over 1,000 square meters of excavation area have been penetrated in the settlement. It is unlikely that sampling error is a major problem.

The third scenario is less readily dismissed and may in part explain the number of burials recorded from this restricted area and their absence from other locations in the settlement. Nevertheless, the fourth hypothesis is understood to be the best explanation for the lack of burials in the settlement.

By way of example, a Postclassic cache accompanied by an infant burial on Structure 4A was revealed in an advanced state of decay. It was placed in a less "ceremonial" context within limestone rubble construction fill, a building medium identical to most house mounds reported at Cerros. Only the crowns of this child's unerupted molars bear witness to the burial. Although the unerupted teeth may have been deliberately smashed away from the jaw for inclusion in the cache, it is more likely that the entire skull was offered. If this sort of decomposition has taken place in the last five hundred years when associated with limestone construction fill, then the last two thousand years would leave next to nothing.

The survival of the thirty-one burials from the area underlying the central precinct is attributable to the manner and location in which these burials were interred. The dense burial concentration on the shoreline is sealed by a 2- to 3-meter-thick plaza deposit overlying the fine silts and clays defining the burial matrix. These burials are less subject to water percolation due to the fine soil fraction around them, which reduces erosion and decay. This condition is generally not the case in the settlement. Nearly all Tulix phase mounds are composed of unsealed limestone rubble fill, which promotes water percolation and the condition described on Structure 4A. In addition, at those sites where Late Preclassic burial populations are preserved in house mounds (Altar de Sacrificios, Barton Ramie, Cuello, and Tikal), the mound fill is generally earth fill. Earth fill is the major component for most building operations in Northern Belize (Hammond 1973, 1975).

STRUCTURE DATA

Structure 9

Structure 9 is defined as a large rangelike structure and the extensive split-level plaza area on which it rests. Structure 9B is the Type 4 range structure located in a *huamil* setting. It is oriented toward the central precinct, lying 180 meters south of Structure 6B. The paved plaza Structure 9A extends north to the foot of plaza Structure 7A and as far south as the Structure 10 Group. The more elevated northern half of the plaza is further defined by the present shoreline and the western margin of plaza Structure 8A. The southwestern limits of the plaza are less distinct, although the western shoreline is again suggested (a portion of it may have been recently removed for rock fill). Its southeastern edge is defined by Structures 13,

14, and 15, which rest on it. Plaza Structure 9A covers approximately 26,400 square meters.

Structures 9A and 9B have been assigned a Tulix phase date, although there is Late Postclassic reoccupation. Structure 9B is understood to have served a civic/ritual function based on its imposing size, proximity to the center, and associated ceramic inventory (Fig. 4.1).

Structure 9A/Feature 33A (Operation 107a and b)

Feature 33A represents a flat test excavation approximately 90 meters southwest of Structure 9B. An uprooted coconut tree revealed the location of this feature within plaza Structure 9A. Operation 107 was excavated during the 1976 field season in anticipation of midden debris. A 2-meter by 4-meter unit was exposed to a maximum depth of 1.0 meter. The long axis of the unit was oriented to magnetic north (Fig. 4.2).

Six naturally defined and two arbitrarily defined levels were divided into nine lots. The surface levels consisted of a loose gray humus loam intruded by boulder-sized rubble fill. This 40-cubic-meter-thick surface rubble deposit represented plaza Structure 9A and contained Tulix phase ceramics. No flooring

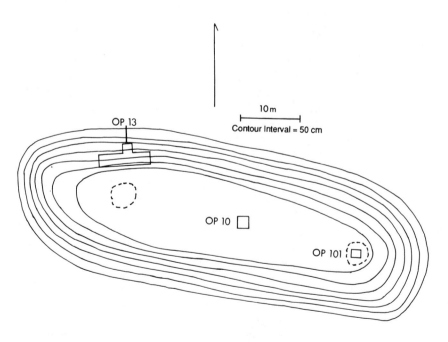

Figure 4.1.   Contour map of Structure 9B.

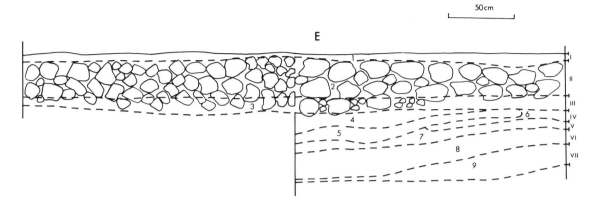

Figure 4.2.   Profile from Structure 9A/Feature 33A (Operation 107a&b).

was apparent because of the exposed nature of the plaza.

Levels 3 and 4 were arbitrary lots consisting of a loose, moist, dark gray clay intruded by angular limestone gravel underlying the plaza. This deposit was excavated in 10-centimeter vertical units due to the abundance of midden debris collected. Sherds, charcoal, ash, bone, and shell were present in high frequencies. A high percentage of ceramic diagnostics, together with thermoluminescence dating (Belew 1978), indicates that the midden was deposited immediately prior to the extension of Tulix phase Plaza 9A and a short time after the later midden deposition defined in Operation 1 (Cliff 1986). This trash has been assigned a firm C'oh phase date.

Level 5 consisted of a compact, moist 5-to 10-centimeter-thick *sascab* floor mottled by the overlying gray clay trash deposit. Predictably, the trash inventory decreased substantially on exposing the house floor. Level 6 was defined as a compact, moist, well-sorted beige clay underlying the floor. It was intruded by a discontinuous band of severely eroded pebble- to cobble-sized hearting stones. A posthole was located in the southeastern portion of the unit apparently associated with the *sascab* floor. (Neither the hearting stone intrusion nor the posthole is visible from the profile Fig. 4.2.) In section the posthole was found to be 14 centimeters in diameter and to extend approximately 20 centimeters below the *sascab* floor surface. The *sascab* floor appeared to feather out on two of the four sides of the unit. Although the perimeter of the structure could not be traced, evidence suggests that our test unit may have straddled the edge of the

structure. Artifact densities inside and outside the structure were not revealing.

Level 7 consisted of a compact, moist, well-sorted blue clay gumbo. The water table was contacted at 80 centimeters BSD. This matrix contained a few unidentifiable sherds and is suggested to be a riverine clay deposit associated with the earliest occupation at the site (Cliff 1986). Level 8 was the decomposing yellow granular caprock deposit. Chemical and physical soil analysis has been carried out on levels 6, 7, and 8 (Appendix B).

Feature 33 has produced a significant information base. The underlying C'oh phase midden deposit and ground-level structure as well as the underlying clays further support the hypothesis that Cerros developed from an Ixtabai/C'oh phase village adapted to a riverine economy. The presence of Tulix phase plaza Structure 9A corresponds to a major sociopolitical adjustment at Cerros. By the Tulix phase the intrasite area as defined by the main canal had taken on a civic community character unlike earlier occupations. The ceramic analysis of the C'oh component indicates Feature 33 to have been a small elite residence.

Structure 9B (Operations 10a and 13a)

Structure 9B is 70 meters long, 24 meters wide and 3.5 meters high. It has a potential floor space of 480 square meters and an absolute volume of 3,948 cubic meters. A medial outset staircase appears on the north side of the structure.

Operation 10a was excavated during the 1974 field season. A test pit was placed near the center of the mound between two slightly elevated superstructural platforms at either end of the east-west oriented mound. This 4-square-meter exposure was excavated to a depth of 2.3 meters in an attempt to date the mound by means of a primary associated cache. Although no dedicatory offerings were located, a stratigraphic sequence was discernible.

A scattered Postclassic component was located within the humus horizon and underlain by white marl and rubble fill. A brown, sandy matrix was encountered approximately 90 centimeters BSD. Rubble fill severely intrudes this matrix. Three additional marl lenses, also intruded by rubble fill, were noted before terminating the exposure. The marl concentrations were extremely ephemeral and mixed with a sandy matrix, making them difficult to isolate. This suggests that the fill for the mound was thrown together rather than deposited in clean, fine lenses.

At approximately 1.05 meters BSD one of the marl layers was found to be better defined, being continuous across the horizontal exposure. It was 2 centimeters thick and contained burned limestone chunks. Little in the way of artifactual diagnostics was recovered. This lens lay at approximately the same depth as the marl lens reported in Operation 101a (Structure 9C). Unfortunately, we cannot yet confirm this lens as being as continuous. An abrupt increase in sherd fill was noted at 1.5 to 1.9 meters BSD. This appears to be a Late Preclassic component, but the limited exposure did not allow primary contextual control for an unequivocal date.

Operation 13a was excavated during the 1974 field season. It was a trenching operation located on the northwestern slope of the mound. The 2-meter-wide by 9-meter-long exposure was excavated parallel to the long axis of the mound on its upper slope. An additional 1.35-meter by 1.5-meter exposure extended below and perpendicular to this trench. This T-trench exposure was excavated in anticipation of architectural features, with the surface debris suggesting later trash deposits. On removing the fill overlying the structure, a crude upper riser was exposed. It was defined by five uncut limestone slabs placed vertically as a retaining wall for the cobble-sized rubble and marl fill composing the mound. The sherd inventory overlying this feature contained a high percentage of Postclassic censer ware and chert flakes and a low frequency of obsidian blade fragments. Fish and sea turtle bone in addition to numerous ceramic fish net weights (Eaton 1976, 1978) were also found in this context.

The T-trench further exposed a Late Preclassic cut stone wall 1.7 meters BSD behind and to the west of the riser. The cut stone wall consisted of a four-to five-course chinked wall exposure with a basal molding. Each cobble-sized stone was rectilinear in form. Bits of plaster and *sascab* suggest that the surface was covered to prevent the exposure of the irregular arrangement of stone coursing. The height of the wall was 80 centimeters at its best-preserved location. The basal molding consisted of horizontally bedded cut stones extending out from the wall. The lateral extent of the molding and the underlying floor could not be determined. The sherd inventory collected behind and under these features dates to the Tulix phase exclusively.

Structure 9C (Operation 101a)

Structure 9C is a slight superstructural feature at the top eastern side of Structure 9B. The superstructure is poorly defined by a rectilinear single-course arrangement of limestone blocks approximately 2 meters east-west by 4 meters north-south. It appears to be associated with a Late Postclassic occupation of the site.

Operation 101 was excavated during the 1975 field season. It was a restricted 1-meter by 2-meter exposure excavated in an attempt to date the feature. A marl matrix intruded with large limestone blocks was located on penetration of the mound. It was in turn underlain by large dry-laid rubble fill. The marl deposition may represent an occupational event, but little associated debris was collected. Some evidence of construction pauses within the fill of the mound is suggested by the appearance of a sandy soil sandwiched between the rubble fill at 1.5 meters BSD.

Structure 10 Group

The Structure 10 Group is composed of Structures 10B, 10C, 10D and the constricted raised plaza area, 10A. It contains over 8,000 cubic meters of fill and represents the largest mound cluster in the settlement. The entire Type 2 structure group rests on the southern flank of the low-lying plaza Structure 9A, south of Structure 9 within a *huamil* setting. It is located near the northern terminus of the western *sacbe* (dike) (Feature 126), with both its southern and western margins near the depressed *zacatal* setting. The mound group appears to be oriented toward the central precinct in a manner not unlike Structures 13, 14, 15, and 16—all structures in the immediate vicinity of the Structure 10 Group. Although the structure has been assigned an Early Classic Period date, the underlying subplaza Structure 9A was constructed during Tulix times.

The imposing size and complexity of Group 10 suggest that it served a nonresidential function. Given the paucity of Classic architecture at the site, the Structure 10 Group was one of the major foci of Classic Period activity following the reoccupation of the center (see Fig. 4.3).

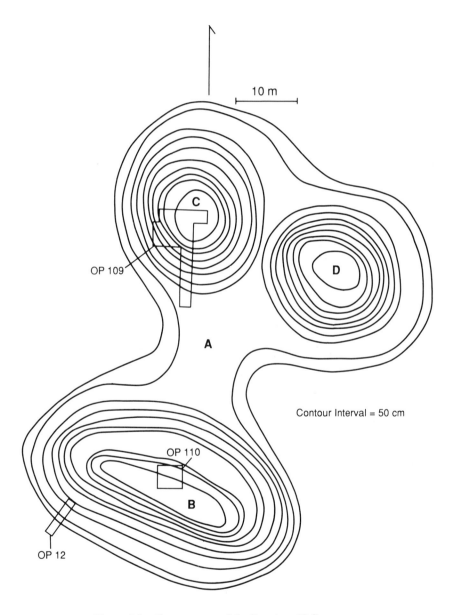

Figure 4.3. Contour map of the Structure 10 Group.

54   *SETTLEMENT EXCAVATIONS*

Structure 10B (Operations 12a and 110a–d)

This structure is the largest and southeasternmost mound in the group. It is 45 meters long, 27 meters wide, and 5 meters high. It has a potential summit floor space of 270 square meters and an absolute volume of 3,713 cubic meters. In addition, an apparent *chultun* was located 10 meters south of Structure 10B and outside the *plazuela* group. It seems to have been cut into the limestone bedrock, with only a small constricted orifice visible from the surface.

A 6.75-meter by 1.5-meter trench (OP12a) was put into the southwestern edge of the mound in anticipation of uncovering trash deposits and/or a retaining wall during the 1974 field season. Unfortunately, neither a retaining wall nor a plaster melt was encountered. Mound layering, however, was evident, with the bulk of the mound consisting of dry rubble fill underlain by a lens of larger rubble within a light gray loam. If a retaining wall existed, it was composed of uncut rubble that has long since been destroyed. The small artifact inventory contained a mixture of Late Preclassic and Classic material.

Operation 110 a–d, a 16-square-meter exposure, was opened at the summit of Structure 10B during the 1977 field season. These excavations were conducted along the medial axis of the mound immediately above what appeared to be an outcropping stairway section. Anticipating a range structure, given the size and elongated shape of the mound and its similarity to Structure 11B (another Type 2 *plazuela* group structure, discussed below), masonry walls and plaster floors were predicted. This prediction was plainly disconfirmed. Instead, a 30-centimeter-thick lens of hearting gravel underlain by boulder-sized fill stones was defined. Although Late Preclassic ceramic diagnostics were identified, the most recent debris from within the unsealed hearting was Classic Period utility ware.

Structure 10C (Operation 109a–i)

Structure 10C is one of two conical mounds approximately 22 meters north of Structure 10B. It is 28 meters long, 25 meters wide, and 5 meters high. It has a potential summit floor space of 80 square meters and an absolute mound volume of 1,950 cubic meters.

Operation 109 was excavated during the 1977 field season in anticipation of architectural features and trash concentrations. Part of this operation consisted of a 2-meter by 10-meter proximation trench excavated to

a depth of 1.4 meters. It extended from the lower plaza up to the edge of a crude platform. Unfortunately, this suboperation provided only minimal information. The absence of any sign of a masonry stairway on the medial axis of the mound, however, suggests that there never was one.

A more productive suboperation in which 43 square meters were excavated to a depth of 1.7 meters was conducted on the summit of the mound. Artifactual debris was recovered in low frequencies and no primary features were located. However, one concentration of utility ware ceramics dating to the Classic Period was recovered approximately 20 centimeters above the surface of the platform.

The platform appears to be D-shaped in plan with its straight face oriented into the plaza. The front exposure was four courses high and composed of crude, undressed stones set in a marl grout. The backside of the platform was defined by a poorly preserved curvilinear, single-course alignment. The platform appears to have projected above the frontal slope of the mound. Willey et al. (1965:97) indicate a similar condition for BR123 Period 3. The tendency of the Maya during all periods to level previous mound occupations in making way for subsequent structures suggests that another occupation, as yet unrevealed, underlies this platform. The apparent use of only a portion of the total mound surface area available to the platform builders indicates this to have been the case.

Five ill-defined "clean" marl lenses within 1 meter of vertical exposure and sandwiched between layers of rubble fill indicate that the interior of the structure was artificially raised above the lower retaining wall, probably in the Classic Period. It should be noted that the nearly clean white marl and rubble fill of Structure 10C contrasts sharply with the trash-laden fill of Structure 11B (below) as well as with the tan topsoil overlying the rubble core of Structure 10B. This difference relates Structure 10C to the conventions of construction found in the monumental public architecture of the central precinct, where clean fill is strongly preferred (Freidel 1977). Although it is difficult to estimate the floor space provided by the platform, the exposed western side of the retaining wall enclosed an area of 12 square meters. Symmetry would suggest a similar platform wing area to the east in an area which has yet to be excavated.

The age of this platform is puzzling. A Preclassic date was initially assigned based on little more than general morphological similarities with those of

Structure 11B. Subsequent analysis, however, suggests a Classic Period date. Although there is a meter of overburden capping the site, there is no clear weathering horizon. This indicates that the platform may be Classic Period in date, particularly since the group as a whole dates to this period.

Our inability to obtain a firm date for this platform necessitated a revision in our sampling technique. Limited postholing on the back and lateral sides of this and other poorly dated mounds was carried out in an attempt to locate associated midden deposits (after Fry 1969). However, the limited number of sherds collected from the preliminary postholing program, even when accompanied by controlled test pitting operations, forced a return to sealed construction fill contextual dating. (See Rice and Rice 1980:438 for brief discussion of these techniques.)

Structure 11 Group

Group 11 is composed of three structures on a raised plaza labeled Structures 11B, 11C, and 11D (Fig. 4.4). This Type 2 structure group rests within a *huamil* setting flanked on three sides by depressed *zacatal* and thorn-scrub savanna. The present shoreline is less than 40 meters to the northwest. The largest mound, Structure 11B, is oriented to the west and the two other structures appear to be directed toward this better-preserved structure. The structure group has been assigned to the Tulix phase, although there are indications of an Early Classic Period reuse. A Late Postclassic Period reoccupation of the structure is also apparent.

Although, based on the formal field evidence presented below and the functional assessment of the ceramic assemblage (Scarborough and Robertson 1986), the Structure 11 Group is thought to have had an elite residential function during the Tulix phase, Lewenstein (1986, 1987) has presented evidence suggesting a different interpretation. Drawing from an insightful contextual analysis of stone tools and related debris, she argues that the largest mound in the *plazuela* Structure 11B indicates evidence for male-dominated craft activities such as woodworking and hide processing to the exclusion of household tasks such as food preparation or storage. The suggestion that Structure 11B could be an association house for men does not necessarily contradict other evidence. Given the elaborate facading noted at this locus coupled with an architectural plan similar to that of the civic

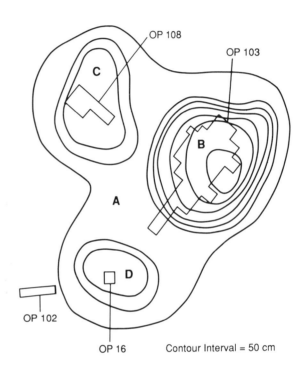

Figure 4.4. Contour map of the Structure 11 Group.

temples Structures 29, 30, and 31 at Tikal, the formal field evidence may support a men's house function. Further, the functional ceramic analysis would have had difficulty discriminating an elite residence from a special-purpose house of this kind. Men occupying the house would likely be served in elite residence vessels, which would not be different from ceramic assemblages recovered from actual elite houses. Nevertheless, the adjacent Structures 11C and 11D contain debris which appears to have household functions (Garber personal communication). Lewenstein's analysis does suggest that Structure 11B was a special-purpose structure; however, it seems to have been maintained by a family occupying the lesser mounds in the *plazuela*.

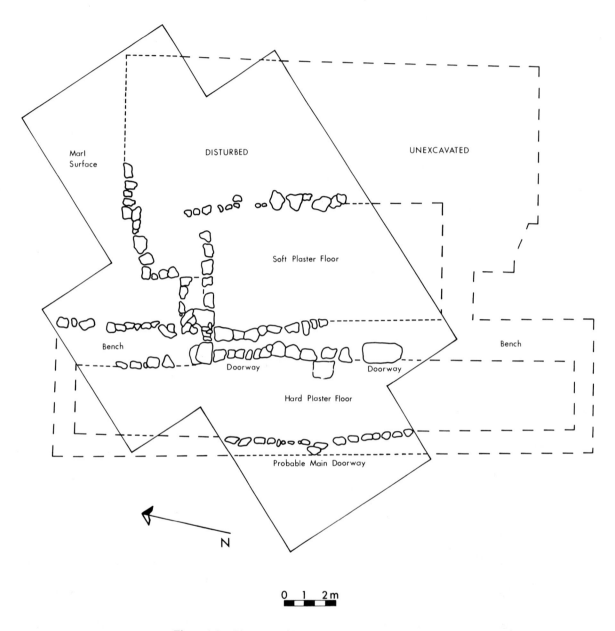

Figure 4.5.   Plan map of Structure 11B (Operation 103).

Structure 11A (Operation 102a)

Structure 11A is the raised plaza area supporting the three associated substructures. Operation 102a was excavated during the 1976 season in order to obtain midden debris while documenting the construction history of the *plazuela* group. The 1-meter by 5-meter trench was located on the backside of Structure 11D.

Assuming the prevailing winds had not changed over time, the location of the trench downwind and behind the plaza area was thought to be ideal for trash deposition. Unfortunately, true primary depositional trash was not located.

The trench was also extended into the raised plaza area. The data indicate that the plaza may have been

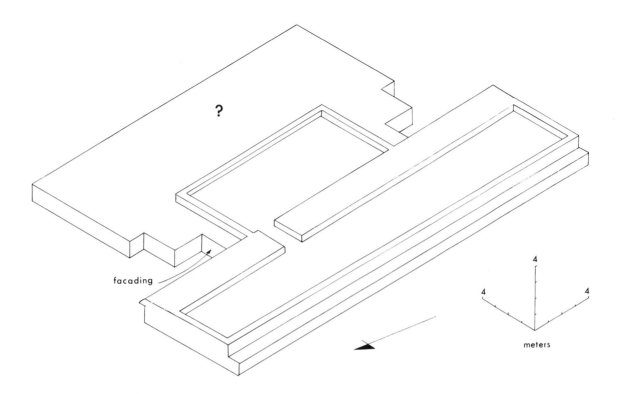

?

facading

4

4   4

meters

Figure 4.6.   Isometric plan of Structure 11B. The back third of the mound was not preserved, and no doorway could be defined.

paved with a dark soil matrix in the Late Preclassic Period. An overlying Late Postclassic Period humus was underlain by this Late Preclassic pavement, which was in turn supported by a loosely packed limestone rubble core. The plaza construction fill appeared to be less tightly packed than that of the mounds themselves.

Structure 11B (Operation 103a–ii)

Structure 11B is approximately 2 meters higher and east of the adjacent mounds in the Structure 11 Group (Figs. 4.5, 4.6). It is 25 meters long, 20 meters wide, 3.5 meters high, and oriented west. It has a potential floor space of 130 square meters and an absolute volume of 1,103 cubic meters. The plan of Structure 11B is not unlike a scaled-down version of Structures 29, 30, and 31 at the North Acropolis of Tikal (Coe 1967), each oriented to the west and perhaps dating to the Early Classic Period in their final form.

During the 1974 field season a 1-meter by 3-meter unit was excavated to a depth of 2.15 meters from the summit of the mound. This exposure provided a

degree of stratigraphic control for subsequent work on the mound. During 1977 the mound was excavated horizontally in an attempt to expose architectural and artifactual associations. More than 125 square meters or nearly all of the northwestern half of the platform were exposed and mapped to a maximum depth of 2.3 meters. A 2-meter by 2-meter arbitrary grid control was maintained during the course of excavations to ensure accurate horizontal as well as vertical provenience for anticipated activity area relationships (see Lewenstein 1986, 1987).

The earliest construction activity is represented by a friable lens of reddish-brown clay underlain by trash, soil, and gravel ballast. This event appears to represent the leveling of an earlier occupation in preparation for the next constructional episode. Because this lens is at the same elevation both inside and outside the overlying platform, it is suggested that the entire mound surface was prepared by the builders responsible for the subsequent platform. Ceramic diagnostics from the trash deposit underlying the lens date to the Late Preclassic Period.

The elaborate building platform overlying this leveling event was Preclassic in date as well, although no primary caches or burials were found. The building platform was composite in plan. A large rectangular west room fronting the plaza was connected to an eastern rear room by a constricted accessway. The masonry was more substantial than many other architectural contexts in the settlement zone. The chinked walls were composed of rectangular stones that were covered at one time by a thick coat of red and white plaster. The backside of the platform may have been curvilinear in plan, possibly indicating a building convention similar to that revealed in Structure 10C. Unfortunately, the rear portion of the platform was badly deteriorated, preventing the testing of this hypothesis.

Near the northwestern corner of the platform, a recessed wall niche (1 meter by 1 meter) was exposed (Fig. 4.7). It appears to have been adorned by a relief panel of plaster, molded on carved stone and painted red, buff, black, and white. This polychrome molded stucco facade was probably supported by four tenoned

and grooved stones projecting from an upper course in the niche which have since collapsed. Excavation of the niche also produced an interior south wall behind the wall supporting the relief, indicating that the building platform was originally constricted an additional 80 centimeters. It should be noted that fragments of a smashed jade bead and a portion of a jade ear flare found in the collapsed niche debris may indicate an elite termination ritual associated with the abandonment of the mound during the last hours of the Tulix phase at Cerros (see Garber 1983).

Although the front of the building platform was only surficially examined, a stairway probably ascended from the plaza to the building. A plaster floor extended over the building platform on the front, or plaza side, of the niche, creating an enclosed rectangular space separated from the main building and stairway by wall stub alignments. Three plaster floors were accounted for on this verandalike frontal room, one immediately overlying another. The main, or rear, superstructural room was not as well preserved, but

Figure 4.7.   Exterior platform wall niche of Structure 11B.

two temporally separated plaster floors were discernible. The stones defining the front and side walls of the main room appear to be well-dressed loaf-shaped blocks similar to those found in the central precinct and dating to the Late Preclassic Period. Although the rear wall was not discovered, the main room must have been over 4 meters wide by 6 meters in length. In addition, the verandalike frontal room was 3 meters wide by at least 8 meters in length. The southern third of the mound was not excavated, preventing the recording of exact dimensions for these rooms.

Associated evidence indicates that the two rooms were originally at the same elevation. They were defined by stone foundation walls with perishable upper walls. No postholes, postmolds, or post-impressed briquettes were recovered. The rooms were connected by two or more entranceways. At a later time, the main eastern room was raised and the doorways were modified with the addition of steps. The Tulix phase date accepted for these events was derived from diagnostic ceramics taken from sealed floors in the front and back rooms, from sealed wall fill representing sequential modifications of the building plan, and from construction fill incorporated into the building platform.

An Early Classic occupation of the mound is suggested by the appearance of Tzakol basal flange bowl fragments in extremely low frequencies. These five sherds would appear to suggest the presence of a rather ephemeral reuse of the site by an Early Classic group, not unlike that found in other contexts within the central precinct. The proximity of Classic materials to the final Preclassic construction phase coupled with the absence of any subsequent construction datable to the Classic Period suggests that the building platform was still largely visible and reused by Classic Period occupants.

The most recent pre-Columbian occupants of this site appear to have been Late Postclassic groups, represented by a poorly defined rectilinear wall stub and patches of poorly preserved plaster flooring. This structure and hypothesized perishable room extensions may have covered most of the level mound surface. The occupants appear to have constructed their foundation on top of the earlier Preclassic wall stub foundation. The floor within the wall alignment seems to have been underlain by large flat-laid limestone ballast. This type of flooring may be similar to Wauchope's description of "embutido" (1938:15), in which large flat stones were irregularly placed in a matrix of lime and marl. A

threshold area was located along the medial axis of the structure. A small dedicatory cache of Postclassic affinity was discovered immediately outside the structural wall alignment to the west.

A trash deposit on the southeastern slope of the mound contained a high frequency of lithic debris. Lewenstein (1986, 1987) suggests that this location was the locus for fishing net production, given the character of the lithic edge wear and the frequency of ceramic fishnet weights (*mariposas*). Further, a concentration of Postclassic sherds apparently from a single pot were found strewn over the northwestern wall foundation, suggesting postoccupational reuse. A chlorite schist ax was also collected from this context.

The dry-laid rubble defining the northeastern portion of the mound suggests that the Postclassic occupants may have purposely buried the underlying retaining wall or platform (see Willey et al. 1965:69; Bullard 1973:236). The wall alignment overlying this disturbance indicates that between the Late Preclassic/Early Classic and the Postclassic periods, a large portion of the Preclassic component was destroyed and subsequently overlain by a substantial amount of rubble fill.

Even though Structure 11B lacks diagnostic household features (Haviland 1970), its form and size and its relationship to the ancillary *plazuela* Structure 11C and Structure 11D indicate affinities to other domestic structures in the Maya area. The elaborate nature of Preclassic Period architecture at Structure 11B suggests a strong social linkage to the central precinct located approximately 460 meters to the northeast. Although the differential consumption of luxury ceramics, lithics, and exotic materials must await further analysis, the evidence at hand supports at least a part-time residential occupation of this group.

Structure 11C (Operation 108a–c)

Structure 11C lies approximately 15 meters northwest of Structure 11B. It is 25 meters long, 22 meters wide, and 1.5 meters high. It has a potential floor space of 192 square meters and an absolute volume of 557 cubic meters.

During the 1977 season a 24-square-meter exposure was excavated to a depth of 1.2 meters. Instead of employing a proximation trench, a contiguous horizontal exposure was opened at the summit of the mound. The low, flat appearance of Structure 11C and the absence of raised masonry retaining walls associated with other small mounds in the settlement made this type of excavation preferable. Although smaller in size than the other structures, Structure 11C was excavated in an attempt to elucidate variability within the *plazuela* group.

The building platform was composed of light gray marl intruded by cobble-sized and larger stones. The excavation produced a sizable sample of Postclassic lithic debris (after Rovner 1975) as well as Late Preclassic and Late Postclassic ceramic diagnostics. Unfortunately, architectural features were not defined for any period. No ceramics were found in primary deposits, although a Late Preclassic component appears to have been encountered approximately 50 centimeters below the surface.

Structure 11D (Operation 16a)

Structure 11D is located approximately 15 meters southwest of Structure 11B. It is 20 meters long, 15 meters wide, and 1.5 meters high. It has a potential floor space of 140 square meters and an absolute volume of 330 cubic meters. During the 1974 field season a 2-meter by 2-meter test unit was excavated to a depth of 2.0 meters at the summit of the mound, to establish a stratigraphic column.

The mound was constructed of dry-laid rubble overlying a deposit of dark brown clay (5 to 10 centimeters thick) containing Tulix phase ceramics at 1.4 meters below the summit of the structure. The depth of this lens corresponds to the same absolute elevation at which trash and dark soil were recovered from Structure 11B. This suggests that an extensive, though poorly preserved, component was occupied or simply deposited before the *plazuela* mounding occurred. This stratum corresponds to the earliest leveling event described for Structure 11B. A thin marl lens underlies this deposit and appears to be a preparatory surface overlying the sterile paleosol.

Structure 13

This Type 4 structure rests on the eastern flank of the low-lying plaza Structure 9A south of Structure 9B within a *huamil* setting. The mound appears to be oriented toward the central precinct in a manner similar to Structures 14, 15, 16, and the 10 Group; all are structures in the immediate vicinity of Structure 13. The structure lies on the western flank of a shallow runoff channel draining the southwestern central precinct

plaza. The structure is understood to have been a residential facility during the Tulix phase. Further, ceramic analysis indicates that the mound served a nonelite family group. Excavations have revealed three distinct construction phases on this mound, the most recent being a meter-thick mantle dating to the Postclassic Period. The earlier events are associated with a clear Tulix phase construction (Fig. 4.8).

Structure 13A (Operation 125a)

This structure is 26 meters long, 22 meters wide, and 2.5 meters high. It has a potential summit floor space of 25 square meters and an absolute volume of 746 cubic meters. During the 1978 field season a 2-meter by 2-meter unit was excavated to a maximum depth of 2.7 meters. The unit was located on the southwestern slope of the structure, southeast of the predicted medial axis for the mound. A slight ridge trending southwest from the summit of the mound and facing Structure 14 was argued to be the remains of an outset staircase. The excavation was placed in the adjacent inset to obtain midden debris as well as substructural walls. The unit was oriented to magnetic north (Fig. 4.9).

The strata were lotted into seven naturally occurring levels. The surface level consisted of a dark brown loam A-horizon intruded by fall stones. Level 2 was defined by a friable brown loam intruded by gravel- to boulder-sized ballast. Although this matrix is understood to be mound construction core for the reoccupation of the site during Postclassic times, a few faced stones were noted in the fill. Level 3 consisted of a light brown loam, intruded by small boulder-sized rubble in the northern portion of the unit. It graded laterally (south) into a grayish brown loam containing few fill stones. At the base of the level, a marl construction pause or decomposed floor was apparent.

Level 4 was defined as the ballast under the construction pause. The southern portion of the unit revealed gravel-sized hearting packed in a thick marl matrix. This in turn rested on a soft plaster, or *sascab,* floor (F1). In the southeastern corner, an ancient tree root disturbance had been truncated by the construction pause leveling event. To the north, the soft plaster floor (F1) was found to lip up onto a four-course high (50 centimeters) platform retaining wall. The wall was oriented southwest-northeast through the center of the unit. It was composed of crudely faced limestone cobbles. The wall was sectioned and found to retain a

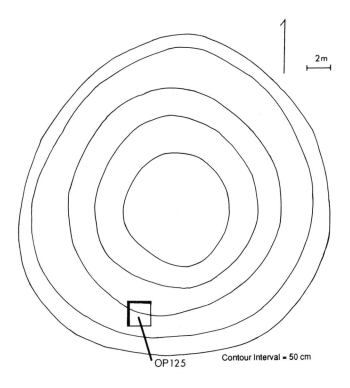

Figure 4.8. Contour map of Structure 13.

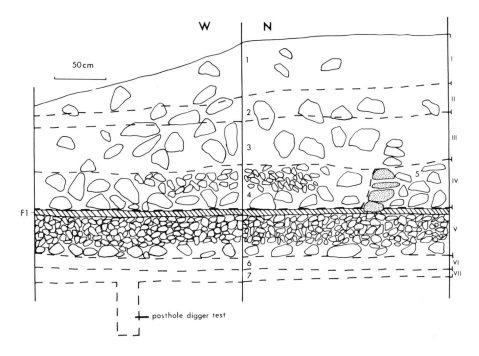

Figure 4.9. Profile from Structure 13A (Operation 125a).

pebble- to cobble-sized ballast packed in a white marl matrix resting on a continuation of the exterior soft plaster floor (F1) outside the wall.

Level 5 consisted of the 5- to 7-centimeter-thick soft plaster floor (F1) as well as 35 centimeters of tightly compacted pebble-sized hearting underlying the floor. The lower reaches of this fill contained cobble-sized ballast. This level is thought to be the subplaza Structure 9A and was found to underlie most of the mounds in this area. It should be noted that a possible construction pen wall of small boulder-sized stones was removed from the fill. It would have been oriented north-south in our exposure, as indicated in the northern profile. All ceramics sealed behind the retaining wall and below the floor (F1) date to the Tulix phase.

Level 6 consisted of a dark brown silty clay intruded by a few ballast stones from above. The 10-centimeter-thick lens represents a primary midden deposit containing large and numerous fragments of Tulix phase pottery, charcoal, bone, and shell. Level 7 was defined as the sterile underlying paleosol clay. It was posthole probed to determine its 15-centimeter-thick depth as well as the presence of the underlying parent material.

Structure 13 demonstrates four constructional events. The underlying midden deposit is thought to be associated with an early Tulix phase ground-level occupation. The ballast, including the *sascab*/plaster floor (F1), is understood to represent the southeastern portion of subplaza Structure 9A. This feature underlies most of the structures in this quadrat. The retaining wall is a feature associated with the initial construction of Structure 13. The most recent construction event was a later occupation associated with the Postclassic reuse of the site. The Tulix phase retaining wall was razed except for the extant four courses, and correspondingly, the adjacent area outside the wall was raised. Stratigraphically, this occurred sometime after Tulix phase abandonment, as evidenced by the truncated tree root disturbance. The overlying fill was poorly consolidated.

Structure 14

This Type 4 structure rests on the eastern margin of subplaza 9A within a *huamil* setting. The mound shares the same orientation toward the central precinct as the adjacent Structures 13, 15, 16, and the 10 Group. A shallow, poorly defined runoff channel draining the main plaza lies to the east. The imposing size, limited

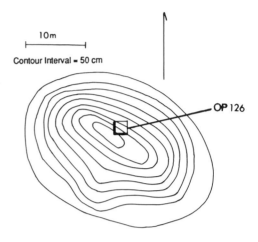

10m

Contour Interval = 50 cm

OP 126

Figure 4.10.   Contour map of Structure 14.

summit space, and spatial disposition to other mounds suggest that it is not a residential locus. Unfortunately, the ceramic inventory was too small to be of any use. It should be noted that the southwest side of the mound appears to be terraced. The structure has been assigned a Tulix phase date, although C'oh phase ground-level structure may also be suggested (Fig. 4.10).

Structure 14A (Operation 126a)

This structure is 33 meters long, 22 meters wide, and 4.5 meters high. It has a potential summit floor space of 40 square meters and an absolute volume of 1,724 cubic meters. During the 1978 field season a 2-meter by 2-meter unit was placed high on the northeastern slope of the structure and excavated to a maximum depth of 4.8 meters. The unit was positioned in this area to expose midden debris or architectural detail east of the projected medial axis for the mound. The unit was oriented to magnetic north (Fig. 4.11).

Strata were lotted into nine naturally occurring levels. The surface level consisted of a dark brown clay loam A-horizon which graded into an arbitrarily defined second level. The latter was a friable grayish brown loam. Both were intruded by fall stones and surface accumulation.

Level 3 was defined by a gray loam intruded by cobble-sized rubble fall. The matrix was lighter in hue than level 2. It appears to represent the fall debris from the final mound construction. Level 4 consisted of a thick white marl-melt deposit intruded by boulder-sized

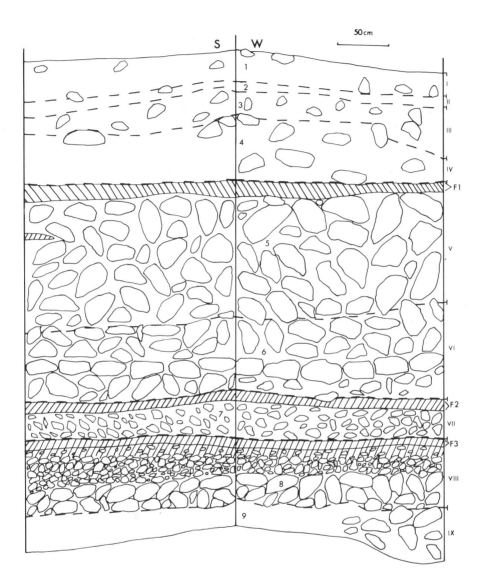

Figure 4.11.   Profile from Structure 14A (Operation 126a).

fall stones. The plaster deposit was thicker to the south than to the north, contouring to the slope of the mound. It rested on a soft plaster floor (F1).

Level 5 was a 15-centimeter-thick soft plaster floor (F1) and an underlying 1.2-meter-thick boulder-sized dry-laid ballast. A sealed Tulix phase date was obtained from this fill. The floor consisted of a gravel ballast incorporated into the soft plaster. This is understood to be a postdepositional occurrence resulting from the settling of the floor under the porous dry-laid rubble. A construction pause 60 centimeters below the soft

plaster floor (F1) was apparent in the western portion of the unit, but it feathered out into the eastern rubble fill. The upper portion of the fill produced numerous fragments of painted hard plaster, including one large molded piece. The colors included red, buff, and green and indicate the presence of a rather elaborate facade. The disarticulated and buried nature of the facade is reminiscent of the ritual events found immediately above Structure 5C 2nd.

Level 6 consisted of a friable grayish brown loam intruded by cobble-sized rubble fill. It was approximately 60 centimeters thick. Level 7 was defined by a compacted white marl lens (F2) 10 centimeters thick. It was underlain by a 30-centimeter-thick gravel-sized ballast layer packed in a friable off-white marl. Although the white marl lens was not as hard as exterior flooring operations found elsewhere in the settlement, it was comparable to the interior floors of some of the structures (Structures 11B and 10C). The tightly packed gravel-sized hearting supporting the lens further suggests that this was an interior floor associated with the initial platform construction at this location.

Level 8 was a polished hard plaster floor (F3), together with its underlying tightly packed hearting. This floor (F3) was 10 to 15 centimeters thick and was supported by a thin underflooring event of friable white marl. The gravel hearting was 15 centimeters thick and underlain by 30 centimeters of cobble-sized ballast. A sealed Tulix phase date was obtained from the ceramic fill. This flooring operation is understood to be an extremely well preserved section of the original subplaza Structure 9A.

Level 9 represents the brown-gray clay paleosol underlying the site. A thin discontinuous lens of white marl capped the paleosol and may represent a "preparatory surface" laid down for the plaza construction. A ceramic inventory from the upper reaches of the paleosol was much larger than expected and dates to the C'oh phase exclusively. This artifactual debris may be associated with an earlier ground-level occupation prior to the plaza construction of Tulix times.

Structure 14 is understood to be a Tulix phase nonresidential structure. However, a smaller platform resting on the underlying subplaza Structure 9A is suggested. This latter structure was stratigraphically constructed in the early Tulix phase. The plaza appears to be contemporaneous with the small platform. The earliest evidence for occupation of this locus comes from the paleosol surface underlying the plaza and dating to the C'oh phase.

Structure 15

This Type 4 structure rests to the immediate northeast of Structure 16 within a well-drained *huamil* setting. The mound lies on the southeast margin of subplaza Structure 9A. The major intrasite *zacatal* depression lies to the south. The mound is oriented toward the central precinct, in keeping with the other mounds resting on subplaza Structure 9A. The structure dates to the Late C'oh phase and is underlain by the same type of midden debris exposed under Structure 16. The mound is believed to be a residential facility due to its size and ceramic inventory. The ceramic analysis further indicates an elite residential function for the structure. The underlying midden deposit argues for functional continuity through time and space. Tulix phase occupation is also indicated (Fig. 4.12).

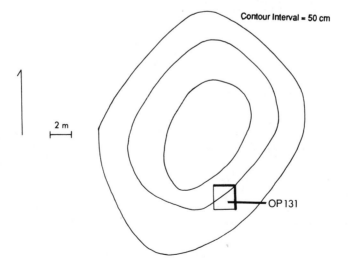

Figure 4.12.   Contour map of Structure 15.

Structure 15A (Operation 131a)

This structure is 42 meters long, 39 meters wide, and 1.7 meters high. It has a potential summit floor space of 96 square meters and an absolute volume of 1,474 cubic meters. During the 1978 field season, a 2-meter by 2-meter unit was excavated to a maximum depth of 2.4 meters. The unit was placed on the southwest portion of the structure to reveal architectural detail as well as potential midden debris. Neither expectation was realized in association with the final construction phase. The unit was oriented to magnetic north (Fig. 4.13).

The strata were lotted into four naturally occurring levels. The surface level was defined by a dark brown loam intruded by fall stone. A layer of flat, bedded, cobble-sized stones covering the entire unit was defined at the base of the level. This appears to be a Tulix phase modification of the original C'oh phase mound. Level 2 was defined as a light tan silty loam intruded by rubble fill. The limestone cap was removed and found to be underlain by an ephemeral lens of white marl, which graded into the rubble fill. Level 3 consisted of a white marl matrix intruded by very few stones. At the base of this matrix a single course of small boulder-sized foundation stones was found to cover the entire unit.

Level 4 represented a primary midden deposit underlying the mound construction. Although no clear flooring event could be isolated, a red stain was apparent in a discontinuous distribution across the unit. The dark midden clay contained charcoal, ash, bone, and ceramic debris. The dark brown gumbo paleosol was identified immediately below the midden clays. It was posthole probed and found to be approximately 30 centimeters thick and underlain by the ubiquitous gray parent material.

Structure 15 is viewed as a C'oh phase house mound associated with Structure 16. Both structures antedate subplaza Structure 9A, although Tulix phase occupation is suggested. The underlying midden deposit is similar to that identified under Structure 16. It is postulated to be associated with a ground-level occupation similar to Feature 33 (Operation 107) and to that underlying Structure 16. It should be noted that the ground-level occupation underlying subplaza Structure 9A appears to be more dispersed than the nucleated village defined under subplaza Structure 2A.

Structure 16

This Type 5 structure rests at the southeast margin of the subplaza Structure 9A within a *huamil* setting

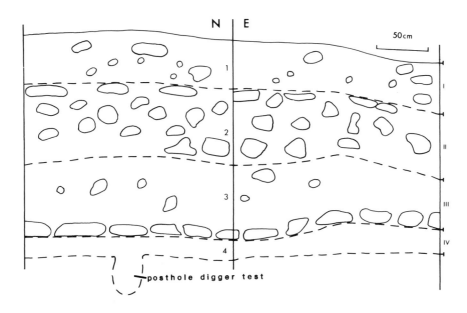

Figure 4.13. Profile from Structure 15A (Operation 131a).

but immediately north of the depressed *zacatal* near the center of the core site area. This relatively small rangelike structure is oriented toward the center in a manner similar to that noted in Structures 13, 14, 15, and the Structure 10 Group, all in near proximity. The mound and underlying ground-level floors date to the Late C'oh phase. Although no features were exposed, this structure is hypothesized to be a domestic facility due to its size and the suggestion that the underlying domestic occupation resulted in a later mounded residence. Tulix phase occupation is also suggested. Ceramic analysis indicates that the Late C'oh occupation represents an elite residence (Fig. 4.14).

Structure 16A (Operation 130a)

This structure is 23 meters long, 11 meters wide, and 1.0 meter high. It has a potential platform summit space of 48 square meters and an absolute volume of 151 cubic meters. During the 1978 field season a 2-meter by 2-meter unit was excavated to a maximum depth of 170 centimeters. The unit was placed on the north slope of the mound in anticipation of an axial staircase and/or associated midden debris. Only the second proposition was partially fulfilled. The unit was oriented to magnetic north (Fig. 4.15).

The strata were divided into seven lots consisting of three arbitrary and four natural levels. The upper three

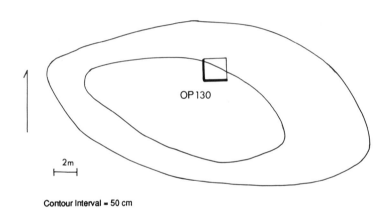

Contour Interval = 50 cm

Figure 4.14.   Contour map of Structure 16.

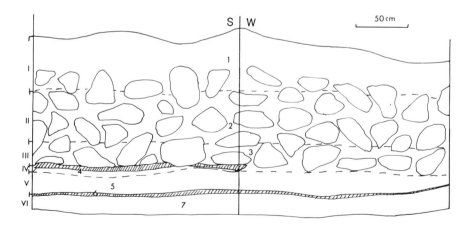

Figure 4.15.   Profile from Structure 16A (Operation 130a).

levels were arbitrarily separated in an attempt to seriate the construction events responsible for the structure. The upper reaches of the mound consisted of a dark brown loam intruded by small boulder-sized fall and fill. It graded into a light brown clay loam intruded by slightly smaller rubble fill.

Level 4 was naturally defined by a 15-centimeter-thick white marl cap. It appears to be a "preparatory surface" underlying the mound construction. Midden debris intruded its lower reaches. Level 5 represented a complicated series of sealed lenses associated with ground-level occupation prior to mound construction. These dark brown midden deposits contained ash and charcoal debris as well as bone and shell fragments. The level was terminated on a lens of dark midden clay defined by a surface of horizontally bedded sherds and a possible *tierra quemada* flooring event. In addition to charcoal, bone, and sherd debris on the floor, a bit of hard plaster associated with red earth stain was noted. Although this primary midden debris was very dense, level 5 was only 15 centimeters thick.

Level 6 was defined as the underlying black gumbo paleosol. It contained a bit of sherd debris filtering down from above. The gray parent material was found to underlie this matrix.

Structure 16 is a Late C'oh phase domestic facility at the margin of subplaza Structure 9A. Structure 9A appears to be a Tulix phase construction which did not quite extend to Structure 16. The underlying ground-level structure would appear to be contemporaneous with the Feature 33 exposure (Operation 107) underlying subplaza Structure 9A and only slightly earlier than the postulated Tulix phase ground-level occupations under Structures 13 and 14. It should be noted that the floors exposed under Structure 16 appear identical to those defined under subplaza Structure 2A of the central precinct, which in part date to the C'oh phase.

Structure 18

This Type 5 structure rests in the western portion of the core site area. It lies in the northwestern margin of the largely depressed thornbush and *zacatal* zone at the center of the site. This structure is positioned in a less well drained *huamil* setting. The mound has been assigned a Tulix phase date, although a Late Preclassic modification of the structure is apparent. The mound has been defined as a small residential locus. Tulix

phase ceramic analysis suggests an elite residential facility (Fig. 4.16).

Structure 18A (Operation 11a)

This structure is 15 meters long, 12 meters wide, and 0.8 meter high. It has a potential summit floor space of 80 square meters and an absolute volume of 130 cubic meters. During the 1974 field season a 2-meter by 2.5-meter unit was excavated to a maximum depth of 1.7 meters. The long axis of the exposure was oriented east-west. The unit was placed at the summit of the structure to obtain a sealed construction fill date (Fig. 4.17).

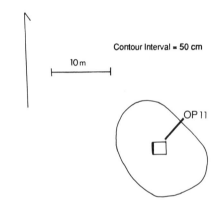

Figure 4.16.   Contour map of Structure 18.

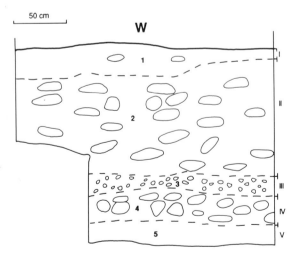

Figure 4.17.   Profile from Structure 18A (Operation 11a).

The five natural strata were divided into ten arbitrarily defined levels. The surface humus (level 1) was underlain by cobble-sized flat-laid rubble encased in a dark brown clay loam (level 2). A human burial (burial 6) was found 40 to 60 centimeters BSD within this matrix. This poorly preserved adult was lying on its left side in a semiflexed position with its head oriented to the west. Although no accompanying furniture was found, a notched chert point was located near the area of the groin. The burial has been assigned a Late Postclassic date.

The next natural stratum, lying at 120 centimeters BSD, consisted of a black clay loam intruded by gravel-sized stone. A high sherd concentration was associated with this 20-centimeter-thick lens and appears to define an earlier near-ground-level occupation. A viscous gray clay paleosol intruded by cobble-sized and smaller limestone chunks underlay the black clay loam. It in turn was underlain by sterile white decomposing caprock.

This structure is understood to be a Tulix phase manifestation, although a Late Postclassic modification of the structure is suggested. A residential facility is indicated. Further, the ceramic inventory supports an elite residential function during the Tulix occupation.

Structure 19 Group

This Type 3 structure group rests in a well-drained *huamil* setting near the western margin of the core site area. A depressed *zacatal* setting lies in proximity. The structure group was selected for excavation because of its imposing size and unique form. This structure group has been more severely damaged than any other structures in the settlement. Bulldozer action has removed the southern third of range Structure 19C and perhaps disturbed the adjacent southern portion of plaza Structure 19A. Informants participating in this damage relate that the fill removed from Structure 19C was used to infill a portion of the western segment of the main canal. Inspection of the ragged profile resulting from the bulldozer damage suggested a single-phase construction event. The size and elaborate form of the structure group indicate that this mound was a nonresidential facility. The large platform area of Structure 19B may suggest a storage facility of some kind. Excavations demonstrate a Tulix phase date from sealed construction fill for the bulk of this mound. Ceramic analysis further indicates that

this structure functioned as a civic/ritual facility (Fig. 4.18).

Structure 19B (Operation 124a)

This structure is 45 meters long, 34 meters wide, and 3.5 meters high. It has a potential platform summit space of 1,280 square meters and an absolute volume of 4,918 cubic meters. During the 1978 field season a 2-meter by 2-meter unit was excavated to a maximum depth of 2.95 meters. The unit was located on the western slope of Structure 19B. Although architectural detail was anticipated at this location, associated trash outside the final construction retaining wall was also predicted. In addition, we anticipated isolating the construction technique of the underlying subplaza Structure 19A. The test unit was oriented to magnetic north (Fig. 4.19).

The strata were divided into nine lots consisting of seven naturally occurring levels. The surface level was defined by a dark brown loam grading into a lighter loam matrix intruded by rubble fall. Level 2 represented construction ballast packed in a gray loam. The eastern portion of the unit was composed of pebble-sized hearting, which graded laterally into large rubble fill. Level 3 was defined by a well-made construction pen wall to the northeast and small boulder-sized ballast in a friable grayish brown loam to the southwest. The latter underlay the hearting stone defined in level 2. The construction pen wall was five to six courses high (1.15 meters in elevation) and oriented northwest-southeast through the northeast corner of the unit. The boulder-sized stones were crudely faced and slightly stepped back one above the other to contain the bulk of the platform. The wall was not sectioned because of the danger of side wall collapse.

Level 4 represents a compacted layer of grayish brown loam intruded by gravel-sized ballast. This 15-centimeter lens appears to be a foundation deposit over which the large ballast was laid. Level 5 consisted of a 5- to 7-centimeter soft plaster floor (F1) and an underlying 20-centimeter-thick gravel-sized hearting support lens. This floor (F1) was found to underlie the construction pen wall and is understood to be the subplaza surface Structure 19A. Level 6 consisted of a thin lens of white marl "preparatory surface" underlying the plaza construction. It in turn overlay a 20-centimeter-thick deposit of brown silty loam containing a sizable quantity of Tulix phase ceramics. This latter deposit may indicate the presence of a ground-level Tulix phase

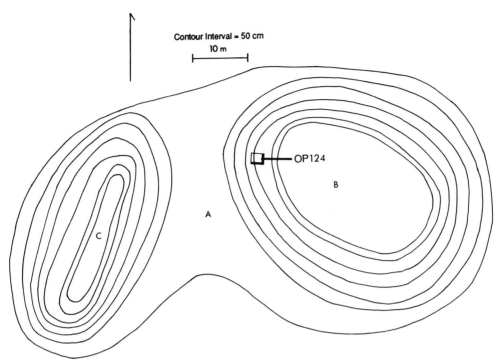

Figure 4.18. Contour map of the Structure 19 Group.

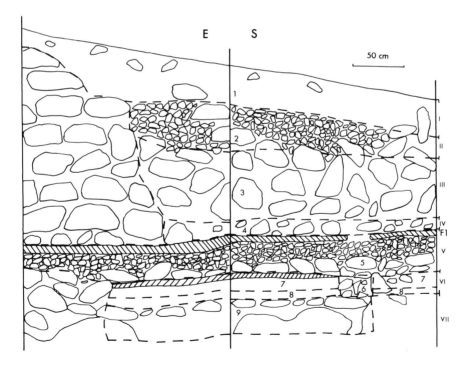

Figure 4.19. Profile from Structure 19B (Operation 124a).

dwelling in proximity to our exposure, but the inventory was not dense enough to argue for primary midden deposition. In the southwest corner of the unit at 238 centimeters BSD, we isolated a Tulix phase "beer mug" (Matamore Dichrome; Matamore Variety), cached and sealed below the plaza floor (F1). The pot was placed in a cavity fashioned from dry-laid ballast and dark gray loam. A few additional large sherds were found in association but no other complete vessels were found. The cache was not covered by a preparatory surface and would appear to date the plaza construction.

Level 7 was defined as the base of the mound and consisted of the dark gray gumbo paleosol found elsewhere at the site. The gray decomposing parent material was less than 10 centimeters thick and immediately underlain by indurated caprock. A solution cavity was evident in the basal matrix.

The Structure 19 Group is understood to be a Tulix phase nonresidential facility based on the size and complexity of the group as well as the functional ceramic assessment. Structure 19B demonstrates a single Tulix phase construction event, although some evidence exists for a domestic occupation prior to the underlying plaza construction during a stratigraphically earlier Tulix moment.

Structure 21

This Type 4 structure rests in a fork of the main canal at the northwest edge of the core site zone, 30 meters south of the bay. It is surrounded by *zacatal* and *hulub*, but occupies an island of well-drained caprock. A tentative Tulix phase date has been assigned to this structure, although the ceramic inventory was very small. Given the imposing size and position of this mound at the entrance of the canal system, this structure is suggested to have functioned as a civic facility (Fig. 4.20).

Structure 21A (Operation 105a and b)

This structure is 32 meters long, 25 meters wide, and 5.0 meters high. It has a potential summit floor space of 70 square meters and an absolute volume of 2,175 cubic meters. During the 1976 field season, two 1-meter by 2-meter units were excavated at the summit and on the western flank of the mound to a depth of 180 centimeters and 170 centimeters, respectively. These unit locations were selected to obtain sealed

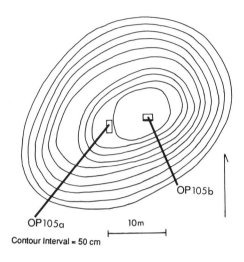

Figure 4.20.   Contour map of Structure 21.

construction fill dating samples as well as possible architectural detail. Both units were oriented to magnetic north (Fig. 4.21).

The summit exposure was divided into seven lots consisting of five natural levels. The first two levels consisted of a humic horizon underlain by a gray marl matrix intruded by pebble- to small-boulder-

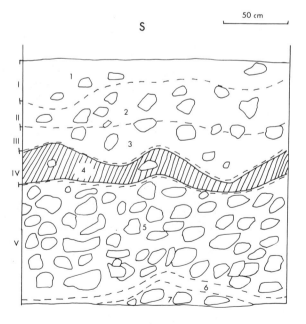

Figure 4.21.   Profile from Structure 21A (Operation 105b).

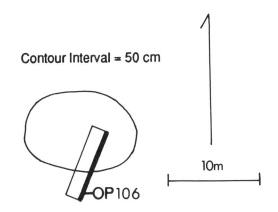

Contour Interval = 50 cm

10m

OP 106

Figure 4.22. Contour map of Structure 22.

sized rubble. Level 3 was defined by a friable light gray clay containing bits of pottery, charcoal flecks, ash, and *sascab*.

At 70 centimeters BSD, level 4 was defined as white marl/*sascab* containing abundant charcoal flecks, fire-cracked limestone, and ash. Although the exposure was limited, this 10 to 15-centimeter-thick lens may be the remains of an early poorly preserved house floor. Level 5 was a mottled light gray marl immediately underlying the *sascab* lens. No hearting ballast was noted and only boulder-sized rubble made up the mound fill. A thin, discontinuous lens of dark friable clay appeared in the unit at 170 centimeters BSD. It may represent a construction pause. It in turn was underlain by rubble fill.

The western flank exposure consisted of four lots excavated from three naturally defined levels. The surface level consisted of humic loam and gravel-sized stone. Level 2 was composed of cobble-sized ballast in a gray marl matrix. These stones were underlain by small-boulder-sized rubble. Level 3 was defined by

boulder-sized rubble containing little soil matrix. This appears to be the dry-laid core of the mound.

Structure 21 provided little architectural or functional evidence from our limited test excavations. The Tulix phase date is derived from a construction fill context.

Structure 22

This Type 6 mound structure is located 40 meters south of the present bay in the northwest portion of the core site area. The mound is located in well-drained *huamil*, but flanked to the west by *zacatal*. The structure has been assigned to the Tulix phase and has been defined as a small house mound. Ceramic analysis indicates a nonelite residential function (Fig. 4.22).

Structure 22A (Operation 106 a–d)

This structure is 12 meters long, 9 meters wide, and 0.5 meter high. It has a potential summit floor space of 16 square meters and an absolute volume of 31 cubic meters. During the 1976 season, a 2-meter by 8-meter trench was excavated up the south side of the mound to a maximum depth of 1.0 meter. Both midden debris and architectural detail were anticipated, but neither was realized. An attempt was made to strip the exposure and at the same time maintain a 2-meter by 2-meter grid provenience control (Fig. 4.23).

Four arbitrary levels were defined during excavation. Levels 1 and 2 were defined by a dark humic loam underlain by a light brown clay. Levels 3 and 4 consisted of a light brown clay intruded by cobble-sized rubble fill. The entire exposure was mottled by vertical intrusions, making the dating of the structure suspect. The ceramic inventory consisted of C'oh and Tulix phase ceramics.

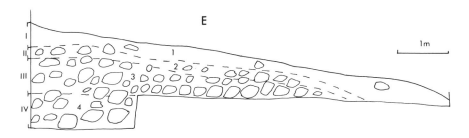

E

1m

Figure 4.23. Profile from Structure 22A (Operation 106a–d).

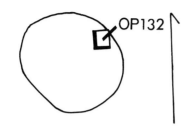

Contour Interval = 50 cm

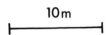

10 m

Figure 4.24.   Contour map of Structure 24.

Structure 22 is a poorly understood structure, in spite of a sizable excavation area. It has been tentatively assigned a Tulix phase date and is understood to have been a residential facility.

Structure 24

This Type 6 structure rests at the northern end of the Sacbe 1 (Feature 126) on the margins of the depressed *zacatal*. The structure lies in a well-drained *huamil* setting at the southern reaches of Plaza 9A. Structure 24 is interpreted as a Late C'oh phase construction reoccupied in Tulix times. The function of the mound is equivocal, but its small size and association with Structures 13, 14, 15, and 16 at the edge of Plaza 9A suggest an outbuilding or service population

residence. Ceramic analysis indicates the presence of a nonelite residence, adding further support to the formal field identification (Fig. 4.24).

Structure 24A (Operation 132a)

Structure 24 is 11 meters long, 10 meters wide, and 0.5 meter high. It has a potential summit floor space of 16 square meters and an absolute volume of 32 cubic meters. During the 1978 field season a 2-meter by 2-meter unit was excavated to a depth of 1.0 meter. It was located on the eastern flank of the structure in anticipation of midden debris and/or architectural exposure. The unit was oriented to magnetic north (Fig. 4.25).

The strata were divided into five lots consisting of four naturally occurring levels. The surface level was a dark brown humic loam intruded by cobble-sized fall stones. This level was underlain by the edge of a stone platform in the western portion of the exposure. The platform margin was poorly defined but seems to have been covered by small tabular boulders a course or two high (20 centimeters maximum height). The matrix outside and east of this stone concentration was the same humic deposit as found above. This feature is argued to be associated with the Tulix reoccupation of the mound.

Level 2 consisted of a gray clay loam intruded by cobble-sized construction fill. A couple of large stones in the southwestern corner may be the remains of a C'oh phase retaining wall, but additional exposure is necessary. Associated at the foot of these stones (level 3) was a thin midden deposit not unlike those defined elsewhere under plaza Structure 9A. Charcoal and

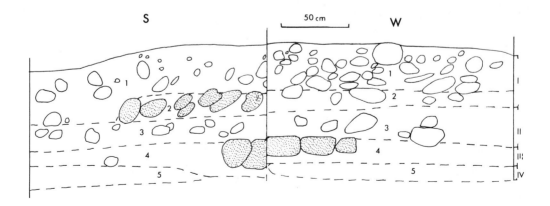

Figure 4.25.   Profile from Structure 24A (Operation 132a).

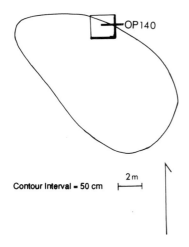

Figure 4.26. Contour map of Structure 26.

Contour Interval = 50 cm   2m

bone were collected. Level 4 was identified as the underlying sterile gray parent material. No "preparatory surface" or paleosol was noted.

This structure was excavated because of its size and proximity to the relatively large mounds of this zone. The absence of a paleosol suggests the deliberate removal of this topsoil prior to construction. Again, it may suggest the premium placed on the soil itself, and its relocation to agricultural plots. The C'oh phase construction of this hypothesized nonelite house mound appears to be near ground level. A subsequent Tulix phase modification of the structure is also apparent.

Structure 26

This Type 6 mound is located in a *huamil* setting in close proximity to Structures 25, 27, and 28. The caprock in this area is exposed in some locations. The soil overlying the caprock is quite moist, apparently because of the drainage depressions surrounding the area. The mound is interpreted as a domestic dwelling constructed during the Tulix phase, although a ground-level C'oh occupation is indicated. Although the structure has been disturbed by postdepositional agents, the test excavation unit was placed away from the most obvious disturbances, to the south. This mound was selected for excavation because of its formal and spatial affinity to the other mounds in proximity (Fig. 4.26).

Structure 26A (Operation 140a)

Structure 26A is 12 meters long, 12 meters wide, and 0.5 meter high. It has a potential summit floor space of 24 square meters and an absolute volume of 42 cubic meters. During the 1978 field season a 2-meter by 2-meter unit was excavated to a depth of 95 centimeters. The unit was placed on the northern flanks of the mound to avoid the obvious disturbed portion of the structure. The unit was oriented to magnetic north (Fig. 4.27).

The strata were lotted into four naturally occurring but poorly defined levels. The surface level consisted of a dark clay loam A-horizon intruded by gravel-sized

50 cm

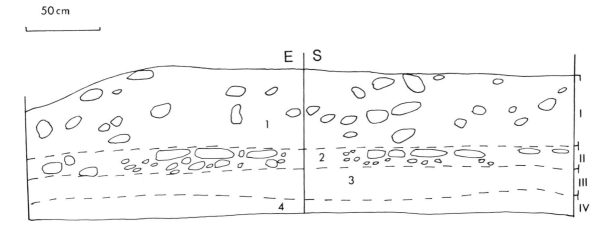

Figure 4.27. Profile from Structure 26A (Operation 140a).

fall. This graded into the second level, or gray clay loam intruded by cobble-sized and larger rubble fill. The southern portion of the mound was defined by a gravel-sized construction core. Level 3 consisted of a light gray clay marl understood to be the decomposing parent matrix, although a few migrating sherds were collected. The basal level defined the upper reaches of the solid limestone caprock. The absence of a paleosol suggests its deliberate removal.

Structure 26 appears to represent a nonelite residential facility dating to the Tulix phase. Ceramic analysis has provided the precise function for the structure. A ground-level C'oh occupation is suggested immediately following the removal of the paleosol. The absence of a paleosol indicates the deliberate removal of this deposit, perhaps in a manner not unlike that suggested for Structure 38 (see p. 80).

Structure 29

Structure 29 rests in the elevated *huamil* of the southeast portion of the core site area. Its spatial relationship to the two ball court groups (Structure Groups 6l and 50) is unique in that its western medial axis bisects a north-south trending line between the two courts. This same north-south line continues through the alleyway between Structure 4 and Structure 6 of the central precinct and appears to define a midline bisecting the entire core zone. Structure 29B is the most prominent Tulix phase civic monument in the settlement (outside the central precinct) and will be treated in its entirety in another presentation (Freidel 1986a and b). The subplaza Structure 29A oriented to the west is the subject of this narrative. This plaza area dates to the Tulix phase and was selected for excavation because of the possibility that an extensive stratigraphic column for the settlement zone would be present. Additionally, architectural detail was anticipated. Only the latter expectation was partially realized. An ephemeral Postclassic reuse of the platform was also indicated (Fig. 4.28).

Structure 29A (Operation 134a)

This structure is 100 meters long, 80 meters wide, and 1.5 meters high. It has a potential floor space of 8,000 square meters and an absolute volume of 12,000 cubic meters. During the 1978 field season a 2-meter by 2-meter unit was excavated to a maximum depth of 2.15 meters. The unit was placed at the foot of Structure 29B on the medial axis of the structure. It was oriented to magnetic north (Fig. 4.29).

The strata were divided into seven lots consisting of three arbitrary and four naturally occurring levels. The surface level was defined as a dark brown clay loam A-horizon intruded by limestone fall as well as an apparent Postclassic earthen mantle. Level 2 represented the definition and removal of a well-defined hard plaster floor, which sealed the remainder of the plaza fill. The floor (F1) was 5 to 9 centimeters thick and underlain by a comparable thickness of pebble-sized hearting. The southern portion of the floor was less well preserved than the northern three-quarters of the unit.

Levels 3, 4, 5, and 6 were artificially leveled lots and can be viewed as one naturally occurring level. These lots were separated to maintain stratigraphic control throughout the unit. The 130 centimeters of fill underlying the plaster floor and hearting support consisted of thick, discontinuous lenses of dense white *sascab* alternating with light brown clay loam mottled by the *sascab* fill. In the upper reaches of the deposit, isolated pockets of dark brown loam containing burned limestone gravels intruded the *sascab* matrix. In the lower reaches of the exposure, thin lenses of black granular soil mottled the *sascab*. Very few stones intruded the plaza fill. However, along the western excavation wall, a well-constructed four- to five-course-high wall (130 centimeters in elevation) retained the earthen plaza fill. This wall is a construction pen wall similar to those defined in the central precinct.

Level 7 was defined as the dark brown paleosol found under most of the structures in the settlement. Although a few sherds were found in association with this matrix, they are understood to be a consequence of vertical migration. The paleosol was 10 centimeters thick and underlain by a yellow granular parent material.

Plaza Structure 29A was constructed as one event during the Tulix phase. The absence of stone fill for this structure may be a result of its low massive form which required less rigidity than taller structures. Even so, it is considered anomalous when compared to other structures of similar form at the site. It is suggested that the fill for Structure 29A came from the depressed thornbush and *zacatal* setting to the west. Once the maximum quantity of stone from throughout the settlement was removed, further

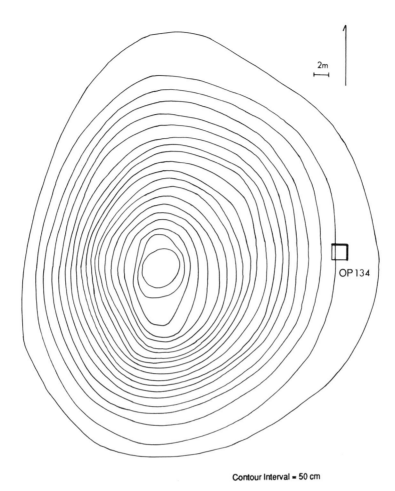

2m

Contour Interval = 50 cm

Figure 4.28.   Contour map of Structure 29.

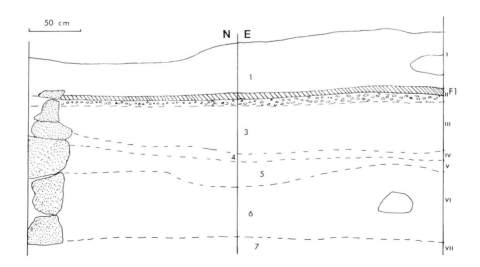

Figure 4.29.   Profile from Structure 29A (Operation 134a).

excavation is postulated to have occurred into the *sas-cab* parent matrix, which underlies the caprock. The depressed condition of the *zacatal* is understood to be in part a consequence of this subplaza Structure 29A.

Structure 34

This Type 5 structure rests in a well-drained *huamil* setting associated with the scoured and pitted caprock relief of the northeastern intrasite area. The southern margin of the mound is flanked by an apparent runoff ditch issuing into the main canal. Structure 34 is oriented N45°W of magnetic north so that its primary axis is directed toward the central precinct. The structure has been assigned a Late Tulix phase date. Although the construction appears to have been initiated during the Late Tulix phase, significant modifications occurred during the Terminal Preclassic Period. The mound was reused in Early Classic times as well. However, the structure is viewed primarily as a Tulix phase domestic facility. Residential trash such as groundstone, ceramic net weights, and sherd lid covers further suggest a Tulix phase domestic occupation. The formal field data as well as the ceramic analysis suggest a residential function for the structure (Figs. 4.30, 4.31).

Structure 34A (Operation 118 a–n)

Structure 34A is 16 meters long, 14 meters wide, and 1.0 meter high. It has a potential summit floor space of 36 square meters and an absolute volume of 130 cubic meters. During the 1978 field season a 2-meter by 2-meter unit was placed on the northern flank of the structure. It was excavated to a maximum depth of 1.4 meters. On exposure of two retaining wall features and an exterior plaster floor, Structure 34 was selected for further lateral excavation. The horizontal exposure revealed 53 square meters on the northern half of the structure to a maximum depth of 1.7 meters. A 2-meter by 2-meter arbitrary grid control was maintained to ensure accurate horizontal and vertical provenience for the anticipated activity area relationships. These data were to be compared and contrasted with Structure 11B and other less extensive excavations (Fig. 4.32).

The earliest component at this site locus is a Tulix phase ground-level occupation. Architecturally, it is not well documented, although, ceramically, the inventory included large sherds and other trash debris in and overlying the sterile black gumbo paleosol. A

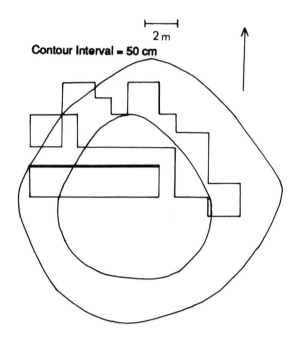

Figure 4.30.   Contour map of Structure 34.

discontinuous 5-to 10-centimeter-thick lens of gravel-sized hearting stone capped the paleosol and probably represents the original flooring for the structure. The overlying small-boulder-sized rubble coring together with the thick concentration of *sascab* melt may represent the razed remains of this dwelling.

The next component has been defined as a simple rectangular Late Tulix phase platform. It was approximately 6.95 meters long by 5.70 meters wide and attained a maximum preserved height of 90 centimeters (six to eight courses in elevation). The chinked retaining wall was composed of rectangular stones set in a thick marl grout. The construction fill consisted of a dry-laid small-boulder-sized rubble overlain by a cobble-sized ballast encased in an intruding humus fill. No flooring was associated with the platform surface. It was apparently stripped away during the subsequent modification of the mound. An exterior hard plaster floor was associated with the base of the platform along the northern side.

The major construction phase on Structure 34 was a two-step Terminal Preclassic platform with an outset staircase or ramp. It was approximately 7.75 meters long, 6.60 meters wide, and attained a maximum height of 90 centimeters. The outset was 3.75 meters

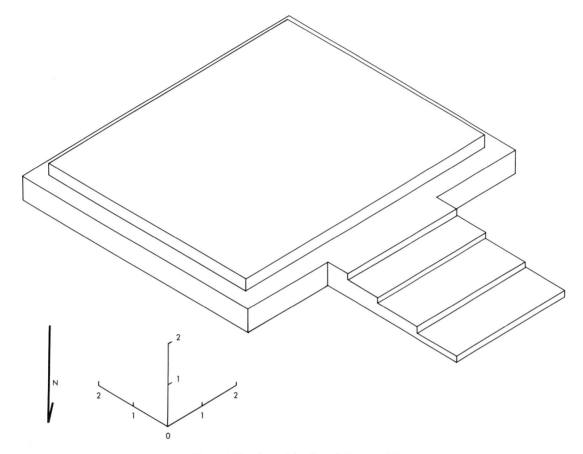

Figure 4.31. Isometric plan of Structure 34.

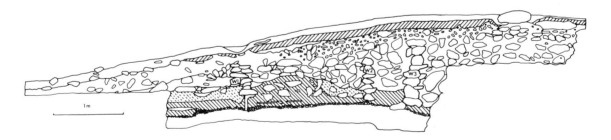

Figure 4.32. Profile from Structure 34A (Operation 118a–n).

long and 3.20 meters wide. The treads and risers were severely damaged. The structure incorporated the Tulix phase platform by adding an additional retaining wall to the entire structure. This outer wall was placed 30 to 50 centimeters from the inner wall, running parallel to its N45°W orientation. It was constructed with the same rectangular stones set in a marl grout as identified for the inner wall. The fill between the two walls consisted of cobble-sized coring packed in a white marl matrix. The outer wall was one to two courses lower than the inner wall, thereby providing the stepped appearance of the structure. Excavation did not reveal preserved plaster associated with the platform; however, an exterior plaster floor was found preserved within the inset corner areas of the outset staircase as well as at the eastern corner of the structure. Traces of flooring were also noted along the northeastern side of the structure, suggesting that the area immediately outside the structure generally had been plastered. Hearting stones 5 to 7 centimeters thick were found to underlie the better preserved portions of this floor.

The outset staircase was hung on the northwest side of the outer platform wall. It was composed of the same rectangular stone masonry as found in the other two walls. At the juncture of the outer platform wall and the outset, the staircase attained a height of six courses (60 centimeters). The fill within the outset was the same cobble-sized ballast as found between the platform walls, but it also contained a large percentage of *sascab* and plaster melt (Fig. 4.33).

A substantial Early Classic reuse of the structure was evidenced by a continuous clean marl cap or lens (5 to 10 centimeters thick) covering most of the platform. One possible posthole, 10 centimeters in diamater and similar to those defined on Structure 50D

(chapter 5; Scarborough et al. 1982), was located between the two platform walls and approximately 1.0 meter northeast of the southwest inset. A Tzakol basal flange bowl was found at a shallow depth along the medial axis of the mound and 50 centimeters southeast of the inner wall. It was badly crushed and does not appear to have contained any additional offering.

Structure 34 has been identified as a dwelling. Its orientation and location on a plastered plaza argue that it was an elite residence during Late and Terminal Preclassic times. The ceramic analysis supports this interpretation (Scarborough and Robertson 1986).

Structure 38

This structure rests within a well-drained *huamil* setting. The ground is generally elevated but riddled with pits and shallow quarry scars. It appears to have undergone limited quarrying activity, perhaps as a consequence of the exhaustion of other caprock locations in proximity. Structures 37 and 105, both within

Figure 4.33. Exposure of northern portion of Structure 34. The view is eastward.

100 meters of Structure 38, appear to be stockpiles of limestone construction fill rather than occupation facilities. Two poorly defined well-like features occur immediately southeast of Structure 38 in addition to an amorphous depression speculated to have been a *sascabera*. Structure 38 is one of the larger structures in this location, but unlike mounds of this size it appears to be constructed primarily of earthen fill.

The mound has been assigned a Late C'oh phase date, which suggests that extensive quarrying of the caprock was seldom undertaken in this phase, perhaps reflecting the absence of social mechanisms necessary to prevent damage to the fragile natural drainage system at the site. Earth fill is obtainable by simply scraping the surface of the decomposing caprock over a rather extensive area. However, this practice would eventually force the occupants to quarry for new mound fill, as the earth fill would be exhausted relatively quickly. A Tulix phase reoccupation of the mound was demonstrated as well. Judging from the trash lens of C'oh phase debris, the mound is identified as a house locus. The ceramic analysis indicates a nonelite occupation of the structure. A shell scoop and a digging stick weight have been identified from our exposure. This is a Type 4 mound (Fig. 4.34).

Structure 38A (Operation 119a)

Structure 38 is 28 meters long, 24 meters wide, and 1.3 meters high. It has a potential summit floor space of 100 square meters and an absolute volume of 502 cubic meters. During the 1978 season a north-south–oriented 2-meter by 2-meter unit was located on the northeast slope of the mound. This location was selected because of the possibility of contacting architecture (i.e., a retaining wall) as well as midden debris. The site map and lateral stripping excavations elsewhere in the settlement suggested that many of the features in the core zone were oriented to the central precinct rather than to true north. Given the prevailing southeasterlies, midden debris was predicted at this location. This latter hypothesis was realized but only by a moderately dense sheet midden deposit (Fig. 4.35).

Five naturally occurring levels were lotted into six corresponding subunits. The surface level was a thin, dark gray clay A-horizon underlain by a poorly developed, friable, light gray B-horizon. The profile was

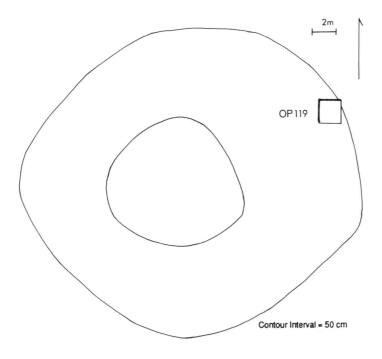

Figure 4.34. Contour map of Structure 38.

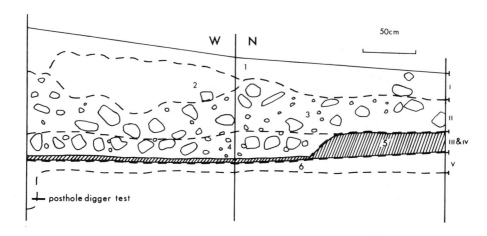

Figure 4.35.   Profile from Structure 38A (Operation 119a).

quite mottled and subject to leaching. The second level was a tan marl, intruded by unworked fall stones. These stones are thought to be associated with the original Preclassic superstructure of the mound, while the surface level is understood to be associated mantle.

The third level was unsealed construction fill consisting of light gray marl intruded by limestone gravel. It was differentiated from the above matrix by a smaller size and greater quantity of stone as well as a slight color distinction between the two lenses. Nevertheless, the boundary between the two matrices was not abrupt, indicating the mixed context of all recovered debris from these lots.

Level 4 represented the same light gray marl, but containing cobble-sized and larger rubble coring to the west, or the interior of the mound, and unintruded clays to the east. Although no retaining wall was defined, this lateral matrix division may correspond to the original limits or perimeter of the mound. The debris isolated from both contexts reveals a clear phase date for this construction. The interior lot of level 4 was underlain by a thin (2 centimeters thick) white marl "preparatory surface" as defined elsewhere in the settlement. The outside, or eastern exposure, produced no such deposit.

The lowest level was a sterile black paleosol, which was underlain by a yellowish parent limestone material. Although these depths were only probed with a posthole digger, the interior, or southwestern, corner of the exposure revealed the black paleosol to be 40 centimeters thick, while the southeastern probe indicated a shallow 5-centimeter-thick paleosol. This may suggest a deliberate attempt to infill an interior depression

underlying the mound prior to the construction of the substructure by simply scraping the adjacent ground surface for fill.

Although Structure 38 was not completely composed of earth fill, the bulk of the mound is suggested to have been light gray marl. This matrix would have been easily obtained from the adjacent ground surface without a concentrated quarrying effort, suggesting the constraints placed on monumental architecture during this C'oh phase.

Structure 46 Group

This Type 3 *plazuela* group of two mounds lies approximately 50 meters outside the canal to the southeast. It is 70 meters east of a causeway or check dam bridging the canal. The group rests in a *monte alto* setting, but it is flanked on three sides by *huanal*. The structures face one another northeast-southwest and rest on a raised plaza. This orientation runs parallel to the nearby canal axis. Although Tulix phase ceramics were well represented in the excavation, a clear Early Classic date has been obtained for this group from a sealed construction fill context. Although the *plazuela* was constructed in the Early Classic, the amount of Late Preclassic debris suggests the presence of a Tulix phase construction in this vicinity. However, without stronger evidence, the mixed Tulix assemblage cannot be directly associated with the Structure 46 Group. Ten fishnet weights have been collected from this structure and suggest the continued exploitation of riverine resources into the Early Classic Period (Fig. 4.36).

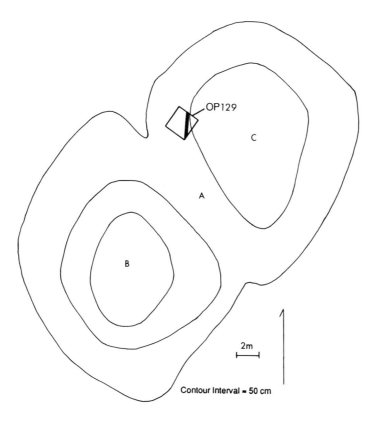

Figure 4.36.   Contour map of the Structure 46 Group.

Structure 46C (Operation 129a)

Structure 46C is the smaller and northeasternmost structure in this *plazuela*. It is 25 meters long, 16 meters wide, and 1.1 meters high. It has a potential summit floor space of 80 square meters and an absolute volume of 264 cubic meters. During the 1978 field season a 2-meter by 2-meter unit was excavated to a maximum depth of 1.4 meters. It was located on the southwestern margin of the structure. This location was estimated to straddle the margin of the platform (Structure 46C) as well as a portion of the lower plaza (Structure 46A). Both architecture and midden debris were anticipated. The unit was oriented N45°W, in keeping with the orientation of the group (Fig. 4.37).

Five naturally occurring levels were divided into seven lots. The surface was defined by a well-developed dark brown clay loam A-horizon intruded by cobble-sized and larger fall. The second level consisted of a light gray clay loam heavily intruded by fall in the upper reaches and gravel ballast in the lower reaches. A substructural retaining wall was revealed in the eastern portion of the unit. This inset-outset alignment consisted of three segments cornering at right angles running perpendicular and parallel to magnetic north. The wall was only a single course high (except for two courses along a short segment in the north), but was composed of finely faced stones. Although weathered and mixed from above, the masonry appears to have been chinked with sherds and covered by plaster. A very poorly preserved flagstone floor appears to have abutted this retaining wall. It in turn was underlain by 25 centimeters of gravel ballast. The level was terminated on exposing a hard plaster floor which extended across the entire unit and under the above retaining wall. This floor, however, was not well preserved in the western portion of the unit.

Level 3 was defined as the construction fill underlying and including the hard plaster floor (F1) understood to be the raised plaza surface (Structure 46A).

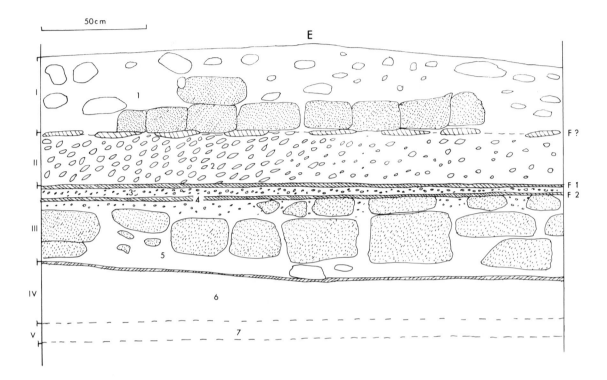

Figure 4.37.   Profile from Structure 46A (Operation 129a).

Six centimeters below this floor lay a yet harder floor. Although this latter surface may represent under-flooring, its hardness suggests that the plaza area may have been refurbished at a later date. The southern portion of the floor was again poorly preserved.

The lower floor (F2) was underlain by 5 to 10 centimeters of hearting gravel in a friable light gray clay loam. A gray loam intruded by loosely packed small-boulder-sized rubble underlay the floor ballast. A crude two-course-high construction pen wall was located in the center of the unit trending north-south and parallel to the substructural retaining wall. This construction wall secured the plaza surface and apparently prevented slumpage of the floor in the eastern portion of the unit. The base of level 3 was defined by a thin white "preparatory surface," which was apparent in the northern portion of the unit.

Level 4 was defined by dark gray midden clay loam intruded by cultural debris. This 25-to 30-centimeter-thick deposit dated to the Early Classic Period. This midden deposit underlying the plaza suggests both an early and a late construction and occupation of this

area during the Early Classic Period. The basal level consisted of a dark gray to brown paleosol, which was underlain by sterile gray clay parent material.

The Structure 46 Group is the only well-documented and unequivocal Early Classic small structure reported at Cerros, although reoccupation or reuse of Late Preclassic Period mounds is apparent elsewhere. Two construction/occupation events are documented at this structure. The earliest is associated with the midden debris. Whether or not it is a primary or secondary context deposit, it implies that the immediate vicinity was lived on by Early Classic residents prior to the construction of the plaza and Structure 46C. The later construction reflects a continuous occupation of the area culminating in the exposed architecture. The "preparatory surface" suggests an affinity to the Late Preclassic practice of spreading this white marl across a house site before the onset of construction.

The Early Classic occupation of the settlement is not well defined and usually quite ephemeral. However, the presence of the Structure 46 Group may suggest a continuity in tradition from the Preclassic florescence at Cerros. If reduced Early Classic populations maintained small, well-drained plots and were perhaps directed by a few managerial families, then the Structure 46 Group may represent a "rural elite" residence.

Structure 53

This structure is a Type 4 structure located in the same relationship (to the south) with Structure 29 and the ball court Structure 50 Group as Structure 65 is to Structure 29 and the ball court Structure 61 Group (to the north) (Fig. 3.9). The structure is nearly surrounded by depressed *zacatal* and thorn-scrub savanna. Except for a strip of elevated ground to the south, the structure can be viewed as an island. The large size and isolated location of the structure suggest that it was not a residential locus but a civic facility during the Tulix phase. Ceramics taken from construction fill indicate an initial C'oh construction followed by later Tulix phase modifications. Formal field excavations did not identify the function of the structure. However, ceramic analysis suggests that the underlying C'oh phase construction is associated with an elite residence, while the subsequent Tulix phase modifications indicate a civic facility (Fig. 4.38).

Structure 53A (Operation 123a)

Structure 57 is 32 meters long, 30 meters wide, and 3.0 meters high. It has a potential floor space of 72 square meters and an absolute volume of 1,548 cubic meters. During the 1978 field season a 2-meter by 2-meter test unit was excavated to a maximum depth of 1.9 meters. The unit was placed on the northwest flank of the structure next to an outset medial ridge on the west side of the structure. This inset location was anticipated to yield midden debris in addition to architectural detail. Neither expectation was fully realized. The unit was oriented N45°W (Fig. 4.39).

The strata were divided into eight lots within four naturally occurring levels. The surface level was defined by a dark brown A-horizon loam intruded by gravel and fall stones. Level 2 was defined as a gray brown loam surrounding cobble-sized and larger rubble coring. This level composed the bulk of the mound, it being 130 centimeters thick and underlain by a thin preparatory surface. The upper fill in the eastern portion of the unit consisted of compacted

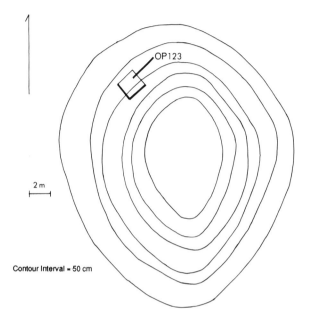

Figure 4.38. Contour map of Structure 53.

gravel-sized ballast suggestive of the hearting used below a floor. However, no plaster was noted. A crude, poorly defined alignment of boulders was discernible in the western portion of the unit trending north-south through the base of the level, although no true retaining wall was identified. The ballast in the lower reaches of level 2 graded into a tan loam intruded by gravel-sized ballast.

Level 3 consisted of a 3- to 5-centimeter-thick lens of dark gray loamy clay identified as a preparatory surface overlying the sterile paleosol. Level 4 was defined as the sterile matrix below the mound. The paleosol was a nonsticky, mottled, light-gray clay loam unlike that found elsewhere. Our posthole probe indicated that it was approximately 40 centimeters thick and underlain by decomposed parent material. Forty centimeters below the surface of this yellow material, an underground solutionlike cavity was detected. It was shallow and dry as a consequence of the dry season.

The excavation did not identify the function of the structure. However, its size, isolation, and relationship to Structure 29 and the Structure 50 Group suggest that it had a civic function during the Tulix phase. Moreover, it appears to have been a near ground-level house during C'oh times, given the functional ceramic analysis.

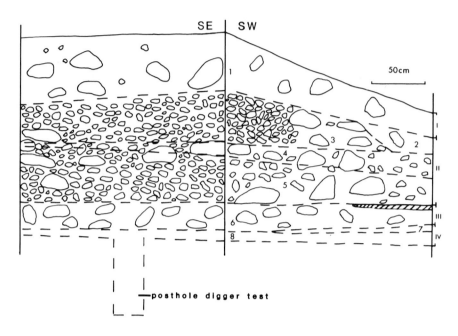

Figure 4.39.   Profile from Structure 53A (Operation 123a).

Structure 54

This Type 4 structure rests at the north end of the eastern *Sacbe* 2 or plaza edge (Feature 51). The structure lies in an elevated *huamil* setting, although thorn-scrub lies in the immediate vicinity. The structure was tested because of its imposing size as well as its location at the end of the *sacbe*. The site is understood as having served as public architecture. The mound was constructed during the Late Tulix phase, but was occupied during the Early Classic Period, too. This construction date accords well with Structure 29 at the south end of the *sacbe* (or plaza edge) and provides a tentative date for the *sacbe* itself (Fig. 4.40).

Structure 54A (Operation 121a)

This structure is 29 meters long, 24 meters wide, and 3.5 meters high. It has a potential summit floor space of 80 square meters and an absolute volume of 1,358 cubic meters. During the 1978 field season a 2-meter by 2-meter unit was placed on the southeast flank of the mound in an attempt to isolate an architectural retaining feature as well as to expose trash deposits immediately outside the structure. The unit

was oriented to magnetic north and excavated to a maximum depth of 3.2 meters (Fig. 4.41).

The strata were divided into six lots taken from three naturally defined levels. The surface level consisted of a dark brown A-horizon loam grading into a poorly developed gray B-horizon clay loam. A few fall stones were removed from this matrix. The level was terminated on exposing four well-defined risers, each consisting of three to four courses of loaf-shaped stones. The lower two risers were better preserved than the upper two, each attaining a maximum height of 50 centimeters. The treads were not well preserved, except for a white marl lens at the foot of the lowest riser. The entire feature appears to be an eastern-facing staircase, although the mound contours may suggest that it is an uninterrupted decorative technique flanking the four sides of the mound. It should be noted that an ill-defined alignment of faced stones was located in the northern profile trailing east-west down the structure and overlying the risers. This alignment may be nothing more than fall stones, but by way of analogy, Late Preclassic balustrades have been reported at Komchen (Andrews V 1981) and Uaxactun (Ricketson and Ricketson 1937).

Level 2 represents the rubble core of the structure underlying the exposed architecture. This matrix

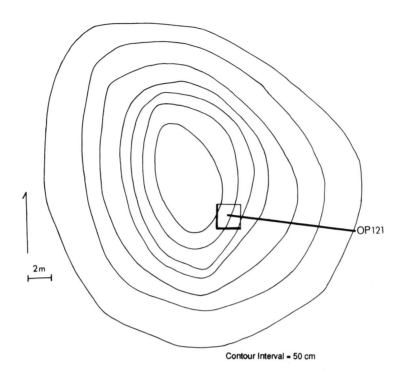

Contour Interval = 50 cm

Figure 4.40.   Contour map of Structure 54.

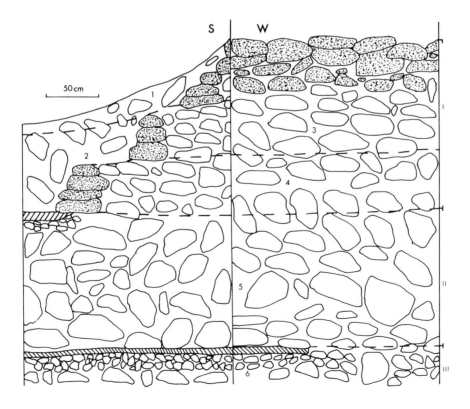

Figure 4.41.   Profile from Structure 54A (Operation 121a).

consists of cobble-sized and larger ballast, roughly flat-laid and packed in a friable light gray loam grading to a viscous grayish brown loam. A well-defined construction pause was identified immediately underlying the basal riser and corresponds to the marl surface at the foot of the basal riser noted in level 2. The rubble underlying the construction pause was larger and more randomly placed than that above, although the marl flooring associated with the basal riser was supported by a 10-to 15-centimeter-thick lens of gravel hearting. At 2.9 meters BSD the level was terminated on exposing a thin lens of soft white *sascab/* plaster. The northern edge of the unit did not reveal this lens, so it was leveled off somewhat arbitrarily.

Level 3 was defined as soft plaster and underlying gray silty clay. The soft plaster was 5 to 7 centimeters thick and immediately supported by a thin deposit of gravel hearting. The underlying gray silty clay was found to overlie the dark brown gumbo paleosol. An increase in sherd debris may indicate that this soft plaster was an earlier ground-level residential facility. Nevertheless, this surface dates to the same ceramic phase as the overlying mound and may reflect an elaborate preparatory surface for the structure.

Structure 54 is believed to be a Tulix phase civic facility. The date is not unequivocal because of the presence of Early Classic debris in low frequencies on the upper reaches of the mound. However, these sherds are argued to be a consequence of vertical migration due to the decomposed nature of the upper tread surfaces. Only Tulix phase ceramics were taken from the lower 2.2 meters of fill.

Structure 57

This Type 6 structure rests near the center of the *sacbe,* or plaza edge, defined in the eastern core zone (Feature 51). The mound lies in a *huamil* setting, but at the margins of a thorn-scrub setting. The structure was tested to augment the Type 6 sample as well as to provide a cross section of the underlying *sacbe* on which it rests. The sherd inventory from unsealed construction fill suggests that the mound dates to the Tulix phase, as does the underlying *sacbe.* Originally, the structure was understood to be a nonresidential facility because of its diminutive size and its central position on the *sacbe.* However, recent functional ceramic analysis suggests a nonelite residential function for the building. Comparing the floor space of other

nonelite residential structures with that of Structure 57 indicates a comparable floor area. No household features were identified, but most domestic activities, when associated with these modest dwellings, would have been conducted outside the structure.

The structure's position on the *sacbe,* or plaza edge, probably signals a Late Tulix phase occupation at the time of the center's collapse. This occupation occurred during a period when public ceremony presumed associated with a core zone "processional way" would have disappeared. Alternatively, the *sacbe* was actually a plaza edge with little civic/ritual function from the outset (Fig. 4.42).

Structure 57A (Operation 144a)

This structure is 13 meters long, 9 meters wide, and 1.0 meter high (including the underlying *sacbe*). It has a potential summit floor space of 16 square meters and an absolute volume of 67 cubic meters. During the 1978 field season a 2-meter by 2-meter unit was excavated to a maximum depth of 1.2 meters. The unit was placed at the summit of the mound in anticipation of features, but none were realized (Fig. 4.43).

The strata were separated into six lots consisting of six levels. The surface level was a dark brown loam A-horizon intruded by fall and surface accumulation. Level 2 represented construction fill consisting of gravel-sized ballast and defined by the same brown

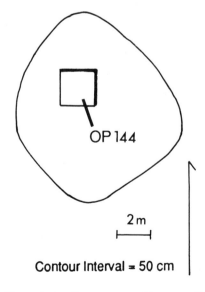

Figure 4.42. Contour map of Structure 57.

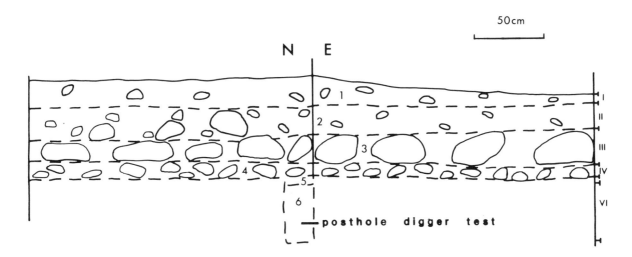

Figure 4.43.   Profile from Structure 57A (Operation 144a).

loam as identified in level 1. Level 2 was terminated on the *sacbe,* or plaza edge, surface. The mound was less than 50 centimeters in depth.

Level 3 consisted of a viscous brown loam intruded by cobble-sized and larger rubble. Although the exposure was limited, many of these stones were tabular and horizontally laid in a manner not unlike that noted for the western Sacbe 1 (Feature 126). Level 4 consisted of the same viscous brown loam, but mottled by the underlying dark clay paleosol. Gravel-sized stone ballast contributed to this matrix. Level 5 represented the thin sterile paleosol, and level 6 exposed the yellowish gray parent material. These latter two levels were simply probed using a posthole digger.

Structure 57 was initially positioned to be a shrine or outbuilding of unknown function resting on the *sacbe.* More recent ceramic analysis suggests that the structure was a nonelite residential facility. The surface of the underlying *sacbe* was ill-defined except for the appearance of the flat-laid cobbles.

Structure 65

Structure 65 rests on an elevated *huamil* setting shared with Structure 120. This area is surrounded by thorn-scrub with an elliptical catchment basin defining the southern margin of the elevated *huamil.* In plan, the mound bears a northern orientational relationship to Structure 29 and ball court Structure 61

Group similar to that of the more southern Structure 53 to Structure 29 and ball court Structure 50 Group. This Type 4 mound was selected for study because of its position in the settlement (Fig. 3.9).

Although no midden debris was isolated, sealed construction fill has provided a Late C'oh construction date. The mound was also occupied into the Tulix phase (Fig. 4.44).

Structure 65A (Operation 138a)

Structure 65 is 31 meters long, 23 meters wide, and 1.5 meters high. It has a potential summit floor space of 108 square meters and an absolute volume of 161 cubic meters. During the 1978 season, a 2-meter by 2-meter unit was placed on the south-central margin of the mound. This is believed to be the backside of the structure. Again, the strategy was to define midden debris outside the structure as well as architectural features within. The unit was oriented to magnetic north (Fig. 4.45).

Five naturally defined levels divided into six lots made up the identified strata. The upper dark brown humus loam was intruded by cobble-sized and larger fall stones. This level graded into an underlying light brown loam intruded by additional fall and plaster melt. In the northwest corner of the unit a 20-centimeter-thick deposit of melt was isolated. It appears to have slumped away from a superstructure located a meter or less to the northwest, higher up on

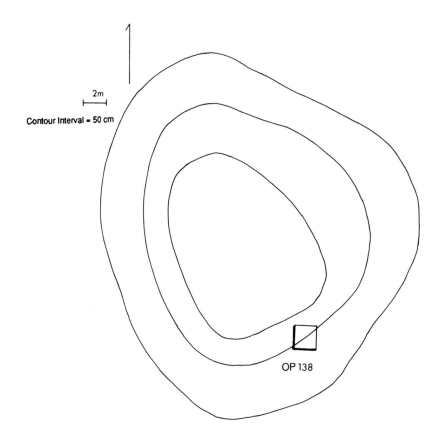

Figure 4.44.   Contour map of Structure 65.

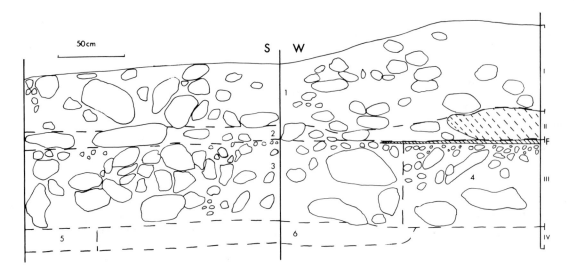

Figure 4.45.   Profile from Structure 65A (Operation 138a).

the mound. The consolidated chunks of plaster melt, as well as the remainder of the level, lay on a hard plaster floor. The 3-centimeter-thick hard plaster floor was well preserved over the northern three-quarters of the unit but disintegrated and slumped to the south. However, sufficient quantities of decomposed plaster were isolated to indicate that the entire unit was formerly covered by plaster flooring.

Level 3 underlying and including the plaster floor was lotted into two discrete subunits. This matrix was approximately 60 centimeters thick and rested on sterile clays. The northern three-quarters of the unit was separated from the southern portion in order to obtain a sealed ceramic sample. A friable light gray clay loam intruded by numerous pebble-sized gravels defined the upper 10 centimeters of hearting underlying the floor. This matrix graded into a cobble-sized and larger fill, loosely packed in the same light gray clay loam. The southern portion of the level was slightly darker in hue, probably as a consequence of root and soil disturbance intruding from above through the poorly preserved portions of the plaster floor.

The basal level was defined by the sterile, granular, light gray loam parent matrix. Except for a small patch of dark brown paleosol restricted to the southeast corner of the unit, the bulk of the mound appears to overlie the decomposing caprock surface. This suggests that the surface of the caprock was scraped clean of its topsoil accumulation prior to mound construction. Although this thin, organically rich deposit may have been removed for any number of unknown cultural preferences (see Structure 38), it is speculated that at least some of this fill was relocated and used on adjacent agricultural plots (see Harrison and Turner 1983).

Structure 65 is postulated to have functioned as a nonresidential civic facility. This identification is based on very slim evidence, but is suggested on grounds of the spatial relationship it manifests with the structures mentioned above. Although the hard plaster floor unassociated with domestic trash can be argued to represent sampling error, it is predicted that little midden debris will be collected from this mound if further exposure is undertaken. The ceramic sample was too small to clarify the situation.

Structure 66

This structure rests on an elevated island of well-drained *huamil* flanked by broad runoff thorn-scrub

depressions. This raised ground is suggested to have been surrounded by the drainage depressions channeling the central precinct runoff. The mound was test excavated because of its isolated position with respect to the number of large mound clusters in this vicinity. Structure 66 is a Type 4 mound argued to be a Tulix phase construction. Judging from the amount and kind of debris, the mound has been identified as a house. The ceramic analysis supports an elite residential function (Fig. 4.46).

Structure 66A (Operation 122a)

This structure is 24 meters long, 17 meters wide, and 1.5 meters high. It has a potential summit floor space of 80 square meters and an absolute volume of 366 cubic meters. During the 1978 season a 2-meter by 2-meter test unit was located on the northwest slope of the mound. Subtle surface contours suggested the possibility of an outset staircase along the north-south side of the structure. The excavation unit was placed within the inset of this postulated feature to expose trash and fall trapped in this context. Again the test unit was located both to maximize architectural detail and to obtain datable trash. The unit was oriented to magnetic north (Fig. 4.47).

The test unit was divided into three levels consisting of four lots. A dark brown clay loam A-horizon

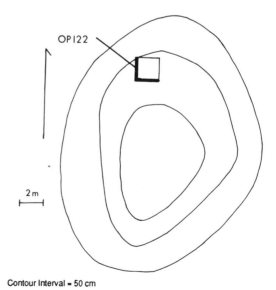

OP 122

2 m

Contour Interval = 50 cm

Figure 4.46. Contour map of Structure 66.

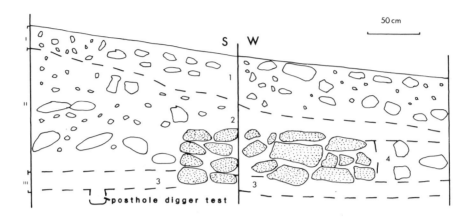

Figure 4.47.   Profile from Structure 66A (Operation 122a).

intruded by cobble-sized and larger fall defined the surface level. This matrix graded into a light, friable, loamy clay intruded by decomposing fall. This second level appears to represent architectural fall from the initial occupation of the mound, in addition to later occupational mixing. Some of the fall may be associated with an underlying western wall exposure as well as the summit superstructure.

Level 3 was defined by two culturally significant lots. A 20-centimeter-thick, dark gray clay lens of primary midden debris was isolated and removed (lot 4) outside a crudely faced wall. Bone, ash, and charcoal were collected from this context. The other lot represented the sectioning of the wall exposure. This latter operation demonstrated that the midden deposit was associated with the wall construction and did not underlie the wall. The wall was oriented north-south in the western profile of the unit. It was 40 centimeters high and consisted of cobble-sized and larger stones composed of three ill-defined courses. It was caked with poorly preserved plaster melt, or *sascab*. A portion of red painted plaster was collected. The matrix outside the wall contained faced fall stones overlying the darker midden clays. No white marl preparatory surface was identified underlying the structure. The dark gray clay loam was underlain by the sterile light gray parent matrix. The slight slope of the original land surface suggests that the mound was raised on a slightly elevated setting initially.

Although little can be made of the exposed architecture relative to the surface contours of the mound, the position and orientation of the wall fragment is not unlike the patio wings or extensions revealed on Structure 11B. The wall fragment may be the interior inset behind and below a western-facing veranda.

Structure 76 Group

This structure group represents the focus for a complex of eight separate mounds within 100 meters of Aguada 1 (Feature 79). Structure 76 can be classified as a Type 2 mound group, although its form and orientation are unlike that defined elsewhere in the settlement. It lies within the *monte alto* setting. A Late C'oh or Tulix construction phase date has been assigned, with a subsequent Early Classic occupation noted. Aguada 1 appears to be a Late Preclassic Period artificial reservoir formed as a consequence of the fill necessary in constructing Structure 76. The clustering of the mounds around Structure 76 as well as their proximity to Aguada 1 may suggest a degree of water management at the southern margin of the *hulub bajo* setting.

Although our sample of the Structure 76 Group is very small, the absence of household midden debris indicates a nonresidential function for this group. Surely the size and relative dominance of this structure compared to the adjacent structures would argue for a different function. Moreover, the pottery suggests a civic or ritual orientation (Fig. 4.48).

Structure 76B (Operation 112a and b)

Structure 76B is 34 meters long, 33 meters wide, and 4 meters high. It has a potential floor space of 320 square meters and an absolute volume of 2,884 cubic

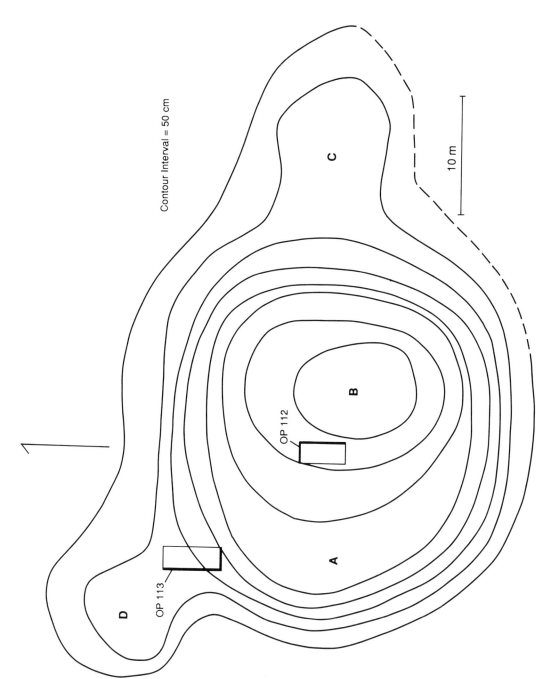

Contour Interval = 50 cm

10 m

Figure 4.48. Contour map of the Structure 76 Group.

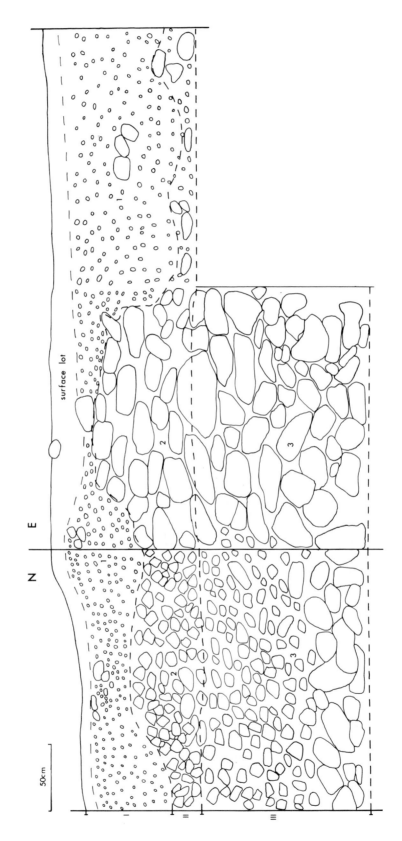

Figure 4.49. Profile from Structure 76B (Operation 112a&b).

meters. This site was selected for excavation because of its imposing size and its distance from the central precinct. During the 1978 field season a 2-meter by 4-meter trench was positioned on the sloping western margin of this acropolislike platform, which rests on an elevated substructure (Structure 76A). The excavation is believed to have intersected the medial axis of the structure. The long axis of the unit was oriented N10°W. The trench was excavated to a maximum depth of 2.4 meters, with the southern half of the unit being terminated at a depth of 1.15 meters (Fig. 4.49).

Although the unit was lotted into three natural excavation levels, no floors or architectural features were revealed; they apparently weathered away long ago. The upper stratum was defined by a friable dark gray clay loam intruded by numerous limestone gravels. This matrix graded into gravel-sized ballast packed in a friable light gray marl. The thickness of the ballast varied throughout the exposure, with the northern third attaining a depth of 2.0 meters BSD, although the lower 1.3 meters of fill was essentially dry-laid. The southern and eastern portions of the unit changed to cobble-sized and larger dry-laid rubble fill within 30 centimeters of the surface. The remainder of the unit below 2.0 meters was also dry-laid cobble-sized and larger rubble coring.

These excavations suggest that the northern and western portions of the unit supported a ramp or stairway connecting Structure 76B (to the northwest) with the raised substructure (Structure 76A), as evidenced by the thickness of the hearting within the trench. Although no evidence for plaster surfacing was recovered, a thick, dense ballast would be expected in this location. The large rubble fill near the surface in the southern portion of the unit may indicate that less traffic was directed across this surface. Although erosional agents may account for some of the missing hearting, the slope angle of this location is not critical and would not seem to be greatly affected by wasting. The profiles further suggest that the acropolis, or Structure 76B, was not a later addition to the structure but was part of the initial form.

Structure 76D (Operation 113a, b and c)

Structure 76D is 20 meters long, 12 meters wide, and 1.8 meters high. It has a potential floor space of 64 square meters and an absolute volume of 274 cubic meters. This structure lies to the immediate northwest of Structure 76B. Although the summit trench (OP112)

provided an unmixed Late C'oh phase date for the structure group, the sherd sample collected was from an unsealed content. During 1977, we located a 2-meter by 5-meter trench between the northwest margin of Structure 76A and the southeast edge of Structure 76D in anticipation of sealed construction fill as well as architectural detail. The long axis of the unit was oriented to magnetic north. The trench was excavated to a maximum depth of 2.0 meters. This location was selected because slope wash and wasting from above had apparently settled in the trough between the two structures quite early on. This overburden was believed to have lessened the surface deterioration of the original structure, unlike the unprotected summit exposure. In addition, a portion of the hypothesized ramp or stairway between the two structures suggested by our summit trench was anticipated at this location (see Fig. 4.50).

Eight lots and four natural levels were excavated. The surface stratum consisted of a dark brown humic clay intruded by roots and fall stones. This was underlain by a poorly developed B-horizon of dark friable clay intruded by gravel-sized and larger limestone. The northern third of the unit was underlain by gravel-sized ballast thought to be an Early Classic reoccupation mantle.

The second natural level consisted of dark friable clay intruded by gravel- to small-boulder-sized limestone. A hard plaster floor was defined 1.2 meters BSD. Plaster chunks associated with a clean white marl were found throughout the matrix. Although this stratum represents fill and fall associated with the final occupation of the mound, some of the debris resting on the floor is probably associated with the original construction and initial occupation of the structure.

The hard plaster floor associated with the base of this level did not continue into the southern third of the trench, although the same level was arbitrarily defined through excavation. The fill in the southeast portion of the unit was a very friable marl matrix intruded by few gravels. To the north, this matrix graded to a gray clay marl intruded by numerous gravels. Pockets of marl and plaster melt appeared throughout. The presence of the thick marly matrix corresponds to a diagonal break in the hard plaster floor. Even though preservation was very poor, it is hypothesized that this latter deposit reflects the approximate position of a connecting ramp.

The third natural level was defined as the matrix below and including the 5- to 7-centimeter-thick hard plaster floor. Sixty to seventy centimeters of dry-laid hearting gravel were underlain by a continuous single

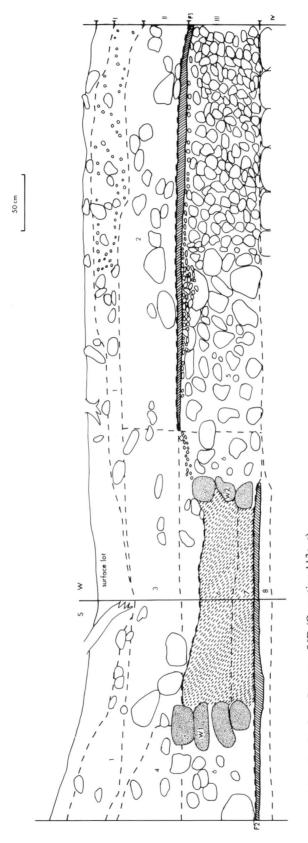

Figure 4.50.   Profile from Structure 76D (Operation 113a–c).

layer of dry-laid limestone boulder rubble. In the south-eastern portion of the unit, gravel- to cobble-sized limestone packed in a friable light gray clay was found to underlie the floor as it feathered out.

A poorly preserved four-course-high retaining wall (Wall 1) was contacted in cross section in a southern excavation wall. To the southwest, a thick, dense deposit of *sascab* melt containing sizable chunks of plaster was isolated in front (west) of this retaining wall. A second crudely faced retaining wall (Wall 2), three courses high, located in the western profile, defined the northernmost extent of the plaster melt. The two retaining walls are interpreted to have joined in forming an inset corner between Structures 76A and 76D. The plaster melt outside the poorly preserved walls is argued to represent the razing of a superstructure or facade from the summit of Structure 76D. The hard plaster floor appears formerly to have overlain and defined the edge of the retaining walls.

Level 4 consisted of a 2-centimeter-thick white marl lens underlying the rubble core of the construction and overlying a dark brown paleosol. To the north the white marl was replaced by a dark friable clay loam intruded by the rubble. Both Structures 76A and 76D are believed to have been underlain by this white marl preparatory building surface.

Structure 77

This Type 6 structure rests 60 meters east-south-east of plaza Structure 8A in a well-drained *huamil* setting. The mound occurs in an area of disturbed relief, probably as a consequence of high winds and uprooted trees. A portion of the main plaza runoff depression passes to the immediate west. The water table appears to rise in this vicinity, as evidenced by the mottled gleilike condition of the soils and the graham cracker consistency of the ceramic retrieved. This is further supported by the presence of a recently abandoned well site to the immediate west. This area is unusual in this respect and may have provided suitable drinking water for a segment of the prehistoric population. The mound was dug as much to increase our Type 6 mound count as to test the prospect that some of these very small mounds were not the result of human energies. The majority of sherds collected from the mound date to the Late Postclassic Period, and the mound is understood to have been a deliberate human construction (Fig. 4.51).

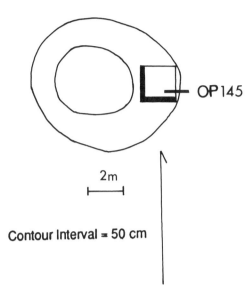

Figure 4.51.   Contour map of Structure 77.

Structure 77A (Operation 145a)

This structure is 8 meters long, 7 meters wide and 1.0 meter high. It has a potential summit floor space of 9 square meters and an absolute volume of 33 cubic meters. During the 1978 field season a 2-meter by 2-meter unit excavated to a maximum depth of 1.0 meter was located on the eastern flank of the mound. The position of the unit was a rather arbitrary decision, although midden debris was anticipated in this area based on the distribution of surface debris (Fig. 4.52).

Although the exposure was badly mottled, two natural levels were discernible. The upper dark humus clay loam A-horizon was a poorly defined accumulation of fall debris and construction fill. The support ballast was gravel-sized and loosely packed. The yellow and brown mottling of the soil horizon suggested the effects of a high seasonal water table. The lower level graded into a viscous gray clay not unlike the sediment removed from the infilled canals. These clays were strongly influenced by waterlogging. The mound was underlain by the gray clay parent material defined elsewhere in the settlement. The absence of a dark paleosol was noted.

This mound is understood to be a Late Postclassic house platform at the foot of the main plaza. Although the high water table may have posed some problems for the occupants, the proximity of a potentially potable

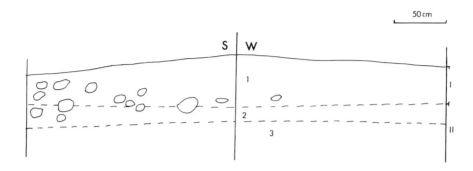

Figure 4.52.   Profile from Structure 77A (Operation 145a).

water source may have out weighed any disadvantage. The absence of the paleosol this close to the main plaza during the Late Preclassic occcupation of Cerros might be predictable, but its absence during the ephemeral Postclassic occupation is more puzzling. Although the construction ballast was neither dense nor homogeneous, the feature is argued to be a deliberate domestic facility.

Structure 84

This structure represents one of eight isolated structures surrounding the Structure 76 Group. It was selected for excavation because of its diminutive size in relation to the Structure 76 Group and because of a greater sherd scatter on the surface than reported from the other small Type 5 and 6 mounds in the vicinity. The mound rests in proximity to a *huanal* setting, although *monte alto* defines the immediate surrounding. The structure has been assigned an Early Classic Period date, although Postclassic reoccupation is suggested. It has been tentatively identified as a house locus (Fig. 4.53).

Structure 84A (Operation 143a)

This Type 5 structure is 15 meters long, 12 meters wide, and 50 centimeters high. It has a potential summit floor space of 18 square meters and an absolute volume of 50 cubic meters. During the 1977 season a 2-meter by 2-meter test unit was located near the southeastern margin of the mound. The location was selected to contact a possible retaining wall or associated floor as well as to expose midden debris. Neither of these objectives was realized, but enough pottery was collected from the

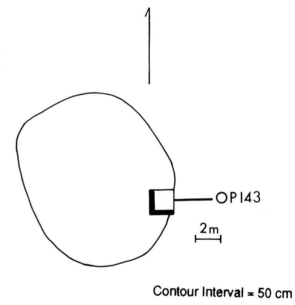

Figure 4.53.   Contour map of Structure 84.

construction fill to provide an Early Classic date for the structure (Fig. 4.54).

The strata were lotted into two natural levels. Both levels were poorly defined and seriously disturbed by root action and leaching. The surface stratum consisted of a dark clay loam A-horizon intruded by small-boulder-sized fall and gravel fill ballast. The lower stratum graded into a light brown loamy clay intruded by dense concentrations of gravel-sized ballast. The base of the structure was defined by crude tabular limestone boulders within and overlying a thin, viscous, brown paleosol. Sterile, calcareous clay having an undulating surface underlay the exposure. The water table

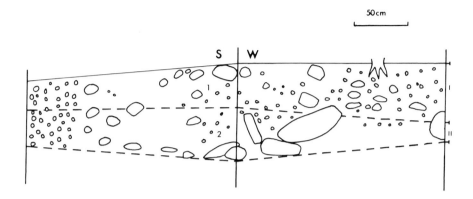

Figure 4.54.   Profile from Structure 84A (Operation 143a).

was defined at the base of the exposure. No marl preparatory surface was associated with this Early Classic construction.

Although few of our expectations were met in the examination of this mound, an apparent cultural selection for an environmentally depressed setting was made by the builders of this mound. The depressed and undulating paleosol was stabilized by laying down foundation stones to prevent mound settling in this area.

Structure 94

This Type 5 mound lies within the *huanal,* approximately 40 meters south and outside of the canal. The diminutive size and isolated position of the mound coupled with the presence of Postclassic debris suggest that Structure 94 was a farmstead constructed during the Late Postclassic Period. Over two dozen Postclassic fishnet weights have been collected from this mound (Fig. 4.55).

Structure 94A (Operation 135a)

This structure is 17 meters long, 11 meters wide, and 0.4 meter high. It has a potential summit floor area of 187 square meters and an absolute volume of 75 cubic meters. During the 1978 field season a 2-meter by 2-meter unit was placed on the eastern flanks of the mound. We located the unit next to a surface concentration of limestone rubble in an attempt to reveal an underlying retaining wall. Unfortunately, no architecture and little midden debris was

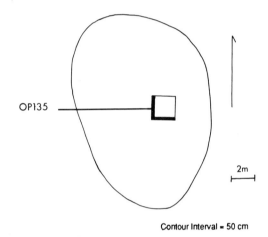

Figure 4.55.   Contour map of Structure 94.

identified. The unit was oriented to magnetic north (Fig. 4.56).

Only two lots and two levels were defined in the 80 centimeters of vertical exposure. The upper-level matrix consisted of a dark brown clay loam A-horizon grading into a lighter B-horizon. Both horizons were intruded by fall stones and rubble coring. The western portion of the unit contained a greater frequency of gravel-sized ballast than the eastern portion, indicative of construction fill. This suggests that the excavation unit straddled the edge of the substructure, although no formal architectural feature was apparent. The lower excavation level consisted of a black clay paleosol underlain by a gray clay parent material. The bulk of the mound rested on this undisturbed surface. No preparatory surface was identified.

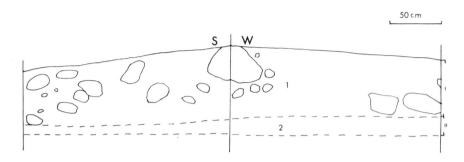

Figure 4.56.   Profile from Structure 94A (Operation 135a).

The mound appears to have functioned as a residential facility during the Late Postclassic Period. The presence of Tulix phase ceramics suggests that this zone was also utilized in the Late Preclassic, but we found no architecture or related features associated with this period.

Structure 98

This Type 4 structure rests in a *huamil* setting in the southwestern margin of the core site area. It lies 10 meters north of the main canal. The structure was selected for investigation because of its small size and commanding position on the bank of the canal. The structure has been assigned a Tulix phase date and is argued to be a residential facility. The ceramic evidence further indicates that the structure was occupied by elite residents (Fig. 4.57).

Structure 98A (Operation 141a)

This structure is 24 meters long, 19 meters wide, and 1.5 meters high. It has a potential summit floor space of 160 square meters and an absolute volume of 462 cubic meters. During the 1978 field season a 2-meter by 2-meter unit was placed on the southeastern flank of the mound and excavated to a maximum depth of 130 centimeters. The unit was oriented to magnetic north. Architectural detail and midden debris were anticipated, but only the latter expectation was realized (Fig. 4.58).

The strata were divided into three levels consisting of four lots. The surface level was defined by a dark brown loam humus heavily intruded by pebble-sized and smaller limestone ballast. No platform flooring was preserved. Level 2 consisted of boulder-sized and smaller rubble fill packed in a moist, compacted gray clay. Most of the limestone was severely weathered

and appears to have suffered from waterlogging. High $CaCO_3$ salt concentrations were distributed throughout the exposure. The level was terminated on uncovering a complete Tulix phase vessel (Cabro Red: Cabro Variety) resting in the southwestern quadrant of the unit. Although the water table does rise seasonally and may inundate a major portion of this mound, the fill associated with this level is unlike most other mound excavations, with the exception of Structure 38. However, the sediment fill removed from within the canal as well as the eroded adjacent caprock chunks appear very similar (see OP 116, 151, 152, and 153).

Level 3 consisted of the same moist, compacted gray clay as defined in level 2, but unintruded by rubble fill. It was excavated in two lots to maintain provenience control. The southwestern three-quarters of the unit contained a high frequency of middenlike debris. Large sherds, bone, charcoal, ash, and fire-cracked rock were collected. Some fragments of human bone were also apparent. The concentration of debris was most dense in the southwest corner of the unit. This debris may correspond to the position of an outside platform retaining wall, as a few crudely dressed stones were noted in the area. The decomposing yellow granular caprock defined the bottom of the exposure.

Structure 98 is a Tulix phase mound. Given its proximity to the canal and the nature of its fill, it is argued that the structure was constructed from a dredging event in the canal's prehistory. Some of the larger limestone rubble may have been removed from the banks of the canal in an effort to widen or deepen it. The canal construction was initiated in the C'oh phase, but continued in use during the entirety of the Tulix phase. A *terminus post quem* for the canal has been derived from the Cabro Red vessel buried by dredged canal sediments. Structure 98 represents a Tulix phase house mound. Ceramic indicators also suggest that the structure was occupied by elite residents.

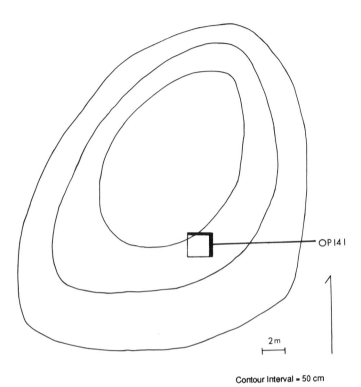

OP 141

2 m

Contour Interval = 50 cm

Figure 4.57.   Contour map of Structure 98.

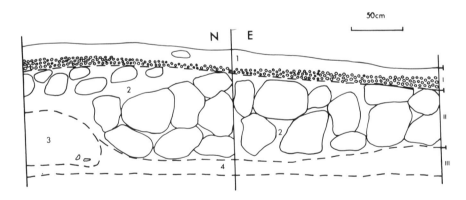

Figure 4.58.   Profile from Structure 98A (Operation 141a).

Structure 102

This Type 5 structure lies in the western portion of the site 180 meters outside the main canal and 90 meters south of the bay. The setting is well-drained *huamil*. The mound was selected for excavation in part to increase the structure sample from the western portion of the site. A Late Tulix phase date has been assigned to this

apparent domestic facility. In addition, an Early Classic occupation of the mound is indicated (Fig. 4.59).

Structure 102A (Operation 142a)

This structure is 20 meters long, 14 meters wide, and 0.5 meter high. It has a potential platform summit space of 36 square meters and an absolute volume

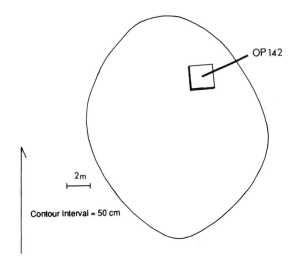

Figure 4.59.   Contour map of Structure 102.

and restricted to the western half of the unit. Sherds, lithic debris, and charcoal were collected. This deposit may be associated with a ground-level structure, given its location under the bulk of the mound. Level 4 was defined as the underlying dark clay gumbo paleosol. It rested on the decomposing yellow granular caprock, which undulated slightly across the unit.

Structure 102 is considered a Tulix phase construction. Further, an Early Classic occupation of the mound is suggested. The structure has been tentatively identified as a house mound.

Structure 112

This structure lies on the edge of the present bay, approximately 200 meters east of the main plaza. It rests on a well-drained *huamil* setting and is flanked on three sides by *hulub*. An apparent runoff channel passes south of the structure and may drain into the main canal. The structure was selected for excavation because it was uniquely located on the shoreline, suggesting direct involvement in maritime exchange. The entire structure dates to the Tulix phase. In addition to the mound, our excavations demonstrated the presence of ground-level occupation during the Tulix phase sealed by the overlying structure. It should be noted that the northeastern portion of the mound may have been robbed of rubble fill in recent history (Fig. 4.61).

Structure 112A (Operation 117a)

This Type 4 structure is 32 meters long, 18 meters wide, and 1.6 meters high. It has a potential summit

of 79 cubic meters. During the 1978 field season a 2-meter by 2-meter unit was placed on the northeastern flank of the mounds and excavated to a maximum depth of 120 centimeters. The unit was excavated in anticipation of architectural detail and/or midden debris. Neither expectation was realized. The unit was oriented to magnetic north (Fig. 4.60).

Four natural levels were defined and excavated. The surface level was identified as dark brown humic loam intruded by eroding fall debris. Level 2 consisted of a tan silt loam intruded by boulder-sized limestone rubble fill. This matrix comprised the bulk of the mound core. Level 3 was defined as a 20-centimeter-thick black loam trash deposit. It was located 80 centimeters BSD

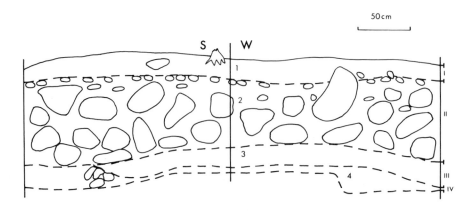

Figure 4.60.   Profile from Structure 102A (Operation 142a).

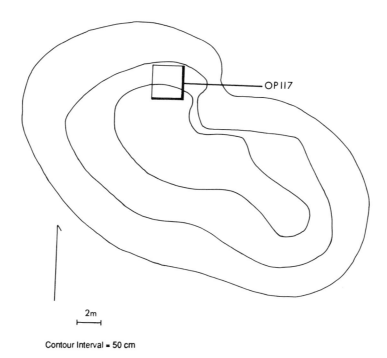

OP 117

2m

Contour Interval = 50 cm

Figure 4.61. Contour map of Structure 112.

floor space of 98 square meters and an absolute volume of 539 cubic meters. During the 1978 field season a 3-meter by 3-meter unit was initially opened to a depth of 1.7 meters. At this elevation the unit was reduced to a 2-meter by 2-meter exposure located in the southwest corner of the unit and further excavated another 20 centimeters. The location of the unit was on the northern flank of the structure. Although no architecture was visible, our test unit straddled an outset "ridge" trending north-south down the medial axis of the mound. We anticipated midden trash preserved in the hypothesized inset of the staircase or ramp as well as a retaining feature. Neither expectation was met. The unit was oriented to magnetic north (Fig. 4.62).

The strata were separated into nine lots consisting of six naturally defined levels. The surface level was defined as a friable dark gray loam A-horizon intruded by pebble-sized and larger fall and construction fill. Although no architecture was revealed, the western portion of the unit (corresponding to the hypothesized outset) consisted of a light gray loam containing compacted pebble-sized ballast. The second level was defined by a gray clay grading to a white marl intruded by gravel and small-boulder fill. This level was taken

down 1.4 meters BSD and represents the bulk of the mound core. Level 2 was terminated on exposure of a soft *sascab* floor (F1) underlying the mound. The matrices underlying level 2 were quite moist as a consequence of the nearby bay water levels.

Level 3 was a friable light gray loam including and underlying the 3-to 5-centimeter soft floor (F1). Twenty centimeters of gravel-sized ballast were located overlying a second *sascab*/plaster floor (F2). The ballast supporting the upper floor (F1) was best defined in the western third of the unit. The southwest corner was disturbed by a postdepositional intrusion apparently occurring before the mounded feature was constructed.

Level 4 was defined as the light grayish brown loam including and underlying the second floor (F2). Less gravel ballast was found to support this floor than the upper floor (F1). The floor (F2) was mottled and poorly preserved throughout the unit, although the western portion was slightly better defined. The surface of the floor exposed patches of gray and yellowish orange discoloration associated with burning, not unlike the *tierra quemada* floors of the buried midden village (Cliff 1986). The southwest corner was disturbed by the same postdepositional intrusion as mentioned above.

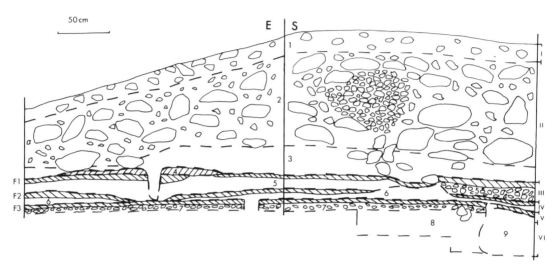

Figure 4.62.   Profile from Structure 112A (Operation 117a).

Level 5 represents a poorly defined soft plaster/ *sascab* floor (F3) and an underlying midden debris ballast. The floor appears to have been smoothed over the unleveled ballast, as indicated by the variable depth of the floor across the unit. The midden debris does not appear to be a primary deposit, judging from the small size of the sherds. Charcoal as well as fire-cracked limestone ballast were noted, indicative of an earlier *tierra quemada* flooring event. The intrusion in the southwest corner of the unit consisted of a gray sandy marl and gravel at this level.

Level 6 was defined by the dark gray clay paleosol found under most of the structures at Cerros. Although usually sterile, a few artifacts were found to have migrated down from the upper levels. A human burial was isolated in the southwest corner of the unit below F3, but intruding into the paleosol and the underlying sterile parent material. The disturbance noted above through the three floors (F1, 2, and 3) is not associated with the burial. The burial appears to be associated with an event immediately before the third floor (F3) was established, although the floor (F3) was very poorly preserved above the burial and the ballast support for the floor was lacking. The matrix encasing the individual was a mottled mixture of dark gray clay, white marl, and brown loam. The burial was taken from the level of the water table and was not well preserved. The sex, age, and stature are unknown at this writing. The individual was interred without furniture in a semiflexed position with the cranium oriented to the northeast.

Structure 112 presents a rapid developmental sequence involving four constructional events occurring within the Tulix phase. Although the precise function of the mound is not well understood, the docking facility hypothesis cannot be discounted. A possible limestone anchor weight was reported from this structure (Garber personal communicaton). The underlying three floors and the associated burial best describe a ground-level residential locus early in the phase. Most researchers suggest that burials in small structures indicate a household function for a mound. Analysis reveals in this and other contexts that C'oh and early Tulix phase ground-level dwellings later had mounded structures built over them. This practice would appear to be a comment on kin spatial continuity through time. The mounds in these cases probably represent the establishment and assertion of greater family authority within the community.

Structure 115 Group

This Type 2 group of three structures lies 150 meters south of the Structure 116 Group and rests east and outside the main canal segment. The *plazuela* group is located on an elevated *monte alto* setting and is surrounded by *hulubol*. The orientation of the group may be toward the central precinct. The group has been defined as a residential facility analogous to the Structure 116 Group. Immediately to the west of the *plazuela* is a problematic mound, which may be the remains of an ancient raised-field platform. It was entirely circumscribed by linear depressions. A Tulix phase date has been assigned to the construction of the structure group, although an ephemeral Early Classic Period occupation is apparent. Ceramic analysis corroborates the household function and further suggests an elite residence for the group (Fig. 4.63).

Structure 115B (Operation 128a)

Structure 115B is the largest and easternmost mound in this *plazuela*. The structure is 19 meters long, 14 meters wide, and 1.2 meters high. It has a potential summit floor space of 100 square meters and an absolute volume of 200 cubic meters. During the 1978 field season a 2-meter by 2-meter unit was located on the southwestern slope of the structure and excavated to a maximum depth of 1.1 meters. The unit was positioned to reveal both architecture and trash debris just off the estimated medial axis of the mound (Fig. 4.64).

Four naturally defined levels were divided into seven lots. The surface level consisted of a dark brown clay loam A-horizon intruded by limestone gravel and root disturbances. A poorly developed gray clay B-horizon intruded by additional gravel defined the next level. These upper strata represented a mixed surface accumulation of fall debris.

Level 3 was defined by the exposure of a single-course ramp of foot stones trending northeast to southwest and contouring to the slope of the mound. The ramp consisted of five smooth, tabular, small boulders oriented in a line from the summit of Structure 115B toward the foot of Structure 115D. The matrix outside (or to the southeast) of the ramp was a dark gray clay grading to a dark brown clay containing few limestone inclusions. The lower reaches of this deposit appear to represent a 25-centimeter-thick midden concentration. Small concentrations of ash, bone, and shell were collected in addition to the Tulix phase ceramics. The deposit was mottled by flecks of *sascab* that apparently weathered from the eroded superstructure above. The matrix inside and underlying the ramp stones was a gray clay loam intruded by gravel-sized ballast. Although we have tentatively identified an underlying

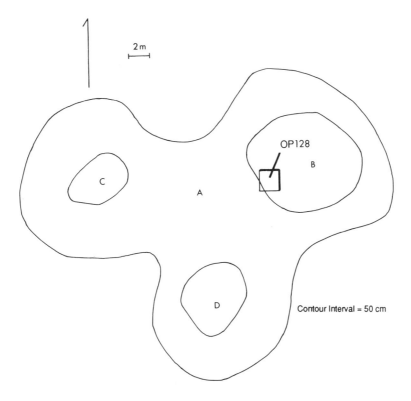

Figure 4.63.   Contour map of the Structure 115 Group.

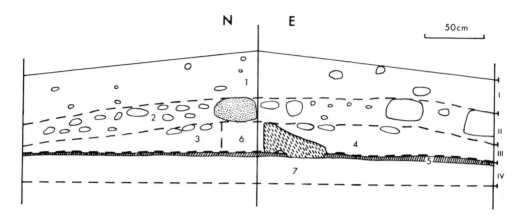

Figure 4.64.   Profile from Structure 115B (Operation 128a).

deposit of dark brown paleosol contaminated by sherd migrations from above, a thin deposit of middenlike soil may underlie the interior of the ramp area as well. The matrices at the basal level of this exposure were badly leached and mottled as a result of the fluctuating high water table. A thin, poorly defined white marl preparatory surface was identified and found overlying the paleosol. The sterile, decomposing gray clay loam parent material was found under the paleosol.

This mound group is postulated to have functioned as a residential area for an elite kin unit. Despite the small size of the *plazuela* and the poor quality of the architecture, elite ceramic material is present. The proximity of the adjacent *bajo* suggests that the occupants secured a living from the *bajo* setting. The high ground on which the Structure 115 Group rests is argued to represent the easternmost extent of potential canal maintenance and quarry area at the site. It is unlikely that the managerial elite at Cerros would have placed an elite residence as characterized by the Structure 115 Group in this setting if the area were not at a premium for agricultural use and/or construction fill.

Structure 116 Group

This Type 1 structure group rests within the *hulub bajo* outside and northeast of the main canal. The four structures in the group appear to be oriented to the cardinal directions (or toward the central precinct) and rest on a low platform. Judging from our test unit, the elevated platform is perhaps best seen as the original ground surface, with the surrounding matrix having

been culturally or naturally removed. The group was tested because of its architectural complexity and position outside the canal and within the poorly drained *hulubol*. Its proximity to the coast was also considered important, given the trade network postulated for Cerros. The group is argued to have functioned as a residential *plazuela*, perhaps monitoring raised-field agriculture outside the canal. A Tulix phase date has been assigned to the group, although the sherd inventory collected was small (Fig. 4.65).

Structure 116B (Operation 127a)

Structure 116B is the largest and westernmost mound in the group. It is 23 meters long, 22 meters wide, and 2.2 meters high. It has a potential summit floor space of 120 square meters and an absolute volume of 689 cubic meters. During the 1978 season a 2-meter by 2-meter test unit was placed on the southwestern backside of the mound and excavated to a maximum depth of 1.6 meters. The test unit was positioned to expose both architecture and midden debris located on the slope of the mound. Neither of these objectives was well realized. The unit was oriented to magnetic north (Fig. 4.66).

The strata were lotted into three naturally occurring levels. The upper level was a dark brown loamy clay A-horizon heavily intruded by roots and much small-boulder-sized limestone fall. The level was badly disturbed and may have included construction fill. The consistency of the limestone rubble was more dense than recorded in other excavations. This may suggest a slight change in the

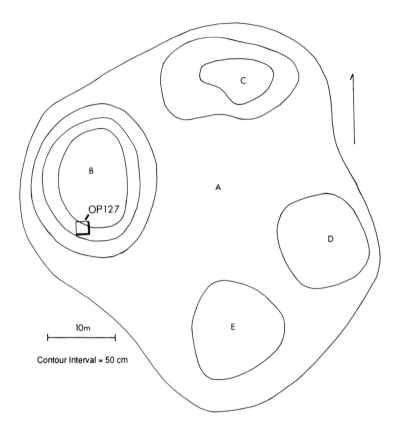

Figure 4.65.   Contour map of the Structure 116 Group.

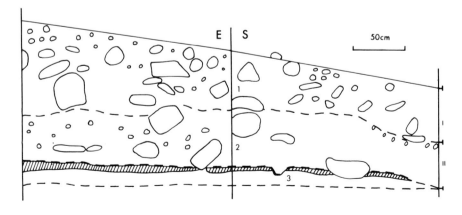

Figure 4.66.   Profile from Structure 116B (Operation 127a).

properties of local limestone caprock taken from the eastern margin of the site.

Level 2 consisted of a mottled light gray clay loam intruded by assorted limestone ballast. This level defined the construction core of the mound. Pebble-sized hearting was concentrated in the northern (or mound interior) portion of the unit. The southwestern portion of the unit contained an off-white marl with few limestone inclusions.

The third level defined the base of the mound. The preparatory surface was isolated as a continuous granular yellow clay ranging from 2 to 3 centimeters thick. The underlying dark brown paleosol was 10 to 15 centimeters thick and was in turn underlain by the sterile gray clay parent material.

The structure did not reveal a dense midden deposit or clear architectural detail. However, given its distance from the center and, by analogy, from other *plazuela* groups in the lowlands, it is thought to have functioned as a rural residential cluster. The structure group's position within the *bajo* suggests its role in raised-field agriculture. The size and formal complexity of the group may indicate that a managerial elite resided at this location. Even allowing for subsidence and erosion of the shoreline, the proximity of the group to the coast would have permitted petty riverine exchange.

Structure 165

This Type 6 mound rests on the margins of the *hulubol* and the depressed thorn-scrub savanna setting at the eastern periphery of the core area. It lies on the immediate banks of the canal and was excavated to expose a ground-level structure in the dispersed settlement. The structure's stratigraphic relationship to the main canal was also understood to be useful in interpreting the function of the canal (chapter 6). The feature has been tentatively identified as a ground-level residence dating to the Tulix phase.

Structure 165 (Operation 154b)

This structure is 5 meters long, 4 meters wide, and 0.10 meter high. It has a potential summit floor space of 16 square meters and a negligible absolute volume of fill. During the 1981 field season a 2-meter by 2-meter unit extended over the structure. This exposure was associated with an adjacent trench operation excavated across the main canal (OP 154a and b). The elevated caprock at this location was anticipated to yield posthole molds of perishable structures. Additionally, the fill from the flanking canal was understood to produce abundant midden debris associated with the occupation of the structure. Only the latter expectation was realized.

Only one stratum and associated lot was retrieved from the excavation of the structure. This surface level was defined by a thin, viscous, brown humic loam intruded by shallow rootlets. The matrix was less moist and viscous than the adjacent canal sediments. The exposed caprock was not pocked or pitted and did not reveal evidence of aboriginal postholes. A possible single course alignment of stones was reported at the western edge of the exposure and may indicate the remains of a house wall. Unfortunately, preservation was too poor to argue strongly for the presence of a foundation wall. The abundant midden debris taken from the canal exposure suggests that these materials were deposited in the canal by the occupants of the structure. Ceramic analysis indicates that Structure 165 was a Tulix phase residence. It should be noted that a possible tread carved down into the bank of the main canal was revealed immediately in front (east) of the structure (see chapter 6).

5. LATE PRECLASSIC BALL COURTS AT CERROS

The competitive ball game played on a masonry court has long been considered a characteristic feature of Mesoamerica, having probable origins in the rubber-producing lowlands (Stern 1949:4). Although the wide distribution of related ball games suggests an origin and dissemination during the Preclassic Period (de Borhegyi 1980; Kubler 1975:41; Stern 1949:76), most of the masonry ball courts which have been excavated and reported in the Maya Lowlands to date have been associated with the Classic and Postclassic periods.

Two ball courts have been excavated in the settlement at Cerros. These single major construction phase courts are morphologically more similar to one another than to other known ball courts, although formal analogies to other sites can be drawn (Scarborough in press). Evidence indicates that these structures are two of the earliest ball courts in the lowlands, further suggesting that the eastward diffusion of the ball court "theme" out of the Veracruz-Tabasco area was a more dynamic process than commonly presumed (see Parsons in press; Scarborough and Wilcox in press).

INTRASITE RELATIONSHIPS

Structure Groups 50 and 61 were utilized at the same time during the Tulix phase, although the latter court was initiated by the Late C'oh phase. Both structures were oriented north-south and lie on the north-south medial axis bisecting the site as defined by the canal perimeter and the pyramidal Structure 5C (the latter structure located at the northern end of the central precinct). In addition, the westward orientation of Structure 29 and its associated plaza axis were found to intersect the medial site axis at a point equidistant between the ball courts. Although the areas in immediate proximity to the courts were well drained, the location midway between the two structure groups is understood to have been a catchment reservoir. The overall layout of the courts supports the idea that much of the settlement was planned and constructed during one moment in time, although the architectural and/or

astronomical import of this spatial design is less well understood (see Fig. 3.9). (Portions of the following presentation describing the two ball courts at Cerros have appeared elsewhere [Scarborough et al. 1982].)

Excavations in the Structure 61 Group

The playing alley of the Structure 61 Group lies approximately 200 meters N5°W of the Structure 50 Group and approximately 100 meters N170°W of the medial staircase on Structure 3. The Structure 61 Group is composed of two parallel ranges, Structure 61B to the west and Structure 61C to the east. No well-defined north-south boundary could be demonstrated for the Group, although the raised alleyway (Structural Feature 61A) appears to have dropped away at the same north and south location as the structures themselves. It should again be noted that no standing architecture has been exposed on any structure in the settlement zone at Cerros (Figs. 5.1, 5.2).

The playing alley, Structural Feature 61A, was mapped and briefly examined in 1978 by a 2-meter by 2-meter test unit. Two hard plaster floors supported by limestone ballast and underlain by midden debris were located. In addition, a sizable hole, 1.65 meters in diameter, was identified and found intruding through both floors. The Structure 61 Group was not interpreted as a ball court until the 1979 season, when the original test unit was extended to form a 2-meter-wide trench crosscutting the ball court along its central axis with extensions to the south along the bench feature of Structure 61B and to the north along the bench feature of Structure 61C. Twenty square meters were horizontally excavated within Structural Feature 61A, 22 square meters were exposed within Structure 61B, and over 51 square meters were laterally excavated within Structure 61C. While excavation was aimed primarily at architectural exposure of the surface, the 2-meter-wide east-west trench across the alleyway was excavated to sterile paleosol, a 2-meter by 4-meter unit at the foot of the east-side stairway on Structure 61C was

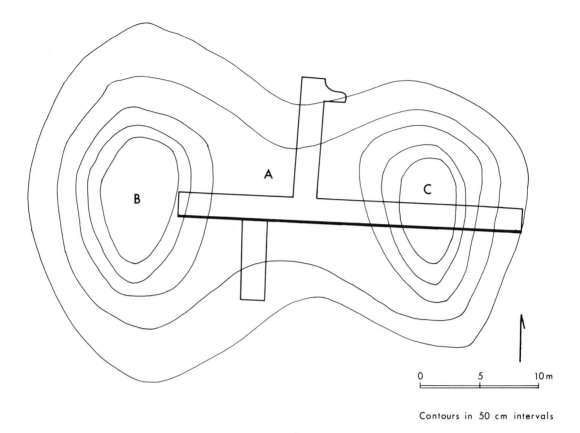

0   5   10 m

Contours in 50 cm intervals

Figure 5.1.   Contour map of the Structure 61 Group.

excavated to the paleosol, and a probe 50 centimeters wide was placed through the west-side bench of Structure 61C. The deeper penetrations yielded the sealed ceramic samples of the Late C'oh phase in association with the construction of the ball court. Tulix phase modification of the structure was also indicated. Excavation and recovery techniques involved the excavation and screening of architecturally and naturally defined levels.

Structures 61B and 61C are approximately 2.7 meters high in their present state of preservation. At the base, they were 22 meters north-south by 18 meters east-west, with inclined benches on their interior faces. These benches flanked a narrow alley 4.1 meters wide, which was oriented approximately N1°E. (Directional data must be considered as only a close approximation of the original alignment due to the effects of weathering on the exposed masonry. All bearings were referenced to true north.) The substructural range structures

may have supported perishable buildings, as no evidence has been found of masonry superstructures.

The masonry of the range structures consisted of coursed stones chosen for general consistency in size and shape. There were no finely dressed stones. The stones ranged from an average of 20 to 25 centimeters across for the loaf-shaped stones of the benches and upper wall on Structure 61B to an average of 35 to 40 centimeters across for the masonry of the staircase and upper wall on Structure 61C. This type of masonry was common throughout the site. The benches were constructed of horizontal courses stepped back to form a slope over a core of rubble and marl. Small, irregularly shaped flat stones formed a discontinuous layer over the stepped courses. These stones were set into a compact, light gray, mortarlike matrix which covered the stepped courses. A smooth sloped surface to the benches was achieved when the exposure was covered with hard plaster. This same bench construction

Figure 5.2.   Playing alley and benches of ball court Structure 61 Group. The view is toward the north.

technique was employed in building the Structure 50 Group ball court.

The alleyway and end zone floors were paved with well-preserved hard plaster. In addition, some plaster remained on the benches and on the upper wall of the western range, Structure 61B. Although no preserved paint was recovered from the *in situ* plaster, two pieces of plaster which were found in fall debris were surfaced with a deep red pigment. Two fragments were collected near the benches of each range structure.

The sloping face of the benches formed an angle with the alleyway floor of between 20° and 30°. As a consequence of preservation, it is unclear whether or not there once was a sharp angle between the face and

the top of the benches. The small patch of preserved flooring at the top of the benches showed a very slight batter (2° or less). These surfaces rose an average of 1.02 meters above the alleyway floor on Structure 61C and 1.06 meters above the alleyway floor on Structure 61B. The width of the bench tops was approximately 2.5 meters.

The upper playing walls of the two ranges differed somewhat. In addition to the larger stone masonry used in the upper wall on Structure 61C, its angle (81° from the horizontal as measured on the masonry) was quite different from that of the upper wall on Structure 61B (36° as measured on the plaster). Time did not allow a trench through the upper walls; it may be that the exposed wall of one of the ranges was a later addition which was never constructed or simply not preserved on the other structure.

The east-west trench which revealed the above playing surfaces extended down the backside of Structure 61C. A staircase was exposed and is approximated to have been 4 meters wide. It had a central landing and a small patch of flooring still adhering to the foot of the lowest riser. Although the stairway was not cornered, its disposition relative to the building clearly indicates that it was outset. A rough construction wall (Wall C; see below) was found underlying the stairway that may mark the edge of the mound. If this is so, then the stairway was outset about 2 meters.

Structure 61 Group was an open-ended ball court. The full extent of the plaster flooring within the end zones beyond the benches has not been determined. Further excavation may reveal some type of boundary around the end zone area, such as a line of stone (see Stern 1949:36). However, there are no obvious walls or platforms defining end zone boundaries. The alleyway playing area may be roughly defined by the margins of the most recent alleyway floor surface (F1A). This floor ended in an irregular line drawn between each bench corner, with the underlying floor (F1B) continuing beyond it. This is analogous to the latest building phase at the Structure 50 Group.

No marker stones or niches were found in the ball court. However, the initial test unit excavated during the 1978 field season revealed a circular depression in the alley floor. It was 1.65 meters in diameter and 1.0 meters in depth and contained pebble-sized limestone packed in a marl matrix. This fill was distinguishable from the surrounding platform fill. The purpose of the pit is unclear, although similar depressions were exposed in the alleyway floor of the Structure 50 Group. It is suggested that a connection exists between these features and the ball court function of the structure groups.

Based on the size and shape of the depression, it is argued that this was the location of an alleyway marker of the type common in the Maya Lowlands (Blom 1932:4; Satterthwaite 1933:1; Kubler 1975:133). The stone marker would have been removed at the time of abandonment. Ritual abandonment of the ball court and the removal of the marker stone may have been equivalent to the ceremonial defacing of the many buildings in other Late Preclassic contexts at Cerros. It should be noted that the pit was not precisely located on either central axis of the ball court but was centered

1 meter south and 75 centimeters east of the midpoint for the court. This noncentral location is a feature shared with the depressions in the alleyway of the Structure 50 group.

One feature on the bench top of Structure 61B may indicate the position of another smaller ball court marker. The plaster on top of the bench was sectioned at a curiously high spot. A postholelike feature approximately 20 centimeters in diameter and 10 centimeters in depth was found patched with the same white plaster of the overlying floor. The surrounding matrix underlying the bench surface was a light gray clay loam, which may represent an earlier destroyed flooring event. The depression appears to have been associated with this earlier surface. The depression may have held a tenoned marker that was removed and filled with plaster during the process of laying down the later floor. This feature was south of the medial court axis, but placed on an approximate east-west line with the alleyway depression immediately below it.

Construction Sequence

The 1978 testing operation was specifically geared to determining the stratigraphic sequence and the ceramic inventory for the Structure 61 Group. The excavation unit was taken down to sterile soil. The 1979 operation concentrated on lateral exposure to obtain as much information as possible on ball court form and dimensions. Moreover, the area of the playing alley within the 2-meter-wide east-west trench was excavated to within 25 centimeters of the sterile paleosol. Further, a 2-meter by 4-meter unit at the rear of Structure 61C was excavated below the floor level following the removal of the lower four risers of the staircase. Finally, a 50-centimeter-wide test trench was excavated through the bench on Structure 61C.

The construction sequence in the alleyway is the most complete and will be discussed initially (Fig. 5.3). The first cultural deposit above the basal, sterile, black gumbo paleosol is a 3-centimeter-thick, white marl lens designated F3. This was laid as a foundation for subsequent construction, elsewhere referred to as "preparatory surface." The layer was exposed only in the initial test unit 90 centimeters below the alleyway floor (F1A). Immediately overlying this lens was a dark gray midden layer 12 centimeters thick. Although it remains uncertain whether this was primary midden deposit associated with a house or a secondary deposit brought in as fill, there is evidence for ground-level structures during

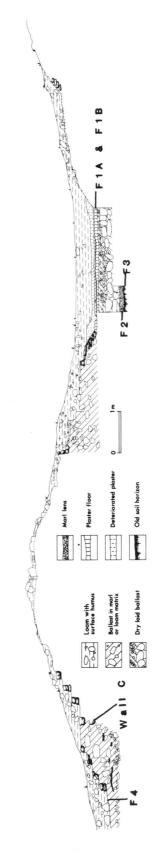

F 1 A & F 1 B

F 3

F 2

Wall C

F 4

Marl lens

Plaster floor

Deteriorated plaster

Old soil horizon

Loam with surface humus

Ballast in marl or loam matrix

Dry laid ballast

0   1 m

Figure 5.3.   Southern profile from Structures 61C, A, and B.

the C'oh and Tulix phases elsewhere in the settlement. Only C'oh phase ceramics have been found associated with this level. Capping the midden debris was a patchy marl layer 3 centimeters thick (F2).

The next level clearly constituted platform fill. It consisted of one to two layers of cobble-sized rubble set in a thin, discontinuous, reddish brown soil overlain by pebble-sized, dry-laid floor ballast. This level was 50 to 60 centimeters thick and again dated to the C'oh phase.

Overlying this fill was a 6- to 10-centimeter-thick layer of hard plaster (F1B). This floor extended to the edges of the two north-south trench extensions and underlay Structure 61C at least as far east as the upper playing wall. A small patch of flooring in front of the Structure 61C staircase (F4) was found at the same level as F1B. However, at this same elevation under the staircase itself no flooring was found, only a marl construction pause. It appears that F1B was laid down before the benches were constructed but not as a base for the entire structure. A logical building sequence would have the ranges built first, then F1B laid, and finally the benches added. Further support for this expectation was indicated by the wear pattern on the floor. F1B was quite worn and pitted in the alleyway area but smooth and unworn under the bench. It should be noted that our trench into the bench of Structure 61C revealed only rubble fill under the upper playing wall, with no indication that it extended down through the rubble to the level of F1B. The bench does not appear to be hung from an extension of the upper playing wall.

Overlying F1B in the alleyway was a 1-centimeter-thick lens of gray marl. Immediately above this marl was another hard plaster floor (F1A). This floor extended laterally to the edges of the bench masonry. F1A consisted of plaster only, without gravel ballast, and appears to date to the Tulix phase.

The plaster lip extending up onto each bench was added after F1A was laid down. These plaster wings extended out 30 centimeters from the bench masonry and provided the surficial face of the bench batter. A small test on a well-preserved part of the bench on Structure 61B demonstrated that there were two layers of plaster on the bench face, both associated with F1A.

One feature on F1B suggests that at one time there was another earlier plaster bench surface associated with this floor. In front of both benches there was a strip of well-preserved F1B plaster, like that under the bench of Structure 61C before the worn

appearance of F1B began in the alley. This strip corresponds closely to the extent of the plaster lip associated with the later F1A. While it is possible that the very edge of the floor received less abuse than the center of the court during play, the clarity of the line between worn and well-preserved plaster indicates that the floor was protected by some type of surface beginning at this line. It is argued that a plaster lip, similar to that associated with F1A, was removed at the time the new alleyway floor (F1A) was added. Apparently, the benches could not be replastered without first removing the earlier plaster lip; this prevented the narrowing of the alleyway and suggests a degree of standardization for the width of the court. However, the possibility of ritual defacement of an entire bench surface associated with the renovation of an alleyway should be kept in mind as an alternative explanation. The previously mentioned resurfacing of the bench top associated with Structure 61B may further reflect a greater investment in architectural modifications than our present evidence conservatively allows.

Although the 1978 test unit yielded a good number of exclusively Late Preclassic sherds, the sealed sample recovered from the alley in 1979 was disappointingly small. In order to enlarge the sample, a trench was opened through the staircase of Structure 61C. The removal of the staircase and underlying rubble fill revealed the marl construction pause previously mentioned (an extension of F4). In addition, a north-south trending wall (Wall C) was found resting on this marl pause just underlying the middle of the staircase landing. The rough masonry of the wall suggested that it was a construction pen wall employed to hang the lower outset portion of the staircase. Construction pens incorporating walls of large, roughly cut stone were a common feature of construction at Cerros (see Structure 50B). Wall C was not removed because it corresponded closely to the western line of our 2-meter by 4-meter unit, acting as a buttress against side-wall collapse. Below the marl pause associated with the construction wall was a pebble-sized ballast similar to that underlying F1B in the alleyway. It was less tightly packed and set in a matrix of buff-colored marl. This layer was 40 to 50 centimeters deep, terminating on the exposure of a yet earlier marl construction pause. This latter pause corresponds in depth to the marl lens designated F2 in the alleyway. Apparently associated with this latter pause was another construction wall (Wall D) running in an east-west direction from the line of Wall C and continuing at

Figure 5.4. Aerial view of ball court Structure 50 Group. The low-lying *zacatal* lies in the center field and the bay in the upper left margin.

Figure 5.5. Ball court Structure 50 Group on partial clearing of the *huamil*. The view is toward the north from Structure 50D with the playing alley excavated. The white outcrop in the upper right is Structure 29B.

least as far east as the edge of our trench. This crude wall was only two courses high and was immediately overlain by the upper marl pause.

F2 evidently formed the base for the entire ball court. On this foundation, the structures were built of a wet-laid fill retained by construction pen walls in the east and a more dry-laid fill to the west. The exact line between these two types of construction and the reason for the difference can only be determined through further excavation.

Excavations in the Structure 50 Group

The Structure 50 Group consists of four range structures, labeled clockwise 50B through 50E, with the southernmost range flanking the bank of the main canal. The central plaza area and playing alley are termed Structural Feature 50A. The playing court is defined by the two parallel ranges, Structure 50C to the east and Structure 50E to the west. The largest mound of the Group, Structure 50B, delimits the northern extent of the Group. The southern basal riser of Structure 50B lies 38 meters north of the alleyway center, although a shallow plaza depression separates it from the other structures. Structure 50D is located 26 meters south of the alley center and is linked to the alley by continuous raised plaza fill.

Structures 50C, 50E, and Structural Feature 50A

The Structure 50 Group was initially located, mapped, and briefly tested during the 1978 field season. At that time a 2-meter by 3-meter test unit was excavated at the northwest corner of Structure 50E. Two walls were revealed in the exposure. Wall A was constructed of two courses of finely cut block masonry oriented N95°W. Wall B was constructed of vertically set slabs which faced away from Wall A. Wall B appeared to be unassociated with Wall A and part of a later building event. A hard plaster floor found on the north side of Wall A concealed the lowest course of this wall and suggested earlier flooring events associated with the basal course of the wall. Ceramics sealed by the floor were found to date exclusively to the Tulix phase.

Structures 50C and 50E as well as plaza Structural Feature 50A were extensively excavated during the 1979 field season (Figs. 5.4, 5.5). The excavations carried out on Structure 50E exposed 42 square meters

on its western flank, 45 square meters on its northern side, 26 square meters on the playing bench, and a 2-meter-wide medial axis trench across the structure. More than 113 square meters of lateral exposure were excavated. Structure 50C exposed 38 square meters on its eastern side, with a 6-square-meter extension at the northeast corner and an 8-square-meter exposure on the bench. Fifty-two square meters were horizontally excavated on this structure. In addition, a total of 68 square meters of the playing alleyway area were revealed. Ceramic trash in association with the building was uniformly sparse, but reasonable pottery samples of the Tulix phase were obtained from the sealed context of the dismantled stairway on Structure 50E, the excavated flooring bordering the northern edge of this building, and the selective probes associated with the alleyway area (Structural Feature 50A). As was the case with the Structure 61 Group, our recovery techniques involved the excavation and screening of architecturally and naturally defined strata from within a 2-meter by 2-meter control grid (Figs. 5.6, 5.7).

Structures 50C and 50E were rectangular ranges, each a mirror image of the other. Both were preserved to a height of 2.1 meters, with a 4.2-meter-wide alley separating the two structures and oriented N4°E. Each structure consisted of three terraced platforms with each basal terrace measuring 18 meters north-south by 14.5 meters east-west.

The basal terraces consisted of sloping benches facing onto the playing alley. The benches were 1.1 meters high and had a batter of 50°. The tops of each bench were poorly preserved except for a small area of plaster flooring associated with Structure 50C. It remains unclear whether or not these surfaces were level or slightly canted. On the back side of Structure 50E, the terrace stepped down 30 centimeters to an associated exterior plaster floor. The back and side wall corners of the basal terraces were inset with apron moldings. Several fragments of painted and molded plaster were located in the fall behind Structure 50C, suggesting that facading decorated the back sides of these structures. Unfortunately, the precise location of this plaster decoration is unknown, as no *in situ* plaster was exposed. The fragments show elements similar to those found from the facades flanking the monumental architecture elsewhere at Cerros (Structures 5C and 29B; Freidel 1977, 1981, 1986a and b).

The upper playing walls facing the alleyway were located on the second terraces. They were inclined at a 70° angle, rose to a height of 50 centimeters, and

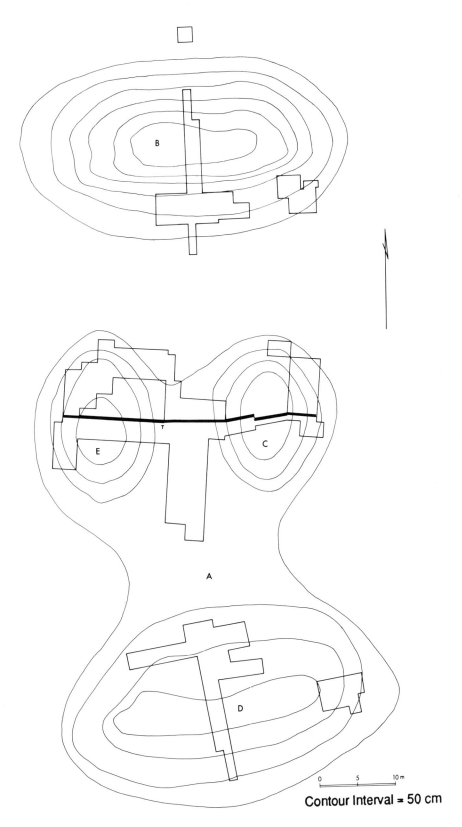

B

E   T   C

A

D

0   5   10 m

Contour Interval = 50 cm

Figure 5.6.   Contour map of the Structure 50 Group.

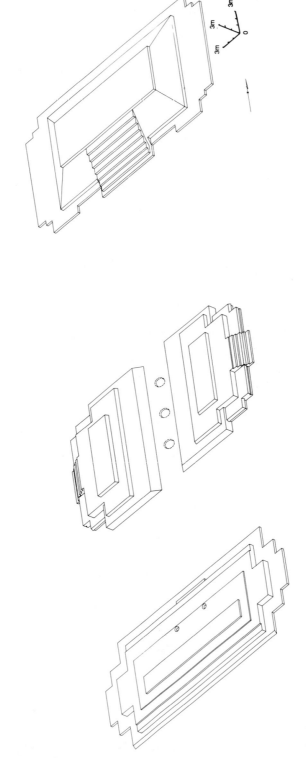

Figure 5.7   Isometric plan of the Structure 50 Group.

rested recessed 3 meters behind the lower bench faces. These terraces were T-shaped in plan, with broad staircases, 4.6 meters wide, extending off the backside of each structure. The staircases were outset 1 meter from the back walls of the structures. Fragments of six risers were found behind Structure 50E. Only the lower steps were preserved on Structure 50C.

The uppermost terraces on both structures were small rectangular platforms that probably supported perishable superstructures. These terraces were recessed 2 meters behind the upper courses of the upper playing walls. The upper playing wall and the alley-facing side wall of the upper terrace were found in good condition on Structure 50C, although neither was preserved on Structure 50E. The uppermost terrace wall on Structure 50C was inclined like the underlying upper playing wall (60°) and preserved to a height of 50 centimeters. None of the uppermost platform side walls were exposed, so the north-south length of these platforms is conjecture. The back walls of the uppermost platforms were identified on both structures, providing an east-west width of 4 meters for the platforms. A fragmentary wall stub oriented at right angles to the back wall on Structure 50E may have formed part of a bench on top of this upper platform. The poorly preserved nature of the wall, however, prevented a positive identification, and a similar feature could not be located on Structure 50C.

Several types of masonry were used in the construction of Structures 50C and 50E. Finely cut limestone blocks were used in the construction of the back and side walls of the lowest terraces and on the staircases. The blocks used in Structure 50C were smaller than those in Structure 50E. The facing stones identified in Structure 50C averaged 10 centimeters high by 15 centimeters long, as opposed to the 15-centimeter by 25-centimeter blocks in Structure 50E. The steps of the staircase were constructed of various block sizes, ranging from small stones 10 centimeters by 15 centimeters to blocks 25 centimeters by 50 centimeters. In addition, a number of the large, finely shaped stones were recovered from the fall around the backs and sides of the two structures. Since these stones were only found *in situ* when associated with the staircase, their original location cannot be determined. This fine block masonry was unusual at Cerros, where most of the masonry consisted of loaf-shaped stones. Although this might on first appraisal suggest that the Structure 50 Group was built later than other structures at Cerros, the masonry in Structures 50B and

50D (which are contemporaneous with Structures 50C and 50E on the grounds of proximity, spatial orientation, and ceramic inventory) contains poorly dressed stones. Apparently, several types of masonry were incorporated simultaneously. The upper playing walls as well as the uppermost terrace walls were constructed of relatively small, irregular, flat stones to produce the sloping surfaces mentioned. Loaf-shaped stones were also used in the stepped support walls found under the bench faces.

The bench faces were built of a layer of hard plaster overlying a core of marl and small ballast, as was the case with the Structure 61 Group. This core was in turn supported by a stepped wall. The bench construction was slightly different from the Structure 61 Group, where a layer of small, irregularly shaped, flat stones was found between the stepped construction wall and the plaster surface. Little construction fill or core was sandwiched between the underlying wall and the plaster surface in the Structure 61 example. The bench face on Structure 50E was well preserved to a height of 35 centimeters above the alley floor, while only a small patch of the plaster bench face remained on Structure 50C. The original height of these benches—approximately 1.1 meters—has been estimated from the elevation of the underlying stepped support wall and from the sections of plaster floor resting on top of the benches. The preserved plaster on the bench face of Structure 50E formed a 50° angle with the alley floor, an angle steeper than the 20 to 30° angle recorded for the Structure 61 Group. However, the stepped support wall underlying the bench surfaces of both Structures 50C and 50E formed an angle of approximately 30°. Such an angle is more in keeping with that identified in the Structure 61 Group and suggests some degree of bench face modification for the Structure 50 Group.

As in the Structure 61 Group, there was poor preservation at the corners of the bench faces. Nevertheless, the southeast corner of Structure 50E provided some information on the appearance of these corners. Although the plaster of the bench face was not preserved in this area, the stepped support wall was in fairly good condition. This wall formed a rounded corner back to the west for approximately 1 meter. Time limitations prevented further excavation of the southern side wall of the structure. Through analogy with the northern side wall, which was almost completely excavated, it appears that within 2 meters of the corner, the stepped support wall of the bench met the vertical retaining wall of the platform. The corner and bench face may have been slightly outset from the side wall.

The Structure 50 Group is an open-ended ball court in its final construction phase. No definite north-south alleyway boundary was found, although excavations extended 3 meters beyond the southern edge of the benches. The hard plaster floor of the alley was well preserved for 2 meters south of the benches, with the floor ballast extending to the edge of the excavation unit. The elevation of the alleyway floor surface was within 10 centimeters of the elevation recorded for the hard plaster plaza floors in front of Structures 50B and 50D, as well as those behind Structures 50C and 50E. The playing limits of the court may have been marked by paint or in some other medium which has long since disappeared (Fig. 5.8).

The initial construction phase of the Structure 50 Group ball court was nearly identical to its final manifestation, with the exception of an earlier sunken playing alleyway. Sections excavated through the alley and into the plaza on the north side of Structure 50E, as well as its staircase, demonstrate that these structures were not modified when the playing alley was raised. In the initial construction phase, the alley was 30 centimeters lower than the surrounding plaza. This lower alley was bound at its southern edge by a sloping plaster surface which graded into the elevated plaza. If a similar boundary were located to the north, the alleyway would have extended north-south for 18 meters. The southern boundary rose at a 35° angle from the lower alley floor (F1B). A section through these surfaces showed that each was constructed of a hard plaster layer supported by a marl and pebble-sized ballast core. No boulder- or cobble-sized ballast stones were found. Prior to the excavation of the upper alley floor (F1A), the location of the buried southern alleyway boundary was suggested by an irregular break at that end of the alley floor. F1A had separated from the adjoining plaza floor and was slightly higher along the break. This upper alleyway floor had been constructed without disturbing the lower sloping boundary surface. Nevertheless, the bench faces of this earlier court

Figure 5.8.   Ball court Structure 50 Group playing alley. Structure 50C lies to the right and Structure 50E lies to the left. The view is toward the north.

associated with Structures 50C and 50E were removed before F1A was constructed. Only one small plaster fragment of this earlier bench remained *in situ* on the stepped support wall of Structure 50E. The second bench face was constructed at the edge of F1A. It simply involved the resurfacing of the upper portion of the underlying stepped support wall.

No stone or plaster markers were found in the Structure 50 Group. As in the Structure 61 Group, large holes were found in the playing alley. The first hole excavated was positioned on the medial east-west axis of the alley and set 1 meter closer to Structure 50C than to Structure 50E. A second hole was located 3.5 meters south of the first and again closer to Structure 50C. The holes were oval in shape and measured 1.5 meters east-west by 1.0 meter north-south. Both of these depressions were associated only with the later court. Apparently, markers were located in these holes.

F1B was preserved under these depressions. However, earlier holes were identified and associated with this earlier alley. The later marker locations had shifted slightly when the alley was raised. The holes through F1A were southeast of those in F1B. Because the northern part of the alley was not excavated, it is unknown whether a third marker was located in that area. The markers were apparently removed as part of the ritual abandonment of the site. No postholes were found on either of the bench tops. It should be noted, however, that on Structure 50C a small, roughly circular area of raised plaster was found in front of the playing wall. This feature was located north of the medial east-west axis and cannot be positively identified as a marker.

Construction Sequence

The construction sequence of Structures 50C and 50E was determined by excavations through the playing alley and plaza at the southeast corner of Structure 50E, a section through the staircase of Structure 50E, and the previously mentioned test unit excavated in 1978. As discussed earlier, the structures defining the court were constructed in one phase. The only later modification to the court was the raising of the playing alley, although the bench face surfaces may have been periodically altered (Fig. 5.9).

A layer of black, silty clay gumbo was found at the base of all sections. This layer is the ancient ground surface and has been observed in other excavations at Cerros immediately below the base of a mound. The layer is usually sterile, although in some of the

Structure 50 Group sections a few sherds were found near the surface of the deposit. These artifacts were probably deposited during the construction episode, although it is possible that the sherds are associated with some other type of occupation in this part of the site predating the construction of the ball court.

Initial construction activity consisted of a thin layer of marl laid on the paleosol surface. The marl lens was less than 2 centimeters thick and, like the initial construction in the Structure 61 Group, it probably served as a foundation for construction.

The marl lens was covered by a layer of cobble-sized dry-laid ballast ranging in thickness from 15 centimeters to 25 centimeters. This ballast layer graded into a deposit of pebble-sized hearting. Both ballast layers were found underneath the structures and the plaza. The surface of the hearting layer was covered by a 2-centimeter-thick lens of compact gray marl in the plaza areas, which was found to extend laterally for approximately 2 meters underneath the structures themselves. The lowest course of the platform walls was built on this upper marl lens, as was the hard plaster surface of the first (sunken) playing alley (F1B). The southern boundary of the first alley and the associated bench faces were built on the plaster surface of this initial alleyway. The plaza around the structures was raised, with a layer of pebble-sized ballast in a matrix of loosely packed marl. This ballast deposit was surfaced with a layer of hard plaster. The plaza floor and underlying ballast layer were 40 centimeters thick and buried the basal two courses of the original side and back walls at the foot of Structures 50C and 50E.

The second construction episode consisted of raising the alley floor. The first alley floor (F1B) was covered with a layer of pebble-sized ballast packed in a marl matrix. The markers were reset in slightly different locations and the alley way then covered with a layer of hard plaster (F1A). As in the Structure 61 Group example, the bench faces were built slightly over the edges of the associated plaster floor.

A final episode of construction on Structure 50E apparently postdates its use as a ball court. As mentioned earlier, the test unit excavated in 1978 uncovered a wall constructed of vertically set slabs (Wall B) which postdated Wall A (a platform wall of the ballcourt). The area to the south of Wall A was cleared and Wall B was found to be part of a square-walled, cistlike feature. The walls of the feature were constructed of vertical slabs faced toward the interior of the feature.

Figure 5.9. Northern profile from Structures 50E, A, and C.

Traces of plaster were found on the walls, suggesting that they were covered with a lens of plaster. The floor of the feature was paved with a layer of flagstones set in a matrix of compact white marl. The feature appears intrusive into the construction fill of Structure 50E.

The cistlike feature was 1.9 meters by 2.1 meters in plan and oriented at a 45° angle to the layout of the ball court. The walls of the feature were 1.5 meters high. A high density of pebble-sized ballast in a gray loam matrix along the back and northern side of Structure 50E suggests that this area was artificially raised as part of the construction episode associated with the feature. Since this ballast layer covers a number of finely trimmed stones, which were part of the fall debris from Structure 50E, the feature seems to postdate the abandonment of Structure 50E as a ball court.

The function of this feature is unclear. In the eastern half of the cist a large number of sherds were collected, including the fragments of a complete vessel and probably most of a second one. They appear to date to the Late Classic Period (David Pendergast and Robin Robertson personal communication), although many of the sherds are quite weathered. In the western half of the feature a concentration of cobble-sized stones was found, together with a soil matrix containing charcoal. The haphazard distribution of the sherds and related debris throughout the matrices within the cist indicate that the final function for the feature was as a trash dump. The original design of the cist was clearly too elaborate to have been intended for use as a trash pit. More probably, it represents a looted cist burial which was only subsequently used as a trash pit. Alternatively, the concentration of stones and charcoal may indicate that they were used as an *in situ* hearth, now poorly preserved, and suggests the intriguing possibility that the feature functioned as a sweat bath. If so, it was associated with a reuse of the Structure 50 Group after its abandonment as a ball court. A correlation between ball courts and the sweat bath has been suggested at other sites in the Maya area (Coe 1967; Ruppert 1952; Satterthwaite 1944).

Structures 50B and 50D

The north and south ends of the Structure 50 Group are defined by Structures 50B and 50D, respectively (Figs. 5.6, 5.7). Structure 50B was initially examined during the 1978 field season. A 2-meter by 2-meter test unit was excavated near the south-central base of the structure. A single major construction episode was defined by a hard plaster exterior floor in association with two risers. Both risers consisted of two courses measuring 25 centimeters high and composed of loaf-shaped masonry. A sizable Early Classic ceramic inventory was collected from above these features, but a pure Tulix phase collection was taken from under the sealed floor. Structure 50D was not tested at this time.

Form and Construction Sequence of Structure 50B

At its base, Structure 50B has been shown to be 34 meters long by 18 meters wide and approximately 3 meters high. Eighty-nine square meters of horizontal exposure has provided information concerning the south face of the structure. More limited, although revealing, evidence for Late Preclassic architecture was gleaned from the summit and back side of the structure.

Structure 50B rests on a marl lens or preparatory surface, on which subsequent construction activities occurred. Although this lens could represent an earlier ground-level domestic structure, no associated features were discernible. The off-white marl layer was spread discontinuously over the original ground surface to a depth of 3 centimeters. The underlying black gumbo paleosol was not removed from the area.

The mass of Structure 50B was initiated and finalized in one construction phase, although minor refurbishing events did occur. The exterior of the structure was defined by a 4-meter outset staircase, of which the lower two treads were well preserved and the third tread was at least traceable (Fig. 5.10). The remainder of the staircase had been completely destroyed. Judging from the absence of shaped stone in the overlying fall debris, it is suggested that this stone was deliberately removed from the structure to another, as yet unknown, location. The lower risers were composed of loaf-shaped masonry within a marl grout. The risers were two courses high and apparently covered with hard plaster, as indicated by an *in situ* fragment recovered from the basal tread. A hard plaster exterior plaza floor lipped upward from the base of the structure to the lowest riser, although the floor was only well preserved within 2 meters of the front side of the structure. The floor appeared to extend the length of the southern face of the structure, however, and measured 10 centimeters in thickness. It was underlain by 25 centimeters of pebble- and cobble-sized

Figure 5.10.   Ball court Structure 50B. The outset medial staircase is pictured. The view is toward the east across the front side of the structure.

ballast packed in a light gray marl overlying the sterile paleosol.

At the flanks of the outset staircase were recessed panels 50 centimeters high. The exposed eastern panel was composed of small loaf-shaped stones. Extending 50 centimeters out from the base of the panel was a 20-centimeter-high basal molding. The lateral extent of the panel was not identified and no facading was discernible either in the fill or adhering to the wall.

At the southeast corner of the structure, we exposed a rather elaborate inset corner apparently associated with the base of the substructure only (Fig. 5.7). The previously defined hard plaster exterior plaza floor was found associated with the corner, although a later resurfacing was also revealed. It should be noted that there was an indication that basal molding was employed in the construction of this corner.

The summit of the structure received limited attention as a consequence of time restrictions and our previous experience elsewhere with the settlement in defining poorly preserved superstructural features. Nevertheless, a surficial east-west trending wall was located. The southern face of this wall delimited the northern edge of our deep axial trench. Although the wall is thought to have been the foundation for a superstructural feature, it also descended into the core of the structure to provide substructural support. This lower construction pen wall, composed of small limestone boulders, appears to have cornered in our eastern profile, exposing two of the four construction pen walls. The pen was 1.4 meters at its maximum height. Underlying this pen construction was another construction pen wall, revealed in our eastern and southern trench walls. This lower construction pen was also 1.4 meters high and filled with a dry-laid limestone pebble- and small-cobble-sized ballast. The position of the lower construction pen indicates that these building units of undetermined horizontal dimensions were offset or staggered one on top of the other, presumably for additional support. Our axial trenching operation was terminated on exposing the marl preparatory surface and the underlying sterile paleosol.

Form and Construction Sequence of Structure 50D

Sixty-four meters south of the outset staircase on Structure 50B and bounding the southern end of the ball court plaza lies Structure 50D. It was 34 meters east-west by 16 meters north-south and 2.2 meters in height. One hundred twenty-five square meters were laterally exposed on the northwest face and the southeast corner of Structure 50D. A 2-meter-wide axial trench provided the construction sequence for the mound.

This structure presents little evidence for a ground-level dwelling preceding and underlying the bulk of the mound, although a marl preparatory surface was identified under the hard plaster floor and support ballast at the foot of the structure. This 3-centimeter-thick lens was laid directly on the sterile black gumbo paleosol.

Structure 50D was raised in a single construction episode. The front or north side of the substructure consisted of three tiers running the length of the structure, although the lower platform extension continued beyond the upper two substructural tiers. A shallow step restricted to 4 meters in length was defined on the medial axis of the structure between the first and second tiers. Both the tiers and the step were three courses high. The masonry was composed of loaf-shaped stones secured in a marl grout. Immediately in front of the medial axis step or riser was a soft decomposing plaster cap thought to be a later refurbishing operation. A fragment of *in situ* hard plaster was found below and abutting the base of the earlier shallow step.

The summit of the structure received more lateral attention than other structures in the settlement as a consequence of locating a stone-lined posthole within our axial trench. This feature was 50 centimeters in diameter and defined by a tabular, horizontally bedded stone at its base. A slit trench to the east exposed another stone-lined posthole of similar diameter and depth located 4 meters away. Each posthole was positioned immediately behind an upper superstructural terrace retaining wall. The two postholes rested 2 meters east and west of the medial axis of the structure. The width and orientation of the Structure 50 Group alleyway corresponds closely to the position of the postholes.

In addition to a lower superstructural terrace, the summit appears to have accommodated an upper recessed rectangular platform area. Although no plaster was identified, a dense hearting stone matrix was enclosed by a single-course retaining wall.

The rear, or south side, of Structure 50D lies approximately 20 meters from the canal. The south exposure of the structure had the same tiered arrangement as found on the northern face, although our excavations were quite limited. The basal foundation wall was very well preserved, having a batter of 40° and consisting of five well-defined courses. A hard plaster exterior plaza floor was found to lip upward onto the bottom course. A section through this floor revealed only Tulix phase ceramics in association. No preparatory surface was defined under the floor and associated ballast. However, the complete absence of a paleosol at this location suggests the removal of the humic layer in the likely attempt to facilitate passage to and from the canal before the Structure 50 Group was initiated. No rear staircase was identified on Structure 50D, although the graded tiers of the structure may have permitted access.

The southeast corner of the structure was examined in an attempt to locate midden, define the dimensions of the structure, and further assess architectural complexity. All of these objectives were attained, although the midden debris appears to be temporally mixed (see Lewenstein 1987). An elaborate inset corner was found associated with a hard plaster floor. Elevations indicate that this floor was the same plaza floor defined in the front and the back of the structure. The architectural form of the corner was analogous to that defined on Structure 50B.

The trenching operation into the bulk of the structure was carried out in three test units positioned on both sides (front and back) of the structure and at the summit. No construction pen walls were defined. The structure was composed of 70 centimeters of wet-laid cobble-sized ballast underlain by small-boulder-sized dry-laid rubble. The marl preparatory surface was only located under the northern plaza floor exposure.

INTERPRETIVE NOTES

The excavations outlined above have provided temporal and spatial control for two Late Preclassic ball courts. The degree of similarity between the two courts strongly suggests a standardization of the ball game at this time and place. Although certain minor differences between the courts are apparent in terms of range construction and court dimensions, the amount of variability within each structural group would appear to be as great (table 9; see Scarborough in press). In addition, some of the between-site variability at Cerros may be attributable to the various degrees of preservation in which we have found the features discussed.

The ball game played in a masonry court is a characteristic feature of Mesoamerican civilization (de Borhegyi 1969, 1980). This game had both religious and social significance and many times was associated with elite activities (Scarborough and Wilcox in press). Drawing specific analogies from other areas in the Maya Lowlands to Cerros has been difficult because of the lack of comparable Late Preclassic Period data to be found elsewhere. The only other Late Preclassic ball court reported in the Maya area comes from the nearby site of Colha (Eaton and Kunstler 1980), where subsequent Late Classic reuse of the court has obscured many of the earlier architectural details. The previously suggested Late Preclassic ball court at Nohmul has now been shown to date to the Terminal Classic (Hammond et al. 1987). Outside the Maya area, early ball courts have been

located at sites which also show evidence for the development of social complexity, including monumental architecture. An examination of the distribution of these courts suggests that the game may have spread as a complex of iconographic and ideological traits from the lowlands of Tabasco and Veracruz into the Maya region.

The earliest suggested evidence for a pre-Columbian ball court comes from the Stirling Group at the Olmec center of La Venta (Wyshak et al. 1971). Although ball-player figurines from San Lorenzo suggest the appearance of the game earlier (1150–900 B.C.; Coe 1970), excavations at La Venta indicate the formal presence of a ball court radiocarbon dated to 760 B.C. (Wyshak et al. 1971). Little is known of the form of this court other than that it appears to be of the open-ended type. Three sites in Southern Chiapas which date to the Modified Olmec Escalera phase (650–550 B.C.) are also known to have ball courts (Agrinier in press; Lowe 1977). These sites, Finca Acapulco, Vergel, and San Mateo, have a linear arrangement of monumental architecture similar to that at La Venta. Dating to about this same period is a court at the site of San Lorenzo (Coe 1970; Coe and Diehl 1980). This court dates to the Palangana phase (600–400 B.C.) and is part of renewed construction

TABLE 9

Cerros Courts Compared

| | Bench Face | | Bench Top | | Ratio | Playing | Alley | | | | |
| | | | | | | Wall | | Alley | | Ratio | Ends |
Ball Court	H (m)	Slope (°)	W (m)	Slope (°)	H/W	H (m)	Slope (°)	L (m)	W (m)	L\W	
Cerros 61	1.02	20	2.5	1–2	0.42	0.60+	36	16.0	3.8	4.20	Open
Cerros 50	1.10	50	3.0	0	0.37	0.50+	70	18.0	4.2	4.30	Open
Cerros 50-sub	1.33	35*	3.0	0	0.44	0.50+	70	18.0	4.2	4.30	Closed & Sunken
Monte Albán (dated M.A. III)	1.0	49	1.8	0	0.56	6.5	33	26.0	5.0	5.20	Closed & Sunken
Piedras Negras (RII)	0.8	33	2.5	0	0.32	3.0	36	18.0	4.3	5.14	Closed
Yaxchilán I	1.4	28	3.0	2	0.47	2.75	58	19.0	4.5	4.20	Open
Yaxchilán II	1.0	27	4.0	7	0.25	2.4	39	18.0	5.0	3.6	Open
Chijolom 3-4	1.0	49	2.9	0	0.34	1.25	67	17.5	4.2	4.17	Open
Copán	0.7	75	7.0	25	0.10	1.0	90	26.8	7.0	3.8	Open
Palenque	0.9	90	2.5	0	0.36	3.0	58	22.0	2.7	8.1	Open

NOTES: After Quirarte 1972: Appendix.
   H = Height; W = Width; L = Length
*Angle taken from south end of sunken batter surface.

activity at the site, following a hiatus at the end of the Olmec occupation there. This phase shows ceramic ties to the Middle Preclassic Mamom of the Maya Lowlands. Unfortunately, detailed information is not available on these courts, but all appear to have been open-ended.

At Monte Albán in Highland Oaxaca, the earliest of two superimposed courts dates to Monte Albán II times (Acosta 1965) or between 200 B.C. and A.D. 200. Another ball court recorded briefly from the same area, at San José Mogote and dating to the Monte Albán II period, is argued to be so similar to the late Monte Albán III example at Monte Albán that a standard plan for these courts has been suggested (Flannery and Marcus 1976). Recently, Kowalewski et al. (1983) have indicated from survey data that eleven of the sixteen Monte Albán II ball courts within the Valley of Oaxaca rest along the valley's periphery. These authors suggest that the ball game institution had evolved to resolve conflict associated with the expanding margins of an early Zapotec state by this early date. To date, these Oaxacan courts appear to be the only ones contemporaneous with the courts at Cerros. It should be noted that the ball courts recently identified by Agrinier (in press) for Chiapas may have a Late Preclassic affiliation.

In Quirarte's typology of ball court architecture (1972), the Monte Albán III court represents a Type II structure (see table 9). Although the Cerros ball courts do not fit precisely into Quirarte's scheme, they perhaps best resemble his Type II or IIa. This similarity in profile and plan between the Oaxacan example and the Cerros courts is further supported by the stepped stone masonry underlying the plaster batter surfaces of both groups of courts. In addition, the presence of possible outset bench corners and the sunken playing field of the initial Structure 50 Group has strong affinities at least to the Monte Albán III court and perhaps to the San José Mogote case.

Although ball courts are rare in the Maya lowlands until the Late Classic, two Early Classic courts have been reported. At Copán, the earliest court dating to the Early Classic period is the first of a series of three superimposed courts at the site (Stromsvik 1952). Although it is open-ended like the courts at Cerros, the bench tops are slanted in a manner most similar to later Copán courts. In addition, both the Copán and the Monte Albán ball courts share with the Cerros courts a marked north-south orientation. In this vein, it should be noted that in the Guatemala Highlands, Brown (1973) has reported Early Classic or Middle Classic ball courts at or near Kaminaljuyu which maintain this same north-south orientation. Palenque is the second site in the lowlands reported to have a court dating to the Early Classic Period (Rands 1977). Also oriented north-south, this court appears to be a Type IIa variety in Quirarte's classification scheme. Little more is available concerning this court. Generally speaking, the scarcity of Early Classic as well as Late Preclassic ball courts is probably due to their subsequent burial at most sites by later construction episodes.

6. LATE PRECLASSIC CANALS AT CERROS

Water management is a recurrent theme in prestate and state development and must be considered an important element in the evolution of Late Preclassic Period Cerros. The canal survey and excavations were conducted to better discern the hydrology at Cerros. The precise areas selected for intensive investigation were determined by the fortuitous identification of an earthen platform complex associated with a southern section of the main canal, and geographically widely spaced trenches placed across the main canal. (Portions of the following presentation examining the Cerros canal system have appeared elsewhere [Scarborough 1983a; Freidel and Scarborough 1982]).

CANALIZATION

The main canal circumscribed the densest and most massive concentration of structures at the site (Fig. 6.1). It extended over 1,200 meters to form a great arc with its focus at the central precinct. The 37-hectare area enclosed by the canal contained ninety-five mounded features. This area is comparable to that enclosed by the Late Preclassic (Pakluum phase) ditch at Becán, Campeche (Ball and Andrews V 1978; Webster 1976).

Surface elevations indicate a gentle gradient of less than 1 meter descending from west to east across the site from within the infilled canal. Little consistent drop in elevation can be detected along the banks of the canal or at other adjacent areas of high ground. In plan, the form of the canal is sinuous, with a lobate bank that periodically projects into the body of the depression. The eastern end of the canal most strongly manifests this appearance.

The canal traverses three microenvironments in its swing around the site. Much of its course passes through the depressed *bajo*-like setting characterized by *hulub* (*Bravaisia tubiflora*), entanglement, and poorly drained dark gumbo soils. The *hulub bajo* setting dominates the eastern and far-western portions of the main canal, although most of this setting lies outside it. The southern section of the canal is less depressed, being defined by thorn-scrub savanna (see Wiseman 1978), thin clayey topsoils inside the core area, and patches of better-drained high ground (*monte alto*) outside. The canal is wider and generally less distinct in the *hulub bajo* localities.

The canal was initially discovered as a result of its low-lying appearance, in spite of two millennia of infilling, and its relatively sparse cover of vegetation (Fig. 6.2). The latter is a function of the impermeable clays which have infilled the canal as well as the depth

Figure 6.1. Aerial view of main canal before bush clearing activity. This eastern segment was the best defined in the settlement.

Figure 6.2.   Ground view of eastern segment of main canal prior to bush cutting.

of the present trough. These two factors have prolonged the annual period of ponding and prevented many plant species from adapting to the condition. Another factor affecting the visibility of the canal has been the recent removal of the climax vegetation, although secondary and tertiary seres have moved in rapidly. Even conventional aerial photography has helped verify the extent of canalization at Cerros, where the elevated forest canopy has been cut down.

Narrow damlike features were recorded bridging the canal at various locations. Six of these features have been identified and measured approximately 5 meters wide prior to excavation. These causeways were distributed more or less uniformly around the course of the canal, although an absence of causeway construction along the eastern leg of the canal may indicate the disuse of the eastern site periphery following the Late Preclassic abandonment of the site. The causeways were constructed during the Early Classic Period. They were best defined along the southern section of the canal in areas of less-depressed terrain.

Lateral canals issue from the main canal at seven locations, diverging at nearly any angle. These feeder canals were wider and shallower than the main canal, but varied in length, with the longest being over 100 meters. Most of these laterals required extremely fine mapping procedures to locate their course. Their visibility was obscured in the extreme western end of the site as a consequence of recent land modifications, but in the south and east visibility was obscured as a function of siltation processes over the last two thousand years.

The focus of the raised-field research has been in the southwestern portion of the core zone. The major lateral canal draining this area issues north of the main canal. It is well defined and clearly distinguishable in aerial photographs. It is approximately 80 meters long and 10 meters wide and leads to the margin of the raised-field complex. A reservoir 30 meters in diameter separates it from the known field locus. Another system of laterals was intensively mapped in the eastern core area. Although these less well defined features probably provided drainage control across the community, formal raised-field agriculture seems unlikely. The more apparent topographic relief coupled with the pronounced rectilinearity of the depressions found in the southwestern portion of the site suggest that the eastern core area was probably not involved in raised-field agriculture.

The known field plots are shallow rectangular platforms, heavily eroded and much reduced from their original height. The dimensions of the plots range from 14 meters by 28 meters to 22 meters by 40 meters. They are oriented to the cardinal directions. (See Siemens [1982:222, 1983a, 1983b] for other oriented raised fields in Mesoamerica.) At least five fields compose the southwestern core complex, but another four may be present, if badly eroded. Each earthen platform is circumscribed by a narrow, shallow channel.

In addition to the raised fields in this depressed thorn-scrub and *zacatal* setting, there was a system of reservoirs. In two instances, the lateral canals connected into small elliptical depressions. Within the greater survey area, numerous depressions or small seasonal reservoirs were recorded. Although some of these features may have been *dolinen,* or sink holes, and partially attributable to natural processes (Sweeting 1973; Siemens 1978:136), most were deliberately constructed for water storage. Further, the quarrying data introduced earlier (chapter 3) demonstrate the purposeful excavation of the many depressions at Cerros. This is indicated in part by the association of these reservoirs with concentrations of mounded features.

Three discrete catchment basins were apparent in the vicinity of the fields. Moreover, the mapped and excavated basin canal segments circumscribing the plots functioned in a similar way. The basal contours of the lined basin canals are discontinuous and terminate before issuing into the main lateral, suggesting the impoundment of water for drier months. In addition, a shallow gradient system of elevated drainage canals is suggested by our contour map and is understood as having diverted excess runoff into the main canal.

A *sacbe,* or dike, separated the agricultural plots from the remainder of the intensively mapped area. Northwest of the *sacbe* were two of the three reservoirs as well as the southern margin of a large 40,000-square-meter subplaza (Structure 9A). It is likely that the runoff from the plaza space was directed into the reservoir system behind the *sacbe.* This arrangement would have provided adequate potable water and prevented the contamination of this drinking water by the fields to the southwest.

Additional evidence for water management and raised-field agriculture has been suggested elsewhere in the settlement. Seven earthen platforms defined by a shared system of channels have been pace and compass

mapped at the margin of the New River's northeast floodplain zone. They are oriented perpendicular to the present shoreline (N115°W), rather than to the cardinal directions, and rest nearly 1,100 meters southwest of the main canal. These platforms vary in dimensions and fall within the range of those described in the center. The New River platforms occupy a more severely depressed setting than the fields closer to the main canal. House mound density drops off significantly as one approaches the first river terrace and the location of these platforms. No controlled excavations have been conducted in this area, but surface collections from the eroding shoreline suggest an Early Classic occupation.

EXCAVATIONS

Excavation and recovery techniques involved the excavation and screening of naturally defined levels. All exposures were hand-dug and controlled by contiguous excavation units no larger than 2 meters by 2 meters. Flotation samples were run from most strata in the field and limited statements addressing the collected microfossils have been made (Appendix C). To determine the origin and fertility of sediments taken from the canals and field platforms, chemical and physical soils tests have been evaluated (Appendix B). Moreover, pollen samples from several contexts including the water system at Cerros, are currently under study (see Crane 1986).

Main Canal

Excavation of the main canal has been carried out at five locations perpendicular to its long axis. Each trench was positioned to retrieve specific information about the immediate surroundings in which the excavation was carried out, while addressing the overall function of the canal system.

The West Trench

The westernmost trench (OP157) was placed at the foot of the 5-meter-high Structure 21 (Figs. 4.20, 6.3). This location was selected because of (1) the promise of obtaining midden debris from the structure in the canal, (2) the possibility of defining a water-control device in proximity to this large sentinel-like structure and the beginning of the main canal, and (3) the prospect of stratigraphically

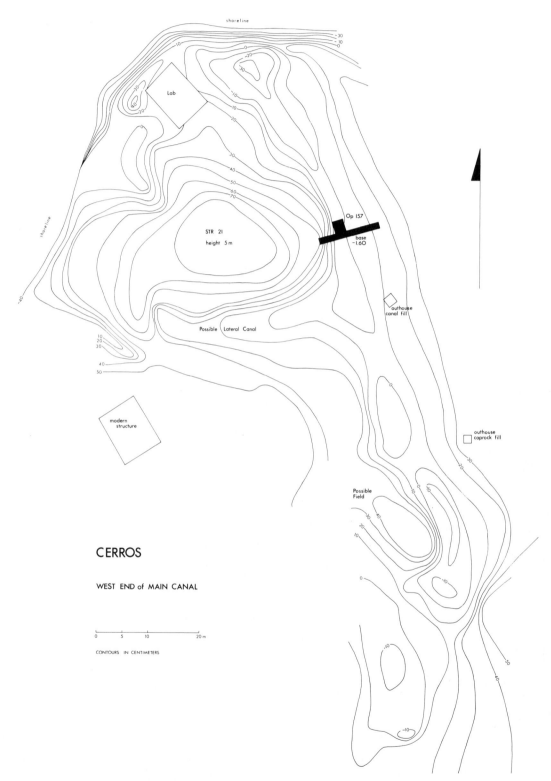

Figure 6.3. Contour map of the Western Canal Segment.

linking the canal with the previously dated Tulix phase Structure 21.

The trench exposed 16 square meters to a maximum depth of 1.60 meters. The main canal at this location was defined by a deeply buried caprock canal bank which dipped to form a symmetrical, U-shaped cross section. The canal cut at this location was approximately 6 meters wide and only 1 meter deep (the latter relative to the arbitrary main canal map datum), although the original height of the canal bank walls may have been higher. The bottom of the canal was exposed by means of three posthole probes. The dry season water table at this location was within 35 meters of the present shoreline and, depending on conditions over Corozal Bay (i.e., dry *norte* disturbances), the trench would fill and hold half to full capacity of the original canal volume.

The basal matrix was typified by the same sterile, friable, white marl or clean *sascab* to be noted from the other canal exposures. Above the original canal cut lay 1 meter of friable, blocky gray clay silt. Most of the matrix examined was taken from the upper 50 centimeters because of the rising water table. The entire matrix was heavily intruded by pebbles to small limestone boulders, although the western half of the exposure contained a greater concentration of debris than the eastern portion. Fall stones are believed to have slumped from the adjacent Structure 21 and probably indicate a contemporaneous abandonment of both the mound and the trough. Near the bottom of the exposure the clays were more compacted. The sediments were severely recemented, making microstratigraphic control impossible. Overlying the lower gray clays were 40 centimeters of viscous dark gray clay. The western three-quarters of the canal trough was again heavily intruded by pebbles to small limestone boulders.

The eastern bank area was composed of friable light gray clay with small gravel-sized inclusions of white marl. These clays appear to have been retained behind a crude alignment of small-boulder-sized stones. It was difficult to identify the original sterile decomposed caprock behind the stone concentration, because of the mottled nature of the matrix. However, at approximately 1 meter below the present surface, indurated caprock was encountered behind the stone alignment.

In the far western portion of the exposure, indurated caprock was found at approximately 80 centimeters from the surface. Again, a concentration of stone, two to three courses high, was apparent at the edge of

the canal bank. The matrix behind the concentration consisted of a viscous dark gray clay similar to the sediments in the canal. The matrix near the caprock was less intruded by large cobbles to small boulders than was that higher in the stratigraphy. Generally, the darker clays in this region were more mottled by intrusions and mound fall than elsewhere in the exposure. The artifact inventory was greatest in the higher reaches of the western side of the exposure. The entire trench was covered by a 10-centimeter-thick viscous black loamy clay intruded by pebble- to small-cobble-sized limestone gravels.

The exposure indicates that the main canal was excavated to a more shallow depth at the western end of the core area than at other locations. Although a severe amount of siltation buried the main canal course, the amount of soil overlying the caprock at both sides of the cut suggests the former presence of raised fields. This is argued on two points. First, the height of the main canal bank would have been considerably greater and more in keeping with the critical depth of the main canal from other exposures if the banks of the canal were raised and defined by flanking field plots. Second, the degree of siltation at this locus is significantly greater than at other locations, suggesting the erosion of raised-field sediments into the main canal. This line of argument is further supported by the concentration of stones found at the edge of the canal bank, which may represent the lower courses of buttresses supporting the field platforms as those are defined elsewhere in the settlement.

In any case, the canal seems to have been infilled from its adjacent banks. Some of the sediment was derived from the margins of the canal, but the substantial amount of rubble limestone suggests a colluvial origin for the rest, probably from the summmit of Structure 21. Preliminary examination of the ceramic collection from the cut indicates a mixed Late Preclassic/Early Classic date. In addition to pottery, a small amount of bone and charcoal was noted from the matrix.

The absence of bay beach sands in the basal sediments of the canal suggests a change in the present shoreline (see chapter 3). The proximity of the present beach sands and the elevated position of the bay level relative to the bottom of the canal indicate that the main canal would have been invaded by the bay if the bay level were the same today as in the past. It is suggested that the land mass at Cerros was formerly at least 1 meter higher along the coast or that the water level was a comparable amount lower.

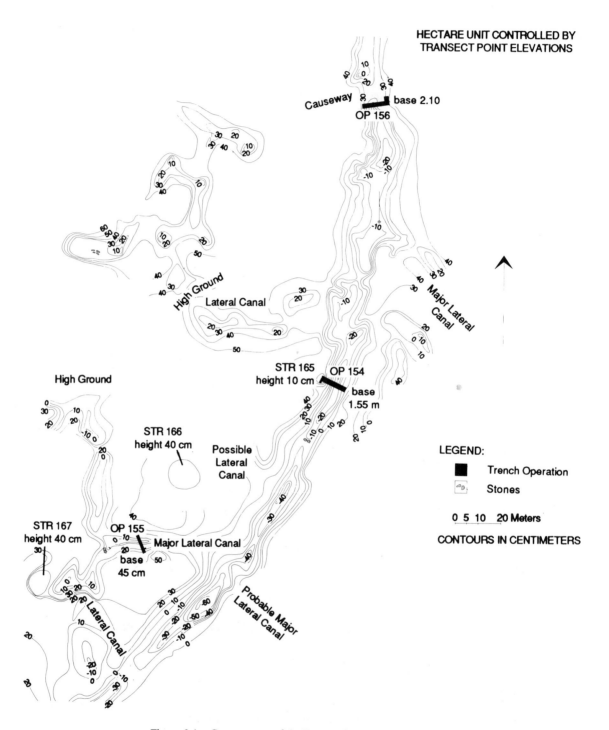

Figure 6.4. Contour map of the Eastern Canal Segment.

The East Trench

Another trench (OP154) was placed on the eastern margin of the core zone (Fig. 6.4). A small ground-level structure (Structure 165, chapter 4) on the immediate margin of the canal bank had been revealed during the intensive mapping of the main canal. The trench location was chosen to define the nature of ground-level occupation with specific reference to the main canal. Abundant midden debris was anticipated within the canal trough.

The trench exposed 25 square meters to a maximum depth of 1.55 meters. The canal cut was a symmetrical U-shape, although the bank sloped downward at a gentle angle before dropping abruptly into the canal (Fig. 6.5). The canal exposure at this location was 3.20 meters wide and 1.70 meters deep relative to the arbitrary main canal vertical datum used for the entire canal system. The bottom of the canal was defined by the sterile clean white marl, or *sascab,* exposed at the base of the caprock. The basal sediments were covered by the dry season water table, and the bottom of the canal was discernible only through postholing.

The bulk of the sediment in the canal consisted of a blocky gray clay loam containing numerous gypsum crystals. The matrix was severely recemented through the effects of percolating ground-water charged with calcite or dolomite. *Pomacea* burrows further disrupted the stratigraphy. A significant inventory of midden debris was retrieved from the exposure, with the greatest concentration of material coming from the western margin of the unit immediately outside and below the ground-level structure. Pottery, chert, bone, charcoal, and ash were collected and identified. The eastern portion of the unit exposed additional concentrations of sherd debris at the edge of the canal. Toward the center, the matrix graded imperceptibly into a lighter gray clay loam containing a lower concentration of gypsum crystals and a greater frequency of limestone gravels. It contained some cultural debris. The bedding plane of the sherds indicated a lateral slope wash deposition for this sediment.

The canal was capped by a 10-centimeter-thick viscous black gumbo clay containing few limestone gravels. At the boundary between this humic horizon and the underlying gray clay loam was a diminutive U-shaped trough in the center of the canal. It represents a stone-lined canal segment constructed some 1.20 meters above the base of the original canal cut and after the major siltation process at Cerros. It

may be associated with the Early Classic reuse of the canal system.

Because of the narrow width of the canal at this location, a sizable area of canal bank was exposed in our 12-meter-long trench. The eastern bank revealed a pavement of tabular limestone gravels. The pavement did not rest on a paleosol or a lens of gray clay loam, which suggests that the caprock was scraped of soil before the pavement was laid. The pavement, not revealed at other canal bank locations, is similar to plaza surfaces exposed elsewhere in the settlement. A thin veneer of light gray clay loam overlay the pavement and in turn was capped by the black gumbo.

On the west bank the ground-level Structure 165 was identified, but no architectural features were apparent. This type of poor preservation has been frequently reported in the settlement. Even though the structure had been placed directly on the caprock, no clearly defined postholes were noted. The quantity and quality of midden debris at the foot of the structure within the canal suggest that the structure was a domicile. In addition, a possible step into the canal trough was indicated during our excavation of the bank. However, the advanced deterioration of the canal bank at this location did not allow a positive identification. A thin humus covered the exposure.

Ceramics in this exposure indicate a Late Preclassic date for the initiation of the feature. The original canal cut is associated with a constriction in the canal, perhaps made necessary as a crossover point from the core area into the periphery of the site. The possible step in the western canal bank may be the location of a former log bridge (after Wilken 1969). The pavement on the east side may be the continuation of a stone path into the eastern *hulub bajo.* The location of a structure on the west bank might be expected, given a degree of controlled access to the core area. Following the infilling of the canal system, a minor "echo" canal (after Haury 1976:149–150) was crudely constructed to collect water in a manner not unlike that demonstrated at the southern margin of the core area.

The Northeast Trench

At the northeastern end of the visible main canal segment, another trench (OP156) was placed across an area of high ground (Fig. 6.4). The unit rests approximately 150 meters south of the present shoreline. This location was selected to (1) examine the terminus of the present canal trough and (2) reveal, in part,

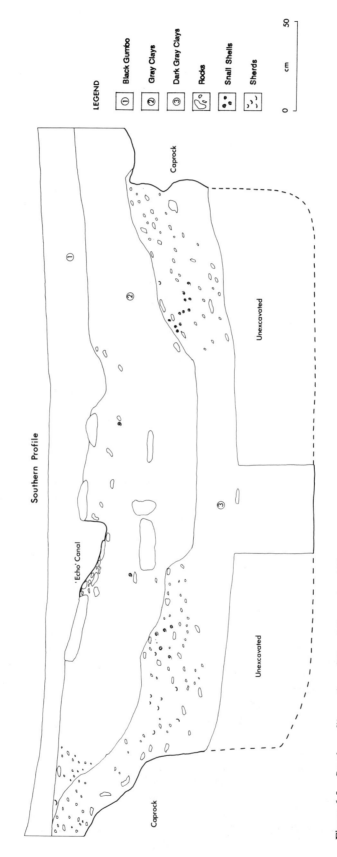

Figure 6.5.   South profile section of Canal Operation 154.

the function of the canal by excavating at a potential raised causeway location.

This operation was the most complex in the canalization program (Fig. 6.6). The trench exposed 30 square meters to a maximum depth of 1.80 meters, the latter relative to the arbitrary main canal vertical site datum. The canal cross section revealed a stepped, asymmetrical U-shape with a broad platform or sill positioned at the eastern base of the canal (Fig. 6.7). The canal dimensions at this location were approximately 5 meters wide and 2.10 meters deep relative to the vertical site datum. The canal bottom was defined by the same sterile white marl, or *sascab,* reported from the other exposures. It was located 40 centimeters below the dry season water table and was demonstrable by the positioning of 13 postholes within the canal banks. The postholing also revealed the nature of the basal

Figure 6.6. Northeast canal trench across main canal (OP154).

platform or sill which projected from the eastern bank approximately 2.25 meters before abruptly dropping 75 centimeters to the bottom of the canal channel. In plan, the sill ran diagonally across the floor of the canal from the southeast side of the exposure into the northwest profile. In addition, the east canal bank revealed two carved steps inset into the indurated canal bank caprock. Although severely weathered, they appeared clearly in the south profile exposure. The west bank of the canal was poorly defined but appears to have been stepped, dropping precipitously into the canal course. It seems to have had one step but no projecting sill.

The matrix within the canal consists of a dark gray clay flecked with white marl. It was severely recemented and affected by worm casts. *Pomacea* intruded throughout the matrix. The soils were generally better sorted in this exposure than elsewhere, though a few limestone gravels were apparent near the bottom. The highest incidence of gravel was reported at the flanks of the canal bank. Although little cultural debris was recovered from on the sill, a great deal of trash (pottery, flint, bone, charcoal, and ash) was collected from the basal course of the canal trough. Little debris was found directly on the canal floor; rather, it lay 40 centimeters above the present canal bottom. Most of the sherds were horizontally bedded or bedded in the plane of the canal bank contour. At the banks of the canal, the matrix was a more sandy texture but mottled by gray clay fill.

The unit was excavated in three vertical strips containing numerous horizontal levels and lots. In carrying out the excavation in this manner, we recovered a whole red slip collared jar (Tuk Red-on-Red Trickle: Tuk Variety) sealed 1.50 meters below a presumed Early Classic walkway bridging the canal following the infilling process (Fig. 6.8). This Tulix phase vessel was found upright and resting 20 centimeters above the sill at the east end of the canal bank. Other large sherds, dating to the Late Preclassic, were collected from this area as well.

On the western margin of the canal another vessel was isolated, although it was broken and disarticulated. This pot was a slightly larger version (12 centimeters in diameter) of the same form reported at the east end. It was resting upside down and may originally have been placed on a steplike contour noted in the west canal bank. Neither of these vessels contained offerings and, judging from the context, were portable water containers.

In addition to a sizable inventory of ceramic debris, a good bit of limestone gravel was removed from the

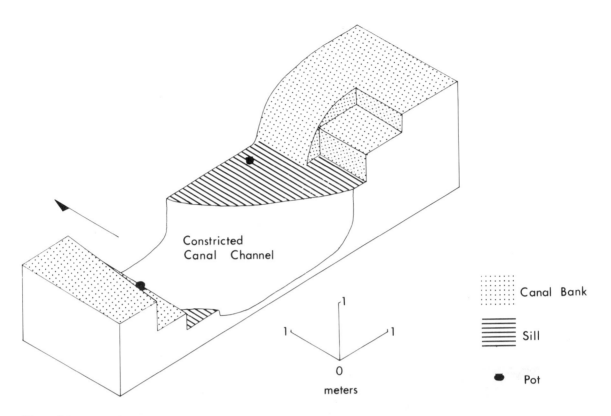

Constricted
Canal Channel

Canal Bank

Sill

Pot

meters

Figure 6.7.   Isometric reconstruction of northeastern canal section. The two vessels date to the Tulix phase and were found
sealed by an overlying Early Classic walkway.

Figure 6.8.   Northeast canal trench (OP154). A whole pot rests *in situ* immediately above the canal sill. The flagstones to the
right capped the infilled canal sediments.

west canal flank. The west bank of the canal appears to have partially slumped away from the more indurated caprock to produce a shallow niche in the western profile. This is likely a consequence of groundwater action, but may have been accelerated by the weight exerted from the overlying walkway traffic.

At approximately 1.70 meters above the basal sediments in the canal trough, and overlying the bulk of the canal matrices, was a narrow limestone walkway about 1 meter wide and 10 meters long (Fig. 6.9). The stones were water-smoothed, small tabular limestone boulders, a single course high, laid horizontally across the high northern end of the main canal. At the west end of the walkway on the caprock bank, a dense concentration of coarse limestone pebbles was

Figure 6.9. Northeast canal trench (OP154). The flagstone path across the infilled canal segment appears to be Early Classic. The diminutive stone grid to the lower right postdates the walkway.

isolated. Their distribution was restricted to the north side of the walkway in a 2-meter by 2-meter area. These stones were related to the construction of the causeway and may represent an infilling repair operation associated with the slumping of the underlying bank.

Also on the west bank, to the immediate south of the walkway, another concentration of stone was identified. This concentration of medium-sized pebbles consisted of a single-course gridiron alignment corresponding to the orientation of the walkway. The stones were placed in the viscous black gumbo clay humus, slightly above the caprock bank. The entire exposure was capped by the same black gumbo humus found throughout the depressed canal trough.

The stratigraphy generally illustrates the nature of the main canal. Although lateral lensing was not clearly visible, the apparent concentration of sherd debris at the margins of the canal bank suggests that the matrices were entering the canal from the bank and not longitudinally down the canal course. The sill identified in the cross section is understood to be a landing or platform used during the dry season to obtain water from the deeper canal channel to the west. The lower canal course might be viewed as a dipping pool, attainable by resting on the low-lying sill. The canal cut is quite narrow at this lower location, approximately 2 meters wide from the edge of the sill to the western canal bank. This constriction is interpreted to have been a device for controlling the amount of water in a larger pool located immediately south of our trench, as revealed by the contour map (Fig. 6.4).

The pots in the canal are believed to have been deposited during a rapid infilling event in association with the abandonment of the system. Both vessels appear to have rested on carved caprock treads and subsequently to have slipped into the muck early in the collapse of the adjacent field system. Although the type and presence of other pottery fragments in the canal may have some ritual significance (Garber 1981, 1983), the excavation data point to a more mundane explanation. The canal sediments are believed to have been deposited over a generation or more during the Terminal Late Preclassic phase. The extreme amount of sediment in this exposure and the complete infilling of the canal segment north of this location may indicate the presence of additional eroded fields.

The walkway is argued to be Early Classic in date due in part to the apparent attraction of this locus during the Late Preclassic Period. It is interpreted as

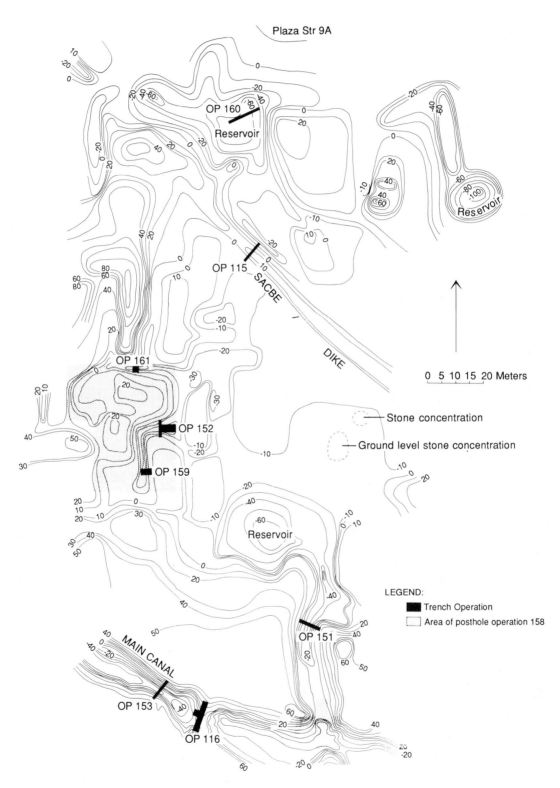

Figure 6.10.   Contour map of the west-central core area. The known raised fields lie to the south and west of the *sacbe*.

a crossover point during the Late Preclassic Period because of the constricted form of the canal at this location. Our survey and excavation program has demonstrated the continued presence of a sizable population subsequent to the halt in nearly all private and public construction at the end of the Late Preclassic Period. The Early Classic population would have used this location as a crossover point because of the greater infilling and the accessibility of features reoccupied in the periphery. The diminutive stone grid alignment on the west bank of the canal, whose function is enigmatic, is believed to be Late Postclassic in origin. Given the amount of lateral erosion from the sides of the main canal, it is unlikely that this formation would be preserved unless it were quite late in the sequence. The Late Classic and Early Postclassic periods are not demonstrable at Cerros.

The Southern Trenches

This location was selected because the canal relief contour was well defined and in proximity to the known earthen field platforms. One of the two trenches at this location was placed across and parallel to the long axis of one of the damlike features (a causeway). A second trench was placed 14 meters west of the first to reveal any local variability between the two sections. The original canal cut was excavated through limestone caprock to a depth of 2 meters and a width of 6 meters (Figs. 6.10, 6.11).

The First Trench. Our initial trench across the damlike feature (OP116) exposed 26 square meters to a maximum depth of 2 meters (Figs. 6.12, 6.13). The basal canal sediments were exposed in a 1-by 2-meter exposure only. The bottom of the canal was defined by a sterile white friable marl as well as by the dry season water table (Fig. 6.14). All canal sediments were moist. A 5-centimeter-thick dark blocky loamy clay overlay the parent material, although it feathered out near the center or bottom of the canal. This matrix was not viscous as identified elsewhere in the settlement. Overlying and intruding into this layer was a 20-centimeter deposit of decomposing angular limestone gravel, in the form of small cobbles overlain by pebble-sized gravels. Again, the concentration of gravels was thickest on the southern side of the exposure and found to pinch out toward the center or bottom of the canal.

Figure 6.11. Aerial view of southwest portion of core area. The main canal circumscribes the major architecture as well as the known raised fields. The fields are best identified by the dark patches of *muk* separated by narrow channels of savanna grass.

The next stratigraphic level represented the bulk of the canal sediments. Most of the 1.5 meters of friable blocky gray clays were removed from the entire horizontal exposure. These clays graded from darker to lighter value (after Munsell chart) as the profile was ascended, although no boundary between the sediments was discernible. No microstratigraphic control of these sediments was possible, as chemical recrystallization and the effect of burrowing snails (primarily *Pomacea flagellata*) had altered their appearance. The darker gray clays near the base of the exposure were more compact than those deposited later. A pure C'oh phase sherd sample was taken from these gray clays. In addition, fragments of bone, charcoal flecks, and stone debitage were recovered.

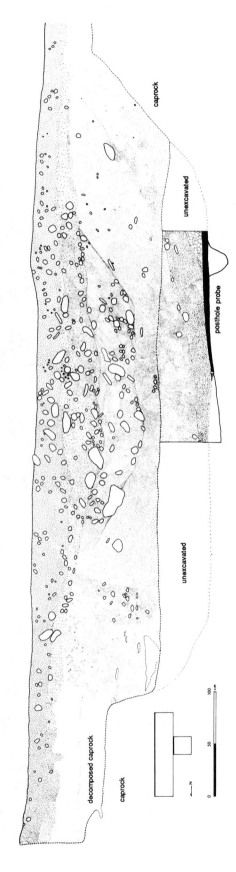

Figure 6.12.   East profile section of Canal Operation 116.

Figure 6.13.   Southern trench (Trench 1) across main canal (OP116).

Figure 6.14.   Close-up of southern trench (Trench 1, OP116). The dry season water table is apparent at the bottom of the canal.

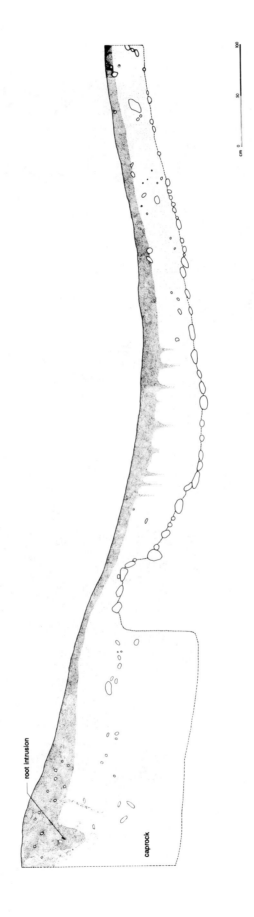

root intrusion

caprock

cm 0   50   100

Figure 6.15.   East profile section of Canal Operation 153.

Some of the carbonized material associated with the upper 50 centimeters of this level has provided a date of 2300 ± 150 years B.P. (350 B.C.) (SMU 774 [5,568-year half-life]). Calibrating on the basis of tree-ring data at the 95% confidence interval (Klein et al. 1982) provides a calendar date of 403 ± 377 years B.C.

Capping and intruding into the canal sediments at this location was an infilled lazy-U-shaped deposit, 3 meters in length and 80 centimeters in maximum depth, grading from a dark loamy clay at the top to a light gray clay near the bottom. The sediments were a loose, blocky clay heavily intruded by limestone gravel ranging in size from pebbles to large cobbles. Although the texture, structure, and consistency of the fill seemed similar throughout the deposit, the upper 40 centimeters was of a darker value and faintly segregated from the lower 40 centimeters by a gradually smooth boundary. A somewhat similar deposit to that described for the lower 40 centimeters of light gray clay within the infilled U-shaped lens was found to intrude into the underlying gray clays near the northern margin of the canal profile. It was intruded by coarse-pebble-sized limestone gravel to a depth of 80 centimeters (Fig. 6.12). Early Classic ceramics were the most recent diagnostics taken from this infilling operation.

Decomposing limestone and gravel were found on the immediate northern and southern margins of the canal cut. Thin discontinuous lenses of granular friable yellow marl issued from the upper decomposing northern limestone caprock defining the vertical bank or side wall of the canal. Our excavation through 40 centimeters of the decomposing limestone caprock revealed the massive indurated caprock defining the lower reaches of the canal side walls. The original canal cut profile was U-shaped with a less steep southern slope forming an approximate 45° angle with the flat bottom of the trough. Overlying the decomposing upper caprock at the banks of the canal was a continuous 10-centimeter-thick layer of mottled gray clay similar to that defined within the canal. These clays spilled into the canal section. The complete excavation exposure was capped by a dark, viscous, blocky, loamy clay intruded by pebble- to small-cobble-sized limestone gravels.

The Second Trench. The second trench was placed across and perpendicular to the long axis of the main canal (OP153). Its precise location was selected to explain an apparent constriction in the width of the canal at this location. It was also anticipated that

less energy and time would be expended in obtaining an additional cross section, given the narrowing of the canal at this location. The excavations exposed 8 square meters to a maximum depth of 1.6 meters (Figs. 6.15, 6.16). The same blocky, friable, light gray clays found partially sealed by the damlike feature in the first trench represented nearly all the fill in this exposure. Although we were unable to define the basal sediments in the canal, we did identify the near-vertical northern canal side wall. It consisted of the same granular, friable, yellow decomposing limestone as revealed in the first trench. The yellow limestone matrix was again found to spill into the gray clay canal sediments to produce thin, discontinuous lensing. Below this lensing and within the gray clays was collected a pure, although obviously unsealed, Late Preclassic

Figure 6.16. Upper lined section of southern trench (Trench 2, OP153). Dating to the Early Classic. The Late Preclassic canal cut underlines the exposure.

ceramic sample. A large chert blade was also recovered (not to be confused as a biface).

South of the northern exposure, a shallow single-course concentration of small-cobble-sized limestone gravel was identified. These stones lined the remainder of the exposure, which extended approximately 6 square meters to the south. These cobbles formed a lazy asymmetrical U with a steep northern side wall in cross section. The sediments probed below this feature revealed the same light gray clays as located to the north of the stone lining. The sediments overlying the stone feature were a slightly darker gray clay of the same texture, structure and consistency as those below. Overlying the entire deposit was a 10-centimeter layer of dark, blocky, viscous clay loam. Soil cracking was apparent at this level and chemical recrystallization and intrusive snails (principally *Pomacea*) were present throughout the light gray clays. An Early Classic date has been assigned to the debris taken from above the stone lining.

The south segment of the main canal, excavated at two locations (OP153 and OP116), revealed a 2-meter-deep, 6-meter-wide U-shaped canal cut. It was later modified by an Early Classic check dam and stone-lined catchment pond. The bottom of the canal at this location is 1.60 meters below the arbitrary main canal vertical datum. The sediments associated with the Late Preclassic infilling of the canal, given their depth and lateral lensing, strongly suggest a raised-field origin. The soil matrices are similar to those reported in the other three exposures within the main canal and appear to have the same depositional history.

Figure 6.17. Ground view of Southern Lateral Canal (OP151). The white backdirt pile identifies the trenching operation.

Lateral Canals

The Southern Lateral Canal Trench

Forty-five meters northeast of the damlike feature exposed in the southern trench of the main canal (OP116), another trench (OP151) was positioned across a lateral canal draining into the main canal (Fig. 6.17). This lateral canal lies at a right angle to the main canal and extends northward for over 70 meters. At its northern end, the channel takes an abrupt dogleg to the west. The contour map of the locality indicates a small reservoir or catchment basin near this bend in the channel's course (Fig. 6.10).

This lateral canal was selected for investigation because it connected the identified earthen field platforms of the core area to the main canal. The trench was positioned at a well-defined location of the eastern canal bank, which was anticipated to provide a convincing profile of the canal. The construction of this canal was not modified through time, as was the case with the main canal. The lateral, approximately 90 centimeters deep and at least 8 meters wide, was much shallower and wider than the main canal (Fig. 6.18). The bottom of the canal was also 80 centimeters below the arbitrary main canal vertical datum. It was defined by a shallow dish-shaped cross section cut into the limestone caprock, although the excavations did not extend far enough west to define the exact nature of the opposite bank. The flat bottom of the canal rose at a 45° angle in forming the eastern bank.

Figure 6.18. Southern Laterial Canal Trench (OP151).

Eight square meters of deposit were removed to a maximum depth of 90 centimeters. The fill was the same homogeneous blocky gray clay defined in the main canal section, although it appeared to be of a slightly lighter value. The fill was not heavily intruded by limestone gravel. The sediments were recrystallized and affected by gastropod intrusions (*Pomacea*). No microstratigraphy was evident. Overlying the 80 centimeters of gray clays was a 10-centimeter cap of blocky dark clay loam topsoil. The boundary separating these two layers was not abrupt but graded between levels. The underlying parent material defining the trough of the canal consisted of the same yellow limestone found overlying the indurated caprock in the southern trenches of the main canal (OP116). Although the ceramic sample was a small, mixed one, the great majority of identifiable sherds date to the Late Preclassic Period.

The Eastern Lateral Canal Trench

On the eastern side of the core area, we traced the course of an apparent drainage network. The survey team followed a lateral canal into the interior core of the community (Fig. 6.4). Only the depressed linear troughs were recorded, because the amount of vegetation limited visibility. The canal-like depressions appeared to be oriented to the cardinal directions. No field platforms were identified, but a few ground-level structures were reported.

The eastern lateral canal trenching operation (OP155) was placed northeast-southwest across the course of a lateral canal approximately 35 meters west of the main canal, into which runoff was directed. A trench in this location was predicted to yield information about (1) the amount of quarrying that occurred generally in this area, (2) the presence of raised fields, and (3) the relationship between ground-level residential space and the core area drainage system. Unfortunately, our limited exposure did not reveal as much information as anticipated.

This trench exposed 14 square meters and was excavated to a maximum depth of 60 centimeters. As was the case with the shallow lateral exposure in the southwestern portion of the core area (OP151), only a limited amount of caprock appears to have been removed to produce the trough. The base of the ill-defined feature was approximately 2.5 meters wide by 30 centimeters deep. However, the upper banks of the trough were separated by as much as 8 meters, producing a dish-shaped cross section 80 centimeters deep. The bottom of the trough relative to the vertical main canal site datum rested 45 centimeters below datum. The base of the trough was defined by indurated caprock with a thin deposit of granular limestone sand eroding from the caprock. The depression fill was identified by a dark, viscous, gray clay intruded by bits of limestone gravel. The gray clay on the high ground contained more limestone gravel than the trough. No buttress stones were located, as revealed elsewhere in the settlement. The entire exposure was capped by black gumbo clay humus. Late Preclassic slipped wares predominated in the sparse identifiable ceramic collection.

The exposure is interpreted to be the remains of a shallow canal established to drain this area of the site. Raised fields were not demonstrable from our exposure. Kitchen garden plots were likely to have been present in this area, but clear archaeological associations were lacking. Given the presence of ground-level

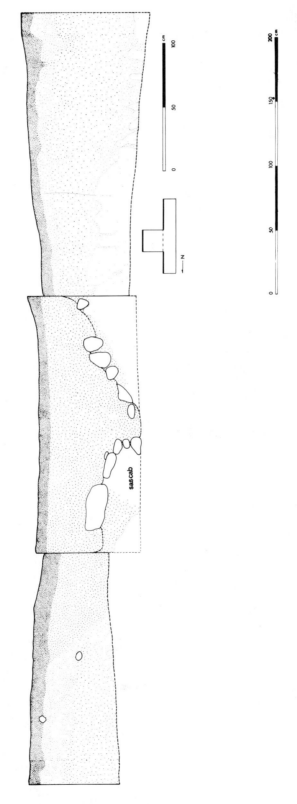

sascab

Figure 6.19.   East profile section of Basin Canal (OP152).

structures in this area, it is suspected that these minor canals diverted water away from residential space and into the main canal. Most of the thin layer of topsoil in the area is thought to be soil development subsequent to the Late Preclassic abandonment of the site.

Fields and Associated Features

More survey and excavation was conducted in the west-central portion of the core area (Figs. 6.10, 6.11), which was the focus of our raised-field research. The greater visibility of these features in this area, both on the ground and by means of aerial photographs, permitted an examination of the raised-field drainage system in microcosm.

Basin Canal 1A

Excavations carried out within and between two earthen platforms during the 1979 field season revealed a narrow, shallow channel (1 meter wide and 1 meter deep) initially believed to circumscribe each platform (see Freidel and Scarborough 1982). Our trench (OP152) was positioned to expose both the matrices of the earthen platforms and the profile of a minor feeder canal. The exact location of the trench was chosen because of the relief found at this point. Nine horizontal square meters of deposit were removed to a maximum depth of 80 centimeters (Fig. 6.19).

The canal section was defined in part by a sterile, off-white, granular, friable marl (Fig. 6.20). Excavations into the flanking platforms indicated that this sterile sediment may have been intentionally mounded in forming the side walls of the canal, although the matrix was quite mottled and difficult to identify clearly. Positioned above and intruding into the off-white clay were smooth, although pitted, cobbles and small-boulder-sized limestone gravels resting to form an ill-defined, lazy, asymmetrical, U-shaped cross section. Although the canal is thought to have been defined by these uncut stones, some of the stones had fallen

Figure 6.20. Raised-field excavations in progress, Basin Canal 1A (OP152). The parallel-running buttress stones define the width of the Basin Canal through the center of the photograph. The view is toward the east.

from their original position. Overlying and settling between them were dark, blocky, friable gray clays similar to those identified in the other canal sections. These sediments accounted for 80 centimeters of canal fill and, in turn, were capped by a 10-centimeter-thick lens of dark, blocky, viscous, organically rich clay loam topsoil. Again, the sediments appeared to be recrystallized and intruded by snails, although some lateral lensing was apparent. Ceramic debris taken from within the canal was badly mixed, spanning all early periods of occupation represented at Cerros.

The adjacent platforms were exposed on either margin of the stone concentration (Fig. 6.21). Excavations were taken down to a depth comparable to that reached in exposing the flanking canal segment. Exposure of the northern edge of the southernmost platform revealed the off-white granular friable clay overlying the decomposing yellow limestone caprock. Although the off-white clay marl (*sascab*) was severely mottled by the same postdepositional agents responsible for the

condition of the canal sediments, the lens was thicker at the canal bank margin and found to contour upward with the position of the overlying stone concentration. The southern end of the lens gradually sloped down and out of the profile.

The sediments overlying the mounded canal bank deposit were a lighter, blocky, friable clay identical to those sediments within the canal, except for a slight color difference. This maximum 1-meter-thick deposit was severely mottled but graded smoothly from the basal light clays to the surficial dark clays. High phosphorous readings were recorded in this southern platform (Appendix B). The surface of the platform was covered by a 10-centimeter-thick blocky, viscous, organic topsoil, with soil cracking in part responsible for the mottled appearance of the sediments. The exposure on the northernmost platform was excavated to a level 30 centimeters higher than the maximum depth elsewhere in the operation. Nevertheless, the exposure in both platforms was taken down to the same

Figure 6.21.   Basin Canal 1A (OP152). The Basin Canal is defined by the concentration of stone, with the earthen platforms identified by the extended arms of the T-trench. Note the conspicuous absence of stone from the platforms. The view is toward the south.

level as the basal rubble lining of the ditch and found not to reveal even one stone in their fill.

The ceramic sample from the two platforms, while small (less than one hundred sherds), was exclusively Late Preclassic in date (Robertson personal communication). These sherds were large, unweathered, and accompanied by additional trash in the form of bone and lithic debris. The ceramic sample from within the ditch defined by the rubble linings included both Late Preclassic and Early Classic diagnostics. These sherds were badly weathered (Robertson personal communication). Given that the platforms were artificially constructed and contain only Late Preclassic diagnostics, we infer that the fields were built during this period. The presence of Early Classic material in the ditch is not surprising, because nearby mounds show evidence of ephemeral reoccupation during this period. The weathered quality of the sherds in the ditch proper suggests that the silting-in process was a slow one and that the ditch was still open following the Late Preclassic abandonment of Cerros as well as during the Early Classic Period.

In the 1981 field season, we expanded the trench to clarify the course of the feeder canal. In extending the unit east, we found that the stone lining or buttressing terminated at the juncture of three apparent platforms. The sediment inside the canal basin was again the same as that on the adjacent fields. The *sascab* did not appear to be mounded up on the east side of the canal basin, as observed elsewhere in the canal cross section, but the buttress stones were well defined. The entire matrix was mottled by *Pomacea* burrows.

The matrix inside the canal consisted of a gray clay that had undergone severe recrystallization. Outside the canal, in the platform matrix, the sediments were similar to those found in the canal. Below these gray platform clays the matrix was defined by severely eroding caprock. It consisted of a granular, yellowish gray sandy clay which overlay the indurated caprock, with the decomposing caprock in this area being 30 to 40 centimeters thick. The ill-defined boundary between the platform soils and the underlying matrices indicated some *in situ* soil development, suggesting only minor modification of the original ground surface. The quantity of soil identified relative to other exposures in the settlement (including OP155 and that underlying the excavated house mounds), coupled with the presence of lined canal segments and high phosphate readings, suggested that this area was

intensively exploited for agricultural purposes. The entire exposure was capped by a thin lens of viscous black gumbo clay.

Basin Canal 1B

At the other end of this canal basin (12 meters south-southwest), another trench (OP159) was excavated to further define the dimensions of the feature. The 5-square-meter exposure at the termination of the visible trough revealed a cul-de-sac depression. The canal basin was shown to terminate with boulder-sized limestone caprock defining the feature's southern margin. The northern canal profile revealed a 1-meter-wide canal section excavated to a maximum depth of 70 centimeters. The base of the canal was 55 centimeters below site datum. Solid caprock defined the east bank of the canal basin but it was quarried out on the east platform side of the exposure. The solid caprock bank appeared as a vertical dike supporting or containing the eastern platform matrices. The western platform buttress stones were similar to those reported in the first trench (OP152) but were less well preserved. The matrices in the canal were the same mottled gray clays identified elsewhere in the canal system. However, the eastern field platform was composed of a series of 3-centimeter-thick *sascab* lenses separated by 10-to 20-centimeter-thick gray clay lenses to a depth of 1 meter. No stone intruded into the field exposures.

Canal Basin 1 trenches A and B defined the northern and western margins of one field platform as well as the course of the adjacent canal basin. The canal appears to have been formed partly by the removal of the caprock and partly by the introduction of soil to the fields. The platforms were buttressed by small boulders and, in one case, by natural caprock quarried to form an apparent dike support. The area to the south and west of the second trench (OP159) appears to be a less impacted and more elevated unquarried caprock zone. It may have been modified to catch and direct runoff into the otherwise closed canal catchment basin.

Basin Canal 2

To confirm the association of stone buttressing with linear depressions, we excavated a 2-meter by 2-meter unit on the north side of an adjacent platform (OP161). The southeast side of this large platform had been examined by our 1979 trench (OP152). Our new unit exposed a lazy, asymmetrical U-shaped cross section of the canal basin, approximately 1.2 meters wide and 1 meter deep, with its base 70 centimeters below site datum. The basin fill was the same recemented gray clay defined elsewhere, with the decomposed caprock underlying the exposure. *Pomacea* burrows and root intrusion severely mottled the profile. A small amount of badly eroded unidentifiable cultural debris was collected. The entire unit was overlain by a 15-centimeter-thick lens of viscous black gumbo clay topsoil.

The trench confirmed the presence of another canal basin flanking and defining the north side of this large field platform and the south ends of the two other probable platforms. The canal sediments apparently represent former raised-field platform fill.

Reservoir Trench

Within the survey area, numerous depressions or seasonal reservoirs have been recorded. On the northeastern side of the *sacbe* (Fig. 6.10), a large amorphous depression was identified and examined to determine its depth and form relative to the other features in this area. Some of the largest structures in the settlement lie to the immediate north of this feature (e.g., the Structure 10 Group), and their occupants are believed to have used the basin as a catchment zone. The eastern side of the basin was clearly defined, in part by six small tabular limestone boulders resting at a 45° angle against the bank of the feature. They appear to be the remnants of a retaining feature defining the edge of the reservoir.

The trench OP160 exposed 4 square meters at the edge of the reservoir and demonstrated that the entire reservoir was not lined. The matrix was the same gray

clay intruded by small limestone pebbles as well as *Pomacea* burrows, with the impermeable caprock only 80 centimeters below the stone-lined retaining feature. The entire exposure was capped by the black gumbo clay topsoil.

The reservoir was in a position to have held a great deal of runoff water from the low-lying plaza Structure 9A and probably functioned as a catchment basin. The rather limited amount of fill at the margins of this depression appears to be associated with the northern plaza runoff rather than with eroded raised-field platforms. This suggests their absence in the vicinity.

Sacbe Trench

The Sacbe 1, or raised causeway (Feature 126), connects the ball court Structure 50 Group with the plaza area on which Structures 10, 13, 14, and 15 rest (Fig. 6.10). It traverses the most low-lying *zacatal* in the settlement, and is well defined across 210 meters of clay gumbo or *yax'om* soils. In plan, the *sacbe* is not altogether straight but reflects a slight bow or curve. The actual orientation of the feature is approximately N46°W. In addition to facilitating travel, the *sacbe* may have functioned as a dike or partition separating the private water source of the reservoir and greater *zacatal* from the more public water sources of the raised fields and major canal. Our trench (OP115) was positioned within the northern third of the feature across a well-defined segment perpendicular to the long axis. The exposure was intended to provide information about (1) the extent of quarrying carried out in this area and (2) the form and possible function of the *sacbe*.

The trench exposed 8 square meters to a maximum depth of 50 centimeters (Fig. 6.22). The surface level was defined by a 10-centimeter-thick lens of black

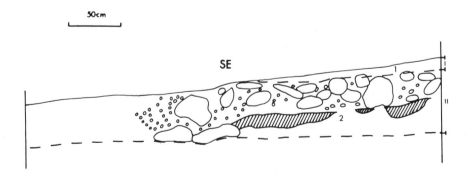

Figure 6.22.   Profile from Feature 126A (OP115a).

viscous clay or gumbo analogous to that defined in adjacent *bajo* settings. The top of the causeway appears to have been covered by these sediments during the seasonal inundation of the greater depression. The black gumbo was thicker on the easternmost end of the feature than on the western end, possibly reflecting a more recent siltation of the deeper *bajo* located on this side of the *sacbe*. The first excavation level was terminated on encountering the continuous layer of limestone cobbles and small boulders defining the present surface of the *sacbe*. The width of the *sacbe* revealed in plan was 6.8 meters, although the absence of well-defined curbstones suggests that the width was somewhat exaggerated as a consequence of lateral slumpage.

The lower excavation level represented the construction core of the feature. Only the eastern half (1 meter by 4 meters) was sectioned. The rubble cap (30 centimeters thick) was found to overlie a light gray glei clay. The original surface of the feature suffered from severe erosion, which produced a leached and mottled profile. The dark gumbo clay characteristic of the upper *bajo* sediments filtered through the profile, which was also extensively penetrated by rootlets. However, there is some evidence for an extremely mottled paleosol capping the underlying sterile matrix. An underlying thin gray clay lens was found to grade immediately into the decomposing caprock.

The *sacbe* rises above the flanking *bajo* by a meter or more, but it extends less than half a meter above the silting *zacatal* setting. The field data indicate that the basal sediments in our exposure have not been altered or built up. The causeway was deliberately isolated as a linear island following the postulated quarrying activities on either side of it. The limestone rubble cap stabilized the surface, which was less cambered than it is today. We have assigned an early Tulix phase date to the *sacbe*, even though the sherd inventory was very meager. The Tulix phase dates for the Structure 50 Group as well as the contemporaneous date assigned to Structures 13–16 further support a Late Preclassic construction date.

Postholing Program

More than fifty postholes were systematically placed over the earthen platforms and adjacent canal basins covering a 1,600-square-meter area (OP158). A north-oriented grid system controlled the placement of postholes at 5-meter intervals. The posthole data produced a series of idealized profiles which confirmed

our excavation data. A subsurface contour map of the original indurated caprock surface underlying the platforms was drafted in an attempt to illustrate the nature of the raised-field complex (Fig. 6.23). A comparison of the surface (Fig. 6.10) and subsurface maps has led us to believe that the largest platform is underlain by elevated caprock.

It is argued that the margins and perhaps the planar surface of the underlying caprock were altered for agricultural space as well as quarried for monument fill. The field platforms were formed in part by simply excavating the margins of the high caprock, although some reworking of the soil matrices is also suggested. The flanking canal basins were lined water reservoirs with buttress stones used to support the bulk of the adjacent and overlying platform sediments. A thick lens of *sascab* overlying the gray clays, apparent at the north end of the southeasternmost platform, may be a concentration of *sascab* used in the reworking of some of the field soils. The source of this white marl is at a depth below the indurated caprock. Because this *sascab* matrix was localized in its distribution, we cannot equate our field platforms with the elevated *sascab* platforms defined by Puleston (1977) on Albion Island. However, there is a suggestion that the flat and more depressed area to the east of the postholing operation may represent deliberate raised earthen platform space that has collapsed over time. Unfortunately, our postholing program only examined the margins of this area, and no trenching has been carried out.

The confluence of the main canal with the major lateral canal in this same southwestern portion of the core zone was also probed with posthole diggers. This area seemed to have potential for locating floodgates or related control devices. Limited testing indicated an abrupt drop into the main canal from the lateral, but precise elevational data were not available. The pronounced elevational difference between the two canals, however, suggests a drainage function for the canal system rather than flow irrigation into the fields.

In the east, postholing was conducted to determine the degree of lobate form to the main canal plan. A series of postholes were placed across the main canal between the northeast trench (OP156) and the east trench (OP154) to assess the width of the main canal plan. Although the bottom of the canal could not be determined, the banks dropped rather abruptly. Our results indicate that the original main canal cut had irregular lobate walls. This is understood to be related to the ponding of water for easy access during the dry season.

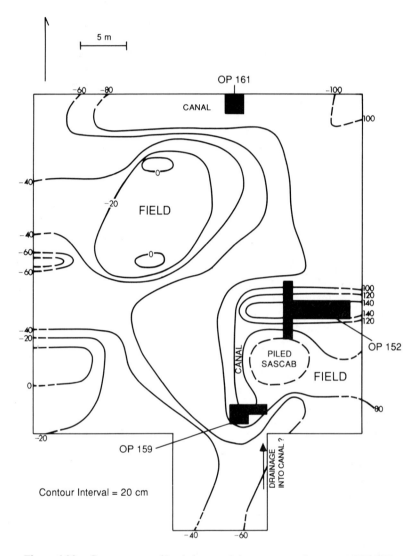

Figure 6.23.   Contour map of buried caprock in west-central core area (OP158).

INTERPRETATIONS

The canal system at Cerros was specifically designed for the semitropical setting of the Late Preclassic Period. The system functioned primarily for drainage and was a simple and harmonious adaptation to the environment. The main canal was constructed during the C'oh phase (200 to 50 B.C.) at which time it may have had a defensive function. This date was derived from postcanal construction sherd deposits resting under the damlike feature noted in the southern main canal

trenching section (OP116) and a *terminus post quem* derived from the deposits of an apparent dredging operation associated with the construction of Structure 98 at the southwest margin of the main canal (chapter 4). A calibrated radiocarbon date of 403 ± 377 years B.C. was obtained from under the causeway.

The main canal was not formed by the natural scouring action of the neighboring New River, as the width of the main canal was much narrower than that of the voluminous river channel. Further, the canal profiles generally reveal a steeply banked U-shaped cross section rather than a lazy, asymmetrical U-shaped profile, as anticipated by a meander at this location (Blatt et al. 1972:136).

Moreover, the fill from the main canal was apparently used in the construction of the various mounded features within the settlement (chapter 3) rather than having been thrown up to support a rampart or parapet of any consequence. The absence of a substantial rampart at Cerros does not deny the existence of a defensive function for the feature, but it does suggest that the fill from the canal was valued more for raised platform space than for protection from outside attack. Wooden palisades are reported during the conquest in the Chan Maya province (Thompson 1977) and the use of thornbushes, such as the various species of *Acacia,* could have provided an adequate deterrent to most intruders. (Millon [1973:40] indicates a possible defensive function for the nopal cactus at Teotihuacan.)

This kind of multipurpose canalization is suggested at Edzna in an examination of the main canal feeding the moat surrounding the "fortress" (Hauck 1973; Matheny 1976, Fig. 3, 1978, Figs. 10.7, 10.8; Matheny et al. 1983). These features relate to emic boundaries of the site and an undeniable barrier to outsiders questioning the perimeters of the site. The short-term benefits of the earthworks would be the obvious defensive advantage during attack. The long-term advantage would be the simple knowledge of its existence to those outside as well as inside.

The lobate form of the canal bank is believed to be a device for collecting and conserving water in the dry season. Given the west-to-east downslope gradient of the main canal, it is believed that the lobate plan functioned in a manner similar to the basin canals directly associated with the raised fields. The main canal trapped water in its lower reaches with the projecting lobes, or sills, separating the elongated reservoirs.

Following the construction of the main canal, the bottom accumulated a thin ephemeral lens of black sediment in at least one section lying on impermeable parent *sascab* (clean limestone marl). This sediment is thought to represent a humate horizon which eroded from the banks of the canal. It is argued that the adjacent fields were abandoned and left unmanaged, which resulted in the present inverted stratigraphy in the canal. The thick, blocky deposit of gray clays is suggested to have been raised-field platform matrix. The gray clays grade from lighter to darker as we descend the stratigraphy, with the expectably richer

humate content occurring in the lower reaches of the profile. The stone and gravel found near the bottom of the canal are in part decomposing bedrock, but may also represent ancient retaining features supporting the earthen platforms that washed out of the suggested collapsed fields.

The argument that these sediments have eroded from the banks of the canal is supported by (1) the absence of microstratigraphy, which may indicate a rapid infilling episode following the abandonment of the site at the end of the Late Preclassic Period, and (2) the slight bit of lateral lensing from the upper reaches of the canal, as well as the thinning lateral slope of the basal canal paleosol, as revealed in OP116.

Although high winds and turbulent water have affected the nearby shoreline, it is unlikely that hurricane activity alone would account for the relatively sorted particle size and gross volume of gray clay loam sediments in the canal bed. We believe that the infilling occurred over more than one hundred years, when Early Classic occupants continued to maintain as much of the system as they could coordinate socially. The Tulix phase vessels underlying the presumed Early Classic walkway at OP156 indicate the initiation of Late Preclassic abandonment at Cerros.

Following the partial infilling event of the main canal, there was a period of restoration and reuse which culminated in the damlike feature in the southernmost Trench 1 (OP116), the stone walkway over the northeasternmost trench (OP156), the later stone-lined canal segment overlying the gray clays in the southernmost Trench 2 (OP153), and the "echo" canal identified above the gray clays in the easternmost trench (OP154). The damlike feature (OP116) has provided a somewhat sealed context for dating the abandonment or disuse of the initial canal. From this southernmost trench we have obtained sherds dating exclusively to the C'oh phase. In addition, we collected a carbon sample from near the top of the gray clays in anticipation of a *terminus post quem* for the abandonment of the initial canal construction. The calibrated radiocarbon date (after Klein et al. 1982) of 403 ± 377 years B.C., however, may suggest the relocation of earlier trash believed associated with the initiation of the main canal (C'oh phase). It should also be noted that numerous *Pomacea* shells were capped by the dam, suggesting the freshwater environment in which these gray clays were deposited.

The two southern trench exposures suggest contemporaneity in terms of complementary architectural form, as well as in the appearance of basal flange bowl elements for the first time in the canal sediments. The latter occur in the stone fill of the damlike feature and above the stone-lined canal segment. It is argued that at this later moment in the prehistory of the canal, this segment between our two trenches functioned as a minor catchment basin for runoff from the deflated and collapsed field area. The absence of stone lining associated with the foot and adjacent area of the damlike feature suggests that the narrow, shallow lining defined in the southernmost Trench 2 was designed as the constricted mouth of a small reservoir. The elevated position as well as the constricted mouth would trap a considerable amount of water during the dry season following the rains of May through October. The position of the feature suggests that the water filling the reservoir entered from the west. Given that these features date to the Early Classic Period, it is tempting to consider the ephemeral Early Classic component at Cerros as responsible for modifying the infilled canal to partially reclaim the previous drainage properties. The absence of substantial amounts of the presumably redeposited raised-field gray clays above the exposed features suggests little concern with intensive agricultural management during these later periods. This thesis is in keeping with the less-structured population aggregates revealed by the house mound survey program. It is likely that the later residents of Cerros viewed the original canal as an impediment to traffic and a breeding ground for insect pests rather than a dynamic hydraulic system. The damlike features may have been as important as causeways as they were for any other function.

The lateral canals were defined by a shallow dish-shaped cross section cut into the limestone. Our excavations of the main canal, as well as in other locations where we have contacted caprock, indicate that the upper 40 centimeters of limestone were quite friable as a result of groundwater percolation. It is suggested that once the main canal was established, quarrying activities for building stone may have been satisfied. Further energy expended in the acquisition of additional stone being less necessary, it was easier to remove a wider section from a lateral canal than to excavate deeper into the indurated limestone in obtaining the same water volume capacity.

The expected amount of light gray clays has infilled the lateral canals. These sediments were identical to those defined in the main canal, and in the case of the southern lateral canal (OP151) were also attributed to a suggested raised-field platform erosional

displacement. The absence of a redeposited paleosol at the bottom of the southern lateral canal analogous to that described for the main canal is thought to be a function of the original drainage gradient. The higher elevation of this canal segment would tend to redeposit some sediments into the main canal until a gradient equilibrium could be established. It should be noted that the vast majority of identifiable sherds from this trench dated to the Late Preclassic Period.

No fields were identifiable in the eastern core zone, where our mapping program revealed a possible drainage system serving ground-level and larger residential structures. Attempts to document the relief in the area north and east of the main canal proved unsuccessful. The amount of sedimentation coupled with the dense *hulubol* prevented the detection of significant relief. Given the proximity of the area to the core zone and the presence of two sizable *plazuela* groups (Structure Groups 115 and 116) dating to the Late Preclassic in the middle of the *bajo* area, it is believed that this area was exploited during the Late Preclassic Period.

The amount of canal fill apparent at the north end is so great that the course of the canal is completely obscured. This may be indicative of the amount of field platform matrix that has eroded into the adjacent canals. However, the only well-studied raised-field plots rest in the west-central portion of the core area.

At the north end of the southern lateral canal were positioned the five earthen platforms which have been interpreted as deflated raised-field platforms, although a residential function may also be implied. Each platform was flanked by a system of narrow basin canals. The infilled matrix within each basin canal was identical to the gray clays found elsewhere and believed to have been eroded from the adjacent platforms. Of particular interest were the presence of uncut fragments of boulder-sized limestone resting in a manner that suggested their previous function as stone retaining features supporting flanking platforms, as well as defining the width of the basin canal. Although affected by leaching, the profile in at least one instance (OP152) reveals what appeared to be a shallow *sascab* bank, which may have formed a diminutive levee into which the stone retaining feature would have been buttressed. Functionally, this would have prevented water from saturating the adjacent platform fields (due to the impermeable nature of the *sascab*) and inciting root rot, as well as preventing water from dissipating into the fields in a premature, uncontrolled manner. The retaining features would have aided in preventing the slumping of the fields into the canals, thereby reducing the amount of time and energy necessary for maintenance as well as securing spatial boundaries.

The cross section of the two adjacent fields revealed in OP152 was somewhat discouraging. Lateral slumping and erosion into the system coupled with leaching, wet/dry soil cracking episodes, and snail (*Pomacea*) burrows have produced a mottled profile. The fields are believed to have been raised higher during the Late Preclassic Period but never elevated by *sascab* platforms (Puleston 1977b, 1978). Although the soil tests are incomplete, it is possible that the naturally low phosphate content of the soils on the peninsula (Wright et al. 1959) was increased by mixing beach sand with the naturally occurring clays. This would also produce a more fertile loam than that made available by the indigenous clays.

The ceramic sample obtained from the field exposures has produced a collection of Sierra Red wares. Large sherds, charcoal flecks, bone fragments, and high phosphate concentrations may suggest that kitchen compost was deposited to enrich the soils (see Wilken 1969:231). Our excavations at the margins of presumed house mounds at Cerros have not produced the midden debris reported from other sites (Fry 1969; Haviland 1963; Stoltman 1978). However, isolated postholing programs in depressed locations have frequently produced thin trash deposits or sheet midden. Although domestic trash may have been deliberately redeposited on the fields, its source is unknown. It is possible that the fields were maintained by households residing on the platforms, practicing a form of infield gardening (see p. 38) (Netting 1974, 1977; Wolf 1966).

In sum, the system was designed as a catchment or watershed. During the rainy season, diminutive canals directed runoff into the basin canals and reservoirs throughout the site. Additional water was diverted by a shallow network of runoff canals which followed the present relief into the main lateral and, ultimately, the main canal. None of these minor feeder canals have been clearly identified, but their form is presumed to have been similar to the small, late "echo" canal at OP154 (see OP153).

During the dry season, water would have been conserved in the lined basin canals as well as in the reservoirs and main canal. It is likely that, given the wide, uninterrupted distribution of the canal system, this water would have been available to everyone in the community. However, this water may have been somewhat contaminated by agricultural by-products, residential waste, and the stagnant nature of the system. Community-wide maintenance of the system would

have been necessary during the low water levels of the dry season. There is evidence for the dredging of the main canal during the time of its peak usage.

Private potable water sources complemented the community water system. These reservoirs may have been maintained by households or extended kin units. Such reservoirs would have held a less-contaminated water source for private consumption throughout the year.

The dichotomy between public and private water sources is most evident in the 2 hectares mapped in detail in the west-central portion of the core area (Fig. 6.10). Here the *sacbe* crosses the depressed zone dividing the apparent field loci from the area to the north and east. Two sizable reservoirs and additional low-lying terrain suggest that this area was a large private water source for those individuals associated with Subplaza 9A (Structures 12–16 and the Structure 10 Group). The *sacbe* may have separated the two water sources both functionally and symbolically.

In conclusion, evidence supports the presence of drained fields at Cerros. Information from several contexts in the Maya lowlands clearly demonstrates the extensiveness of water management and intensive agriculture during the Late Preclassic Period (chapters 3 and 8). In the highlands, canalization has been hypothesized as early as the Tzacualli phase (Terminal Preclassic) at Teotihuacán (Sanders 1976) and empirically demonstrated on a diminutive scale in the Santa Clara area of the northern Basin of Mexico by the Middle Preclassic (900–725 B.C.) (Nichols 1982, 1987). At Hierva el Agua in the Valley of Oaxaca, evidence suggests small-scale irrigation during Monte Albán I (Middle Preclassic) (Flannery et al. 1967). Chinampa agriculture as early as the Preclassic Period is suggested near Tlaltenco in the Valley of Mexico with the construction of an artificial island (Armillas 1971). Coe (1964) indicates a similar date. However, canals as substantial as those shown at Cerros or those documented from Late Preclassic Edzna have not been demonstrated elsewhere in Mesoamerica until the Palo Blanco and Venta Salada phases in the Valley of Tehuacán, Puebla (Classic and Postclassic) (Woodbury and Neely 1972), or at Santa Clara Xalostoc in the Basin of Mexico and assigned a pre-Coyotlatelco phase (Classic) date (Sanders and Santley 1977). The Campeche canals of Edzna represent some of the grandest hydraulic works identified for any period in Mesoamerican prehistory (see Chapter 8). It should be noted that Snaketown has revealed well-developed canalization as early as the Pioneer phase, 300 B.C.–A.D. 400, in the American Southwest (Haury 1976).

7. SETTLEMENT PATTERNS

RECONNAISSANCE

During the course of the Cerros Survey Project, considerable reconnaissance was undertaken to better understand the geographic position of the site relative to other centers on or near the Lowry's Bight sustaining area. As time allowed, the crew followed up as many leads as possible concerning the location of additional sites. Most of our initial locational information came from local informants who accompanied us into these remote areas. A Brunton compass and a sharp machete were the only survey instruments employed in this type of data retrieval (Fig. 7.1). The geographic location of the sites identified can be determined by consulting Fig. 2.7.

Two preliminary sketch maps are provided of the central precinct zones of Hillbank (Fig. 7.2) and Saltillo (Fig. 7.3). The site of Hillbank lies 15 kilometers south-southwest of Cerros, between the New River and Freshwater Creek. It is described as a major ceremonial center in Hammond's typology (1973). The Saltillo site lies 6 kilometers to the southwest of Cerros, near the first river terrace of the New River. Hammond (1973) identifies this site as a minor ceremonial center. Gann appears to be the first author to have made reference to Saltillo (Hammond 1973:9). Our cursory collections indicate a Late Preclassic and Early Classic Period occupation at both sites. This date is derived from fill ceramics taken from looters' pits. Hillbank further suggests a substantial Late Classic component.

Figure 7.1.   Foreman of Chunox village workmen, Valerio Tun, during reconnaissance survey through *monte alto/huamil* to the site of Ramonal.

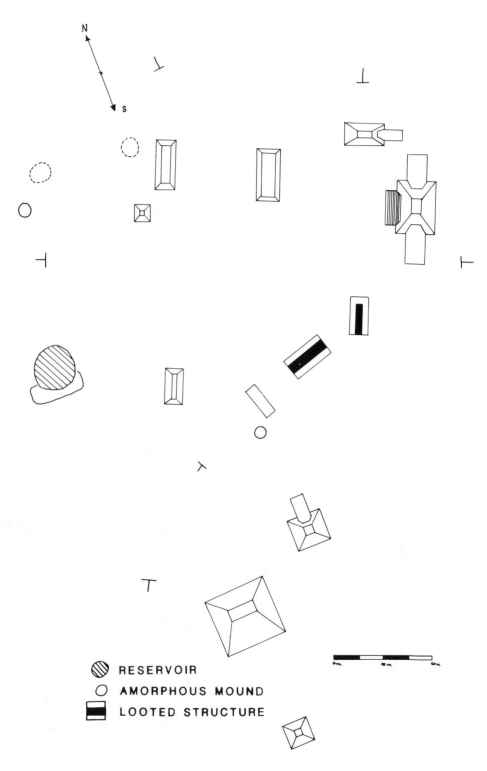

Figure 7.2.   Sketch map of Hillbank.

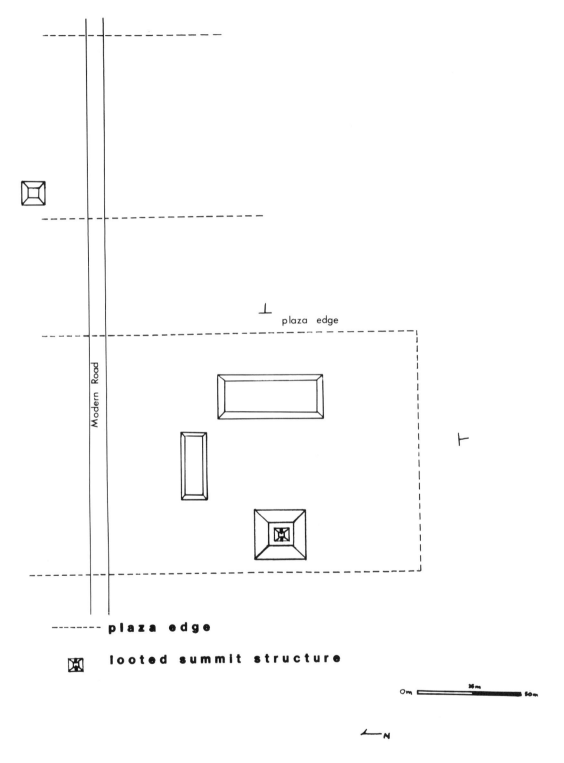

Figure 7.3.   Sketch map of Saltillo.

The previously unreported site of Ramonal received more attention than either Saltillo or Hillbank (Fig. 7.4). This was a consequence of recent bush-clearing activities performed at the site. Resting 5.5 kilometers east-southeast from Cerros, Ramonal had a sizable Early Classic occupation. A transit survey map was drafted of the ruins, although the site was not chained and only transit stadia distances were recorded (Fig. 7.5). The map has been rectified using the Maler convention.

Formal excavations at Ramonal were not possible, but systematic surface collections from each of the identified mounds yielded abundant Early Classic ceramic diagnostics (Robin Robertson personal communication). The presence of Sierra Red wares also indicated an earlier Late Preclassic component. The site area was flanked by savanna to the east and the west and appeared to ride the summit of a low ridge. A substantial canal was reported 1.5 kilometers west of the surveyed site area, but it may be associated with colonial-period logwood harvesting (see Camara 1984; Fig. 2.7).

The areal map is provided to fix the locations of the sites geographically (Fig. 2.7). Hillbank is not located on this map, but Hammond (1973) has it closely approximated. The size of the dot refers to the predicted size of these sites relative to Cerros. Except for the Postclassic community of Esperanza on the opposite side of the bight, all of the sites have a Late Preclassic component, as indicated by the ceramic collections. It should be noted that Point Alegre was not actually visited by members of the Cerros Survey Project. It was plotted with the aid of Roberto Pott of Chunox village, a very conscientious informant, who visited the site and provided the project ceramist with datable surface finds. Recent road cuts indicate Late Preclassic and Early Classic ceramic debris from Chunox and San Antonio. Aventura has been assigned a Protoclassic component as well as a major Early Classic occupation (Sidrys 1983).

The SAR readout has been superimposed on the map to stress the amount of potential canalization in the area (Scarborough 1983b; see Adams et al. 1981). Unfortunately, we have only limited ground-truth

Figure 7.4.   Structure 1 at Ramonal.

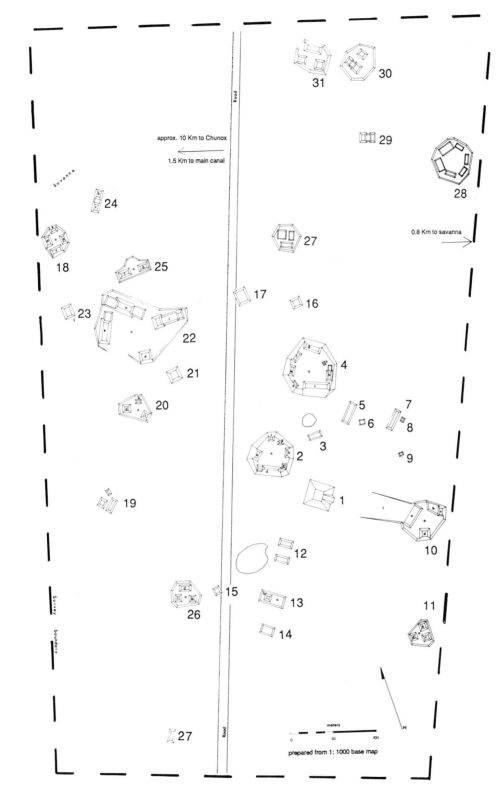

Figure 7.5. Map of Ramonal.

survey data for the presence of many of these lineaments (chapter 2).

Lowry's Bight has been defined as the settlement
sustaining area for Cerros (Figs. 2.6, 2.7). It has been
delimited by an arbitrary line drawn from the mouth of
the New River to the mouth of Freshwater Creek. It was
argued that if a defensive palisade or earthworks existed
at the margins of the sustaining area, it would be most
effectively positioned at this location (Scarborough
1978). In addition to preventing the trespass of landward intruders, it would have allowed tight rein over
maritime traffic using two of the three major rivers
servicing Northern Belize. The sustaining area as defined by this boundary line linking the New River
with Freshwater Creek contained an area of 9.63 square
kilometers.

Our reconnaissance of the Lowry's Bight sustaining
area included a shoreline survey by boat. No mounded
features were identified, but the dense waterline vegetation probably prevented an accurate appraisal. The
extent of the major *bajo* located at the tip of the bight
was confirmed through boat survey.

Reconnaissance along the road to Chunox via
the extant village of Copperbank (near the mouth of
Laguna Seca) indicated a lack of mounded features at
the outer margins of the landward sustaining area. Nor
could evidence be found in support of an artificial
earthworks at this location. A shallow vertical thrust
block fault zone, however, was identified at this approximate location. An examination of the aerial photographs (1:50,000) suggests that this same area was the
former location of an ancient drainage segment probably associated with the New River (chapter 3). Moreover, the SAR data indicate that this low-lying area is
in association with the dendritic patterns thought to
be indicative of raised-field agriculture (Scarborough
1983b).

Drawing on local informants, bush trails were cut
along promising corridors into the interior of Lowry's
Bight. The margins of the large Aguada 2 were examined for mounded features in this manner, although the
northeastern side of the depression was later systematically surveyed. Another short excursion was cut into
the mangrove and *hulub* setting to define the first river
terrace at the end of the western *brecha*. This latter
reconnaissance identified additional raised-field platforms immediately adjacent to those defined by the
systematic survey Transect 1.

An old trail passing through the western margin of
the south-southwest transect (Transect 2) was followed
to its termination at Esperanza Bight (Fig. 2.6). An

Early Postclassic midden deposit, identified by the surface collected ceramic assemblage (Robertson personal
communication) was found near a recently abandoned
wharf at this location. The site of Esperanza extended
along the south side of a shallow embayment and covered an area of approximately 2,500 square meters. No
mounds were identified in the immediate area, nor
were any found at the margins of the embayment. The
dense *hulubol* negotiated in following the latter third of
the trail to Esperanza Bight may in part define the
course of the ancient drainage mentioned previously.
The embayment is believed to have been the mouth of
this ancient river drainage.

No mounded features were noted along the bush
trails into the interior with the exception of one Type
2 *plazuela* group resting about 400 meters south of
our southernmost systematic survey pin on Transect
2. This group lay on the western side of the bush trail
leading to the site of Esperanza and appeared quite
isolated. The setting was well-drained *monte alto,* although a small *aguada* lay to the immediate north of
the feature. This area was located within the featureless terrain thought to be little disturbed by quarrying
activities. However, the *aguada* may reflect the source
of fill for the *plazuela* group. The form and orientation of this *plazuela* was not unlike the Structure 11
Group.

THE SYSTEMATIC SURVEY AREA

Three *brechas,* or transect lines, were positioned
more than 200 meters outside the main canal, radiating from the margins of the main major survey block
surrounding the site. In addition, a contiguous southern block of hectare units was surveyed. The chief
reason for the survey transects was to test the hypothesis that mound density decreased outside the core site
area (Fig. 2.3). No excavation was carried out in this
systematic survey area.

Southern Block

A portion of the systematic survey area outside the
main canal (but within the major survey block) was surveyed during the 1978 and 1979 field seasons. The area
was mapped to better represent mound densities immediately outside the main canal. Twenty-one hectares
along the southern margin of the main site survey block
were mapped in 1979 but were not included in our

spatial sample of mounds for excavation. This area was well-drained *huamil* to the west and poorly drained *hulubol* and *huanal* to the east. The sizable Aguada 3 resting in the southwestern corner of the survey block appeared to be human-made and associated with the complex of structures in the immediate vicinity. This arrangement of structures in association with the *aguada* was not unlike that noted for Aguada 1. In fact, the position of the two *aguadas* equidistant from the main canal and located to the southeast and southwest of the intrasite area further suggests the planned nature of the community. Nine small structures were identified and mapped in this portion of the site.

Transect 1

The initial survey transect line 1 was oriented west-southwest (N115°W) along the present Corozal Bay shoreline. The line issued from a midpoint along the western edge of the major survey block. The transect was designed to be at least 800 meters long and 200 meters wide. As it turned out, it was at least 300 meters wide at most locations, because of the irregular nature of the shoreline. The transect was again positioned to assess the density of house mounds in the western periphery of the site. Both the role of the shoreline and the New River were anticipated to influence the otherwise predicted mound decrease in this zone. A sizable mound component was actually identified. Thirty-one mounds were defined and mapped in the 22 hectares surveyed. This mound density and its distribution are unlike that of other areas in the periphery.

The unordered orientation and small size of these mounds may suggest that they represent house mounds for a segment of the service population at Cerros. Although a bit of Early Classic debris was surface collected from this transect, these structures probably date to the Late Preclassic Period. The settlement design in this area is more similar to the Late Preclassic settlement of Komchen (Andrews V 1981) than to the community disposition inside the main canal. The location of a service population in this portion of the site may suggest the community's dependence on shoreline exchange, even among the sustaining population. Although subsidence and sea level rise have changed the geographic position of the shoreline, an environmental adaptation to a riverine estuary is indicated.

The terrain in this area was generally better drained than were most locations in the periphery, although it continued to be severely pocked and pitted. These shallow scars are thought to be attributable to the quarrying

activities associated with the presumed house mounds. Unfortunately, no excavation has yet been conducted to confirm or disconfirm the presence of household features. There was little indication that a well-organized hydraulic system directly affected the occupants of these mounds.

At the western end of the transect on the banks of the first river terrace, we located at least nine earthen platforms understood to be raised fields. Although no temporal control was established, proximity to the mounds in this area would suggest a coeval date. Nine wells, or *chultun*-like depressions, were located in this area, further indicating a domestic occupation of the western periphery. Five of the nine wells were unassociated with mounded features, suggesting the presence of ground-level structures in the vicinity.

Transect 2

The south-southwestern transect line 2 (oriented N155°W) extended 500 meters from a point near the center of the southern margin of the major survey block. This point of departure was approximately 1 kilometer south of the central precinct at Cerros. The width of the transect was originally intended to be 200 meters, but the area was increased as a consequence of encountering an old trail along the western edge of the transect (the trail to Esperanza Bight). The trail was outside the defined transect area but because visibility was good along its path, an additional 40-meter-wide strip was surveyed at little added expense. The area to the east of the initial transect was also widened to better assess mound density. Because four mounds were encountered on the eastern margins of the transect, we elected to extend the width of the *brecha* systematically another 60 meters to ensure that no mound complex lay in immediate proximity to the concentration. As a routine event, we always examined a radius of 30 meters around a mound which lay at the edge of the systematic survey area. This practice lessened the severity of "boundary effects" (see Hodder and Orton 1976:41) in interpreting the data. The final width of the transect was 300 meters.

The sparse frequency of mounded features suggested that the interior of the bight was not densely occupied. A mound density decrease was apparent. The *brecha* was not extended farther because our reconnaissance along the bush trail previously mentioned did not indicate significant mound densities. However, our survey team did not unequivocally confirm this expectation at this location with additional controlled systematic survey data. Nevertheless, it was deemed more important to augment the sample of Late Preclassic mounded features than systematically survey an area of extremely low mound frequencies, given the overall paucity of house mound data for this period of Maya prehistory.

Transect 2 environs were generally more depressed than in the other transect locations, which may have affected settlement density. Some of the shallow depressions were naturally occurring features, but others may have had a cultural origin. The presence of pits and runnels dropped off significantly at the 12.0-meter contour interval. Scattered surface collections of badly weathered ceramics were noted periodically along the transect, suggesting the presence of ground-level structures. This may be further indicated by the isolated well, or *chultun,* resting 80 meters west-northwest of the nearest mound Structure 150.

Transect 3

The southeastern transect line 3 (oriented N130°E) extended 1 kilometer into the interior from the same point on the southern margin of the major survey block as Transect 2. The line terminated on the southeast side of Aguada 2. The transect was 200 meters wide and shifted 100 meters to the northeast around the *aguada* perimeter to avoid the waterline and to better examine the edge of the *aguada.* The transect was intended to test further the proposition that mound densities decreased as one entered the interior of the bight. The specific direction of the *brecha* was designed to elucidate the relationship between the large *aguada* and the core area. The canal had demonstrated the presence of a sophisticated water management scheme, and the role of the main *aguada* was thought to influence a water management scenario (chapter 3), perhaps at an earlier time in the prehistory of Cerros.

The transect revealed a slight natural ridge running parallel to and within the survey *brecha.* Although this area was elevated above the surrounding terrain and consisted of some of the best-drained land on the peninsula (*monte alto* and *huamil* settings), only three mounds were discovered. The structure nearest the *aguada* lay 200 meters to the north and no structures were noted within 100 meters of the *aguada* margin. However, ceramics dating to the Ixtabai phase were surface collected at the periphery of the *aguada* and may indicate a ground-level community at this location at that time. The presence of a well, or *chultun,* 80 meters southeast of the nearest mound adds further

support for the presence of the ground-level structures. Although reclaimed by the vegetation, the northern margin of the *aguada* had been partially modified by recent construction.

The terrain along the transect was featureless above the 11.5-meter contour interval. North of this contour, the terrain was more pitted and scarred, grading into the thick *hulubol* defined immediately to the east and south of the main canal. Only three mounds were defined in the entire 20 hectares covered by the transect. Mound density clearly decreased into the interior of the bight.

THE SYSTEMATIC SURVEY
AND EXCAVATION AREA

The systematic survey and excavation area was arbitrarily defined during the 1978 field season. The survey design allowed for comparable areal coverage both inside and outside the main canal (tables 6-8). The area inside the canal perimeter has been identified as the core area. It is associated with a more densely occupied residential sector than identified outside the canal as well as with major civic architecture. The area outside the canal perimeter has been defined as the periphery zone. It is understood to be a low-density residential sector (Fig. 2.3). Before discussing temporal trends between these two discrete portions of the site, a specific examination of the various components in the formal settlement is presented.

The Core Area

Inside the core area, eighty-one mounded features have been identified. The various structure types (chapter 4) are represented within the canal perimeter. The overall plan of the core zone reveals a symmetrical layout. The main canal circumscribes the community, forming a great arc with its focus at the central precinct. The canal system has been treated in another section, but suffice it to say here that raised fields do appear within the core zone. A medial site axis ran north-south through the community, intersecting the axes of both ball courts, terminating in the north at the foot of Structure 5C, and dividing the main canal into two nearly equal segments.

Complementing this division of the core zone was the western orientation of Structure 29. An east-west line from the summit of this structure intersected the medial site axis at a point equidistant between the two ball court alleyways. In addition, the two end super-structures at the summit of Structure 29B appear to be facing Structure 65 to the north and Structure 53 to the south, respectively. These two structures are equidistant from the summit of Structure 29B as well as being positioned north-south of one another (Fig. 3.9).

Many of the structures in the core zone were oriented toward the central precinct. This radial pattern of orientation directed toward the major monumental construction at the site further suggests the planned order of the community during the Tulix phase. The base map demonstrates the shared orientation of Structures 13, 14, 15, 16, and the 10 Group within the west-central portion of the core zone. The structures have the same orientation, apparently toward the center. Structure 19 in the western portion of the core zone may exhibit a tendency toward this radial orientation. In the eastern portion of the core zone only the small Structure 34, which was horizontally exposed, can be shown to manifest this alignment toward the center. The mounds in this area were generally smaller and more isolated than those elsewhere in the core area and therefore more difficult to orient. This orientation to the central precinct must be more pronounced than our base map indicates. As a matter of convention, we always oriented the structures to north unless other information suggested differently.

The vacant area in the eastern portion of the core zone was primarily depressed thornbush and *hulubol*. This area appears to have been altered by a limited system of shallow canals that drained into the main canal. Ground-level occupation has also been confirmed in this area (chapters 2 and 4).

Complete description of the excavated structures appears in chapter 4, with additional volumetric and spatial data dealing with all mapped features from Cerros contained in Appendix A. The following inventory of mounds and related features provides additional survey information not found elsewhere for unexcavated features. The presumed function of the unexcavated features is tentative and based entirely on architectural and environmental cues discovered in the field. These judgments have not been incorporated into our predictive sample of excavated features in determining relationships between civic and residential space. The mounds are presented geographically, roughly clockwise, beginning with the eastern coastal margin of the core area. The periphery is treated separately.

The Mounds

The northeastern coastal margin of the site provides evidence for riverine or maritime exchange with the presence of a docklike facility at Structure 112 (chapter 4). Structures 111, 113, and 114 rest at the margins of the *hulubol*. They appear to be house mounds, using the "principle of abundance" (see Willey et al. 1965). Two *chultuns,* or infilled wells, lie between Structures 113 and 114. Structures 34–36 are small house mound structures which are associated with two *chultuns* and a possible *sascabera.* They rest in a drained *huamil* setting. Structure 37 appears to be a limestone construction fill stockpile not unlike the chert stockpiles reported at Becán (Thomas 1974). Structures 30 and 90 also rest within the *huamil*. Both structures are understood to be houses, although Structure 90 lies at the termination of Sacbe 2 (Feature 51) and may have had a civic function as well. Finds exposed by a tree fall at the northwest side of Structure 90 suggest a Late Preclassic date for this mound, although it was not considered in our population estimates derived from formal excavation data. The above structures appear to be drained by two channels issuing into the main canal.

Three low-lying mounds were identified along the canal bank within the eastern core area. Structures 165–167 appear to be house mounds. Structure 165 represents an example of a "hidden" house mound no greater than 10 centimeters high. Structures 39–41 represent a discrete cluster of house mounds associated with a shared ground-level plaza. Structures 42–44 share a similar cluster configuration. These two groups are flanked by drainage channels. Structure 45 lies in the *hulubol* and is understood to be a house mound. The causeway (Feature 161) across the main canal and in proximity to Structure 44 represents one of the major thoroughfares into the interior of the bight from the core zone. Structures 46, 93, and the 76 Group as well as small structures associated with the 76 Group were probably all linked to the center by way of this causeway. The occupants on Structure 44 may have played an important role in regulating the traffic over this bridge. Another causeway (Feature 121) 120 meters west-southwest of the first-mentioned causeway was identified, but the absence of visible occupation to regulate and control access into the center may indicate that it dates to a different period than the former. It should be noted that excavated causeways elsewhere in the settlement (chapter 6) date to the Early Classic Period.

Structure 29 is the most imposing structure in the core area. Pyramidal Structure 29B is drained on its east and south sides by at least three channels running into the main canal. The vacant area to the south of plaza Structure 29A is understood to be a paved ground-level plaza area associated with both the ball court Structure 50 Group and Structure 29. The north and west plaza exposures of Structure 29 drain into the large catchment reservoir defined by the depressed thorn-scrub and *zacatal* at the heart of the core area. Resting just off the medial plaza axis of Structure 29A are two low-lying stone alignments thought to be associated with the Late Postclassic occupation of the site (Freidel personal communication). A linear east-west trending mound lies near the foot of Structure 29B and a circle of stone rests immediately to the west of it. The plaza steps down at its western extension before terminating at the 10.0-meter contour interval. Small Structures 52 and 124 rest on this extension. Judging from their location and diminutive size, they are suggested to be shrines.

It should be noted that Structure 29 at Cerros is not a unique structure in the formative Maya Lowlands. The single-level platform with a pyramidal structure at one end appears in a Late Preclassic context at both Komchen (Andrews V et al. 1981) and Cuello (Scarborough in Hammond 1978). In addition, the westward orientation of Structure 29 without a balancing eastern structure is a recurrent pattern during the Cauac phase on the North Acropolis at Tikal (Coe 1965a).

Running northeast from the northwest upper corner of plaza Structure 29A is Sacbe 2 (Feature 5l). Structures 69, 59, 71, and 57 represent possible shrine features along the course of this less well defined processional road. The functional identification of these mounded structures can only be seen as tentative, given the paucity of remains. The *sacbe* was well defined along its western margin but poorly defined on its eastern flank. It should be noted that Komchen has a similarly oriented *sacbe* also dating to the Late Preclassic Period (Andrews V et al. 1981).

Structures 54 and 90 define the termination of Sacbe 2. Structure 54 is a large multitier structure oriented north-south. It rests on a slightly elevated caprock bench together with Structures 32, 38, 77, 105, 106, 107, 108, and 110. With the exception of Structures 54 and 105, all of these structures are presumed to be house mounds and ancillary structures associated with domestic activities. Structure 107 is associated with a well, or *chultun*. Structure 105 appears to be another stone construction fill stockpile. This caprock bench

area is understood to be one of the last islands of caprock within the core zone that was not stripped or quarried away for monument fill and drainage control. The 10.5-meter contour interval is understood to have been the original ground elevation prior to quarry activities. The planned nature of the site is further suggested by the presence of this unquarried caprock bench in proximity to the central precinct. Quarrying was apparently first initiated some distance outside the central precinct in spite of the restrictive transport costs.

Structures 68, 75, and 81 appear to be house mounds associated with a ground-level plaza. However, this portion of the site has been affected by recent landscaping attempts, which have modified the original appearance of the terrain. Structures 72, 73, and 74 represent another house mound group, probably associated with a ground-level plaza. This area is well drained but appears to have received the major runoff volume from the central precinct. These two groups may have been involved in the channeling of this runoff away from the central precinct.

Structure 66 is surrounded by a complicated system of channels and depressions. These channels appear eventually to drain into the internal catchment basin located in the southwestern portion of the core zone. Structures 67, 25, 26, 27, and 28 occupy a similar setting to the west and southwest of Structure 66 on relatively elevated ground. These structures are considered house mounds. A substantial amount of recent landscaping has occurred in this area, with its most pronounced effects manifest in the depression between Structures 25 to 28 and the ball court Structure 50 Group. This zone has been badly disturbed and may represent the former remains of a small mound cluster. Further comment on the original appearance of this cluster cannot be made because of its present condition.

The two ball courts, Structure 61 Group and Structure 50 Group, rest in elevated and well-drained settings. The Structure 50 Group is drained on its eastern and southern flank by the main canal and to the north and east by the centrally located depression. The Structure 61 Group appears to drain indirectly into the main catchment basin via the southern and eastern sides of the structure. Structure 53 is nearly surrounded by the main catchment depression, while Structure 65 and the small Structure 120 (both resting to the north) are circumscribed by a drainage issuing into the same catchment.

The catchment basin area is divided by the northwest-southwest trending Sacbe 1 (Feature 126). The area of this depression is 3.75 hectares as defined by the 9.5-meter contour line. Structures 18 and 95 rest at the margins of the depression and are understood to be house mounds. No structures are found within the depression, with the exception of the *sacbe* and the small Structure 17 located at its northern terminus. However, the deflated and eroded earthen platforms defined as raised fields rest inside the margin of this depression (chapter 6). The role of the *sacbe* as a dike in directing the flow of runoff across the site must also be considered.

The *sacbe* connected the Structure 50 Group ball court with the subplaza Structure 9A and associated structures. This link across the central depression or catchment basin would have completed a civic or cere-monial circuit through the core zone over controlled-access plaza space. Clockwise, the circuit may have been initiated in the central precinct and crossed over the caprock bench to Structure 54. Proceeding along Sacbe 2 (Feature 51), the circuit would continue to the *sacbe*'s termination on the plaza Structure 29A and the foot of the elaborate Structure 29B. The pavement between Structures 29 and 50 Group may have di-rected traffic toward the ball court. Sacbe 1 permitted the completion of the circuit across the *zacatal* depres-sion onto Structure 9A and back into the central precinct (Fig. 3.8). During periods of elevated water levels in the canals and catchment basins, all civic and most residential structures in the core area could be comfortably reached.

Structures 13, 14, 15, 16, and the Structure 10 Group are a complex of very large and complicated mounds at the end of Sacbe 1 (Feature 126). They rest on plaza Structure 9A and appear to be civic architec-ture, with the exception of Structures 15 and 16, which are house mounds. Their shared orientation reflects a radial attraction to the central precinct. Structures 12 and 24 rest at the edge of plaza Structure 9A and may be outbuildings or nonelite dwellings. Structure 22 lies on an earthen extension of the same plaza and is a small house mound. The public monument, Structure 9B, de-fined the southern limits of the central precinct as well as delineating the northern margins of the lower south-ern portion of Subplaza 9A. Structure 9B was drained of runoff at its southeastern edge.

The Structure 11 Group was isolated from other structures and plaza space. It rests on unquarried high ground within the 10.5-meter contour interval. This courtyard group appears to have been an elite resi-dence. The presence of Structure 11B on the east side of the *plazuela* may have significance in addressing a Late Preclassic residential origin for the later Classic Period

residential shrine/oratory structure at Tikal (Becker 1971).

Structures 96, 97, 98, and the 19 Group are located on an extensive tract of unquarried high ground. This 1.5-hectare unit has been disturbed by heavy equip-ment landscaping operations, but most of the mounds appear to be intact. Structure 19C, however, has been severely damaged (chapter 4). Structures 96, 97, and 98 are argued to be house mounds, while the Structure 19 Group was a very large civic platform. Although a Late Preclassic date has been established, Structure 19B resembles the storage platforms described for the Late Postclassic Period on Cozumel Island (Rathje and Phillips 1975). Perhaps the entire caprock bench area was used as dry storage, with special surplus stored on the raised platforms.

Structure 21 is bounded by a fork in the main canal. Its imposing position at the western end of the canal would suggest its function as a sentinel in regu-lating traffic into the site. A water control device may have been located in this area but no empirical evi-dence has been revealed. The structure probably had a civic function.

Four additional causeways bridging the main canal must be noted in the southwest and western margins of the core site zone. The two to the west permitted traffic from the densely populated western periphery zone. They are poorly defined as a consequence of the recent landscaping operations in this portion of the site. The two other causeways are probably asso-ciated with the Early Classic Period and the reuse of the abandoned canal segment as discussed in chapters 3 and 6.

The Periphery

The periphery zone was defined by 35 hectares resting immediately outside the main canal. The mar-gins of the survey area were determined during the 1978 field season. Initially, the survey area was to include the large complex of mounded features associ-ated with the Structure 76 Group as well as a 200-meter-wide survey strip located immediately outside the main canal in all directions. Time limitations did not permit the examination of the entire area until the following year. However, an area comparable to that inside the canal perimeter was surveyed and a repre-sentative sample of mounds was eventually excavated. The rectangular survey block immediately south and west of the core area was ultimately excluded from the excavation sample, although it was incorporated into the systematic survey area.

The great tract of land to the east of the canal and defined by the 10.5-meter contour line encompassed an area of 22.9 hectares (including 7.5 hectares outside the systematically surveyed zone which were estimated from aerial photographic coverage). This area was extremely depressed and poorly drained. However, its proximity to the core area and the canal system suggests that raised-field agriculture may have been carried out in the area. The zone was systematically examined for structures, but carefully controlled survey with an eye open for agricultural plots was not undertaken. Given the degree of siltation and plant disturbances influencing this *hulubol* setting during the last 2,000 years, it is not surprising that we have yet to identify field plots. It should be recalled that the present surface relief manifested by the fields that have been identified inside the canal is approximately 20 centimeters. Because our survey contour interval has been routinely 50 centimeters, identification of fields and minor drainage canals may have been masked. The SAR readout did suggest a concentration of lineaments in this area of the site, adding further support to this hypothesis. The dotted canal segment running northwest-southeast through the *hulubol* may be a canal segment connecting the main canal with Aguada 1. However, it is very poorly defined and may have a natural explanation rather than a cultural one. It was in this context of field plot identification that the hectare unit D-12 was systematically point surveyed at 5-meter intervals (Fig. 6.4). Somewhat predictably, no meaningful relief was identified.

The two *plazuela* groups located in the northeastern portion of the periphery zone appear to be typical house mound groups (Structures 115 Group and 116 Group). The position of each within the *hulubol* suggests a role in field maintenance. A problematic mound to the immediate west of the Structure 116 Group may be an actual raised-field platform.

The positions of Structures 46, 93, and the 76 Group locus appear to reflect the location of a prehistoric trail leading from Structure 44 and the causeway crossing at Feature 161 to the interior of the bight. The Aguada 1 (Feature 79) was the focus of activities for Structures 78, 80, 82, 84, 85, 86, 87, 88, and the 76 Group. The form of Structures 82 and 88 with their extended plaza aprons is unique in the settlement. Most of the other structures are very small and are viewed as domestic facilities. However, the imposing Structure 76 Group was a civic facility probably providing cohesion to this

small hamletlike constellation of mounds. The position of the Structure 76 Group as a monumental landmark, midway between the large Aguada 2 (Feature 154) and the core area, may suggest its role as a way station or traffic control point for groups farther into the interior of the Bight.

Structures 94, 99, 100, 101, 102, and 103 are believed to be households in proximity to the canal. Ground-level structures may have been interspersed between these dwellings, as evidenced by a few scattered concentrations of sherd debris.

A SETTLEMENT RECONSTRUCTION

Our excavation within the systematic survey and excavation area permits the discussion of developmental trends at Cerros following the initial occupation of the site during the Ixtabai phase. The following presentation is taken from Scarborough and Robertson (1986:169–173).

C'oh Phase (200–50 B.C.)

In the Early and Middle C'oh phase most of the occupation of the dispersed settlement appears to have been at ground-level. During the Late C'oh, however, there was a substantial amount of residential construction in this area of the site (table 4). Within the core zone, eight of the excavated structures (area count) were built during the Late C'oh phase. Of these, six are house mounds, one is an outbuilding (Structure 24), and one is a ball court (Structure 61). Within the six house mounds, four are elite residences, one is indeterminate, and only one is a nonelite residence. It appears that, with the successful development of intensive agriculture throughout Northern Belize (Bloom et al. 1983; Scarborough 1983a and b; Siemens 1982; Turner and Harrison 1981), the energy investment in the construction of the main canal at Cerros in the Late C'oh phase, and the growth of riverine exchange networks, the emerging elites began to express their authority. They either moved away from the earlier Ixtabai village nucleus or elevated themselves above the nonelite. These elites, however, apparently stayed within the boundaries of the canal, since no residential construction can be identified outside the core area (tables 6 and 7; Fig. 3.7).

Most of the civic architecture dating to this phase underlies the present central precinct (Freidel 1986a).

In the settlement, it was considerably less developed than that of the later Tulix phase. Only two excavated monumental structures, Structure 76 and Structure 61 Group, can be reasonably associated with the Late C'oh phase. (C'oh construction is assumed at Structure 76, although an early Tulix phase date has been assigned to the bulk of the mound.) Structure 76 lies outside the core zone at a location midway between the main Aguada 2 and the main canal. Despite its distance from the core area of the site, the construction fill of Structure 76B contained C'oh pottery. Thus it would seem that there was C'oh occupation in the vicinity of the mound. Its location may indicate that the structure played a role in linking the Early C'oh and perhaps the Ixtabai occupants of these two areas. Even though Structure 61 Group, one of the two ball courts, was most heavily utilized during the Tulix phase, construction was initiated during the Late C'oh phase.

The construction of the main canal was begun during the latter portion of the C'oh phase. It probably was built for rainwater catchment, with the bulk of the removed fill being used in the construction of the civic and residential space, although a defensive role cannot be dismissed at this early date (Freidel and Scarborough 1982; Scarborough 1983a).

The site appears to have been heavily occupied during the C'oh phase. Occupational loci for this phase have been defined as secondary deposits located in construction fill or primary trash sealed below mounded features. In the former instance, the condition of the sherds indicates that they were not transported any great distance. Therefore, they reflect the existence of a nearby ground-level occupation. Based on these criteria, it appears that 39% of the known occupation "area" inside the canal perimeter was utilized during the C'oh phase, while 29% of the known occupation space outside the canal was employed. An infield/outfield agricultural adaptation is posited (Netting 1977), although riverine exchange directed through the central precinct may account for the settlement attraction toward that area and the village nucleus.

Tulix Phase (50 B.C.–A.D. 150)

The Tulix phase occupation of the site represents the period of major civic construction. Nearly all the monumental architecture visible at the site can be shown to have been utilized during this phase, and at least 80% of all civic construction inside the canal dates to this time. Outside the canal the only civic construction was Structure 76D, which was added to the 76 Group, suggesting the overall reuse of this group during this period (tables 6 and 7; Fig. 3.8).

All of this grand construction corresponds with quarrying activities associated with the water management system. The main canal was widened and dredged in at least one location, and raised-field platforms were constructed in the core zone.

In addition to the civic monuments, residential construction was undertaken inside the canal. Approximately 60% of the house mounds inside the canal were constructed during the Tulix phase, indicating that the core was a residential zone. The density of house mound construction and occupation in this zone was 1.21 mounds/hectare, demonstrating that the site was certainly not a vacant ceremonial center. In addition, more than a third of the house mounds in the core area were nonelite residences. In contrast, the house mound density outside the main canal was 0.40 mounds/hectare, suggesting a "dispersed compact" model (Puleston 1973) for the settlement during the Late Preclassic florescence. Even if the entire systematic survey area outside the canal is figured into the total (having an overall density of 0.75 mounds/hectare), a hypothetical figure of only 0.40 mounds/hectare can be derived from a Tulix context, given the 53% occupation total for this phase. It should be noted that the *bajo* area has not been subtracted from the density figures, since occupation did occur in these areas with frequency.

There are, however, variations in the distribution of mounds outside the canal. Although the systematic survey and excavation area was defined during the 1978 season, more recent survey and reconnaissance revealed the sizable concentration of mounded features southwest of the core zone. The mound density of this area, west of an arbitrary north-south trending line from the Structure 146 Group to the canal, is 1.23 mounds/hectare (the nearest mound east of the Structure 146 Group lies 240 meters away, suggesting a less arbitrary division of this area). If 53 of these mounds were occupied during the Late Preclassic (as has been indicated by the sample outside the canal in the systematic survey and excavation area), then an occupation density of 0.65 mounds/hectare is hypothetically projected for this area. Thus the density drop-off outside the main canal is not significant along the coastline and in proximity to the New River until one approaches the first river terrace. In contrast, the two transect lines to the south, into the interior of the bight, indicate a density figure much lower than that provided by the southern block periphery zone. A total density of 0.26 mounds/hectare converts to 0.14 mounds/hectare during the Tulix occupation, indicating a density drop-off in the interior. Consequently, it seems the western concentration represents an adaptation to riverine resources and exchange, with the service population engaged in petty trade along the shoreline.

Generally, this density drop-off outside the canal corresponds best to our understanding of the centralizing forces at work in a Maya center. Local exchange systems would have been coordinated and found to converge at the center. Additional support for this hypothesis comes from the construction of Structures 112 and 19, to the east and south of this area, respectively. Both are within the confines of the canal. Based on its immediate proximity to the shoreline, the presence of a ramplike gradient rising from the shore to the mound's summit, and the generous projected summit surface area of the structure, Structure 112 has been interpreted as a port facility. If this is the case, it contrasts with the earlier, but still functioning, dock previously associated with the village nucleus of the site (Cliff 1982, 1986), in that it has little additional room for the storage of goods. Structure 19, by the same token, with its summit area of 1,280 square meters and slightly greater distance from the center and coast, seems to have been reserved for the storage of goods. (Freidel and Sabloff [1984] discuss structures of similar form and suggest a storage function during the Late Postclassic Period.) Perhaps the elites were exerting control over riverine exchange by controlling not only the reception of goods at the site but their distribution as well. Less supervised and more localized exchange could have taken place along the western shoreline and outside the canal, making settlement at this location advantageous to a subordinate service class. The production of agricultural products outside the canal for internal or external consumption is suggested, but clear empirical evidence is lacking.

Although the purview of this monograph has primarily been the Late Preclassic Period, some discussion of the Classic and Postclassic periods is warranted. This brief treatment permits a clearer picture of later period densities at Cerros and underscores the relatively pure nature of the Late Preclassic components.

Classic Period

The Early Classic Period at Cerros is identified by the construction of only one civic monument, Structure 10 Group, the bulk of which appears to have been built during this period. Overall mound construction at the site dropped to 12% of the total. Although a sizable residential reoccupation was assumed initially, further analysis has shown that these later deposits were ephemeral and not indicative of permanent, long-term settlement. The evidence indicates that once a mound was constructed, it was used by all subsequent groups. Later utilization, however, was usually slight and resembles a sheet midden deposit covering the entire site. Much of this occupation represents use of former civic monuments that had been constructed by the end of the Tulix phase.

Although the zone outside the canal represents a slightly lower density of occupation (0.51 mounds/hectare) than does the area inside (0.76 mounds/hectare), two new house mound areas were constructed on the periphery. The main canal probably did not function as a major water control device, but rather was modified to collect small reservoirs of water. Sections of the canal are breached by causeways or dams, suggesting that the original canal was an impediment to foot traffic (tables 6 and 7; Fig. 7.6).

These data indicate that the site was not abandoned following the Tulix phase occupation; instead, it was based on a different land-use pattern because of an overall population decrease. The Early Classic adaptation probably was similar to the infield-outfield adaptation made during the C'oh phase, even though intensive agriculture in the form of raised fields may have continued in the immediate vicinity of the core zone. The more elaborate hydrology of the Tulix phase, however, was certainly beyond the organizational interests or capabilities of the Early Classic inhabitants. Although local exchange may have continued to support the residential population inside the canal, agriculture must have been the major subsistence mode. The community may have been attracted to the Tulix phase ruins because of the functional advantage of elevated ground near the shoreline, to say nothing of the former beauty and glory of the site. It would seem that the managerial elite had abandoned the site by the end of the Tulix phase. The service population and its descendants, on the other hand, adopted a new, less-structured order.

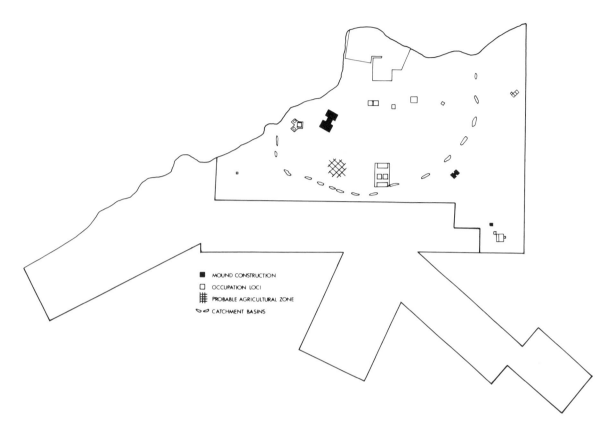

Figure 7.6.   Map of Early Classic occupation.

Cerros was virtually abandoned during the Late Classic Period. A cist containing Terminal Classic trash was exposed on Structure 50E of the ball court group, but no additional evidence for occupation has been found. The abandonment of the site during the Early Classic Period is not well understood, although it will be suggested that exchange networks and political associations circumvented Lowry's Bight (chapter 8). Alternatively, three sites in Northern Belize indicate that a rise in sea level or a complementary landmass subsidence occurred immediately following the Late Preclassic Period (chapter 3; Bloom et al. 1983; Harrison and Turner 1983). Given its proximity to the bay, Cerros would have been severely affected if the relative water level rose even a meter.

On the basis of present information, it may be said that the Early Classic Period occupation of the core area was rather brief and was initiated by the former service population to revitalize the fallen Tulix center. (Ceramic analysis for this period has not progressed far enough to assess clearly the actual length of time the Early Classic occupation may have continued at Cerros.) This effort emphasized the maintenance of the subsistence system to support the local population. With the abandonment of the center by the elites and the loss of centralized authority, however, the civic architecture eroded into disrepair. The canal network underwent sedimentation, and the general water catchment scheme failed. The environmental setting probably reverted to a condition not unlike that found at the site today, making the site nearly uninhabitable. Major reoccupation of the site would have required a considerable energy investment, an investment that was never realized again.

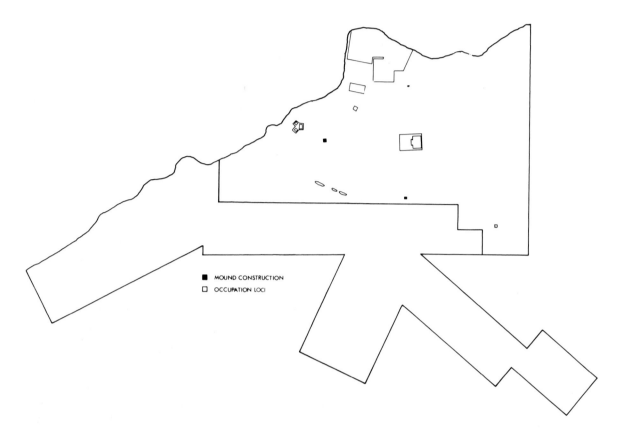

Figure 7.7.   Map of Late Postclassic occupation.

Late Postclassic Period

The Late Postclassic occupation at Cerros may span a greater period of time than the other phases described. Although this may have inflated the density estimates somewhat, these figures appear to indicate the same general trends revealed by the Early Classic occupation (tables 6 and 7). The settlement configuration during this period probably is less reflective of deliberate Postclassic spatial design than it is of simple selection for available high ground (Fig. 7.7). The setting probably was very much like the present, although bush trails and cleared plaza space were likely the rule. No civic construction was carried out at any location in the settlement, and only two house mounds were built. Most of the monumental architecture, however, was reoccupied. An especially dense domestic trash deposit, for example, accumulated at the foot of Structure 9. Because the main canal probably was not utilized

in any significant manner, density figures inside and outside the core zone are less meaningful. The overall density of reoccupation in the systematic survey and excavation area was approximately 0.30 mounds/ hectare. The adaptation made by these occupants is difficult to determine, but a variation of the "merchant pragmatism" model (Sabloff and Rathje 1975) may be suggested by the limited architectural investment (see Harrison 1979) and the rather rich Late Postclassic caches which have been recovered from the larger monumental structures. The Late Postclassic population configuration at Cerros is thought to be related to the growth and dominance of Santa Rita, just 3 kilometers across the bay (Chase 1981; Chase and Chase 1988).

A growth model through time hardly seems appropriate for Cerros. The C'oh phase developed into the Tulix phase, while the Early Classic saw the reoccupation of the collapsed Tulix center. Sparse construction during the Early Classic, coupled with the nearly complete absence of Late Classic debris at the site, strongly suggests that the Early Classic adaptation was not a successful one. An attempt to maintain Late Preclassic traditions, given the new social order, probably spelled the eventual demise of the population. The absence of later Classic Period occupation was a consequence of environmental factors to which the silting-in of the water catchment system contributed. Although the geographically commanding position of Cerros near the mouths of the New and Hondo rivers was not altered, the energy investment necessary to revitalize the water catchment system would have been extremely costly. It was not until the Late Postclassic Period and the rise of the materialistic trading colonies of the Yucatán coast that the geographic position and the potential of an immediate economic return outweighed the physical unpleasantness of the Cerros environment.

8. LATE PRECLASSIC PERIOD COMPARISONS
AND CONCLUSIONS

The archaeological data collected from the Cerros settlement present a set of unique findings. Evidence for several incipient cultural traditions which were later to help define Classic Maya civilization has been identified. Principal among these traditions are (1) intensive agriculture, (2) public ritual as manifest by the native American ball game, (3) a "dispersed-compact" settlement pattern, and (4) town planning as revealed by the monumental architecture in the core area of a community. Complementing these developments are two conditions that have allowed the identification of these incipient traditions: (1) the rapidity at which the site was built during the Late Preclassic Period and particularly during the final two hundred years defining the Tulix phase, and (2) the suddenness of abandonment at the end of this same Tulix phase. Though much has been made of the fortuitous nature of the well-preserved Cerros finds (the lack of Classic Period admixture and the absence of deeply buried Late Preclassic remains), the behavioral implications for the swift rise and fall of the community within a regional context will be the concern of the remainder of the monograph. However, before a summary model of the Late Preclassic Period in the Maya Lowlands can be developed, an examination of other Formative Period communities in the lowlands with data of similar form to those described for Cerros is necessary.

THE LATE PRECLASSIC
MAYA LOWLANDS

Given the paucity of Late Preclassic settlement data, comparisons with Late Classic and Postclassic Maya communities have from time to time been unavoidable. However, such comparisons must be considered much like poorly controlled ethnographic analogy; that is, they contain an indeterminable degree of temporal discontinuity. The site-specific structure densities and monument fill volumes provided below are derived primarily from those communities which have well-documented Late Preclassic activity. Only those sites with controlled settlement pattern data or volumetric information have been considered for this comparative sweep. These two indices allow a reconstruction of population structure as well as the relative energy investment made by a corporate labor pool.

Population structure has a long and widely accepted history in anthropological interpretation and regional analysis (Boserup 1965; Smith 1976; Spooner 1972). However, volumetric comparisons can also become instructive for regional analysis. This is possible because of (1) the pan-regional outlay in monumental architecture made during the Late Preclassic Period and (2) the relatively limited number of universal symbols for the expression of authority at this time, especially when compared to later Classic Period developments (see Schele and Miller 1986). Other symbols of authority, such as portable luxury items, varied widely in form. They become less reliable units of analysis because of noncomparability in raw materials, distance of item from source, quality of craftsmanship, and aesthetic intangibles. Given the widespread use of monumental architecture, volumetrics permit a comparison of similar analytical units by way of like construction materials and building techniques. Volumetrics are a good index of the amount of corporate labor available to a developing elite prior to widespread craft specialization during the Classic Period (Late Preclassic Colha notwithstanding [Shafer and Hester 1983]). The interpretation of these data aid in placing Cerros in the proper temporal perspective and reveals the variety of spatial adaptations made by the Late Preclassic Maya. The coeval regional context of these data permit greater interpretive rigor than do convenient analogies to isolated events of later periods.

Cerros Population Densities Compared

The Tulix phase (50 B.C.–A.D. 150) population density figures from Cerros are comparable to Late

Preclassic concentrations elsewhere. Although structure densities have been previously examined in detail, some attempt at actual human population estimates for the site is presented here. These can be considered conservative but methodologically in line with estimates from other ancient Maya communities. Using a figure of 5.4 persons/structure (after Puleston 1973), a population of approximately 222 would have resided inside the core area, or canal perimeter (1.21 structures/hectare within an area of 34 hectares). Given the same number of occupants/house within the periphery zone at Cerros, a figure of 253 persons is obtained (0.40 structures/hectare). However, in determining the sustaining population for the entirety of Lowry's Bight, the mound densities registered for the two interior transects (Transects 2 and 3) perhaps best characterize overall Tulix population distributions. Given the mound density decrease into the interior along the surveyed transects (0.14 structures/hectare), a conservative sustaining population of 614 persons is estimated for the remainder of the peninsula. (Lowry's Bight has an area of 9.63 square kilometers, of which 16% has been systematically surveyed.) When these figures are combined, the estimated total Late Preclassic population at greater Cerros is 1,089.

Puleston estimates a Late Preclassic Tikaleno population of 8,230 from within a ring encompassing 32 square kilometers (1973:223). The Late Preclassic Zunic settlement system spans the Chuen, Cauac, and Cimi ceramic facets (250 B.C.–A.D. 250). Although the Cerros population is considerably smaller than that of Tikal, the radius of Preclassic occupation in proximity to the core area goes well beyond Lowry's Bight (see "Reconnaissance," chapter 7). However, Tikal would appear to have had a larger and more densely occupied community area during a comparable period. It should be noted that Puleston's Late Preclassic core area covered 3.8 square kilometers and contained 215 structures/square kilometer, though he cautions that the latter may be an elevated figure. The structure density for all mounds, civic and residential, inside the canal perimeter at Cerros converts to 138 structures/square kilometer, excluding the central precinct.

Cerros density figures are comparable to those generated by Rice and Rice (1980) at Lake Yaxha and Lake Sacnab during the Late Preclassic Period (200 B.C.–A.D. 250). The lake region survey data appear similar to the interior transect legs at Cerros. The average Late Preclassic density figures for Lake Yaxha are 19.4 structures/square kilometer. This compares favorably to the

0.14 structures/hectare (14 structures/square kilometer) obtained from the two interior systematic survey *brechas* on Lowry's Bight. Moreover, in a transect operation approximately 500 meters west of the major administrational center of Yaxha, the Rices record a structure density of 48.7 structures/square kilometer, a figure in keeping with the average systematic survey and excavation area outside the canal at Cerros (40 structures/square kilometer). These population data suggest that Yaxha was of the same order of magnitude as Cerros during the Late Preclassic Period. Tikal, on the other hand, was at least twice as large a population center as either Cerros or Yaxha.

Within a core area at Altar de Sacrificios a similar density of nonceremonial structures is documented as reported near Yaxha and immediately outside the core area at Cerros. During the Late Preclassic Plancha phase (350 B.C.–A.D. 150), 28 structures suggest an occupation spread over 66 hectares of settlement space (12 hectares of the site were excluded as central precinct public space). A figure of 42 structures/square kilometer is indicated by Bullard's map (Smith 1972; Willey 1973; Willey and Smith 1969). This figure may reflect the type of settlement periphery aggregate attracted to even a small organizational center during the Late Preclassic period. It does indicate that the size of Altar de Sacrificios was considerably less than that recorded at Cerros, with a density comparable to the peripheral zone immediately outside the canal. This inference is further supported by the overall diminutive area identified as the limits of the community. However, Altar de Sacrificios may have a larger mound population than Bullard's map reveals, as suggested by Puleston (Rice and Puleston 1981) and forcefully stated by Becker (1979).

The heavily fortified community of Becán provides a sizable Late Preclassic settlement population (Thomas 1981). The mound density immediately surrounding Pakluum phase Becán (300 B.C.–A.D. 250) was 439 structures/square kilometer. This figure was derived from a 3-square-kilometer area surrounding the central precinct of the community and excludes about half of the area as uninhabitable *bajo*. Although these calculations may be inflated relative to subsequent periods due to the extreme length of this phase (Thomas 1981:110), they do conform to population estimates reported from Komchen to the far north. Ball and Andrews V (1978) argue that most of the Late Preclassic activity in the central precinct dates to the Late or Terminal Pakluum facets (50 B.C.–A.D. 250), and Thomas (1981:111) indicates that this may be the situation in the surrounding formative settlement.

Barton Ramie reveals an apparent specialized settlement adaptation to the riverine setting along the Belize River. No major monumental construction lies in the immediate vicinity of the site, yet 262 structures have been identified within an arbitrarily defined 2-square-kilometer area (Willey et al. 1965). During the Floral Park phase (100 B.C.–A.D. 300), 50 mounds of the 65 excavated (or 77% of the total) were occupied. Though sampling problems may exist, if three-quarters of the 262 mounds identified were occupied at this time, a density figure of 101 structures/square kilometer is derived. This figure is somewhat surprising, given the absence of a central precinct in proximity. These data suggest that the community made an immediate environmental adaptation rather than a sociopolitical one. A raised-field agricultural advantage near this location (Kirke 1980) and the commercial potential associated with canoe traffic along the river may have allowed Barton Ramie to flourish without a major sociopolitical investment in civic architecture as early as the Late Preclassic Period.

Komchen lies approximately 19 kilometers south of the Gulf of Mexico in northwestern Yucatán. By the end of the Late Preclassic Period (Xculul 1, 300 B.C.–A.D. 150), Komchen covered about 2 square kilometers with an approximate density of 500 structures/square kilometer surrounding centralized monumental architecture (Andrews V et al. 1981). The site had an estimated total population of five thousand (assuming an average of five persons per structure). Komchen is argued to have been an adaptation to salt exploitation along the north coast (Andrews V 1981). The extremely high population densities achieved at Komchen may reflect a centripetal force nucleating the sustaining population as a consequence of regulating the exploitation of the salt beds. The population density is seen as a site-specific settlement adaptation to a labor-intensive economic mode.

The greater community area of Dzibilchaltún provides useful density information, though considerably more is now known about the adjacent Preclassic core area of Komchen. Kurjack (1974) reports that 26% of the 8,390 structures identified within the 19-square-kilometer area surveyed date to the Formative Period (300 B.C.–A.D. 250). This translates into 115 structures/square kilometer during the Late Preclassic Period and suggests a density decrease of the same relative proportions as reported inside versus outside

the major canal at Cerros. Komchen appears to be the civic and residential hub for the more dispersed Dzibilchaltún population. Given the quality of systematic survey and excavation, there can be little dispute that population densities registered in Northern Yucatán are at least four times greater than those revealed in the southern lowlands by the Late Preclassic Period, a condition that never reverses itself.

This information is derived from the restricted settlement data associated with the Late Preclassic Period from throughout the Maya Lowlands. Though the Late Preclassic inventory of materials is generally buried by later Classic construction, these data provide an interpretive window for seeing the Cerros finds in an ordered regional light. It should be noted that no attempt has been made to adjust the population densities recorded from the above communities by time span for comparative purposes. The amount of time associated with each Late Preclassic occupation from the various communities identified varies little, with most periods extending from 400 to 500 years. The two-century span of the Tulix phase at Cerros is the exception, during which time 90% of the monumental architecture and residential space at the site was constructed or occupied. However, if the earlier Late Preclassic Ixtabai and C'oh phase structures are included in the Cerros population totals, a temporal span of 450 years elapses, leaving the comparisons precisely the same. Moreover, the well-controlled sample from Cerros indicates that previously occupied C'oh phase households were subsequently occupied by Tulix phase residents.

This trend is further supported at Altar de Sacrificios, where the Late Preclassic Period has been faceted into an early and a late phase (Smith 1972: table 3). This reoccupational tendency is also apparent from the Barton Ramie data, in which the earlier Late Preclassic Mount Hope phase structures (300–100 B.C.) are subsequently occupied by later Formative Floral Park residents (100 B.C.–A.D. 300) (Willey et al. 1965: table 2). In addition, Thomas (1981:111) indicates that this may be the situation at Becán. Given that the Late Preclassic Period was one of major growth and expansion throughout the lowlands, little sustained abandonment of previously occupied mounded structures is suggested.

Population density comparisons will be made at the areal context of Late Preclassic Northern Belize subsequently (see below), where the quality and quantity of Formative Period material is better known than from any other zone in the Maya Lowlands. Other than

Cerros, communities in Northern Belize have not been examined heretofore so as to permit the later detailed study of one area within the greater Maya Lowlands during the Late Preclassic Period. However, before treating population distributions in Northern Belize, Cerros will be compared to the few well-reported Late Preclassic communities with monumental architecture elsewhere in the lowlands.

Cerros Volumetrics Compared

The total volume of Tulix phase monumental civic construction inside the central precinct at Cerros is 133,104 cubic meters (excluding Structure 9). The volume of Tulix phase civic construction remaining inside the canal perimeter is 61,218 cubic meters. These figures must be considered conservative because paved areas throughout the core area exist but are difficult to evaluate. No attempt has been made to include these areas in the volumetric study. Cerros civic monuments are distributed over 37 hectares inside the canal perimeter with frequent house mounds interspersed.

Less is known about monumental architecture during the Late Preclassic Period from other Lowland Maya communities. However, some comparisons can be drawn. These figures may seem somewhat inflated as a consequence of including underlying structure-fill dating to earlier periods. However, in most cases they should be considered quite conservative, given (1) the extremely limited evidence for monumental architecture during the Early and Middle Preclassic periods and (2) the sampling problems inherent in identifying Late Preclassic construction fill buried by subsequent Classic Period episodes.

The fill volume figures obtained from Tikal were taken from Coe (1965a and b, 1967) and the Tikal map (Carr and Hazard 1961). The North Acropolis at Tikal at A.D. 1 was 45 meters east/west by 40 meters north/south and 9 meters high. It attained a mass of 16,200 cubic meters, which is approximately one-half the fill volume of the largest single monument at Cerros (Structure 4). The Lost World Pyramid, or Structure 5C–54 at Tikal, is considered one of the largest Late Preclassic/Early Classic monuments in the Maya area. It is 76 meters north/south by 62 meters east/west and rises to a height of 30.5 meters. If the summit floor space is 16 meters north/south by 9 meters east/west, then a fill volume figure of 74,054 cubic meters is computed. This is more than twice the volume of the largest pyramid at Cerros. Culbert (1977) notes a

4-meter-thick infilling operation in the Seven Temples plaza during the Late Preclassic Period. The area of this plaza is 104 meters north/south by 76 meters east/west and provides a fill volume figure of 31,616 cubic meters. This is equivalent to the entire volume of Structure 4 at Cerros.

Though the known Late Preclassic monuments suggest that Tikal is at least comparable in size to Cerros, the settlement density figures reveal Tikal to be an order of magnitude larger. The South Acropolis at Tikal goes undated and the extent of Late Preclassic plaza space is unknown. However, Cerros and Tikal share many spatial architectural relationships at this early date. The westward orientation of Structure 29 at Cerros without a balancing structure to the east appears initially in Cauac times (50 B.C.–A.D. 150) on the North Acropolis at Tikal. Further, a center line axis through the entire core zone community at Cerros occurs by the Tulix phase, while Coe (1965a and b) suggests a Cauac phase date for the final center line orientation of the North Acropolis, though Culbert (1977) indicates a slightly later Cimi phase construction date (A.D. 150–250). Courtyards with temples first appear in the Cauac phase (Culbert 1977) at Tikal. Courtyard groups are not well established at Cerros but do appear by the Tulix phase.

One of the most interesting features suggested by the Cerros settlement data and perhaps hinted at in Tikal is the open character of the core area. This is readily apparent from the Cerros map and may reflect an ideal in Late Preclassic community organization. Residential occupation is distributed across the core area, unlike in Maya centers in later periods, where the residential population is generally segregated from the grand monumental construction. Tikal may have had a similar plan during the Late Preclassic Period, given the distance between the North Acropolis and Structure 5C–54. Residential space is likely to have been distributed between these structures and was later covered by civic plaza space and additional monumental architecture. This distance is 500 meters, which compares favorably to the distance at Cerros from the central precinct to the ball court Structure 50 Group. Given the antiquity of these data, it may be more than coincidence when Coe (1977) suggests that Olmec sites had an open appearance as well. Perhaps similar social and environmental conditions resulted in similar civic architectural relationships.

Other sites are less well documented during the Late Preclassic Period due in part to later massive construction events. Though revealing a substantial

Late Preclassic settlement, the significance of Formative Period monument construction at Yaxha is unknown. At Altar de Sacrificios, Structure B-1 Construction B dates to the later Plancha phase. It is approximately 37 meters north/south by 39 meters east/west and rises to a height of 9 meters (Willey 1973; Willey and Smith 1969). The summit platform space is approximately 5 meters north/south by 9 meters east/west. An earthen fill volume of 6,696 cubic meters is approximately two-thirds the fill volume of Structure 29B, the largest mound outside the central precinct at Cerros. No other Plancha phase civic architecture has been reported from Altar de Sacrificios, further suggesting its small size relative to Cerros as previously implied by the settlement densities. Altar de Sacrificios does have domestic occupation in the immediate vicinity of Structure B-1 during the Plancha phase. This reflects an open civic/residential appearance to the center analogous to that at Cerros for this early date.

The site of Becán, Campeche, has revealed Late and Terminal Pakluum phase (100 B.C.–A.D. 250) monumental architecture. The most imposing feature at this site was surely the great ditch and parapet or defensive earthworks surrounding the Late Classic central precinct. Built during the Terminal Preclassic Period, it represents 117,607 cubic meters of quarried fill (Webster 1976). Structure IV-sub is the only Late Preclassic pyramidal structure identified that is of monumental dimensions. Using Potter's illustrations (Ball and Andrews V 1978:11; Potter 1977), the substructure is approximately 20 meters on each side and roughly 11 meters high (14 meters high on the north side and 8 meters high on the south). The substructure platform summit floor space has been approximated to be 120 square meters. These figures provide a fill-volume figure of 2,860 cubic meters. In addition, four small structures, perhaps house platforms, have been identified inside the ditch and date to this phase (Ball 1977c; Ball and Andrews V 1978). Given the presence of these small structures, together with civic architecture circumscribed by a ditch enclosing an area equal to that defined by the core area at Cerros, the previously identified open arrangement between civic and residential space is repeated. The fact that the ditch was constructed at the same approximate time as the canal perimeter at Cerros suggests a similar core area settlement configuration at both sites, though Late Preclassic Becán was buried by subsequent Classic Period developments. Both sites indicate well-defined community limits, a characteristic noted at Muralla de León (Rice and Rice 1981) as well as at El Mirador

(Dahlin 1984), with each understood as dating to the Late Preclassic Period. Becán appears to have been an administrative center of the size and complexity of Cerros. Its clear defensive posture, as evidenced by the ditch and parapet, may have been influenced by the circumscribed position of the site at the geographic center of the Yucatán Peninsula. Down-the-line exchange as well as long-distance trade would have made this location especially active if most communities in the Maya Lowlands were interacting with one another (see Freidel 1979). Militarism would have been one adaptation made for the control of imported resources (see "Model," this chapter).

The Late Preclassic Floral Park component at Barton Ramie is unassociated with large-scale monumental architecture. Two substantial administrative centers, Xunantunich (Thompson 1940) and Baking Pot (Bullard and Bullard 1965; Ricketson 1931), resting in the vicinity, may have more Late Preclassic architecture than is currently documented. However, available evidence from Barton Ramie indicates that sizable Late Preclassic population centers need not be equated with monumental civic centers, a condition not generally documented in later periods.

The Late Preclassic component at Komchen has been shown to be very substantial. Like Cerros, the site appears to have been virtually abandoned following Late Preclassic construction events. By Xculul 1 and probably earlier, platform Structure 500 had attained a height of 2.5 meters and extended over an area 70 meters by 75 meters and produced a fill volume of 13,125 cubic meters. A pyramidal structure, 30 meters by 30 meters and 3 meters high, rested on its south end and accounted for another 2,700 cubic meters of fill. Adjacent platform Structure 450 was 3.5 meters high and extended over 1,400 square meters, yielding a fill volume of 4,900 cubic meters. Moreover, three other sizable platforms are reported at Komchen, but precise volumetric calculations for these structures are difficult without additional data (Andrews V 1981). Nonetheless, Andrews V et al. (1981) indicate that approximately 150,000 cubic meters of architectural fill was associated with the entirety of Komchen.

This figure suggests that Komchen may have been of a comparable order of magnitude to Cerros, but organized very differently. Approximately 200,000 cubic meters of monument fill has been identified within the 37 hectares defining the canal perimeter at Cerros. Although both sites manifest spatial openness, a greater centralization of architecture is juxtaposed with lower population densities when comparing Cerros to Komchen. Further, an examination of the Komchen map indicates little orientational consistency between structures which suggests less overall town planning as compared to the Cerros example. Given a late Middle Preclassic investment in monumental architecture at Komchen and a suggested gradual, less-ordered growth at this site during the Late Preclassic Period, Komchen is seen as a local development with deep indigenous roots. Cerros, with its explosive growth and town planning during the Tulix phase, however, arose without local precedent from within a wider regional field.

These volumetric data are presented to complement the population density information obtained from these same communities. However, several sites in the Maya Lowlands provide data on Formative Period civic monuments but little with regard to settlement distributions. Though these sites allow less complete comparisons, they do provide gross scalar relationships to other communities examined. Three of these communities appear to be at least the magnitude of Tikal.

El Mirador may be the largest city known during any period of Maya prehistory. Evidence indicates that the major construction at the site occurred during the Late Preclassic Period (Dahlin 1984; Matheny 1986). The El Tigre complex rises to a height of 55 meters and contains 495,000 cubic meters of fill, while the Danta acropolis complex contains 563,000 cubic meters of construction fill (Sidrys 1976, from Graham 1967). This latter acropolis complex is nearly three times larger than the entirety of monument fill identified at Cerros. These two complexes combined are comparable to the fill volume of the Pyramid of the Sun at Teotihuacán (see Millon 1973). A cursory inspection of the most recent planimetric map (Dahlin 1984) reveals considerably more architecture than the two above complexes. El Mirador appears to be a full order of magnitude larger than even Tikal.

Río Azul has exposed a large Late Preclassic component (Adams 1986). Settlement data are not yet available; however, acropolis Structure G-103 has been identified and found to be 100 meters on a side and 20 meters high. The summit platform space is 40 meters by 40 meters and provides a construction fill volume of 116,000 cubic meters. The fill volume of this single platform is nearly that of the entire central precinct at Cerros. Additional Late Preclassic civic and residential construction has been identified, suggesting a city on the scalar order of Tikal.

The community of Edzna, Campeche, also provides Late Preclassic evidence. Matheny (1976) argues that most of the grand canalization at Edzna was constructed at this time. Approximately 1,750,000 cubic meters of soil was removed from canal operations, a volume of fill comparable to the combined dimensions of both the Pyramid of the Sun and of the Moon at Teotihuacán (Matheny 1976:642). Further, a moated fortress is understood to be a Late Preclassic development (Matheny et al. 1983) and probably arose as a consequence of the quarried canal matrix in proximity. The quantity of earth manipulated at Edzna suggests a Late Preclassic component comparable to the earth-moving operations at El Mirador, though the actual amount of public architecture is unknown. Hydraulic works of this scale represent major corporate labor expenditures, but the analytical standards for comparing monumental civic architecture with utilitarian waterworks pose difficulties. As stated earlier, monumental civic architecture was a universal symbol of authority during the Late Preclassic Period. Its presence connotes considerable labor costs, but also an offering to sociopolitical and religious solidarity rather than to techno-environmental and techno-economic enterprise. Hydraulic works are generally understood as the latter.

The type site of Uaxactún revealed the first substantial Formative civic architecture in the Maya Lowlands. Pyramid E-VII-sub was first revealed in 1927. Following four field seasons of excavations at Uaxactún, Structure E-VII-sub defined the only well-documented example of Late Preclassic civic architecture for nearly forty years (Ricketson and Ricketson 1937). The elaborate set of eighteen stucco-relief masks flanking the four axial staircases on the three-tiered structure is still unique in the Maya Lowlands. Since the discovery of the structure, however, several sites have revealed polychrome masks and stucco facades dating to the Late Preclassic Period. Although plaza space dating to the Late Preclassic Period has been identified in the Group E sector of Uaxactún, no additional civic architecture has been defined. It should be noted that Smith (1937) does indicate that the Structure A-I complex contained two small superimposed pyramids overlooking the South Court. A small civic center may have been present at this location during the Late Preclassic Period, but considerably more data are necessary before confirming such a hypothesis.

The dimensions of Structure E-VII-sub were 24 meters by 23 meters at the base and rising to a height of 8 meters. The summit floor space was approximately 7 meters by 8.7 meters, providing an area of 61 square meters. The volume of the structure was 2,452 cubic meters or about the size of the Structure 5 Group at Cerros. Structure 5C at Cerros revealed a distribution of grotesque stucco masks on its south exposure similar to those identified on the four flanks of Structure E-VII-sub.

The well-reported excavations at Seibal (Smith 1982) indicate the widespread appearance of public architecture. Both Groups A and D reveal buried plaza and platform space dating to the Cantutse phase (300 B.C.–A.D. 1). Unfortunately, the size or extent of this architecture is not well understood.

Extensive excavation and survey have been carried out at Quirigua (Ashmore 1984; Sharer 1978) and Copán (Baudez 1983; Fash 1983; Webster 1988; Willey and Leventhal 1979), but little substantial Late Preclassic architecture has been reported. These communities clearly show that Classic Period developments at the intrasite level of analysis were not always grounded on formidable Preclassic colonization. These data temper statements suggesting that the Late Preclassic Period was the foundation for all subsequent accomplishments in the Maya Lowlands. Nevertheless, the later Formative Period in the lowlands marks the transition into truly civilized behavior and provides the direction for the cultural trajectory defined as Classic Maya.

Although special local adaptations that affected their population size and investment in civic architecture were made at each of the above sites, Cerros does not seem unique by comparison. Becán, Komchen/Dzibilchaltún, and Yaxha appear to have been of similar size and complexity. Tikal, on the other hand, was considerably larger, as were both Río Azul and Edzna (given the implications of the volumetric data). Preliminary findings from El Mirador indicate this city to be far and away the largest and most influential administrative center in the lowlands, making Tikal, Río Azul, and Edzna second rank order communities relative to this huge site. Altar de Sacrificios, Barton Ramie, and Uaxactún are understood as small Late Preclassic communities, probably smaller and less influential than even Cerros. However, until more is gleaned from the area settlement systems around each of these communities, scalar or hierarchical relationships must be considered tentative.

These population density and volumetric figures reveal that various population aggregates were centralizing during the Late Preclassic Period. With the exception of Barton Ramie, each site contains monumental architecture in a central precinct. Moreover,

comparisons indicate that the highest concentration of residential population at a Late Formative community occurs in an area immediately surrounding each central precinct. This pattern of dense house mound occupation inside a core area heavily laden with civic architecture is later modified at most Maya sites, though later Classic "palace" complexes may represent elite residential space (Adams 1974; Harrison 1970). Classic Period administrative centers demonstrate little residential occupation in the civic core of a community, and no evidence is reported for the nonelite occupation identified at Late Preclassic Cerros. This is not to imply that Classic Period communities were vacant centers, but rather that the civic core area at this time was more delimited and less accessible than in the earlier Formative Period.

The several Late Preclassic communities from Northern Belize have not been examined in this presentation to allow the following analysis of Late Preclassic polity structure within a well-documented and circumscribed area of the Maya Lowlands. The following presentation is a reconstruction of the Northern Belizean sociopolitical climate during the Late Preclassic Period, but it can be viewed as a model for other less well understood areal contexts in the Maya Lowlands at a comparable period of time.

THE VIEW FROM NORTHERN BELIZE

Northern Belize can be seen as a geographical unit for regional analysis, even though it represents a modern political division. The three nearby and parallel-running rivers draining Northern Belize are navigable for much of their length and represent communication and trade avenues for the sites in the area. Additionally, numerous examples of pre-Hispanic intensive agriculture have been systematically identified along these drainages (Bloom et al. 1983; Hammond et al. 1987; Scarborough 1983a; Siemens 1982; Turner and Harrison 1981), providing evidence of a highly productive subsistence system for Maya populations. Overall, the river systems are believed to have bound most communities into a shared regional orientation.

Through the pioneer work of Hammond (1973, 1975), a three-tiered site settlement hierarchy can be derived from the size and distribution of Late Preclassic communities in Northern Belize. Cerros, Nohmul, Colha, and Lamanai are seen as first-order administrative centers, each maintained by an aggregate of smaller villages and hamlets. Hierarchical ranking is based on population structure and public monument volumetrics, the latter again an index of corporate labor investment. In the case of Colha, community-wide specialization in a craft is also considered. Outside Northern Belize, Tikal and Río Azul represent a larger and more complicated scalar divisioning. Moreover, El Mirador, resting less than 100 kilometers west of Northern Belize, may prove to be the primary Late Preclassic center of the lowlands, an analogy based on the supremacy of Terminal Formative Teotihuacán in the Mexican Highlands. Though considerably more systematic mapping and excavation are required, Northern Belize does provide the best example of peer polity interaction (see Renfrew and Cherry 1986) in the Formative lowlands.

By placing Theissen polygons between the four Northern Belizean centers and separating them by sustaining areas, a rhomboidal distribution of polity boundaries results. This patterning is attributable to a riverine adaptation across an otherwise planar resource surface. It is relaxed in figure 8.1 by using ovals rather than rectilinear boundaries, which permits the overlap in territories apparent between Cerros and Nohmul. Given the proximity of these two centers and the location of at least two second-order centers at the margins of either polity, potential conflicts in interest may have existed. Although the major canal at Cerros functioned as a drainage device, it clearly defined territorial limits and may have acted as a military deterrent.

Within the polity divisions, each center was surrounded by second-and third-order communities which probably maintained economic autonomy but were linked by stronger sociopolitical ties to the major centers. The productivity of the agricultural base promoted the independence of the cultivator

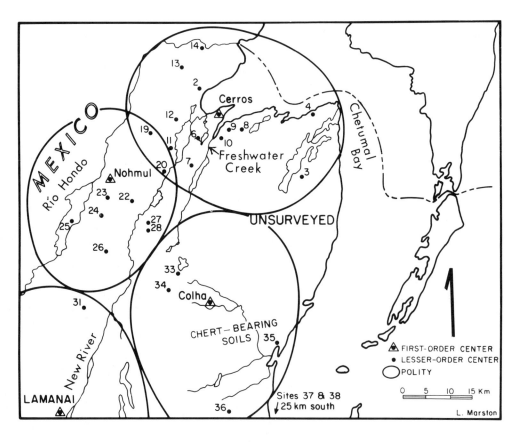

Figure 8.1.   Late Preclassic polities in Northern Belize.

(see Netting 1977). However, allegiance to a sociopolitical center was a practical matter based on strength in numbers as well as on an areal bond of social solidarity and ideological identity. Northern Belizean polities are viewed as loosely organized political units that may have changed their support constituency with time. This again is supported by the very large second-order communities resting between Cerros and Nohmul in a zone that may have been contested.

Figure 8.1 provides the distribution of communities and the proposed limits for the Late Preclassic polities. The large unsurveyed area in the eastern portion of the map represents extensive swamplands and, though the water table may have been lower in the past, substantial occupation in this zone is unlikely. Table 10 further identifies the communities. These data are provided to demonstrate the scalar similarities and differences between sites and to show the level of reliability of the inventoried information. (Note: The site numbers associated with figures 8.1 and 8.2 correspond to those named sites identified in table 10.) Sites with a Protoclassic Floral Park component (A.D. 150–250) as originally defined at Barton Ramie (Willey et al. 1965) have been identified and elsewhere argued to reveal a strong southern highland influence (Hammond 1977; Pring 1977). Table 10 also defines those Early Classic sites reported from Northern Belize. Generally, the Early Classic Period (A.D. 250–450) is associated with statelike institutions, including kingship and the power to sanction others by military coercion (see Schele and Miller 1986). Because the Late Preclassic Period represents the transitional phase into statehood for the Maya, time will be given to reviewing some of the early attributes of Classic Maya civilization. The significance of the Late Preclassic Period can best be appreciated in the context of processual development. A culmination of these processes resulted in the Classic florescence.

Cerros

The Cerros data have already been compared to several other communities found elsewhere in the lowlands. However, greater detail will follow because of the more complete record now revealed for Northern Belize. The geographically commanding position of Cerros by virtue of its river mouth location allowed it gateway community status (after Hirth 1978) into the interiors of Northern Belize and perhaps the northeastern Petén. The sustaining area of the Cerros polity may have been the largest of the polity divisions as a consequence of this riverine and maritime adaptation (see Freidel 1978). Travel time by canoe to second-and third-order communities along the coast in the Cerros territorial sphere was shorter than by trekking on less-direct overland routes.

The Cerros data argue in favor of the concentric zonation model for settlement dispersion during the Late Preclassic Period. However, this compacted settlement design is most convincingly illustrated by the volumetric data. The central precinct contained 63% of all architectural volume at the site with approximately 22,184 cubic meters of fill per hectare used in its construction. Only one-tenth of this architectural volume per hectare was manifest within the remaining core area and only one one-hundredth of this architectural volume per hectare was defined outside the canal. The largest single edifice at Cerros was Structure 4, rising to a height of 22 meters with basal dimensions of 58 meters by 68 meters. The composite fill volume of this monument was 32,038 cubic meters.

The Cerros data also provide insight into the planned spatial disposition of structures and their function. A center line north-south axis through the two ball courts and terminating near the foot of Structure 5C divided the core area approximately in half. As previously discussed (this volume; Scarborough 1983a; Scarborough et al. 1982), a radial attraction toward the central precinct is suggested by the orientation of both residential and civic structures as well as by the curvilinear main canal. The construction or modification of Tulix phase structures within the core area (excluding the central precinct) reveals a ratio of one civic monument to every two occupied residential structures (21:41). Moreover, ceramic studies in concert with the formal architectural identifications indicate that more than a third of these house mounds were nonelite residences (Scarborough and Robertson 1986). Clearly, Late Preclassic communities maintained sizable residential populations in their "ceremonial centers."

The remainder of this section is drawn from a previously published article examining state formation processes in Northern Belize (Scarborough 1985a). Because excerpts from this piece define and examine the three other polities adjacent to Cerros and because the article had a relatively limited circulation, it will be presented at this juncture.

Table 10

Preliminary Inventory of Late Preclassic and Early Classic Sites in Northern Belize

No.	Site	Researcher	Extent of Excavation	Map	Late Preclassic	Protoclassic	Early Classic	Polity	Comments
1	Cerros	Freidel et al.	E	T/A	1	0	2	Cerros	Volume of largest pyramid is 32,038 m^3. Late Preclassic housemound density is 1.21 structures/ha. Ball courts, stucco masks
2	Santa Rita	Chase & Chase; Hammond; Pring	M	T/A	2	L	3	Cerros	Volume of largest pyramid is 14,690 m^3.
3	Shipstern	Hammond; Pring; Sidrys	L	T/A	2	0	3 (?)	Cerros	Volume of largest pyramid is 13,416 m^3.
4	Sarteneja I	Sidrys; Hammond; Pring	L	?	2	0	3 (?)	Cerros	
5	Sarteneja II	Pring	S	0	–	–	2 (?)	Undefined	
6	Saltillo	Scarborough; Gann	S	P/C	2 (?)	?	3 (?)	Cerros	
7	Hillbank	Scarborough; Hammond; Hester et al.	S	P/C	2 (?)	?	2 (?)	Cerros	
8	Ramonal	Scarborough & Robertson	S	T/A	3 (?)	?	2	Cerros	Possible ball court
9	San Antonio II	Scarborough	S	0	3 (?)	?	3 (?)	Cerros	
10	Chunox	Scarborough	S	0	3 (?)	?	3 (?)	Cerros	
11	Benque Viejo	Pring; Hammond	S	0	3 (?)	–	–	Cerros	
12	Aventura	Sidrys; Hammond; Gann; Green	L	P/C	3 (?)	L	1	Cerros	Volume of largest pyramid is 15,300 m^3. Possible ball court
13	Chan Chen	Sidrys	L	P/C	2 (?)	L	2	Cerros	Round structure
14	Santa Elena (Xaman Kiwik)	Mitchum; Hammond	M	T/A	3 (?)	?	2	Cerros	Palacelike structure
15	Kohunlich (Mexico)	Segovia; Andrews	E	T/A	?	?	1	Undefined	Stucco masks, possible ball court
16	Patchchacan	Sidrys; Pring	L	P/C	–	–	2	Undefined	Possible ball court
17	Patchchacan II	Pring	S	0	–	–	3	Undefined	House mounds only
18	Consejo	Hammond; Pring	S	0	–	–	3	Undefined	
19	Louisville	Haberland	L	0	2	?	?	Nohmul-Cerros	Round structure
20	Caledonia	Sidrys; Hammond	L	P/C	2	–	1	Nohmul-Cerros	Volume of largest pyramid is 88,000 m^3
21	Nohmul	Hammond et al.; Chase & Chase; Anderson & Cook; Gann	M	T/A	1	well defined	1	Nohmul	Volume of largest pyramid is 50,400 m^3. Possible ball court
22a	Yo Tumben (Pulltrouser Swamp)	Harrison & Turner	L	T/A	2	–	–	Nohmul	

No.	Site	Source	Extent	Map	Late Preclassic	Proto-Classic	Early Classic	Center	Comments
22b	Kokeal (Pulltrouser Swamp)	Harrison & Turner	L	T/A	2	–	2 (?)	Nohmul	
23	San Luis	Gann; Hammond	L	0	–	L	–	Nohmul	
24	San Lorenzo	Pring	S	0	3 (?)	–	3 (?)	Nohmul	
25	San Antonio I	Siemens et al.; Dahlin	L	0	3	–	2 (?)	Nohmul	
26	Cuello	Hammond et al.; Wilk & Wilhite	E	T/A	2 (?)	–	2	Nohmul	Volume of Structure 35 is 1,100 m³. Late Preclassic population ranges from 2,400–2,940 persons; Early Classic population ranges from 3,063–3,680 persons.
27	San Estevan	Bullard; Hammond et al.; Pring	E	T/A	2	–	1	Nohmul	Volume of largest pyramid is 50,400 m³. Possible ball court
28	Chowacol	Hammond et al.	L	T/A	2	–	2	Nohmul	
29	Yo Creek	Pring	S	0	–	–	3	Undefined	
30	Lamanai	Pendergast; Loten	E	T/A	1	–	primate center	Lamanai	Volume of largest structure is 59,000 m³. Ball court (Late Classic)
31	El Posito	Nievens; Hammond	L	P/C	2	–	2	Lamanai	
32	Colha	Hester et al.; Hammond; Wilk	E	T/A	1	–	2 (?)	Colha	Volume of largest pyramid is 4,500 m³. Late Preclassic population is estimated to be 600 persons. Ball court
33	Honey Camp	Hammond; Pring; Hester et al.	S	0	3	–	3 (?)	Colha	
34	Kichpanha	Hammond et al.; Hester et al.	L	P/C	2	–	3 (?)	Colha	
35	Northern River Lagoon	Hester et al.	L	0	3	–	–	Colha	
36	Altun Ha	Pendergast; Loten	E	T/A	2	–	1	Colha	
37	Kunahmul (New Boston)	Hester et al.	L	0	2	–	–	Colha	(?)
38	Rocky Point	Hester et al.	S	0	2 (?)	?	2 (?)	Cohla	(?)Volume of largest pyramid is 14,400 m³
39	Nago Bank	Hester et al.	S	0	–	–	2	Undefined	
40	Bomba North	Hester et al.	S	0	–	–	2 (?)	Undefined	
41	Will Edwards Lagoon	Hester et al.	S	0	–	–	3	Undefined	
42	Northern River Lagoon South	Hester et al.	S	0	–	–	3 (?)	Undefined	

Key

Extent of excavation:
E = extensive
M = moderate
L = limited
S = surface collections only

Map:
T/A = transit/alidade
? = unknown
0 = none
P/C = pace and compass

Late Preclassic:
1 = first-order center
2 = second-order center
3 = third-order center
? = unknown
– = not represented

Proto-Classic:
0 = none
L = limited
– = not represented
? = unknown

Early Classic:
1 = first-order center
2 = second-order center
3 = third-order center

Nohmul

Nohmul is a multicomponent site lying 26 kilometers southwest of Cerros near the Río Hondo. Unlike Cerros, Nohmul reveals a rich and varied chronological sequence initiated in the Early Preclassic and continuing until the Late Postclassic Period (Hammond 1985; Hammond et al. 1985, 1987). The territorial influence of Nohmul during the Late Preclassic Period may have been slightly less extensive than that of Cerros. However, Nohmul would have been better positioned along the influential Río Hondo corridor into the northeastern Petén core zone. Given the density of second-order sites between those two centers, and the seemingly similar riverine adaptation made by both, it was suggested earlier that the boundary between polities may have been contested. Sites such as Louisville and Caledonia, with significant public architectural investments and located on the boundaries between the two polities, may have vacillated in their alliance.

Late Preclassic architectural volume at Nohmul reveals an extensive energy outlay comparable to that at Cerros. Population estimates are not yet reported, but a systematic survey and testing program is currently under way (Hammond et al. 1985; Hammond et al. 1987). Within the 7 hectares of the central precinct, six structures are over 3 meters high (Structures 1, 2, 8, 11, 55, and 65). The major acropolis, or *nohmul* (Structure 1), has an earthen fill volume of 50,400 cubic meters, including the 14-meter-high Structure 2 resting on its southern margin. The total volumetric expenditure for these structures is approximately 115,000 cubic meters. Although some of these structures may have been initiated in Classic times, Hammond indicates that the central precinct manifests major Floral Park construction and that Structure 1 dates to the Terminal Late Preclassic Period.

The central precinct at Nohmul is less ordered than that found at Cerros, though strict adherence to the cardinal directions is indicated. The dispersed east-west distribution of the monumental architecture is unlike the tightly compacted central precinct design at Cerros, and more akin to the ground plan of El Mirador. The clear north-south axial orientation of the core area at Cerros is in direct contradiction to Nohmul. Hammond shows that the greatest concentration of architecture is divided to the east and to the west and linked by a narrow 300-meter-long connecting plaza. A civic as opposed to elite residential dichotomy is posited for these two architectural complexes by the

Late Classic period (Hammond 1981). Additionally, a north-south-oriented ball court rests immediately to the west of Structure 1. Although it now appears to be Terminal Classic in date (Hammond et al. 1987), the ball court reflects the same orientation as those reported at Cerros as well as the Late Preclassic ball court at Colha.

Lamanai

Lamanai is the third first-order center in Northern Belize and dates to the Late Preclassic Period. Positioned on the northwestern reaches of the New River Lagoon at the headwaters of the New River, Lamanai must rank as one of the most attractive ruins in the tropical world. The site represents a lacustrine adaptation indicated by a ribbon of settlement running along the west bank of the lagoon (Pendergast 1981). Only Barton Ramie, with its linear settlement pattern associated with the course of the Belize River (Willey et al. 1965), appears to have a similar design. However, Lamanai reveals a substantial architectural investment, unlike Barton Ramie. Although Lamanai lacks a focused central precinct, a core area of approximately 35 hectares contains all of the truly massive architecture at the site. The linear orientation of the central precinct had obvious visual appeal to riverine traffic. Loten's survey recorded a total of 718 structures within the 4.5 square kilometers mapped at present. Excavations in the settlement zone are currently in progress. To date, Late Preclassic settlement densities are unreported. What is apparent, however, is that Lamanai was a pivotal community in a regional network of Late Preclassic interactions.

Pendergast (1981) has reported that the tallest structure at the site, Structure N10-43, at 33 meters, was built in the Late Preclassic Period. With a sediment fill volume of 59,000 cubic meters, this structure had a volume comparable to that of the contemporaneous acropolis at Nohmul. Pendergast further indicates that the bulk of the large Structure P9-2 was constructed at this early date.

In addition to architecture, Lamanai shares some striking similarities to its riverine complement at the mouth of the New River. Cerros occupied a lagoon setting (chapter 3; Freidel and Scarborough 1982; Scarborough 1983a), perhaps not unlike Lamanai. Still, Cerros reflects a tighter concentration of structures with a strong north-south orientation into the interior of the community. The iconographic display at both sites at this time reveals strong similarities (Freidel and Schele 1988), with the tripartite summit superstructure of N10-43 having its only clear parallel atop Structure 29 at Cerros, El Mirador notwithstanding. The lone ball court at Lamanai has been securely dated to the Terminal Classic Period (Pendergast 1981). However, its diminutive size and north-south orientation resting only 60 meters south of Structure N10-43 suggest a layout similar to the northernmost ball court, Structure 61 at Cerros. Perhaps an earlier Late Preclassic court was completely destroyed in preparation for the later court. By way of analogy, the Late Preclassic ball court at Colha was entirely rebuilt in Late Classic times (Eaton and Kunstler 1980). Generally speaking, the two sites are understood as representing similar adaptations to a regional interaction sphere. The importance of Lamanai to Cerros is best demonstrated by the central and dominant location of the smaller Structure 29 (9,460 cubic meters) in the core area at Cerros (Freidel 1981) when compared to the larger and commanding Structure N10-43 at Lamanai.

Colha

Colha is the last of the four centers dominating Late Preclassic regional organization in Northern Belize. It rests away from the major drainages servicing much of Northern Belize, reflecting its specific adaptation to another natural resource. Studies directed by Hester, Shafer, and Eaton (1980, 1982) clearly indicate the importance of the community during the Late Preclassic Period. Eaton (1982) estimates a conservative Late Preclassic population of six hundred persons (100 to 120 house mounds per square kilometer) within the 1-square-kilometer area currently surveyed. This figure is in keeping with the settlement aggregate within the core area from Cerros. The monumental center at Colha covers 5 hectares, an area comparable to either Cerros or Nohmul, but containing a far less massive sediment construction fill volume. The largest pyramid at the site, Structure 9, is approximately 10 meters high with a volume of 4,500 cubic meters. Although this structure was initiated in the Late Preclassic, it was severely dwarfed by the massive structures noted from the other three first-order Late Preclassic communities in Northern Belize. The north-south-oriented Late Preclassic ball court (Eaton and Kunstler 1980) rests immediately in front of Structure 9.

The prominence of Colha in a regional analysis lies in its manufacture and distribution of lithic tools. Except for Altun Ha, Colha is the only first-order site at any time to rest in the chert-bearing soils of Belize. Numerous workshop areas cover the settlement and intensive craft specialization is indicated (Shafer 1982; Shafer and Hester 1983). Of the two major standardized classes of Late Preclassic tools, over two million tranchet bit implements were produced and an even greater number of large oval bifaces were made. Moreover, stemmed macroblades, or "daggers," from Colha appear as cache offerings throughout Northern and Central Belize, and they are suggested at Uaxactún and El Mirador (Hester 1982). The utilitarian tool forms appear to have been used in the removal of primary forest and possibly in the preparation and maintenance of raised-field agricultural plots (Harrison and Turner 1983). Wilk (1975b) has suggested that a cottagelike industry may have been at work at the site in which wealthy families marketed their wares regionally. Viewed in this light, Colha would not have required large monumental architecture to attract a constituency or to maintain its centrality as a political and economic node during the Late Preclassic Period.

Colha reflects a singular focus on lithic tool production with a light investment in central precinct architecture. Given a population comparable to Cerros, it is suggested that a different sociopolitical organization was at play than found at the other first-order centers. Colha represents a character of Maya economic organization that has only recently been fully appreciated (Hester et al. 1982; cf. Marcus 1983): site-level craft specialization.

Intensive Agriculture

Intensive agriculture in Northern Belize has been convincingly demonstrated for the Late Preclassic Period at Cerros (this volume; Scarborough 1983a). Although Cerros reveals a "still water," internally drained canal system, most drained-and-raised-field systems in Belize are located on rivers that draw on an external drainage advantage. Late Preclassic debris has been identified with "flow water" riverine canal systems near Nohmul at Pulltrouser Swamp (Hammond 1985; Hammond et al. 1987; Harrison and Turner 1983; Turner and Harrison 1981) and Albion Island (Bloom et al. 1983, 1985; Puleston 1977). Raised fields have been reported immediately to the north of Lamanai, but the extensiveness of this agricultural complex is not yet known (Pendergast 1981). Intensive agriculture has not been clearly defined at Colha, although a considerable amount of survey and reconnaissance has been conducted. This may be an expected consequence of the specialized adaptation made to the production and distribution of stone tools. The importation of food from neighboring communities into Colha may have been the unit of exchange in acquiring these tools used elsewhere in Northern Belize.

Dahlin (1977) has mentioned that Belize may have been the agricultural "bread-basket" for much of the lowlands by way of the extensive raised-field system (Siemens 1982). By the Classic Period Nohmul was squarely in command of an agricultural base unrivaled by other Northern Belizean sites, with the possible exception of Lamanai. Although some new aerial imagery techniques may reveal canal systems in the Petén, few ground-truth surveys have been carried out (Adams et al. 1981). SAR imagery has been ground-truth surveyed over a portion of Northern Belize, where as much as 20% of the lineament imagery covering the Cerros area indicates canalization (this volume; Adams et al. 1981; Scarborough 1983b). Because canals act as boundaries in delimiting plot size, they reflect agricultural units of production. However, present interpretations allow few statements with regard to land ownership or tenure relationships, an area of research that could markedly strengthen the sociopolitical feudal model as presented by Adams and Smith (1981).

Smaller-Order Communities

A number of smaller-order communities are defined within the territories most strongly affected by the four principal centers. Within the Cerros sphere, Hammond (1981:184) maintains that Santa Rita, Sarteneja, and Shipstern were initiated in the Late Preclassic or Early Classic period. Where maps are available from Santa Rita and Shipstern, the main structures at these sites range from 13,416 to 14,690 cubic meters. Orientation of the main pyramid is to the cardinal directions. The remainder of the structures composing these centers are much reduced in size and the areal extent of the ill-defined central precinct is 1 hectare or less. Given the coastal position of these sites, it may be that the central pyramid aided in

navigation as well as defined a central place. Little is known about the residential population size and density of second-order Belizean communities. However, Late Preclassic *plazuela* groups and house mounds unassociated with civic architecture have been identified in each of the polities.

Even less is known of second-order communities within the Nohmul sphere during the Late Preclassic Period. The small Platform Center 109, resting 1.5 kilometers north of the central precinct at Nohmul, may be indicative of the community design supporting Nohmul. This small group of four mounds is again dominated by a main pyramid, though Structure 110, with a fill volume of 1,600 cubic meters, is quite reduced in size from other second-order community pyramids within the Cerros sphere (Wilk 1975a). A cache of Late Preclassic jade heads, similar to a cache identified from the summit of Structure 6B at Cerros, was located in this structure (Hammond 1986).

Structure 277 is located 1.6 kilometers northwest of the central precinct at Nohmul. It has revealed a sizable inventory of Floral Park materials and attained a volume of 9,000 cubic meters (Barry 1975), though a clear Protoclassic date for the entirety of the mound is suspect. This less-pretentious structure carried a humanoid mask associated with a Floral Park assemblage (Gann and Gann 1939), which may have greater affinity to Early Classic modes of symbolic expression. Special reference to the Early Classic human masks on Structure N9-56 from Lamanai and the Early Classic date attributed to the masks of Kohunlich (Freidel personal communication) suggest a tradition rooted in the grotesque mask sculpture from Cerros dating to the Late Preclassic Period (Freidel 1981; Freidel and Schele 1988). The sculptured pyramid tradition would seem to be widely spread throughout Northern Belize and accessible to even minor centers.

Cuello rests 16 kilometers south of Nohmul and reveals a substantial Late Preclassic occupation (Hammond 1978; Hammond et al. 1979). The now famous Platform 34 lies 300 meters southwest of the central precinct. Structure 35, initiated in the Terminal Preclassic period, but encapsulated by an Early Classic pyramid, rests on the western margin of the platform. It rises to a height of 5.5 meters and contains a fill volume of 1,100 cubic meters. In an innovative study, Wilk and Wilhite (1982) examined the settlement pattern at Cuello. From flat excavation tests, they indicate an extremely dense population for this small center. Given the quality and quantity of the artifactual inventory from Platform 34 (eighty-six Terminal Preclassic vessels from cache Feature 6 alone; Cantor 1978) as well as the clear continuity of construction beginning in the Early Preclassic Period, Cuello, unlike other communities discussed, is viewed as a sacred place. It should be noted that Cliff (1982, 1986) has demonstrated a similar occupation density extending over a diminutive area (6 hectares) underlying the central precinct at Cerros. Perhaps a nucleated barrio was located in association with the central precinct of some Late Preclassic centers (Cliff personal communication).

The Lamanai and Colha spheres are only now beginning to reveal Late Preclassic second-order communities. Although Lamanai will surely reveal a sizable number of second-order centers within its periphery, the only reported support center is El Pozito, and it does not reach its maximum size until Late Classic times (Neivens and Libby 1976). However, Group D at San José (Thompson 1936) may be among the constituency supporting Lamanai during the Late Preclassic Period.

The Colha sphere of influence encompasses five known sites during the Late Preclassic Period. Given the considerable investment in reconnaissance around Colha (Kelly 1980, 1982), the infrequency of Late Preclassic remains can be interpreted as negative evidence, rather than as the absence of evidence, in support of a diminutive sustaining population. Altun Ha is suggested to have been a satellite community of Colha, although the relationship at this early date is not well documented. The Late Preclassic pyramid Structure F-8 at Altun Ha (Pendergast 1979) is comparable in volume to the largest structure at Colha, and Late Preclassic occupation is indicated in other zones of the site (Pendergast 1976). Altun Ha plays a more centralized role over the chert-bearing soil region of Northern Belize during the Early Classic Period, when Colha suffers a clear decline.

EARLY CLASSIC DEVELOPMENT

Although the purview of this section has been the Late Preclassic Period in Northern Belize, some discussion of Early Classic Period settlement seems warranted, given the changes attributed to that period (see Fig. 8.2 and table 10). Care must be taken in dealing with the Early Classic Period because of the chronological difficulties involved. Architectural and ceramic

sequential divisions are least satisfactorily understood for this period of Maya prehistory. Nevertheless, a number of Belizean centers underwent a severe decline while a few others experienced a successful restructuring and eventual florescence. Cerros and Colha clearly lost their prominence. Cerros appears to have been reoccupied by a "squatter" population living in part on former civic structures such as ball courts, but little actual civic construction was undertaken (this volume; Scarborough and Robertson 1986). Colha records no Early Classic workshops and only sparse occupation at the site (Eaton 1982).

Lamanai, and perhaps Nohmul, suggest solidification of their support populations and renewed centralization in their central precincts. Nohmul may not have increased greatly in size and may even have suffered an organizational setback, but current research will better elucidate the matter (Hammond et al. 1987). Although Tzakol 2 and Tzakol 3 ceramics may not be well represented in construction fill at Nohmul, Floral Park and Tzakol 1 ceramics are associated with considerable construction in the settlement and central precinct (Hammond 1981; Hammond et al. 1985, 1987). Addressing Lamanai, Pendergast (1981:42) states, "from the evidence at hand it is clear that the 4th through 6th centuries were a time of extensive construction and, one would judge, enhancement of the status of the community . . . achieved in the Preclassic."

Structure P9-25 may have been constructed at this time with a conservative energy investment of 178,200 cubic meters of fill. The fill volume of this one acropolis is comparable to the total volume of monumental architecture at Cerros.

Three or four additional sites with Late Preclassic antecedents emerge as key centers in the Early Classic Period. Altun Ha, San Estevan, Kohunlich (Mexico), and possibly Aventura and Caledonia become less impressive first-order centers within the general Northern Belizean zone. Although limited work has been carried out at Aventura, it has been suggested that remnant populations from Cerros may have relocated there (Hammond 1977). A similar argument has been put forth by Shafer (1982) in addressing the decline in Colha lithic production and the rise of Altun Ha. Platform A-1 at Caledonia, with a fill volume of 88,000 cubic meters, appears to have been initiated in the Early Classic Period (Sidrys 1976). If this early date can be further confirmed, Caledonia will be of critical importance in evaluating the Late Preclassic to Early Classic Period transition.

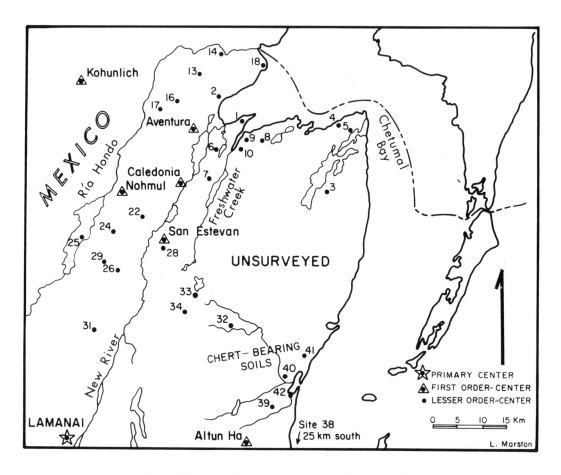

Figure 8.2.   Early Classic communities in Northern Belize.

San Estevan may be the best-preserved Early Classic center in Northern Belize (Bullard 1965), although Hammond (personal communication) has indicated that the north-south-oriented ball court is associated with Tepeu ceramics. Structure 15 reveals an energy outlay of 12,180 cubic meters, a figure comparable to the largest pyramid, Structure A-2, at Aventura (Sidrys 1983).

Numerous second-order centers occur throughout Northern Belize, but hierarchical distance from first-order centers is not great. Generally, with over thirty known sites, the population is believed to have increased slightly over Late Preclassic populations. Clear territorial divisions are not well defined and, except for Lamanai, Northern Belize appears decentralized and best characterized by a number of autonomous communities. Only Lamanai reveals a major increase in size.

THE MODEL

In an attempt to place the Cerros data in an interpretive context and to explain the role Cerros may have had in the Late Preclassic sociopolitical system, a model is presented based on the early introduction of intensive agriculture and interregional interaction. The presentation of the model at the end of the monograph is a consequence of presenting the new data recovered from Cerros. The substance of the model is derived in part from this information. However, confirmation of the new approach must await future field projects. This is a consequence of remodeling our interpretations following the survey and excavations at Cerros. Nevertheless, the thesis outlined below is an explanation for the sociopolitical processes only recently identified for this important period of Maya prehistory.

Cerros has been viewed as one of four regional centers in Northern Belize during the Late Preclassic Period. The development of three of these centers from Middle Preclassic antecedents has been demonstrated (Hammond 1985; Pendergast 1981; Shafer and Hester 1983), but in the case of Cerros, its appearance is not forecasted by a Middle Preclassic component. Nohmul, Colha, and Lamanai have well-documented Middle Preclassic assemblages. However, Hammond (1977) shows that the Middle Preclassic Period in Northern Belize is much less densely occupied than the subsequent Late Preclassic Period. This is to say that new growth in Belize involved not only increasing populations but the establishment of at least one colonizing regional center in an area with little prior history of occupation. The planned symmetry of the Cerros community coupled with the relatively short period of major construction at the site indicates the intensity of regional development. The significance of Cerros goes beyond the unusual abandonment of nearly all public construction projects; the rapidity at which monuments were erected during the short-lived Tulix phase is equally intriguing.

Background

Given the stir of activity in Northern Belize and throughout the greater Maya Lowlands, how do we explain the forces that culminated in the material remains identifying the Late Preclassic Period? Although political systems can only be inferred, some degree of social ranking is indicated as early as the Middle Preclassic Period. At both Altar de Sacrificios (Willey 1977) and Cuello (Hammond et al. 1979), a public building platform has been identified. Moreover, the appearance of obsidian blades traded in from the Guatemalan Highlands indicates access to rare imports at both sites. Further, Andrews V (1981) associates the initiation of Structure 500 at Komchen with late Middle Preclassic developments. Fragments of another imported highland offering, jade, have been reported from the fill of this structure as well. Finally, Puleston (1973:311) notes that Uolantun near Tikal suggests Middle Preclassic civic architecture.

Public works projects and imported luxury goods hint at a degree of social divisioning at all of these communities by Middle Preclassic times. In Northern Belize, this ranking evolved in an environment of considerable abundance, a setting not unlike Xicalango and the heartland of the Olmec (the rivers debouching into Chetumal Bay present an estuarine environment similar in most respects to that found on the other flank of the Yucatán peninsula). Sanders and Webster (1978) argue that the low-diversity, low-risk environment of the Olmec Lowlands set the stage for early ranking. In the Northern Belizean example, Middle Preclassic villages were probably fairly autonomous entities that acquired most of their resources from the immediacy of their surroundings. However, the early suggestion of ranked divisioning in communities would by definition indicate a control over some resources by a select few. Further, some degree of regional social exchange and interaction between communities can be assumed at this time, given the presence of highland stone exotica in the lowland context.

Late Preclassic Population, Agriculture, and Surplus

The Late Preclassic Period was one of major population growth and significant architectural investment. Population growth rates reported from the Middle Preclassic Period to the Late Preclassic Period at Altar de Sacrificios and Yaxha register the greatest increases in the history of these communities (Culbert 1988). Tikal and Barton Ramie indicate correspondingly high growth rates, although slightly less pronounced than those of the early Late Classic Period (A.D. 600–700). (These population figures have been adjusted to account for exaggerated differences in time spans between periods [Culbert 1988: table 4.2].) Further, the amount of public construction during the Late Preclassic Period when compared to the few small Middle Preclassic civic structures known is staggering. No other period in Maya prehistory demonstrates this amount of significant construction when contrasted with a preceding period. This was a formative period in the history of civilization, with little established or codified pan-regional knowledge on which to draw initially.

Food production clearly intensified during the Late Preclassic Period. Raised-and-drained-field systems are not reported in the Middle Preclassic Period, but Late Preclassic wetlands agriculture has been well documented in Northern Belize (Bloom et al. 1983; Scarborough 1983a; Turner and Harrison 1981). These early dates for intensive agriculture coupled with the large-scale construction of hydraulic works such as identified at Edzna and Cerros represent the earliest known evidence for intensification in the tropical lowlands of the New World. The intensification of the agricultural base correlates with the flurry of Late Preclassic building activity in the Maya Lowlands and an increase in population. The planned cultural landscaping of the Late Preclassic environment has been shown at Cerros (this volume; Scarborough 1983a) and population increases throughout the Southern Maya Lowlands demonstrated (Eaton 1982; Ford 1986; Hammond 1981; Kurjack 1974; Puleston 1973; Rice and Rice 1980; Smith 1972; Thomas 1981; Willey et al. 1965).

In the low-risk environments of many portions of the Maya lowlands, intensive agriculture meant considerably higher yields than ever before. Clearly, the increasing caloric demands made by a growing population were great. However, looking to a population pressure model as the causal agent in stimulating agricultural intensification and subsequent social complexity through an involved feedback loop cannot be supported. Population densities were greater than ever before in Maya prehistory but much reduced from the potential carrying capacity of the lowlands, as indicated by the densities recorded during the Late Classic Period. The kind and degree of population stress suggested immediately prior to the Classic collapse (Culbert 1977) can hardly be projected for the Late Preclassic Period, as much as a millennium earlier. Although agricultural production during the Formative Period was only a small percentage of what it was to become, the Maya had already begun to intensify their agrarian base.

Given the apparent abundance available to a dispersed-compact population traditionally adapted to a semitropical rain forest, the incentive for intensification is in need of an explanation. Agricultural intensification in an already productive environment in which population densities were far below the potential carrying capacity of the land are assumed to result in food surpluses. Further, the accumulation of agricultural supplies in a low-risk setting is assumed to allow the conversion of surplus into articles of wealth. Although most agricultural supplies were consumed by the growing population, surplus was less attractively stored for any length of time in the tropical surrounds. The hot, humid conditions of the lowlands excite rapid organic decomposition and, when coupled with the variety of animal pests identified in a tropical regime, the ability to store surplus predictably for extended periods would have been difficult (Reina and Hill 1980).

Goods not in storage, then, were destroyed, consumed, or circulated. Throwing away excess food may have occurred during especially bountiful harvests. However, it would seem maladaptive for the Maya to invest routinely in food production only to destroy food in a potlatchlike ritual, especially given the sociopolitical heights to which they were successfully to aspire. Besides, we have no evidence for such behavior. What we do have evidence for is the widespread appearance of monumental architecture. Perhaps structurally not unlike the show of wealth associated with the potlatch (see Codere 1950), food would have been removed from circulation through its consumption by a labor force responsible for the construction of the monuments.

Architectural construction was more sociopolitically adaptive in promoting a lasting display of wealth for a large supporting population. As Price (1982:731) has indicated, large-scale public monuments are energy equivalents of themselves. From an etic perspective, monuments represent a static edifice to surplus.

Webster (1985) has examined facets of the surplus concept as they relate to the ancient Maya. He indicates that very little need for agricultural surplus existed. The time and labor necessary to construct monumental architecture during the Late Classic is argued to have been accommodated by an extended period between the harvest and sowing months. Labor is believed to have been readily available from the local household and agricultural plot during this period of the agricultural year. However, intensive agriculture as early as the Late Preclassic Period in the Maya Lowlands indicates a need to generate a surplus for a relatively small, dispersed population. Two crops were likely taken during the year, as the intensification process would suggest, making for a full year-round agricultural work cycle. In order to construct civic monuments, time away from fields and field-related activities had to be supported by a previously amassed surplus yield. What conditions would create this excess and how was it consumed or circulated?

Surplus for Status Markers

One condition that may have stimulated surplus production and intensive agriculture was an attempt by newly established elites to legitimize their claim to office and authority. These elites were expected outgrowths of earlier Middle Preclassic social ranking systems. Excavations throughout the lowlands indicate that the abundance of luxury items, or "status tokens," used to symbolically identify controlling individuals or lineages increased markedly during the Late Preclassic Period. The increased appearance of monumental architecture is also seen as a means by which a growing group of elite symbolically and physically identified themselves with the authority to initiate and maintain labor-intensive projects and, therefore, to demonstrate their control over a sustaining population.

However, the agricultural surplus by which elite symbols were obtained could not be physically transferred very far in a primitive economy. The bulk and distances involved in converting crops to luxury items of status and wealth would have been a major stumbling block to an incipient state without inexpensive and efficient modes of transport (see Sanders and Santley 1983). The advantage of carrying food on the backs of human porters for profitable exchange is quickly lost with greater distances traveled, as the load is simply consumed by the bearer.

As a consequence, many short-distance exchange partnerships developed between neighboring communities and polities. These alliances permitted the steady stream of luxury items into the Late Preclassic lowlands principally from Highland Guatemala. Such periodic market exchange would not have involved long-distance trade, but rather a complicated down-the-line exchange network in which a luxury item would be handled and passed along innumerable times before ending up in a particular Northern Belizean context. Long-distance trade always implies a reciprocal set of items in exchange, a problem for scholars since the identification of Olmec "influence" outside the jade- and serpentine-poor Tabasco heartland (see Grove 1984; Santley 1984). The Maya Lowlands, too, had an influence in the highlands probably as early as the Late Preclassic Period (see Freidel 1981), but tangible material remains are little documented, especially when compared to the quantities of obsidian and jade reported from nearly all Lowland Maya sites. Although the perishable nature of some items imported from the semitropical forests of the lowlands into the highlands might be argued with success (Voorhies 1982), this is an assumption based on the absence of evidence, not negative evidence, and probably should be less strongly advanced during the Formative Period, a period long removed from colonial records and industrial market economies.

To Preclassic communities of Northern Belize and the greater Maya Lowlands, as well as in a majority of other primitive sedentary societies, agricultural crops were their most valuable asset. The conversion of these products into luxury items could not be done by long-distance trade as previously defined (see Hammond 1972, 1986; Hirth 1984; Freidel 1979). However, once down-the-line trade was established and the demand for luxury items excited, a "siphon effect" would result, with items moving out of Highland Guatemala, pulled through the Maya Lowlands, and converted for agricultural crops one village to the next. Crops acquired by a village already adequately supplied with foodstuffs could be set aside for laborers during public building projects, or used in the provisioning of military exploits, or perhaps employed to maintain adequate supplies of food for an expanding nonagrarian service class (see Miller and Tilley 1984). Given a demand for luxury items and architectural monuments, for the growing need to set individuals and groups apart within the society, the village-by-village circulation of goods would be expected.

This latter point is illustrated by the number of small centers within the Maya Lowlands that have monumental architecture and rich offerings of luxury goods (note the Late Preclassic Pomona tomb offerings [see Kidder and Ekholm 1951; Justeson et al. 1988]; or the cache of jade heads recovered 1.5 kilometers from the central precinct of Nohmul [see Hammond 1986]; or the recent finds from the small Late Preclassic community of Kichpanha [Gibson et al. 1986]). This economic condition produced a homogeneity of traits and associated ideas throughout the Maya Lowlands, perhaps best typified by the widespread technical redundancy of the Chicanel ceramic sphere itself.

A trait list of material remains recovered from any one region within the Late Preclassic Maya Lowlands is remarkably similar to any other, a condition unlike the regional variation identified during the later Classic Period. The development of the "interaction sphere" responsible for this distribution of characteristics is based on the agricultural success of the period, down-the-line exchange, and the need to administer this newfound bounty and wealth (see below). The origins of writing (Schele and Miller 1986), the singular appearance of the Chicanel ceramic sphere (Robertson-Freidel 1980), and the repeated expression of sculpted polychrome pyramids (Freidel 1986b) each signal the transmission of organizational principles by way of the demand for and movement of goods and services.

Titles to Office

The major advances in complex sociopolitical organization during the Late Preclassic Period arose in part from the Middle Preclassic village exchange system. The number of individuals necessary to organize developing new centers as well as the significant amount of growth associated with old centers indicate that the number of available offices or titles for social control had risen markedly. This condition would have promoted the appearance of at least two social organizational alternatives. The first path would allow any individual with a degree of entrepreneurial skill and familial support to rise to the authority of an office. This approach may have been the adaptation made by Middle Preclassic communities organized in a chiefdomlike manner (Sahlins 1955; Service 1971). A second path would find individuals from specific groups or families groomed by way of selective socialization and ritual knowledge for titled office. This approach requires considerable support from a sustaining population and probably indicates incipient social stratification. Although it is difficult not to characterize these two means of obtaining control over a center and its constituency as evolutionary stages, it is more likely that during a transitional period in the origin of civilization both of these options were available. However, by the end of the Late Preclassic Period, the amount of information necessary to hold and operate a leadership role in society would require longer and longer terms of protracted learning. The acquisition of this knowledge was best communicated by way of hereditary title, a condition clearly in place by the Early Classic Period (Schele and Miller 1986).

With the increased number and size of Late Preclassic centers, the demand for competent functionaries would have been greater than ever before. Given the exaggerated and unprecedented growth and construction during the period, the need for a rapidly trained class or set of lineages to govern these developments is apparent. Autonomous community development would not have provided the leadership roles necessary to keep pace with the explosion of activity in the Maya Lowlands. Unlike the population overshoot model suggested for the Classic Maya collapse (Culbert 1977; Harrison 1977), in which the population surpassed the resources necessary to support itself, the Preclassic florescence provided more disposable resources than could be consumed comfortably.

The need for individuals to fill positions of authority was met by autochthonous elites or newly introduced functionaries from neighboring communities, each with the proper knowledge of tradition and supported by family alliances having the same ritualized regard for these traditions. Although population growth is indicated for the Late Preclassic Period, it was not necessarily an increase initiated at all levels of the social hierarchy. The appearance of intensive agriculture does correlate with Late Preclassic developments, but contemporary comparisons to present-day groups (Wilk 1985; Wilken 1987) suggest that the amount of energy invested in the new technology need not necessarily have required additional labor for greater yields. Better management and coordination of the work projects as designed by the developing hierarchy of elites would not automatically require more labor.

Demographic Structure

The agricultural maintenance tasks needed to support the Late Preclassic socioeconomic context probably did not require sizable sustaining populations. In fact, the nonelite incentive to have large families cannot be argued at this early date. The size of nonelite houses at Cerros, for example, indicates only very limited floor space when compared to elite counterparts. The push for large families among this labor pool, or at least their survivability, was not great. On the other hand, considerable incentive existed for the proliferation of lineages which controlled the ritualized knowledge and authority. The spread of centers across the Yucatán peninsula coupled with the need for individuals knowledgeable enough to lead groups into the new social order produced a population curve heavily weighted toward elite expansionism. The classic demographic profile during the Late Preclassic Period would have been "cylindrical" rather than the expected status-population pyramidal form. Elite functionaries were in demand while the nonelite laborer was less so.

The expansion of elite populations is best demonstrated at Cerros, where the ratio of elite to nonelite occupation was approximately 3:1 inside the core area of the community during both the C'oh and the Tulix phases of the Late Preclassic Period. This is to be compared with the only comparable figures estimated by Adams (1974) for Classic Period Uaxactún. The

Uaxactún population reported as elite within the core area of this important city represented perhaps 1% of the total.

Early Classic Status Regulation

By the Terminal Preclassic/Early Classic Period, several major changes were at work in society. Agricultural production probably continued to increase, as suggested by the extensive tracts of drained fields adjacent to the Early Classic site of Río Azul (Adams 1986). However, major changes in the distribution of populations across the Maya Lowlands are indicated. In Northern Belize, Cerros was abandoned by those elites responsible for public works projects, and most former centers of the Late Preclassic Period experienced notable setbacks, except perhaps Lamanai. These conditions were apparent elsewhere in the lowlands, with some centers commanding and consolidating sizable constituencies, while others lost their support. There is little reason to believe that agricultural production was somehow catastrophically interrupted to produce these demographic shifts. As a matter of fact, some sites, including Río Azul, Lamanai, Tikal, and Yaxha, appear to have experienced a continued burst of activity. Where demographic data exist, both Tikal (Puleston 1973) and Yaxha (Rice and Rice 1980) reveal sustained growth not inconsistent with Preclassic increases.

However, the gap between elite and nonelite was ever widening. This may be most marked in the lavish tombs identified at Tikal and most recently reported from Río Azul (Adams 1986) dating to the Early Classic Period. Studies of skeletal stature at Tikal (Haviland 1967) indicate a trend initiated in the Protoclassic Period and culminating in the Early Classic Period in which elites appear to have lived longer and more healthy lives than their nonelite complement. Moreover, the number of ground-level "hidden" dwellings at Tikal is greatest during the Early Classic Period (Puleston 1973). These structures are usually assumed to be nonelite dwellings. Given the limited energy investment associated with the construction and maintenance of these structures, coupled with subsequent Late Classic population growth at Tikal without a corresponding increase in the number of ground-level dwellings, the gulf between the elite and the nonelite during the Early Classic may have been as broad as it was ever to become.

The Early Classic Period was a turbulent one with graphic depictions of militarism found at many sites throughout the lowlands (Schele and Miller 1986). Defensive earthworks appear at Tikal (Puleston and Callender 1967), Becán (Webster 1976; Ball and Andrews V 1978), and Muralla de León on Lake Macanche (Rice and Rice 1981) by the Terminal Preclassic or Early Classic period and may also be well established at El Mirador by the Terminal Preclassic Period (Dahlin 1984). The struggle between elite ruling lineages is clearly identified. At both Becán and Muralla de León the turbulence during the Early Classic Period apparently resulted in local population declines.

What were the forces that created the instability registerd during the Early Classic Period? In Northern Belize, Early Classic village sites increased slightly in number over Late Preclassic frequencies. Although difficult to extrapolate to the remainder of the lowlands, it is expected that small rural population growth accelerated with the appearance of old and new Early Classic villages and hamlets. However, the shake-ups occurring in the large civic centers throughout the Maya Lowlands suggest that elite lineage control was being challenged. Given the epigraphic data from Early Classic centers, it is likely that most of this strife developed between competing elite lineages (Schele and Miller 1986). This turbulence is understood as a consequence of the proliferation of elite lineages resulting from the creation of the many titles and offices produced during the Late Preclassic Period. Although the need for functionaries and elites to guide the sociopolitical organization of society continued, control became more centralized. Early forms of rigid stratification emerged and are again most evident in the epigraphic record.

Factors in this development were the availability of status tokens, or luxury items that defined groups and individuals and the proliferation of titles near the end of the Late Preclassic Period. The influx of jade and obsidian into the lowlands made it widely available. Too, the amount of monumental architectural construction during this period indicates that crops exchanged for labor projects allowed most elites access to impressive symbols of authority. However, the availability of these symbols and a decrease in the demand for controlling elites and functionaries forced a second major adaptation in the organization of the Maya. Although agricultural resources probably continued to be abundant, a scramble for sociopolitical control of the various polities in the lowlands seems apparent. A "culling" mechanism developed to establish the pecking order associated with stratification. Some elites were eliminated, others simply placed in subordinate or ancillary roles, while a powerful few rose to the kingship and ultimate control of a city or polity.

Garber (1983) relates that the amount of jade found at Tulix phase Cerros was plentiful, but that most of it was recovered from elaborate termination rituals associated with the abandonment of the community. Jade in the Cerros example appears to have been removed from circulation in a ritualized attempt to maintain its value. The importation of jade through down-the-line exchange during the Terminal Preclassic and into the Early Classic periods could not be abruptly discontinued, although the demand for such items decreased. The Cerros termination rituals are one example of an attempt at preventing the dilution of authority by keeping symbols of office costly. It should be noted that the termination rituals at Cerros were just that; the site was abandoned by its elite following these rites. Although other factors surely contributed to the cessation of monument construction and the near abandonment of the community, Cerros was also unable ultimately to stem the inflationary tide of such status tokens.

The disruptions to down-the-line exchange during the later Early Classic Period for luxury items curbed their dropping value. Moreover, the quality of the workmanship in jade coupled with the appearance of new mediums of expression resulted in a new set of status tokens for identifying coercive elites. The appearance of craft specialization in many arenas, being sanctioned by the new aristocracy, would have flowered. Access to these artisans, indeed, the creation of such a class of artisans, would further accent the division between elite and nonelite. By cutting access to Late Preclassic status tokens and controlling the incipient craft specialist, a few coercive elites were able to monopolize the symbols of power.

Demographic Balance

At some point the population "cylinder" model as characterized by the Late Preclassic Period was re-

versed. Especially well-trained and skillful elite lineages or soon-to-be "great families" began to marshal support for themselves. One tactic was to affiliate oneself and one's family with the gods and to proclaim invincibility and immortality through ancestry. This appears to have been a successful maneuver at Tikal (Coggins 1975; Miller 1986) by those who ultimately ascended to power. During this period the amount of attrition between elites would have been considerable. Although some incentive for large families may have continued among the highest stratum of the social hierarchy, large families for lesser elites would not have been promoted (cf. Boone 1986). On the other hand, coercive elites throughout the lowlands began to push their constituency beyond the "moral limit" (Sahlins 1972). Previous Late Preclassic alliances were shaken, with the exchange of functionaries and their knowledge breaking down between smaller communities. Many Late Preclassic centers underwent a decentralization of former elite control, with communities like Nohmul, Colha, Becán, Muralla de León, Komchen/Dzibilchaltún, and Seibal (the last as suggested by Willey 1977) experiencing significant organizational setbacks and Cerros nearly entirely abandoned by the elite.

Closure

The model presented provides a theoretical scaffolding for orienting research in the future. More work is needed to better understand the Early Classic Period. The social distance between the elite and the nonelite during this crucial period will require additional testing. Processual statements concerning the Late Preclassic Period demand an in-depth appreciation for the Early Classic Period. Only by knowing the Early Classic can we reconstruct the immediate trajectory that the Maya of the Late Preclassic Period charted.

APPENDICES

Appendix A
Volumetrics at Cerros

The volumetric assessment presented for Cerros has assumed that (1) the limestone and earth fill for the construction of the civic and residential architecture was quarried within the immediate perimeter of the site and (2) the limestone caprock on which the community rests was homogeneous and approximately flat. Both of these assumptions are examined in chapter 3.

QUARRY VOLUME

The contour map of Cerros provides the critical data for this analysis. An assessment of ground contour depression volume, or removed quarry volume, involved computing the associated area between each of the contour lines. This figure was converted into a volumetric unit by multiplying it by the number of centimeters below the 10.5-meter contour line that the given area occurred. The 10.5-meter contour line was selected as the original surface height of the terrain in the core area because it represented the highest natural ground at the site proper. The area between contour lines was computed using millimeter graph paper placed under the original Cerros Environs Map. The area was measured by counting the number of squares within each zone.

Although siltation has affected the terrain and contours at the site over the last two thousand years, most of these matrices are eroding from high ground in the immediate vicinity of the depressions. This is apparent from the very flat natural topography and suggests that the volumetric comparisons between depressions and structure volumes continue to maintain volumetric comparability.

Karstic features at Cerros are not pronounced, although Aguada 2 is a sizable feature and may be a consequence of karstic erosion. It lies 1 kilometer from the central precinct near the center of the bight and may be related to some other ancient geological process. Within the core site area as defined by the canal, no severe karstic formations have been detected. This is further supported by volumetric studies from within the canal perimeter. In this vein, however, the poor correlation of mound fill with the volume of earth

A-1: Calculated Cubic Meters of Fill Removed from Cerros within the 10.5-Meter Contour Line

Contours (m)	Depression Area (m^2)	Depression Volume (m^3)
10.5–10.0	318,000	159,000
10.0– 9.5	83,200	83,200
9.5– 9.0	36,900	55,350
9.0– 8.5	600	1,200
10.5–10.0*	75,000	37,500
	Total =	336,250

*This figure was derived and estimated from aerial photographs only. It represents a portion of *hulub bajo* outside the systematically surveyed area to the east, but part of the contiguous 10.5-meter contour circumscribing the core site area.

removed from the 10.5-meter contour circumscribing the greater site area would indicate that the zone to the east of the main canal within the *hulub bajo* setting probably was not quarried for house mound or monument fill. The depressed condition of this area would suggest that the zone was naturally low before and after the initiation of occupation.

The calculated cubic meters of fill removed from Cerros are set forth in A-1. Again, the 10.5-meter contour line circumscribing the core area is assumed to represent level and original land surface. These figures include the area underlying each structure.

The calculated cubic meters of fill underlying each structure has been subtracted from the depression quarry volume in A-2. This computation was made because the fill underlying each structure is assumed not to have been removed during quarry activities as indicated by the excavations (chapter 4).

The calculated cubic meters of structural fill for all mounded features within the 10.5-meter contour line circumscribing the site is 213,220 cubic meters. These data then indicate that the calculated fill

A-2: Calculated Cubic Meters of Fill Underlying Each Structure Subtracted from the Depression Volume within the 10.5-Meter Contour Line

Contours (m)	Depression Volume (m³)		Underlying Structure Volume (m³)		New Depression Volume (m³)
10.5–10.0	159,000	–	11,416	=	147,585
10.0– 9.5	83,200	–	1,196	=	82,004
9.5– 9.0	55,350	–	180	=	55,170
9.0– 8.5	1,200	–	0	=	1,200
10.5–10.0*	37,500	–	0	=	37,500
			New total	=	323,459

*This figure was derived and estimated from aerial photographs only. It represents a portion of *hulub bajo* outside the systematically surveyed area to the east, but part of the contiguous 10.5-meter contour circumscribing the core site area.

volume difference between structure volume and depression volume is

$$323,459 \text{ m}^3$$
$$-\,213,220 \text{ m}^3$$
$$\overline{110,239 \text{ m}^3}$$

Nevertheless, this latter total again strongly suggests that a portion of the site was already depressed before quarrying operations occurred. However, if the area within the core zone is considered as the only potential quarried space, then a different set of conclusions may be drawn.

The calculated cubic meters of fill removed from the core area at Cerros, if the core area defined by the main canal represents flat and original land surface, is set forth in A-3. These figures include the area underlying each structure.

A-3: Calculated Cubic Meters of Fill Removed from Cerros within the Core Area

Contours (m)	Depression Area (m²)	Depression Volume (m³)
10.5–10.0	151,200	75,600
10.0– 9.5	71,200	71,200
9.5– 9.0	36,900	55,350
9.0– 8.5	600	1,200
	Total =	203,350

A-4: Calculated Cubic Meters of Fill Underlying Each Structure Subtracted from the Depression Volume within the Core Area

Contours (m)	Depression Volume (m³)		Underlying Structure Volume (m³)		New Depression Volume (m³)
10.5–10.0	75,600	–	11,323	=	64,277
10.0– 9.5	71,200	–	1,196	=	70,004
9.5– 9.0	55,350	–	180	=	55,170
9.0– 8.5	1,200	–	0	=	1,200
			Total	=	190,651

The calculated cubic meters of fill underlying each structure have been subtracted from the depression quarry volume and set forth in A-4. The fill underlying each structure is again assumed not to have been removed during quarry activities, as indicated by the excavations (chapter 4).

Calculated cubic meters of structure fill volume within the core area of the site is 210,986. The calculated fill volume difference, then, between structure volume and depression volume is

$$210,986 \text{ m}^3$$
$$-\,190,651 \text{ m}^3$$
$$\overline{20,335 \text{ m}^3}$$

This figure is more compatible with the understood boundaries of the immediate site area. The additional mound fill for the construction of the monuments within the core area would have been quarried from the margins of the main canal perimeter within the periphery zone.

STRUCTURE DIMENSION DATA

The mound volume data were derived from our 1:50 or better alidade and plane table maps. The mounds were viewed as truncated pyramidal forms for the purposes of the analysis. The length and width of the summit surface space for the structures was taken from the contour maps and has been referred to elsewhere in the monograph as potential platform summit space. It has been provided to better describe mound form.

A-5: Cerros Settlement Volumetric Data—Structures

Structure	h	Bw	B1	Tw	T1	Dist. A	Dist. B	Dist. C	Dist. D	Area (m²)	Type	Volume (m³)
2A[ab]	2.0		(27,500m²)									55,000.0
2B*[a]	3.0	12	15	2	2							276.0
2C*	2.0	14	17	5	5							263.0
3A*[a]	7.0	38	54	23	42							10,563.0
4A*[a]	8.0	58	68	38	52							23,680.0
4B*[a]	12.0	36	38	5	5							8,358.0
5B*	3.0	12	17	3	6							333.0
5C*[a]	6.0	20	38	7	15							1,995.0
5D*	4.0	16	25	6	15							980.0
6A*[a]	8.0	55	64	33	43							19,756.0
6B*[a]	5.0	16	43	6	10							1,870.0
7A[a]	1.0	21	95	21	95							1,995.0
7B*	3.0	13	32	7	23							865.5
7C*	3.0	18	25	8	13							831.0
8A	1.0	50	100	50	100							5,000.0
8B[a]	2.0	13	20	3	7							281.0
8C	2.0	11	32	5	11							407.0
8D	2.0	11	29	2	6							343.0
9A[ac]	0.5		(26,400m²)									13,200.0
9B[ac]	3.5	24	70	12	48	180	308	80	82	1,680	4	3,948.0
10A[a]	1.0	12	20									240.0
10B[ac]	5.0	27	45	10	27	370	350	48	50	1,215	2	3,712.5
10C[ac]	5.0	25	28	8	10	325	348	20	50	700	2	1,950.0
10D[c]	5.0	28	28	8	10	325	328	20	48	784	2	2,160.0
11A[a]	0.5	10	15									75.0
11B[ac]	3.5	20	25	10	13	432	460	23	25	500	2	1,102.5
11C[ac]	1.5	22	25	12	16	440	480	23	28	550	2	556.5
11D[ac]	1.5	15	20	10	14	460	478	25	28	300	2	330.0
12[c]	0.5	4	4	4	4	270	246	20	27	16	6	8.0
13[ac]	2.5	22	26	5	5	265	266	20	21	572	4	1,746.3
14[ac]	4.5	22	33	5	8	280	270	21	27	726	4	1,723.5
15[ac]	17.0	39	42	6	16	314	262	24	38	1,638	4	1,473.9
16[ac]	1.0	11	23	6	8	340	278	24	28	253	5	150.5
17[c]	0.5	10	12	4	4	400	300	45	54	120	6	34.0
18[ac]	1.0	12	15	8	10	425	355	51	54	180	5	130.0
19A[a]	0.5	20	20									200.0
19B[ac]	3.5	34	45	32	40	505	430	48	50	1,530	3	4,917.5
19C[cd]	3.5	17	40	8	30	540	478	48	65	580	3	1,610.0
21[ac]	5.0	25	32	7	10	540	572	97	109	800	4	2,175.0
22[ac]	0.5	9	12	3	3	330	398	40	70	108	6	31.0
23*[a]	3.0	10	17	5						170		307.5
24[ac]	0.5	10	11	4	4	355	306	19	22	110	6	31.5

A-5: (Continued)

Structure	h	Bw	Bl	Tw	T1	Dist. A	Dist. B	Dist. C	Dist. D	Area (m²)	Type	Volume (m³)
25A	0.2	4	4	7	9	298	170	10	26	153	3	3.2
25B[c]	0.5	9	17	9	9	300	160	10	16	110	3	54.0
25C[c]	0.6	10	11	10	6	335	125	24	25	144	6	57.3
26[acd]	0.5	2	12	4	6	345	100	25	30	126	6	42.0
27[c]	0.5	9	14	3	3	315	132	19	24	90	6	33.8
28[cd]	0.5	9	10	5	10							35.0
29A[ac]	1.5	80	100	80	100		430		71	8,000	4	12,000.0
29B[ac]	11.0	38	44	6	8	360	128	68	67	1,672	5	9,460.0
30[c]	0.8	19	24	12	12	300	317	39	45	456	4	240.0
32[c]	1.2	29	32	9	10	382	208	24	42	928	5	610.8
34[ac]	1.0	14	16	6	6	372	228	23	24	224	5	130.0
35[c]	0.4	16	18	16	18	250	240	23	24	299	6	115.2
36[c]	0.3	7	9	7	9	345	250	10	28	63	5	18.9
37[c]	1.0	8	14	4	5	320	254	10	37	112	4	66.0
38[ac]	1.3	24	28	10	10	460	100	28	19	672	6	501.8
39[c]	0.3	10	11	10	11	475	110	15	15	110	6	42.9
40[c]	0.3	7	9	7	9	470	118	12	19	63	6	18.9
41[c]	0.2	9	10	9	10	510	95	12	38	90	5	18.0
42[c]	0.3	12	15	12	15	505	85	12	41	180	6	54.0
43[c]	0.3	9	11	9	11	545	124	38	41	99	4	29.7
44[c]	1.5	22	25	5	6	530	139	52	62	550	5	435.0
45[c]	0.5	22	26	10	12					572		173.0
46A[a]	0.3	4	8	4								9.8
46B[c]	1.5	17	25	7	8	630	230	17	72	425	3	360.8
46C[ac]	1.1	16	25	8	10	630	235	17	78	400	3	264.0
49	0.7	15	25	6	8	1,500	1,484	76	236	375	5	148.1
50A[a]	0.5	10	60									300.0
50B[ac]	3.0	27	44	10	26	486	150	44	47	1,188	1	2,172.0
50C[ac]	2.2	22	24	8	12	530	174	18	38	528	1	686.4
50D[ac]	2.2	27	43	10	26	565	208	33	38	1,161	1	1,563.1
50E[ac]	2.5	20	23	8	12	535	188	18	33	460	1	695.0
52[c]	0.3	2	2	2	2	392	90	18	30	4	6	1.2
53[ac]	3.0	30	32	8	9	432	180	78	108	960	4	1548.0
54[ac]	3.5	24	29	8	10	250	169	30	66	696	4	1358.0
57[ac]	1.0	9	13	4	4	346	79	18	35	117	6	66.5
59[c]	0.4	10	13	10	13	365	58	19	22	130	6	52.0
60	0.5	16	20	10	10	1,432	1,412	76	160	320	5	105.0
61A[a]	1.0	12	12									144.0
61B[ac]	2.5	20	30	8	12	235	224	28	50	600	3	870.0
61C[ac]	2.5	18	22	8	12	237	204	28	24	396	3	615.0
62A	0.2	12	12	3	3	1,274	1,242	10	46	50	3	28.8
62B	0.5	5	10									14.8

62C	0.6	12	12	6	6	1,286	1,251	10	56	144	3	54.0
63A	0.2	8	8	8	10	1,220	1,190	8	52	80	3	12.8
63B	0.3	10	8	8	12	1,228	1,196	8	46	96	3	24.0
63C	0.4	12	8	7	7	1,184	1,176	54	58	49	6	38.4
64	0.2	7	7	9	12	318	188	30	56	713	4	9.8
65[ac]	1.5	31	23	8	10	266	155	50	70	408	4	615.8
66[ac]	1.5	24	17	8	11	255	180	24	49	88	6	366.0
67[c]	0.1	11	8	3	4	376	45	12	22	12	6	17.6
68[c]	0.4	4	3	3	4	376	56	12	22	12	6	4.8
69[c]	0.4	4	3	6	6	870	740	56	68	144	6	4.8
70	0.5	12	12	4	5	352	70	18	19	20	6	45.0
71[c]	0.4	5	4	5	7	174	250	12	13	35	6	8.0
72[c]	0.2	7	5	12	14	180	244	12	13	168	5	7.0
73[c]	0.4	14	12	6	6	188	237	13	13	70	6	67.2
74[c]	0.6	10	7	3	6	205	229	8	8	27		31.8
75[c]	1.0	9	3									22.5
76A	2.5	26	14									910.0
76B[ac]	4.0	34	33	16	20	950	546	24	25	1,122	2	2,884.0
76C[c]	1.0	18	16	10	10	965	564	25	46	288	2	194.0
76D[ac]	1.8	20	12	8	8	927	520	24	46	240	2	273.6
77[ac]	1.0	8	7	3	3	218	228	20	23	56	6	32.5
78[c]	0.8	20	14	7	7	942	545	25	26	280	5	131.6
80[c]	1.3	20	19	7	7	965	570	20	25	380	4	278.9
81[c]	1.0	11	5	3	5	200	232	7	8	55	6	35.0
82[c]	0.4	27	13	13	27	1,035	640	68	72	351	5	140.4
84[ac]	0.5	15	12	3	6	885	481	29	38	180	5	49.5
85[c]	0.5	16	13	4	4	860	464	38	51	208	5	56.0
86[c]	0.3	14	12	12	14	910	509	25	29	168	6	50.4
87[c]	0.4	13	11	11	13	905	320	44	49	143	5	57.2
88[c]	0.4	23	10	10	23	935	322	29	38	230	4	92.0
90[c]	2.0	20	11	6	8	322	142	30	36	220	5	268.0
93[c]	0.9	27	26	17	18	700	296	69	64	702	5	453.6
94[ac]	0.4	17	11	11	17	625	222	100	122	187	6	74.8
95[c]	0.5	8	7	2	2	486	353	68	80	56	6	15.0
96[cd]	0.5	13	9	3	4	542	422	22	56	117	4	32.3
97[cd]	1.3	20	16	4	6	565	440	22	25	320	4	233.6
98[ac]	1.5	24	19	10	16	584	464	25	46	456	5	462.0
99[c]	1.0	16	14	8	10	758	668	20	131	224	5	152.0
100[c]	1.0	20	15	10	10	665	658	32	94	300	5	200.0
101[c]	0.5	19	16	5	6	680	682	32	90	304	5	83.5
102[ac]	0.5	20	14	6	6	762	737	20	90	280	5	79.0
103[cd]	0.5	16	11	7	7	780	757	20	103	176	6	56.3
105[c]	0.8	24	14	4	12	210	278	17	21	336	6	153.6
106[cd]	0.5	5	4	4	5	195	277	17	20	20	5	10.0
107[c]	0.5	11	8	3	3	210	258	38	45	88		23.5
108[c]	0.9	22	16	8	12	252	301			352		201.6

A-5: (Continued)

Structure	h	Bw	Bl	Tw	T1	Dist. A	Dist. B	Dist. C	Dist. D	Area (m²)	Type	Volume (m³)
110[c]	0.2	9	12	9	12	292	290	24	38	108	6	21.6
111[c]	0.9	16	34	8	18	355	373	28	57	544	5	309.6
112[ac]	1.6	18	32	7	14	370	403	28	67	576	4	539.2
113[c]	0.7	15	17	6	12	410	371	38	57	255	5	114.5
114[c]	0.5	16	18	8	8	410	337	38	80	288	5	88.0
115A	0.3	8	10									24.0
115B[ac]	1.2	14	19	10	10	634	494	16	21	266	2	219.6
115C[c]	0.9	13	16	5	5	615	469	14	21	208	2	104.9
115D[c]	0.9	12	13	6	7	630	478	14	16	156	2	89.1
116A	0.4	18	20									144.0
116B[ac]	2.2	22	23	10	12	576	562	25	27	506	1	688.6
116C[c]	1.5	14	22	6	11	590	589	25	31	308	1	280.5
116D[c]	1.0	13	15	10	10	698	584	22	31	195	1	147.5
116E[c]	1.3	19	27	14	14	592	560	22	27	513	1	460.9
120[c]	0.8	19	22	5	5	316	214	30	46	418	5	177.2
124[c]	0.3	4	7	4	7	373	62	12	36	28	6	8.4
128A	0.2	5	5									5.0
128B	0.3	5	6	5	6	1,160	1,178	8	62	30	3	9.0
128C	0.4	7	12	7	12	1,164	1,176	8	54	84	3	33.6
129	0.2	8	14	8	14	1,166	1,140	58	58	112	6	22.4
130A	0.3	15	15									67.5
130B	1.0	15	16	13	13	1,062	1,046	20	52	240	3	204.5
130C	0.4	4	12	4	12	1,076	1,062	20	38	48	3	19.2
131	0.3	8	9	8	9	1,072	1,030	26	32	72	6	21.6
132A	1.0	30	40									1,200.0
132B	1.2	18	20	8	10	1,066	1,036	26	32	360	3	264.0
132C	1.2	12	16	6	8	1,048	1,014	26	26	192	3	144.0
133[d]	0.4	12	16	12	16	1,036	972	18	36	192	5	76.8
134	0.2	4	5	4	5	1,016	954	18	24	20	6	4.0
135	0.5	12	18	6	6	1,004	934	22	24	216	5	63.0
136[d]	0.4	5	8	5	8	986	912	22	24	40	6	16.0
137[d]	0.4	15	19	15	19	972	908	24	34	285	5	114.0
138	0.3	6	9	6	9	912	868	28	28	54	6	162.0
139A	0.2	2	4									1.6
139B	0.5	4	4	2	2	908	878	6	26	16	3	5.0
139C	0.5	4	4	2	2	916	884	6	28	16	3	5.0
140A	0.3	4	4									4.8
140B	0.5	9	12	4	4	896	898	12	60	108	3	31.0
140C	0.6	10	10	4	4	906	902	12	52	100	3	34.8
141	0.3	4	14	4	14	972	964	66	66	56	6	16.8
142	0.2	12	12	12	12	902	982	46	66	144	6	28.8
143	0.3	16	16	16	16	914	940	46	66	156	5	76.8

Structure	h	Bw	Bl	Tw	Tl	Dist. A	Dist. B	Dist. C	Dist. D	Area	Vol.
144A	0.3	25	25	10	10	1,026	934	20	46	625	187.5
144B	2.0	18	25	4	6	1,034	924	20	66	450	550.0
144C	0.4	4	6	6	12					24	9.6
145	2.0	26	28	12	12	1,132	1,058	90	96	728	872.0
146A	0.2	20	20							400	80.0
146B	0.6	4	12	4	6	840	680	16	16	48	21.6
146C	2.0	10	10	8	8	866	694	14	16	100	164.0
146D	0.3	6	6	6	6	888	718	12	24	36	10.8
146E	2.0	20	20	10	10	894	736	24	26	400	500.0
146F	0.3	4	12	4	12	876	710	12	16	48	14.4
146G	1.0	10	13	5	7	858	694	14	16	130	82.5
147	0.6	14	18	7	9	914	610	160	230	252	94.5
148	0.6	18	20	8	10	1,128	752	70	86	360	132.0
149A	0.2	15	10							150	30.0
149B	0.9	12	20	6	10	1,196	824	16	70	240	135.0
149C	1.1	12	12	6	6	1,214	842	16	86	144	99.0
150	1.1	19	24	8	12	1,272	912	86	100	456	303.6
151	0.5	17	17	8	8	1,210	776	68	94	289	88.3
152	0.3	13	13	13	13	1,274	844	60	68	169	50.7
153	0.2	6	6	6	6	1,294	862	60	94	36	7.2
164	0.2	10	12	6	6	800	368	10	32	120	15.6
165	0.1	4	4	4	4	368	218	62	128	16	1.6
166	0.4	10	10	4	4	334	154	62	68	100	23.2
167	0.3	10	12	4	4	320	88	16	20	120	20.4
168	0.3	12	12	4	6	618	364	10	16	144	25.2
169	0.4	18	16	8	10	640	380	16	16	288	109.6
170	0.3	16	16	8	8	640	364	16	28	256	48.0
171	0.8	22	22	4	6	604	332	28	76	484	203.2
172A	0.3	16	8							128	38.4
172B	0.6	16	16	8	10	530	258	4	64	256	100.8
172C	0.4	10	16	8	8	518	243	4	50	160	44.8
173	0.5	20	20	6	8	634	360	14	76	400	112.0
174	0.5	30	30	10	10	608	334	14	42	900	250.0
175	0.3	16	16	10	16	564	284	54	56	256	86.4
176A	0.2	8	20							160	32.0
176B	0.8	18	22	6	6	608	319	10	56	396	172.8
176C	0.4	10	12	4	8	592	300	10	40	120	30.4
177	0.2	16	16	12	12	558	264	40	86	256	40.0

Key

h = height	Tw = width at top	Dist. B = distance to Structure 29B in meters
Bw = width at base	Tl = length at top	Dist. C = distance to nearest neighbor in meters
Bl = length at base	Dist. A = distance to center in meters	Dist. D = distance to nearest second neighbor in meters
		Area = area at base

*Structures 2B-7C, and 23 are in the central precinct, and subplaza height was excluded in all calculations. Plaza height is included in calculations for all other structures.

[a] Excavated structure.
[b] Data for 2A include 5A.
[c] Structure is located within systematic survey and excavation area.
[d] Disturbed.

The final formula employed for calculating mound volume after some experimentation was

$$\frac{(Bl \times Bw \times h) - (Tl \times Tw \times h)}{2} + (Tl \times Tw \times h) = V$$

where: Bl = base length
Bw = base width
h   = height
Tl = top (summit) length
Tw = top (summit) width
V   = volume

A-5 and A-6 present complete metric data for all features recorded by survey methods at Cerros. It also includes distance relationships between mounds for further spatial studies. These latter data are included because of the more precise, large-scale maps available to me.

A-6: Cerros Settlement Volumetric Data—Wells and Depressions

Structure	Depth	Length	Width	Dist. A	Dist. B	Dist. C	Dist. D
20				384	392	20	46
48				1,588	1,574	90	166
79	1.0	100	100	984	578	56	84
83				1,236	812	108	120
89				844	446	32	126
91				830	870	70	70
92				1,300	1,270	40	80
104				164	346	36	64
117				430	344	20	26
118				330	226	12	16
119				1,034	1,010	12	26
123				208	254	6	28
125				796	830	74	86
154	4.0	140	220	1,560	1,120	260	284
155				480	100	4	14
156				1,146	1,078	20	104
162				1,236	906	90	150
163	1.0	80	80	910	808	82	110

Dist. A = distance to center in meters
Dist. B = distance to Structure 29B in meters
Dist. C = distance to nearest neighbor in meters
Dist. D = distance to nearest second neighbor in meters

Appendix B
Soils

Soils analysis from several contexts was conducted at Cerros. Although soil samples were routinely collected from nearly every excavation context, only twenty samples were ultimately examined by the laboratory. These samples were analyzed to better identify the environmental settings found at Cerros. Their significance in defining these microenvironments has been outlined in chapter 3. In addition, the soil samples taken from the canal and raised-field excavations provide substantial support for the interpretations presented in chapter 6. The especially high phosphorous readings from the field plots are viewed as demonstrative of raised-field agriculture.

Sixteen of the twenty soil samples taken for final analysis were collected from our canal operations. The remaining four samples were retrieved from Feature 33A (OP107). One control sample of sterile surface beach sand was collected for analysis from an area immediately north of OP 107 on the present shoreline.

Obtaining control samples unaffected by later cultural disturbance was not an easy task at Cerros, considering the size and duration of occupation. The soils that best qualify were the beach sand sample and the three samples taken from under Structure 9A or the C'oh phase occupation at Feature 33. Moreover, the caprock samples examined from the banks of the main canal were minimally affected by cultural activity.

The locations of the various samples are apparent within the appropriate profile sections. Additional physical descriptions of the matrices are included in chapters 4 and 5. All samples were run at the same time and at the same laboratory for comparability.

The five areas in the settlement chosen for analysis each provided two or more stratigraphically meaningful samples. B-1 through B-4 give the stratigraphic position of the various samples one above another. Samples are identified by operation number, excavation unit, and stratigraphic level from bottom to top.

INTERPRETATION

The soils analysis required a series of chemical tests to reveal trends and relationships. With regard to the nine soil samples taken from the main canal, all four tables indicate a similar distribution of points. This indicates that the sediments within each level of the main canal have undergone a similar set of chemical disturbances. Additional soils tests were run for nitrogen, calcium, and magnesium, but the results were the same throughout all samples across the site. Nitrogen concentrations were low, while calcium concentrations were very high or greater than 4,000 ppm. Some slight variability in the amount of magnesium was detectable in the samples, but all were considered high. Overall, the sodium chloride in our samples is considered a moderate hazard to plants, especially during seed germination, but significant variability between samples was noted. The high salt content is considered a consequence of recent brackish water invading the site setting (chapter 3). All chemical analysis was carried out at the Soil Testing Laboratory, College Station, Texas (the Texas Agricultural Extension Service provides data on minerals that are in a form available to plants).

In addition to chemical tests, consultation with David Shannelbrook, a geologist with Hunt Energy in Dallas, has provided a cursory physical examination of the soils. Grain-size tests were not possible, however, given the recrystallized nature of the sediments and the high calcium carbonate fraction. All samples reacted strongly to hydrochloric acid treatment.

Samples from the Main Canal

Sample 1

The basal sterile *sascab* marl matrix (OP116a-6_1) underlying the caprock indicates a strongly alkaline condition, although leaching action through the canal cut may have partially influenced the reading. The low salt content is indicative of the freshwater source contained by the original canal. Salt concentrations are slightly lower than the present beach sands, the latter representing very well drained matrices.

The sample consisted of extremely fine clay particles. A few root intrusions were apparent, perhaps remnants of riverine grasses and weeds associated with the original canal bottom. A bit of limonite in the sample, indicative of FeS_2 (pyrite) formation,

B-1: Soil Sample Phosphorous Readings (Unfixed)

Sample No.	Soil Sample Operations No.	
Main canal		
1	116a-6_1	
2	116a-6_2	
3	116a-5_1	
4	116a-5_2	
5	116b-4	
6	116b-3_1	
7	116b-3_2	
8	116b-3_3	
9	116b-1	
Caprock		
1	116g-2_1	
2	116g-2_2	
Field platforms		
1	152a-2_1	
2	152a-2_2	
3	152a-2_3	
Basin canal		
1	152a-3	
2	152b-2	
Coastal setting		
1	107b-9	
2	107b-8	
3	107b-7	
Bay sand		
1	Bay sand	

```
       0        25         50        75
     Low      Medium       High
         Phosphorous (ppm)
```

suggests its oxidation in water before the more reduced conditions associated with its present state.

Sample 2

The thin, dark, blocky, loamy clay paleosol (OP116a-6_2) overlying the *sascab* marl matrix indicates a mildly alkaline condition approaching that of fresh water. The higher relative concentration of salt may be a consequence of the underlying impermeable *sascab,* which prevents the leaching of particles through the stratum. Although the phosphorous readings are not high, the trapped nature of this element is further indicated by the potassium readings. It should be noted that the readings for this paleosol are more similar to the surface humate horizon (OP116b-1) than to other samples taken elsewhere in the settlement. This suggests the organic composition of this dark lens.

The sample consisted of loamy clays that underwent recrystallization or recementing through the effects of percolating groundwater charged with calcite and dolomite. Sulfates (calcium sulfate or gypsum) are present, suggesting the organic constituents in the paleosol. The dark, brown color of the lens further suggests an organic component; however, quantifiable tests for organic carbon or organic matter have not been conducted. Nevertheless, the poorly sorted nature of the sediments coupled with the above chemical characterizations indicate this lens to have been an organic paleosol. It is analogous to other paleosols revealed elsewhere in the settlement.

B-2: Soil Sample Potassium Readings (Unfixed)

Sample No.	Soil Sample Operations No.	
Main canal		
1	116a-6_1	
2	116a-6_2	
3	116a-5_1	
4	116a-5_2	
5	116b-4	
6	116b-3_1	
7	116b-3_2	
8	116b-3_3	
9	116b-1	
Caprock		
1	116g-2_1	
2	116g-2_2	
Field platforms		
1	152a-2_1	
2	152a-2_2	
3	152a-2_3	
Basin canal		
1	152a-3	
2	152b-2	
Coastal setting		
1	107b-9	
2	107b-8	
3	107b-7	
Bay sand		
1	Bay sand	

```
0   1   2   3   4   5   6   7   8   9   10
L   M   H       V e r y   H i g h
        Potassium (ppm)
          (in hundreds)
```

L = Low   M = Medium   H = High

Sample 3

The thin deposit of granular, yellow clay associated with decomposing angular limestone gravel (OP116a-5_1) overlying the paleosol has provided readings not unlike those recorded for the caprock samples (OP116g-2). This is in keeping with the argument that these gravels represent eroded or quarried caprock associated with the initial infilling and abandonment of the main canal.

The sample consisted of a yellowish clay sand cemented by fine-grained particles (recystallization). The high water table is in part responsible for this condition. A low percentage of organic constituents is present, an expected result, given the position of the lens relative to the paleosol. The lens is particularly abundant in limonite (producing the yellowish tint), which is indicative of FeS_2, and forms as a consequence of fossil bryozoan or coral breakdown. Although these fossils may occur naturally in the caprock formation, there is the suggestion that some of the bryozoans are of a nonlocal origin. Following this suggestion, intrusive bryozoans would indicate that an outside agent introduced these fossilized remnants into the canal from another marine limestone source. If the two siliceous limestone shoals mentioned earlier (chapter 3) as lying on the New River and south of the site were traced as the source, then a tidy argument could be advanced in regard to the

B-3: Soil Sample pH Readings

Sample No.	Soil Sample Operations No.
Main canal	
1	116a-6$_1$
2	116a-6$_2$
3	116a-5$_1$
4	116a-5$_2$
5	116b-4
6	116b-3$_1$
7	116b-3$_2$
8	116b-3$_3$
9	116b-1
Caprock	
1	116g-2$_1$
2	116g-2$_2$
Field platforms	
1	152a-2$_1$
2	152a-2$_2$
3	152a-2$_3$
Basin canal	
1	152a-3
2	152b-2
Coastal setting	
1	107b-9
2	107b-8
3	107b-7
Bay sand	
1	Bay sand

```
       6.00      7.00        8.00       9.00
                          MiA    MoA   StA
        Acid                    Base
```

MiA = Mildly Alkaline   MoA = Moderately Alkaline   StA = Strongly Alkaline

connection between the canal and the New River. This evidence, however, is not yet available.

Sample 4

A sample was taken from immediately above the gravel deposit and consisted of a poorly sorted clay silt (OP116a-5$_2$). The chemical readings are in concert with the adjacent soils underlying and overlying the sample. They reflect a leached condition. However, the unusually high phosphorous reading (relative to other samples in the main canal) may be attributable to the high phosphorous frequencies recorded on the field platforms (OP152a-2). Given that the canal sediments represent an inverted raised-field profile (chapter 6), the stratigraphic position of this elevated phosphorous reading corresponds well with those located in the present raised-field zones. The subsequent depositional history of the canal sediments accounts for the lower phosphorous reading when compared to the concentrations recorded on the raised-field platforms.

The sample is defined by a light gray clay silt and is apparently lighter in hue as a consequence of the underlying yellow limonite. The grains are poorly sorted and cemented together. A high frequency of worm casts and gastropods is reported as being associated with a post-depositional origin.

Samples 5 and 6

Sample 5 (OP116b-4) was taken from a gray clay silt above Sample 4. The chemical readings are in concert with the adjacent samples and reflect a leached condition. The sample was not well sorted, being cemented

B-4: Soil Sample Salt Concentrations

Sample No.	Soil Sample Operations No.
Main Canal	
1	116a-6_1
2	116a-6_2
3	116a-5_1
4	116a-5_2
5	116b-4
6	116b-3_1
7	116b-3_2
8	116b-3_3
9	116b-1
Caprock	
1	116g-2_1
2	116g-2_2
Field platforms	
1	152a-2_1
2	152a-2_2
3	152a-2_3
Basin canal	
1	152a-3
2	152b-2
Coastal setting	
1	107b-9
2	107b-8
3	107b-7
Bay sand	
1	Bay sand

0 2 4 6 8 1 2 4 6 8 2 2 4 6 8 3 2 4 6 8 4
NaCl (ppm H$_2$O soluble)
(in hundredths)

together. Further, it contained postdepositional worm casts and gastropods. Sample 6 (OP116b-3_1) represented the blocky, dark gray clays overlying Sample 5. The chemical readings associated with Sample 6 are similar to the two previous samples and reflect a further leached condition. The sample is better sorted than the underlying matrix. Little secondary cementing has affected this sample, probably because of its elevated position relative to the dry season water table. The matrix is intruded by recent *Pomacea* shells, but few worm casts are apparent.

Sample 7

A yellow-gray clay deposit is defined near the surface of the caprock edge (OP116b-3_2). A chemical examination of the sample reveals a data set similar to those samples below it. The sediments appear to be well leached with no recrystallization of the matrix. The

stratum is intruded by *Pomacea* shells, but few worm casts are reported. This soil is associated with the most recent canal bank lateral erosion of the caprock. Many of the chemical readings range within the variability of the caprock samples (OP116g-2).

Sample 8

A sample was taken from the upper light gray clay, intruded by pebbles to large cobbles (OP116b-3_3). This matrix was found to overlie the bulk of the blocky gray clay silts within the canal. The sample is associated with the deliberate and final infilling operation of this section of the main canal (the Early Classic causeway construction). The chemical data suggest that there is an increase in the amount of minerals in the soil when compared to the underlying sediments. This may be attributable to the high incidence of decomposing limestone gravels throughout the deposit as well as to the more severe erosional agents apparent near the surface of the exposure. The matrix is friable, showing no evidence for recementing. Organic debris and root cast are present, as are low frequencies of gastropods. The sample is severely leached.

Sample 9

A surface sample was taken from the black gumbo humus horizon (OP116b-1). This loamy clay was intruded by pebble-sized limestone gravels associated with the final infilling operation. The chemical analysis indicates relatively high values for the various elements. A combination of decaying organic debris and a severe erosional attack on the parent limestone gravels have released these elements to the soil. The matrix is better drained, judging from the marked absence of recemented particles and the lower pH value. The higher phosphorous reading may be a consequence of the redeposited trash or midden fill associated with this Early Classic episode. The high organic content is attested to by the numerous rootlets. The chemical affinity this sample has to the basal paleosol is again noteworthy.

Samples from the Caprock

Samples 1 and 2

The caprock soil samples were both taken from the northern bank of the canal exposure (OP116g-2). The chemical analysis provides a controlled sample for assessing the natural composition of this caprock parent material. The effects of leaching appear to account for the higher potassium and phosphorous readings at the ill-defined margins between the solid caprock and the overlying weathering matrix as opposed to the overlying decomposing caprock. The more basic and salt-laden weathering caprock suggests the percolation and redeposition of some minerals at this juncture between the B-horizon and the C-horizon.

The solid, unweathered caprock is an off-white, massive formation. The overlying weathered caprock is a yellowish, iron-rich (limonite) formation. The oxidized state of the weathered caprock is caused by the high water table and capillary action. The leached nature of the formation is indicated by the absence of recemented particles. No worm casts or bryozoans are present and few rootlets have penetrated to this depth.

This description is in keeping with caprock or caliche formation elsewhere in the world (see Reeves 1970).

Samples from the Field Platforms

Sample 1

The earthen platforms were sampled three times, stratigraphically, from the south end of our trenching operation (OP152a-2). A sample was taken from the off-white granular friable matrix immediately overlying the decomposed yellow limestone caprock (OP152a-2_1). Bits of limonite were identified. The chemical readings are high for all the elements analyzed, suggesting some cultural alteration of the field chemistry. The potassium reading coupled with the very high phosphorous percentage indicated that the field platforms were fertilized. The phosphorous readings from this sample and the one stratigraphically above it (Sample 2) are especially significant, given the generally low phosphorous readings elsewhere in the settlement and the deficient readings recorded by Wright et al. (1959) for Lowry's Bight. The moderately high alkalinity of the soil is attributable to the decomposing limestone caprock in the vicinity.

Sample 2

Another sample was taken from a dark gray sandy clay overlying the previous sample (OP152a-2_2). This matrix recorded the highest chemical readings of all samples tested. The extremely high potassium percentages coupled with the highest phosphorous readings in the settlement further suggest fertilization. The high salt content might indicate the development of a K-horizon, but no pisolite concretions are apparent. The textural studies were inconclusive, although *Pomacea* disturbance was pronounced.

Sample 3

A surface sample was taken from near the surface of the platform within a light gray clay loam (OP152a-2_3). The chemical readings are substantially lower than the two previous samples. This appears to be a consequence of the deflated nature of the platforms, which have been severely leached, especially near the surface. The amount of rootlet and related organic debris was high. Recent *Pomacea* disturbance was again apparent.

Samples from the Basin Canal

Samples 1 and 2

Two samples were analyzed from a basin canal circumscribing a field plot. One sample was taken from within the presumably reworked off-white parent material (OP152a-3). Another sample was taken from within the basin canal sediments (OP152b-2). Except for a minor difference between the phosphorous readings, the chemical data illustrate a leaching profile. No quantifiable textural information was retrievable.

Samples from the Coastal Setting

Sample 1

Three soil samples were examined from under the subplaza Structure 9A at Feature 33A. They best reflect the character of the culturally undisturbed soils at Cerros. The basal yellow granular matrix is the decomposing caprock (OP107b-9), which defines the dry season water table. The chemical readings are generally quite low but in the range of other decomposed caprock readings (OP116g-2).

Sample 2

The next sample was taken from a blue-gray clay overlying the caprock (OP107b-8). The chemical readings are markedly higher for this sample than for those above and below it, which may be symptomatic of a leached condition. However, these clays have been argued elsewhere to be riverine in origin (chapter 3) and may have elevated element concentrations as a consequence of the rich sediment load carried by the ancient course of the New River. No grain-size analysis was conducted.

Sample 3

A third sample was taken from the beige clay overlying the alluvial clays and underlying a house floor (OP107b-7). These sediments appear to be associated with the house floor preparation and may be quite disturbed. The low chemical readings suggest comparability to the decomposed caprock elsewhere. No textural analysis was carried out.

A Sample of Bay Sands

The last sample for the site was taken from the present shoreline of Corozal Bay. It was analyzed to provide additional control for the other soil samples. Although constituents of this beach sand suggest a local origin, many of the shell particles are from outside the site area. It should be noted that the phosphorous content is not high enough to account for the very high phosphorous reading on the fields. I have speculated elsewhere that beach sands could have been incorporated into the raised-field soils to increase phosphorous concentrations as well as to permit a more loamy soil than the immediate clays available.

Appendix C
Molluscan Fauna

Molluscan fauna was collected from each stratigraphic lot and level defined in the main canal and raised-field complex. Flotation samples were taken from each of these matrices. The sample sizes were generally small, even though 2-pound bags of earth were floated. Norm MacLeod, an advanced graduate student studying invertebrate paleontology at Southern Methodist University, analyzed the samples from the west-central portion of the core area and provided the following interpretive data. These data are of a preliminary nature, but do support the environmental reconstruction for Late Preclassic Cerros (see chapters 3 and 6).

1. The relative abundance of species which Dr. Lawrence Feldman, the former director of the Museum of Anthropology at the University of Missouri, interpreted as possibly indicative of fresh, moving water, increased from OP152 to OP116 (laterally toward the main canal).

2. The relative abundance of *Pomacea flagellata* increased toward the top of the raised-field platform deposits adjacent to the basin canals.

3. The relative abundance of *P. flagellata* showed a weakly defined decrease toward the top of the matrix which now fills the main canal.

4. *P. flagellata* from the site show a strong bimodality with respect to size, with all specimens falling into two well-defined size groups: 35–50 millimeters (adult shells) or 2–8 millimeters (juvenile shells), the diameter measured through the widest part of the shell. No whole shells were found to fall into the intermediate size range (9–34 millimeters). All other faunal components show a unimodal size distribution centered slightly to the left of the median for their size ranges.

5. Juvenile *P. flagellata* (2–8 millimeters) are thought to be *in situ* owing to their relative abundance at greater depth, their complete lack of a periostracum, and their "old-looking" appearance.

6. The adult *P. flagellata* are understood to be intrusive because of their well-preserved periostracum and their clear association with distinct burrows (the latter observation made in the field). *P. flagellata* occupy stagnant water and depressed swampy settings, being very common at the site today.

Barring major climatic or other environmental variations attributable to nature, they [*P. flagellata*] were also common in the general area of Cerros during Mayan times. Although they were undoubtedly common in the surrounding area, I do not think that *P. flagellata* was a common component of the fauna at Cerros itself during the time of its habitation. This is suggested by the absence of *P. flagellata* from the cultural deposits, given the fact that *P. flagellata* was used as a food source by the Mayan inhabitants of nearby settlements. (Scarborough personal communication)

The smaller *P. flagellata* group (2–8 mm) . . . presence can be accounted for by regarding them as immigrants from surrounding populations (perhaps during the rainy season) that survived in the area for a time by occupying microhabitats of brackish water (perhaps on the raised fields themselves). These immigrants could not attain full size, however, due to the drying up of the microhabitats, or by simply outgrowing the microhabitats. The area in general was not capable of supporting a population of *P. flagellata*. Of course, normal freshwater forms abounded in the canal itself.

After abandonment of the site, drainage modification ceased and natural conditions returned, allowing the local population of *P. flagellata* which had been excluded during habitation to repopulate the area. Adult *P. flagellata* (35–50 mm) are capable of burrowing to horizons which include cultural material and horizons formerly occupied by the canal. This is not only supported by the bimodality of the *P. flagellata* sample and the increase in relative abundance of *P. flagellata* toward the top of the sections generally, but also by direct observation of large *P. flagellata* at the ends of burrows. (Letter to Lawrence H. Feldman from Norm MacLeod, April 7, 1980)

These preliminary data suggest that, during the major construction and maintenance of the canal system, *P. flagellata* were not well adapted to the drained environs at Cerros.

Appendix D
Vegetation Types

D-1: Monte alto/huamil (*acahuales*)

Strong *Monte Alto* Location

Maya/Spanish Name	Latin Name	Comment
Zapote, sapodilla	*Achras sapote*	*, Dominant
Chacah	*Bursera simaruba*	*
Chicoloro	*Strychros panamensis*	
Cranadillo (rosewood)	*Dalbergia cubilquitzensis*	*
Habin	*Piscidia piscipula*	*
Jobo	*Spondias mombin*	*
Jobo	*Spondias purpurea*	
Kenep	*Talisia ulivaeformis*	*
Caoba (mahogany)	*Swietenia macrophylla king*	*, Dominant
Ramon blanco	*Trophis racemosa*	
Ramon rosa	*Brosimum alicastrum*	*
Yaxnik	*Vitex gaumeri*	

*Strong ruin association

D-2: Monte alto/huamil (*acahuales*)

Strong *Huamil* Location

Maya/Spanish Name	Latin Name	Comment
Chacah	*Bursera simaruba*	*
Cylil (persimmon)	*Diospyros verae*	
(Feral calabash)	*Crescentia cujete*	
Guarumo	*Cecropia peltata*	*
Katsim	*Mimosa hemiendyta*	
Negrito	*Simarouba glauca*	
Papayo, patas	*Carica papaya*	*
Pata de vaca	*Bauhinia divaricata*	
Pereskuch	*Croton reflexifolius*	
Pixoy	*Guazuma ulmifolia*	*
Ramon	*Brosimum alicastrum*	*
Sapote	*Achras zapote*	
Subin (bullhorn acacia)	*Acacia collinsii* and *A. glomerosa*	*
Xburut'	*Cucurbita radicans*	
Yaxnik	*Vitex gaumeri*	

*Strong ruin association

Sources for Appendix D: Barrera et al. (1976); Bartlett (1936); Crane (1986); Lundell (1934, 1937, 1938); Standley and Record (1936); Wright et al. (1959).

D-3: Shoreline location

Maya/Spanish Name	Latin Name	Comment
Coco	*Cocos nucifera*	

D-4: Thorn-scrub savanna

Depressed Location

Maya/Spanish Name	Latin Name	Comment
Muk	*Dalbergia glabra*	Dominant
Carrizo	*Arthrostylidium pittieri*	
Chechem negra	*Metopium brownei*	
Katsim	*Mimosa hemiendyta*	
Sac pom	*Cupania glabra*	
Subin (bullhorn acacia)	*Acacia collinsii* and *A. glomerosa*	
Poknoboy	*Batris major*	

D-5: Elevated location

Maya/Spanish Name	Latin Name	Comment
Katsim	*Mimosa hemiendyta*	Dominant
Pixoy	*Guazuma ulmifolia*	
Subin	*Acacia collinsii* and *A. glomerosa*	

D-6: Yax'om soil or hulub bajo (*akalche*)

Maya/Spanish Name	Latin Name	Comment
Hulub	*Bravaisia tubiflora*	Dominant
Chechem de caballo (white poisonwood)	Cameraria *belizensis*	
Ciricote	*Cordia dodecandra*	
Dama de noche	*Cestrum racemosum*	
Manteca ?	*Ampelocera hottlei*	
Palo de sangre ?	*Virola koschuyi*	
Tinta (logwood)	*Haematoxylon campechianum*	
Zapotebobo (provision tree)	*Pachira aquadia*	

D-7: Zacatal

Maya/Spanish Name	Latin Name	Comment
Unidentified grasses		Dominant
Camofillo	*Zamia furfuracea*	
Carrizo	*Arthrostylidium pittieri*	
Cattails	*Typha domingensis*	
Chechem negra	*Metopium brownei*	
Duck flower	*Centrosema Plumieri*	
Pixoy	*Guazuma ulmifolia*	
Santa Maria	*Calophyllum brasiliense*	
Sawgrass	*Scleria bracteata*	
Tulipan	*Malvaviscus arboreus*	
Xcanan	*Hamelia patens*	

D-8: Bajo fringe or huanal

Maya/Spanish Name	Latin Name	Comment
Huano, botan	*Sabal mayarum*	Dominant
Huano (bobwood)	*Anona glabra*	
Camotillo	*Zamia furfuracra*	
Chit	*Thrinax paviflora*	
Escabeche	*Pithecolobium dulce*	
Escoba (give and take palm)	*Cryosophila argentea*	
Granadillo (rosewood)	*Dalbergia cubilquitzensis*	
Habin	*Piscidia piscipula*	
Palmetto	*Acuelorraphe wrightii*	
Pucte (bullet tree)	*Bucida buceras*	
Santa Maria	*Calophyllum brasiliense*	
Xchai	*Jatropha tubulosa*	

D-9: Mangrove shoreline

Maya/Spanish Name	Latin Name	Comment
Mangle colorado	*Rhizophora mangle*	Dominant

BIBLIOGRAPHY

Acosta, R., Jr.

1965   Preclassic and Classic Architecture of Oaxaca. In *Archaeology of Southern Mesoamerica. Handbook of Middle American Indians,* edited by G. R. Willey, Vol. 3, Pt. 2, pp. 814–836. University of Texas Press, Austin.

Adams, R. E. W.

1974   A Trial Estimate of Classic Maya Palace Populations at Uaxactun. In *Mesoamerican Archaeology: New Approaches,* edited by N. Hammond, pp. 285–296. University of Texas Press, Austin.

1980   Swamps, Canals, and the Locations of Cities. *Antiquity* 54 (212):206–214.

1983   Ancient Land Use and Culture History in the Pasión River Region. In *Prehistoric Settlement Patterns: Essays in Honor of Gordon R. Willey,* edited by E. Z. Vogt and R. M. Leventhal, pp. 319–336. University of New Mexico Press, Albuquerque.

1986   The Río Azul Archaeological Project: 1986 Summary Report. Ms. on file, University of Texas, San Antonio.

Adams, R. E. W. (editor)

1977   *The Origins of Maya Civilization.* University of New Mexico Press, Albuquerque.

Adams, R. E. W.; W. E. Brown, Jr.; and T. P. Culbert

1981   Radar Mapping, Archaeology, and Ancient Maya Land Use. *Science* 213:1457–1462.

Adams, R. E. W., and T. P. Culbert

1977   The Origins of Civilization in the Maya Lowlands. In *The Origins of Maya Civilization,* edited by R.E.W. Adams, pp. 3–24. University of New Mexico Press, Albuquerque.

Adams, R. E. W., and W. D. Smith

1981   Feudal Models for Classic Maya Civilization. In *Lowland Maya Settlement Patterns,* edited by W. Ashmore, pp. 335–350. University of New Mexico Press, Albuquerque.

Agrinier, P.

In press   The Ballcourts of Southern Chiapas, Mexico. In *The Mesoamerican Ballgame,* edited by V. L. Scarborough and D. R. Wilcox. University of Arizona Press, Tucson.

Altschuler, M.

1958   On the Environmental Limitations of Mayan Cultural Development. *Southwestern Journal of Anthropology* 14:189–196.

Andrews V, E. W.

1981   Dzibilchaltún. In *Supplement to the Handbook of Middle American Indians,* Vol. 1, *Archaeology,* edited by J. A. Sabloff, pp. 313–344. University of Texas Press, Austin.

Andrews V, E. W.; W. M. Ringle III; P. J. Barnes; A. Barrera Rubio; and T. Gallareta

1981   Komchen: An Early Maya Community in Northwest Yucatán. Paper presented at the Sociedad Mexicana de Antropología, San Cristóbal, Chiapas.

Antoine, P. P.; R. L. Skarie; and P. R. Bloom

1982   The Origin of Raised Fields near San Antonio, Belize: An Alternative Hypothesis. In *Maya Subsistence: Studies in Memory of Dennis E. Puleston,* edited by K. V. Flannery, pp. 227–238. Academic Press, New York.

Armillas, P.

1971   Gardens on Swamps. *Science* 174:653–661.

Ashmore, W.

1981   Some Issues of Method and Theory in Lowland Maya Settlement Archaeology. In *Lowland Maya Settlement Patterns,* edited by W. Ashmore, pp. 37–70. University of New Mexico Press, Albuquerque.

1984   Quirigua Archaeology and History Revisted. *Journal of Field Archaeology* 11:365–386.

Ball, J. W.

1977a   The Rise of the Northern Maya Chiefdoms: A Socioprocessual Analysis. In *The Origins of Maya Civilization,* edited by R. E. W. Adams, pp. 101–132. University of New Mexico Press, Albuquerque.

1977b   An Hypothetical Outline of Coastal Maya Prehistory: 300 B.C.–A.D. 1200. In *Social Process in Maya Prehistory,* edited by N. Hammond, pp. 167–196. Academic Press, New York.

1977c   *The Archaeological Ceramics of Becán, Campeche, Mexico.* Middle American

Research Institute, Tulane University, Publication 43.

Ball, J. W., and E. W. Andrews, V
1978   *Preclassic Architecture at Becán, Campeche, Mexico.* Middle American Research Institute, Tulane University, Occasional Paper No. 3.

Barrera, M.; A. A. Barrera V.; and R. M. López
1976   *Nomenclatura Etnobotanica Maya.* Instituto Nacional de Antropología e Historia, Mexico.

Barry, I.
1975   Investigations of Structure 277 at Nohmul. Operation 309. In *Archaeology in Northern Belize: 1974–75 Interim Report of the British Museum–Cambridge University Corozal Project,* edited by N. Hammond, pp. 109–115. Centre of Latin American Studies, Cambridge.

Bartlett, H. H.
1936   A Method of Procedure for Field Work in Tropical American Phytogeography Based upon a Botanical Reconnaissance in Parts of British Honduras and the Petén Forest of Guatemala. *Botany of the Maya Area,* Miscellaneous Paper No. 1, Carnegie Institution, Publication 481.

Baudez, C. (editor)
1983   *Introduction a la Arqueologia de Copán, Honduras.* Instituto Hondureño de Antropología e Historia, Tegucigalpa.

Beard, J. S.
1944   Climax Vegetation in Tropical America. *Ecology* 25:125–158.
1955   The Classification of Tropical American Vegetation Types. *Ecology* 36:89–100.

Becker, M. J.
1971   *Identification of a Second Plaza Plan at Tikal, Guatemala, and Its Implications for Ancient Maya Social Complexity.* Ph.D. dissertation, University of Pennsylvania. University Microfilms, Ann Arbor.
1979   Priest, Peasants, and Ceremonial Centers: The Intellectual History of a Model. In *Maya Archaeology and Ethnohistory,* edited by N. Hammond and G. R. Willey, pp. 3–20. University of Texas Press, Austin.

Belew, J. S.
1978   Applications of Thermoluminescence Dating to Archaeological Studies at Cerros, Belize, Central America. M.A. thesis, Southern Methodist University.

Belisle, J.; S. Musa; and A. Shoman
1977   The Río Hondo Project, an Investigation of the Maya of Northern Belize. *Journal of Belizean Affairs* (special issue), No. 5.

Blanton, R. E.
1976   Anthropological Studies of Cities. *Annual Review of Anthropology* 5:249–264.
1978   *Monte Albán: Settlement Patterns at the Ancient Zapotec Capital.* Academic Press, New York.

Blatt, H.; G. Middleton; and R. Murray
1972   *Origin of Sedimentary Rocks.* Prentice-Hall, Englewood Cliffs.

Block, M. R.
1963   The Social Influence of Salt. *Scientific American* 209:88–98.

Blom, F.
1932   The Maya Ball-Game *Pok-Ta-Pok* (called *Tlachtli* by the *Aztec*). Middle American Research Institute, Tulane University, Middle American Research Series, Publication 4.

Bloom, A. L.
1971   Glacial-Eustatic and Isostatic Controls of Sea-Level since the Last Glaciation. In *Late Cenozoic Glacial Ages,* edited by K. K. Turekian. pp. 355–379. Yale University Press, New Haven.

Bloom, P. R.; M. Pohl; C. Buttleman; F. Wiseman; A. Covich; C. Miksicek; J. Ball; and J. Stein
1983   Prehistoric Maya Wetland Agriculture and the Alluvial Soils near San Antonio, Río Hondo, Belize. *Nature* 301:417–419.

Bloom, P. R.; M. Pohl; and J. Stein
1985   Analysis of Sedimentation and Agriculture along the Río Hondo, Northern Belize. In *Prehistoric Lowland Maya Environment and Subsistence Economy,* edited by M. Pohl, pp. 21–34. Papers of the Peabody Museum of Archaeology and Ethnology, Vol. 77. Harvard University, Cambridge.

Boone, J. L., III
1986   Parental Investment and Elite Family Structure in Preindustrial States: A Case Study of Late Medieval–Early Modern Portuguese Genealogies. *American Anthropologist* 88(4):859–878.

Borhegyi, S. F. de
1956   Settlement Patterns in the Guatemalan Highlands: Past and Present. In *Prehistoric Settlement Patterns in the New World,* edited

by G. R. Willey. Viking Fund Publication in Anthropology 23:101–106. New York.

1969 The Precolumbian Ballgame: A Pan-Mesoamerican Tradition. *Verhandlungen des 38*. Internationalen Amerikamsten-Kongresses, 1968.

1980 *The Pre-Columbian Ball Games: A Pan-Mesoamerican Tradition*. Milwaukee Public Museum Contributions in Anthropology and History, No. 1.

Boserup, E.
1965 *The Conditions of Agricultural Growth*. Aldine, Chicago.

Brown, K. L.
1973 The B-III-5 Mound Group: Early and Middle Classic Architecture. In *The Pennsylvania State University Kaminaljuyu Project— 1969, 1970 Season*, Pt. 1, edited by J. W. Michels and W. T. Sanders. Pennsylvania State University, Philadelphia.

Bullard, W. R., Jr.
1960 Maya Settlement Pattern in Northeastern Petén, Guatemala. *American Antiquity* 25: 355–372.

1965 *Stratigraphic Excavations at San Estevan, Northern British Honduras*. Royal Ontario Museum of Arts and Archaeology, Occasional Paper 9. Toronto.

1973 Postclassic Culture in Central Petén and Adjacent British Honduras. In *The Classic Maya Collapse*, edited by T. P. Culbert, pp. 221–242. University of New Mexico Press, Albuquerque.

Bullard, W. R., Jr.; and M. R. Bullard
1965 *Late Classic Finds at Baking Pot, British Honduras*. Royal Ontario Museum, Occasional Paper 8. Toronto.

Butzer, K. W.
1976 *Early Hydraulic Civilization in Egypt: A Study in Cultural Ecology*. University of Chicago Press, Chicago.

1980 Civilization: Organisms or Systems? *American Scientist* 68:517–523.

Calnek, E. E.
1972 Settlement Pattern and Chinampa Agriculture at Tenochtitlan. *American Antiquity* 37: 104–115.

Camara, L. M.
1984 Logwood and Archeology in Campeche. *Journal of Anthropological Research* 40(2): 324–328.

Cancian, F.
1965 *Economics and Prestige in a Maya Community: The Religious Cargo System in Zinacantan*. Stanford University Press, Stanford.

Cantor, M.
1978 Late Formative and Early Classic Ceramics Caches from Platform 34 and Structure 35, Cuello. In *Cuello Project, 1978 Interim Report. Archaeological Research Program, Publication 1*. Rutgers University, New Brunswick.

Carr, H. S.
1985 Subsistence and Ceremony: Faunal Utilization in a Late Preclassic Community at Cerros, Belize. In *Prehistoric Lowland Maya Environment and Subsistence Economy*, edited by M. Pohl, pp. 115–132. Papers of the Peabody Museum of Archaeology and Ethnology, Vol. 77. Harvard University, Cambridge.

1986 Preliminary Results of Analysis of Fauna. In *Archaeology at Cerros, Belize, Central America, Volume 1*, edited by R. A. Robertson and D. A. Freidel, pp. 127–146. Southern Methodist University Press, Dallas.

Carr, R. F., and J. E. Hazard
1961 *Tikal Report No. 11; Map of the Ruins of Tikal, El Petén, Guatemala*. Museum Monographs, University Museum, University of Pennsylvania.

Charter, C. F.
1941 *A Reconnaissance Survey of the Soils of British Honduras North of the Central Metamorphic and Igneous Massif*. Government Press of Trinidad.

Chase, D. Z.
1981 The Maya Postclassic at Santa Rita Corozal. *Archaeology* 33:25–33.

Chase, D. Z., and A. F. Chase
1982 Yucatecan Influence in Terminal Classic Northern Belize. *American Antiquity* 47:596–614.

1988 *A Postclassic Perspective: Excavations at the Maya Site of Santa Rita Corozal, Belize*. Pre-Columbian Art Research Institute Monograph 4, San Francisco.

Cliff, M. B.
1982 *Lowland Maya Nucleation: A Case Study from Northern Belize*. Ph.D. dissertation, Southern Methodist University. University Microfilms, Ann Arbor.

1986   Excavations in the Late Preclassic Nucle-
        ated Village. In *Archeology at Cerros, Be-
        lize, Central America, Volume 1,* edited by
        R. A. Robertson and D. A. Freidel, pp. 45–
        64. Southern Methodist University Press,
        Dallas.

Codere, H.
1950   *Fighting with Property: A Study of Kwakiutl
        Potlatching and Warfare 1792–1930.* Uni-
        versity of Washington Press, Seattle.

Coe, M. D.
1964   The Chinampas of Mexico. *Scientific
        American* 211:90–98.
1970   The Archaeological Sequence at San
        Lorenzo Tenochititlán, Veracruz, Mexico.
        In *Contributions of the University of Cali-
        fornia Archaeological Research Facility,*
        No. 8. Berkeley.
1977   Olmec and Maya: A Study in Relationships.
        In *The Origin of Maya Civilization,* edited
        by R. E. W. Adams, pp. 183–196. Univer-
        sity of New Mexico Press, Albuquerque.

Coe, M. D., and R. A. Diehl
1980   *In the Land of the Olmec: The Archaeology
        of San Lorenzo Tenochtitlán,* Vol. 1. Uni-
        versiy of Texas Press, Austin.

Coe, W. R.
1965a   Tikal, Guatemala, and Emergent Maya Civ-
        ilization. *Science* 147:1401–1419.
1965b   Tikal: Ten Years of Study of a Maya Ruin in
        the Lowlands of Guatemala. *Expedition*
        8:5–56.
1967   *Tikal: A Handbook of the Ancient Maya Ru-
        ins.* University of Pennsylvania, University
        Museum.

Coggins, C.
1975   Painting and Drawing Styles at Tikal. Ph.D.
        dissertation, Harvard University.

Collier, A.
1964   The American Mediterranean. In *Natural
        Environment and Early Cultures. Hand-
        book of Middle American Indians,* edited
        by R. C. West, Vol. 1, pp. 122–142. Univer-
        sity of Texas Press, Austin.

Connor, J. G.
1975   Ceramics and Artifacts. In *Changing Pre-
        Columbian Commercial Systems,* edited by
        J. A. Sabloff and W. L. Rathje. Monographs
        of the Peabody Museum, No. 3. Harvard
        University, Cambridge.

Cook, S. F., and R. F. Heizer
1965   *Studies on the Chemical Analysis of Archae-
        ological Sites.* University of California Pub-
        lications in Anthropology, No. 2. Berkeley.

Cooke, C. W.
1931   Why the Maya Cities of the Petén District,
        Guatemala, were Abandoned. *Journal of the
        Washington Academy of Sciences* 21:287.

Covich, A. P.
1983   Mollusca: A Contrast in Species Diversity
        from Aquatic and Terrestrial Habitats. In
        *Pulltrouser Swamp: Ancient Maya Habitat,
        Agriculture, and Settlement in Northern
        Belize,* edited by B. L. Turner II and P. D.
        Harrison, pp. 120–139. University of Texas
        Press, Austin.

Cowgill, U. M.
1962   An Agricultural Study of the Southern Maya
        Lowlands. *American Anthropologist* 64:273–
        286.

Cowgill, U. M. and G. E. Hutchinson
1963   *El Bajo de Santa Fe.* Transactions of the
        American Philosophical Society, New Series
        53, Pt. 7.

Crane, C. J.
1986   Late Preclassic Maya Agriculture, Wild
        Plant Utilization, and Land-Use Practices.
        In *Archaeology at Cerros, Belize, Central
        America, Volume 1,* edited by R. A. Robert-
        son and D. A. Freidel, pp. 147–164. South-
        ern Methodist University Press, Dallas.

Crumley, C. L.
1976   Toward a Locational Definition of State Sys-
        tems of Settlement. *American Anthropolo-
        gist* 78:59–73.

Culbert, T. P.
1977   Early Maya Development at Tikal,
        Guatemala. In *The Origins of Maya Civi-
        lization,* edited by R. E. W. Adams, pp. 27–
        44. University of New Mexico Press,
        Albuquerque.
1988   The Collapse of Classic Maya Civilization.
        In *The Collapse of Ancient States and Civi-
        lizations,* edited by N. Yoffee and G. L.
        Cowgill, pp. 69–101. University of Arizona
        Press, Tucson.

Dahlin, B. H.
1977   The Initiation of the Albion Island Settle-
        ment Pattern Survey. *Journal of Belizean
        Affairs* 5:44–51.

1984   A Colossus in Guatemala: The Preclassic
        Maya City of El Mirador. *Archaeology*
        37(5):18–25.

Darch, J. P.
    1983   The Soils of Pulltrouser Swamp: Classifica-
            tion and Characteristics. In *Pulltrouser
            Swamp: Ancient Maya Habitat, Agriculture,
            and Settlement in Northern Belize,* edited by
            B. L. Turner II and P. D. Harrison, pp. 52–
            90. University of Texas Press, Austin.

Deevey, E. S.; D. S. Rice; P. M. Rice; H. H. Vaughan;
    M. Brenner; and M. S. Flannery
    1979   Maya Urbanism: Impact on a Tropical
            Karst Environment. *Science* 206:298–306.

Denevan, W. M.
    1966   *The Aboriginal Cultural Geography of
            the Llanos de Mojos of Bolivia.* Ibero-
            Americana, No. 48. University of Califor-
            nia Press, Berkeley.
    1970   Aboriginal Drained-Field Cultivation in the
            Americas. *Science* 169:647–654.
    1982   Hydraulic Agriculture in the American
            Tropics: Forms, Measures, and Recent Re-
            search. In *Maya Subsistence: Studies in
            Memory of Dennis E. Puleston,* edited by
            K. V. Flannery, pp. 181–204. Academic
            Press, New York.

Denevan, W. M., and B. L. Turner II
    1974   Forms, Functions, and Associations of
            Raised Fields in the Old World Tropics. *Jour-
            nal of Tropical Geography* 39:24–33.

Donaghey, S.; J. Cartwright; H. S. Carr; C. P. Beetz; P.
    Messick; J. Ward; and N. Hammond
    1979   Excavations in Platform 34, Cuello, May-
            June, 1978. In *Cuello Project, 1978 Interim
            Report. Archaeological Research Program,
            Publication 1,* edited by N. Hammond, pp.
            20–44. Rutgers University, New Brunswick.

Eaton, J. D.
    1975   Ancient Agricultural Farmsteads in the Rio
            Bec Region of Yucatán. *Contribution of the
            University of California Archaeological Re-
            search Faculty,* No. 27. Berkeley.
    1976   Ancient Fishing Technology on the Gulf
            Coast of Yucatán, Mexico. *Bulletin of the
            Texas Archaeological Society* 47: 231–243.
    1978   Archaeological Survey of the Yucatán-
            Campeche Coast. In *Studies in the Archae-
            ology of Coastal Yucatán and Campeche,
            Mexico,* pp. 1–67. Middle American

Research Institute, Tulane University,
Publication 46.
    1982   Colha: An Overview of Architecture and
            Settlement. In *Archaeology at Colha, Belize:
            The 1981 Interim Report,* edited by T. R.
            Hester, H. J. Shafer, and J. D. Eaton, pp. 11–
            20. Center for Archaeological Research,
            University of Texas at San Antonio.

Eaton, J. D., and B. Kunstler
    1980   Excavations at Operation 2009: A Maya
            Ballcourt. In *The Colha Project: Second
            Season, 1980 Interim Reports,* edited by
            T. R. Hester, J. D. Eaton, and H. J. Shafer,
            pp. 121–132. Center for Archaeologi-
            cal Research, University of Texas at San
            Antonio.

Emery, K. O.
    1969   The Continental Shelves. *Scientific Ameri-
            can* 221:107–122.

Fash, W. L.
    1983   Deducing Social Organization from Classic
            Maya Settlement Patterns: A Case Study
            from the Copan Valley. In *Civilization in the
            Ancient Americas: Essays in Honor of Gor-
            don R. Willey,* edited by R. M. Leventhal
            and A. L. Kolata, pp. 261–288. University of
            New Mexico Press, Albuquerque.

Feldman, L. H.
    1979   Snails, Clams and Mayas: The Use of Mol-
            lusks to Measure Ecological Change. Ms. on
            file, Southern Methodist University.

Ferdon, E. N., Jr.
    1959   Agricultural Potential and the Development
            of Cultures. *Southwestern Journal of Anthro-
            pology* 15:1–19.

Flannery, K. V.
    1967   The Olmec and the Valley of Oaxaca: A
            Model for Inter-Regional Interaction in
            Formative Times. In *Dumbarton Oaks Con-
            ference on the Olmec,* edited by E. P. Ben-
            son, pp.79–110. Dumbarton Oaks Research
            Library and Collection, Washington.
    1972   The Cultural Evolution of Civilizations.
            Annual Review of Ecology and Systematics
            3:399–426.

Flannery, K. V., and M. D. Coe
    1968   Social and Economic Systems in Formative
            Mesoamerica. In *New Perspectives in Arche-
            ology,* edited by S. R. Binford and L. R.
            Binford, pp. 267–284. Aldine, Chicago.

Flannery, K. V.; A. V. T. Kirkby; M. J. Kirkby; and W. Williams
 1967   Farming Systems and Political Growth in Ancient Oaxaca. *Science* 158:445–454.

Flannery, K. V., and J. Marcus
 1976   Evolution of the Public Building in Formative Oaxaca. In *Cultural Change and Continuity: Essays in Honor of James Bennett Griffin,* edited by C. E. Cleland, pp. 205–222. Academic Press, New York.

Flannery, K. V., and J. Marcus (editors)
 1983   *The Cloud People: Divergent Evolution of the Zapotec and Mixtec Civilizations.* Academic Press, New York.

Flores, G.
 1952   Geology of Northern British Honduras. *Bulletin of the American Association of Petroleum Geologists* 36:404–413.

Folan, W. J.; E. R. Kintz; and L. A. Fletcher
 1983   *Coba: A Classic Maya Metropolis.* Academic Press, New York.

Ford, A.
 1986   *Population Growth and Social Complexity: An Examination of Settlement and Environment in the Central Maya Lowlands.* Arizona State University Anthropological Research Paper 35. Tempe.

Freidel, D. A.
 1977   A Late Preclassic Monumental Mayan Mask at Cerros, Northern Belize. *Journal of Field Archaeology* 4:488–491.
 1978   Maritime Adaptation and the Rise of Maya Civilization: The View from Cerros, Belize. In *Prehistoric Coastal Adaptations,* edited by B. L. Stark and B. Voorhies, pp. 239–265. Academic Press, New York.
 1979   Culture Areas and Interaction Spheres: Contrasting Approaches to the Emergence of Civilization in the Maya Lowlands. *American Antiquity* 44:36–54.
 1981   Civilization as a State of Mind: The Cultural Evolution of the Lowland Maya. In *The Transition to Statehood in the New World,* edited by G. D. Jones and R. R. Kautz, pp. 188–337. Cambridge University Press, Cambridge.
 1986a The Monumental Architecture. In *Archaeology at Cerros, Belize, Central America, Volume 1,* edited by R. A. Robertson and D. A. Freidel, pp. 1–22. Southern Methodist University Press, Dallas.

 1986b Polychrome Facades of the Lowland Maya Preclassic. In *Painted Architecture and Polychromed Monumental Sculpture in Mesoamerica,* edited by E. Boone, pp. 5–30. Dumbarton Oaks, Washington.

Freidel, D. A., and J. A. Sabloff
 1984   *Cozumel: Late Maya Settlement Patterns.* Academic Press, New York.

Freidel, D.A., and V. Scarborough
 1982   Subsistence, Trade and Development of the Coastal Maya. In *Maya Subsistence: Studies in Memory of Dennis E. Puleston,* edited by K. V. Flannery, pp. 131–151. Academic Press, New York.

Freidel, D. A., and L. Schele
 1988   Symbol and Power: A History of the Lowland Maya Cosmogram. In *Maya Iconography,* edited by E. Benson and G. Griffin, pp. 43–93. Princeton University Press, Princeton.

Fried, M. H.
 1967   *The Evolution of Political Society.* Random House, New York.

Fry, R. E.
 1969   *Ceramics and Settlement in the Periphery of Tikal, Guatemala.* Ph.D. dissertation, University of Arizona. University Microfilms, Ann Arbor.

Gann, T. W. F., and M. Gann
 1939   *Archaeological Investigations in the Corozal District of British Honduras.* Bureau of American Ethnology, Smithsonian Institution, Bulletin 123.

Garber, J. F.
 1981   *Material Culture and Patterns of Artifact Consumption and Disposal at the Maya Site of Cerros in Northern Belize.* Ph.D. dissertation, Southern Methodist University. University Microfilms, Ann Arbor.
 1983   Patterns of Jade Consumption and Disposal at Cerros, Northern Belize. *American Antiquity* 48(4):800–807.
 1986   The Artifacts. In *Archaeology at Cerros, Belize, Central America, Volume 1,* edited by R. A. Robertson and D. A. Freidel, pp. 117–126. Southern Methodist University Press, Dallas.

Gibson, E. C.; L. C. Shaw; and D. R. Finamore
 1986   *Early Evidence of Maya Hieroglyphic Writing at Kichpanha, Belize.* Working Papers in Archaeology No. 2. Center for Archaeological

Research, University of Texas at San Antonio.

Gibson, M.
1974 Violation of Fallow and Engineered Disaster in Mesopotamian Civilization. In *Irrigation's Impact on Society,* edited by T. E. Downing and M. Gibson, pp. 7–20. University of Arizona Press, Tucson.

Geertz, C.
1963 *Agricultural Involution.* University of California Press, Berkeley.

Graham, I.
1967 *Archaeological Explorations in El Petén, Guatemala.* Middle American Research Institute, Tulane University, Publication 33.

Grove, D. C.
1984 *Chalcatzingo: Excavations on the Olmec Frontier.* Thames and Hudson, London.

Hammond, N.
1972 Obsidian Trade Routes in the Mayan Area. *Science* 178:1092–1093.
1973 *British Museum—Cambridge University Corozal Project, 1973 Interim Report.* Centre of Latin American Studies, Cambridge.
1975 *British Museum—Cambridge University Corozal Project, 1974–75 Interim Report.* Centre of Latin American Studies, Cambridge.
1977 Ex Oriente Lux: A View from Belize. In *The Origins of Maya Civilization,* edited by R. E. W. Adams, pp. 45–76. University of New Mexico, Albuquerque.
1978 *Cuello Project, 1978 Interim Report. Archaeological Research Program, Publication 1.* Rutgers University, New Brunswick.
1981 Settlement Patterns in Belize. In *Lowland Maya Settlement Patterns,* edited by W. Ashmore, pp. 157–186. University of New Mexico Press, Albuquerque.
1985 *Nohmul: A Prehistoric Maya Community in Belize: Excavations 1973–1983.* British Archaeological Reports, International Series 250. Oxford.
1986 The Emergence of Maya Civilization. *Scientific American* 254(8):106–115.

Hammond, N.; C. Clark; M. Horton; M. Hodges; L. McNatt; L. J. Kosakowsky; and A. Pyburn
1985 Excavation and Survey at Nohmul, Belize, 1983. *Journal of Field Archaeology* 12:177–200.

Hammond, N.; S. Donaghey; C. Gleason; J. C. Staneko; D. Van Teurenhout; and L. J. Kosakowsky
1987 Excavations at Nohmul, Belize, 1985. *Journal of Field Archaeology* 14:257–281.

Hammond, N.; D. Pring; R. Wilk; S. Donaghey; F. Saul; E. Wing; A. Miller; and L. Feldman
1979 The Earliest Lowland Maya? Definition of the Swazey Phase. *American Antiquity* 44(1):92–110.

Harrison, P. D.
1970 *The Central Acropolis, Tikal, Guatemala: A Preliminary Study of the Function of Its Structural Components during the Late Classic Period.* Ph.D. dissertation, University of Pennsylvania. University Microfilms, Ann Arbor.
1977 The Rise of the Bajos and the Fall of the Maya. In *Social Process in Maya Pre-History: Studies in Honour of Sir Eric Thompson,* edited by N. Hammond, pp. 470–509. Academic Press, New York.
1978 Bajos Revisted: Visual Evidence for One System. In *Pre-Hispanic Maya Agriculture,* edited by P. D. Harrison and B. L. Turner II, pp. 247–254. University of New Mexico Press, Albuquerque.
1979 The Lobil Postclassic Phase in the Southern Interior of the Yucatán Peninsula. In *Maya Archaeology and Ethnohistory,* edited by N. Hammond and G. R. Willey, pp. 189–207. University of Texas Press, Austin.
1982 Subsistence and Society in Eastern Yucatán. In *Maya Subsistence: Studies in Memory of Dennis E. Puleston,* edited by K. V. Flannery, pp. 119–128. Academic Press, New York.

Harrison, P. D., and B. L. Turner II (editors)
1978 *Prehispanic Maya Agriculture.* University of New Mexico Press, Albuquerque.
1983 *Pulltrouser Swamp: Ancient Maya Habitat, Agriculture, and Settlement in Northern Belize.* University of Texas Press, Austin.

Hauck, F. R.
1973 The Edzna Hydraulic Complex: Initial Investigation. M.A. thesis, Brigham Young University.

Haury, E.
1976 *The Hohokam, Desert Farmers and Craftsmen: Excavations at Snaketown.* University of Arizona Press, Tucson.

Haviland, W. A.

1963 *Excavation of Small Structures in the Northeast Quadrant of Tikal, Guatemala.* Ph.D.
dissertation, University of Pennsylvania.
University Microfilms, Ann Arbor.

1966 Maya Settlement Patterns: A Critical
Review. In *Archaeological Studies in Middle America.* Middle American Research
Institute, Tulane University, Publication
26.

1967 Stature at Tikal, Guatemala: Implications
for Ancient Maya Demography and Social
Organization. *American Antiquity* 32:316–
325.

1969 A New Population Estimate for Tikal,
Guatemala. *American Antiquity* 34:429–433.

1970 Tikal, Guatemala and Mesoamerican Ur-
banism. *World Archaeology* 2:186–198.

Hazelden, J.

1973 The Soils and Geology of the Orange Walk
and Corozal Districts. In *British Museum-
Cambridge University Corozal Project, 1973
Interim Report,* edited by N. Hammond,
pp. 74–85. Centre of Latin American Studies, Cambridge.

Healy, P. F.; J. D. H. Lambert; J. T. Arnason; and R. J.
Hebda

1984 Caracol, Belize: Evidence of Ancient Maya
Agricultural Terraces. *Journal of Field Archaeology* 10:397–410.

Healy, P. F.; C. van Waarden; and T. J. Anderson

1980 Nueva Evidencia de Antiguas Terrazas
Mayas en Belice. *America Indigena* 40:773–
796.

Heider, K. G.

1970 *The Dugum Dani: A Papuan Culture in the
Highlands of West New Guinea.* Viking Fund
Publication, No. 49. New York.

Hester, J. A.

1954 *Natural and Cultural Bases of Ancient
Maya Subsistence Economy.* Ph.D. disserta-
tion, University of California, Los Angeles.
University Microfilms, Ann Arbor.

Hester, T. R.

1982 The Maya Lithic Sequence in Northern Belize. In *Archaeology at Colha, Belize: The
1981 Interim Report,* edited by T. R. Hester,
H. J. Shafer, and J. D. Eaton, pp. 39–59.
Center for Archaeological Research, University of Texas at San Antonio.

Hester, T. R.; J. D. Eaton; and H. J. Shafer (editors)

1980 *The Colha Project: Second Season, 1980
Interim Report.* Center for Archaeologi-
cal Research, University of Texas at San
Antonio.

Hester, T. R.; H. J. Shafer; and J. D. Eaton (editors)

1982 *Archaeology at Colha, Belize: The 1981 Interim Report.* Center for Archaeological Research, University of Texas at San Antonio.

High, L. R., Jr.

1975 Geomorphology and Sedimentology of
Holocene Coastal Deposits. In *Belize Shelf-
Carbonate Sediments, Clastic Sediments, and
Ecology,* edited by K. F. Wantland and W. C.
Pusey III, pp. 53–96. American Associaton of
Petroleum Geologists, Tulsa.

Hirth, K. G.

1978 Interregional Trade and the Formation of
Prehistoric Gateway Communities. *American Antiquity,* 43:35–45.

Hirth, K. G. (editor)

1984 *Trade and Exchange in Early Mesoamerica.* University of New Mexico Press, Albuquerque.

Hodder, I., and C. Orton

1976 *Spatial Analysis in Archaeology.* Cambridge
University Press, Cambridge.

Holdridge, L. R.

1967 *Life Zone Ecology.* Revised edition. Tropical Science Center, San Jose, Costa Rica.

Jacobson, T., and R. Mc.C. Adams

1958 Salt and Silt in Ancient Mesopotamian
Agriculture. *Science* 128:1251–1258.

Jacks, G. V.

1954 *Multilingual Vocabulary of Soil Science.*
Food and Agriculture Organization of the
United Nations, New York.

Justeson, J. S.; W. M. Norman; and N. Hammond

1988 The Pomona Jade Flare: A Preclassic
Mayan Hieroglyphic Text. In *Maya Iconography,* edited by E. Benson and G. Griffin,
pp. 94–151. Princeton University Press,
Princeton.

Kelly, T. C.

1980 The Colha Regional Survey. In *The Colha
Project: Second Season, 1980 Interim Re-
port,* edited by T. R. Hester, J. D. Eaton, and
H. J. Shafer, pp. 51–69. Center for Archaeo-
logical Research, University of Texas at San
Antonio.

1982   The Colha Regional Survey, 1981. In *Archae-ology at Colha, Belize: The 1981 Interim Report,* edited by T. R. Hester, H.J. Shafer, and J. D. Eaton, pp. 85–97. Center for Archaeological Research, University of Texas at San Antonio.

Kidder, A. V., and G. F. Ekholm
1951   Some Archaeological Specimens from Pomona, British Honduras. In *Notes on Middle American Archaeology and Ethnology,* Vol. 4 (102):125–142. Carnegie Institution.

Kirke, C.M. St.G.
1980   Prehistoric Agriculture in the Belize River Valley. *World Archaeology* 11:281–286.

Klein, J.; J. C. Lerman; P. E. Damon; and E. K. Ralph
1982   Calibration of Radiocarbon Dates. *Radiocarbon* 24(1):103–150.

Kowalewski, S. A.; G. Feinman; L. Finstein; and R. E. Blanton
1983   Boundaries, Scales, and International Organization. *Journal of Anthropological Archaeology* 2:32–56.

Krader, L.
1968   *Formation of the State. Foundations of Modern Anthropology Series.* Englewood Cliffs, Prentice-Hall.

Kubler, G.
1975   *The Art and Architecture of Ancient America,* 2nd Ed. Penguin Books, Baltimore.

Kurjack, E. B.
1974   *Prehistoric Lowland Maya Community and Social Organization: A Case Study at Dzibilchaltun, Yucatan, Mexico.* Middle American Research Institute, Tulane University, Publication 38.
1976   Pre-Columbian Polities and Communities in Northwest Yucatán, Mexico. Paper presented at the Meetings of the Society for American Archaeology, St. Louis.

Lewenstein, S. M.
1986   Feature 11 and the Quest for the Elusive Domestic Structure: A Preliminary Reconstruction Based on Chipped Stone Use. In *Archaeology at Cerros, Belize, Central America, Volume 1,* edited by R. A. Robertson and D. A. Freidel, pp. 65–73. Southern Methodist University Press, Dallas.
1987   *Stone Tool Use at Cerros: The Ethnoarchaeological and Use-Wear Evidence.* University of Texas Press, Austin.

Lind, A. O.
1961   *Coastal Landforms of Cat Island, Bahamas: A Study of Holocene Accretionary Topography and Sea-Level Change.* Department of Geography Research Paper Vol. 122. University of Chicago, Chicago.

Loten, H. S.
n.d.   Lamanai Postclassic. In *The Lowland Maya Postclassic,* edited by A. F. Chase and P. M. Rice, pp. 85–90. University of Texas Press, Austin.

Lowe, G. W.
1977   The Mixe-Zoque as Competing Neighbors of the Early Lowland Maya. In *The Origins of Maya Civilization,* edited by R. E. W. Adams, pp. 197–248. University of New Mexico Press, Albuquerque.

Lundell, C. L.
1934   *Preliminary Sketch of the Phytogeography of the Yucatán Peninsula.* Carnegie Institution of Washington, Publication 436, Contribution 12.
1937   *The Vegetation of the Petén.* Carnegie Institution, Publication 478.
1938   Plants Probably Utilized by the Old Empire Maya of Petén and Adjacent Lowlands. *Papers of the Michigan Academy of Sciences, Arts, and Letters* 24:37–59.
1940   The 1936 Michigan-Carnegie Botanical Expedition to British Honduras. In *Botany of the Maya Area.* Carnegie Institution, Publication 522. Miscellaneous Paper No. 14.

McDonald, R. D.
1979   Preliminary Report on the Physical Geography of Northern Belize. In *Cuello Project, 1978 Interim Report. Archaeological Research Program, Publication 1,* edited by N. Hammond, pp. 79–87. Rutgers University, New Brunswick.

McKillop, H.
1984   Prehistoric Maya Reliance on Marine Resources: Analysis of a Midden from Moho Cay, Belize. *Journal of Field Archaeology* 11(1):25–36.

Maldonado-Koerdell, M.
1964   Geohistory and Paleogeography of Middle America. In *Natural Environment and Early Cultures. Handbook of Middle American Indians,* edited by R. C. West, Vol. 1, pp. 3–22. University of Texas Press, Austin.

Marcus, J.
1980   Zapotec Writing. *Scientific American* 242:50–79.
1983   On the Nature of the Mesoamerican City. In *Prehistoric Settlement Patterns: Essays in Honor of Gordon Willey,* edited by E. Z. Vogt and R. M. Leventhal, pp. 195–220. University of New Mexico Press, Albuquerque.

Matheny, R. T.
1976   Maya Lowland Hydraulic Systems. *Science* 193:639–646.
1978   Northern Maya Lowland Water-Control Systems. In *Pre-Hispanic Maya Agriculture,* edited by P. D. Harrison and B. L. Turner II, pp. 185–210. University of New Mexico Press, Albuquerque.
1980   *El Mirador, Petén, Guatemala: An Interim Report.* Papers of the New World Archaeological Foundation, No. 45. Provo.
1986   Investigations at El Mirador, Petén, Guatemala. *National Geographic Research* 2 (3):332–353.

Matheny, R. T.; D. L. Gurr; D. W. Forsyth; and F. R. Hauck
1983   *Investigations at Edzna, Campeche, Mexico. Vol.1 Pt. l: The Hydraulic System.* Papers of the New World Archaeological Foundation, No. 46. Provo.

Meggers, B. J.
1954   Environmental Limitation on the Development of Culture. *American Anthropologist* 56(5):801–824.

Miles, S. W.
1957   Maya Settlement Patterns: A Problem for Ethnology and Archaeology. *Southwestern Journal of Anthropology* 13:239–248.

Miller, A. G.
1986   *Maya Rulers of Time: A Study of Architectural Sculpture at Tikal, Guatemala.* University Museum, Philadelphia.

Miller, D., and C. Tilley
1984   Ideology, Power and Prehistory: An Introduction. In *Ideology, Power and Prehistory,* edited by D. Miller and C. Tilley, pp. 1–15. Cambridge University Press, Cambridge.

Millon R.
1973   *Urbanization of Teotihuacán, Mexico, Volume 1. The Teotihuacán Map,* Pt. 1. University of Texas Press, Austin.

Mitchum B. A.
1978   House Forms in the Maya Lowlands: A Comparison of Ancient and Modern Types. Ms. on File, Southern Methodist University.
1986   Chipped Stone Artifacts. In *Archaeology at Cerros, Belize, Central America, Volume 1.* edited by R. A. Robertson and D. A. Freidel pp. 105–115. Southern Methodist University Press, Dallas.

Morley, S. G.
1956   *The Ancient Maya.* Revised by G. W. Brainerd, 3rd Ed. Stanford University Press, Stanford.

Morley, S. G., and G. W. Brainerd
1983   *The Ancient Maya.* Revised by R. J. Sharer, 4th Ed. Stanford University Press, Stanford.

Neivens, M., and D. Libbey
1976   An Obsidian Workshop at El Pozito, Northern Belize. In *Maya Lithic Studies: Papers from the 1976 Belize Field Symposium,* edited by T. R. Hester and N. Hammond, pp. 137–150. Center for Archaeological Research, University of Texas at San Antonio.

Netting, R. Mc.C.
1974   Agrarian Ecology. In *Annual Reviews of Anthropology,* edited by B. J. Siegel, A. R. Beals, and S. A. Tyler, pp. 21–56. Annual Reviews, Palo Alto.
1977   Maya Subsistence: Mythologies, Analogies, Possibilities. In *The Origins of Maya Civilization,* edited by R. E. W. Adams, pp. 299–334. University of New Mexico Press, Albuquerque.

Nichols, D. L.
1982   A Middle Formative Irrigation System Near Santa Clara Coatitlan in the Basin of Mexico. *American Antiquity* 47(1): 133–144.
1987   Risk and Agricultural Intensification during the Formative Period in the Northern Basin of Mexico. *American Anthropologist* 89(3):596–616.

Nye, D. H., and D. J. Greenland
1960   *The Soil under Shifting Cultivation.* Commonwealth Bureau of Soils, Technical Communication, No. 51. Commonwealth Agricultural Bureau, Harpenden.

Olson, G. W.
1977   Significance of Physical and Chemical Characteristics of Soils at the San Antonio Archaeological Site on the Rio Hondo in

Northern Belize. *Journal of Belizean Affairs,* 5:22–35.

Ower, L. H.
1929 *The Geology of British Honduras.* Clarion, Belize.

Parsons, L. A.
In press The Ballgame in the Southern Pacific Coast Cotzumalhuapa Region and Its Impact on Kaminaljuya during the Middle Classic. In *The Mesoamerican Ballgame,* edited by V. L. Scarborough and D. R. Wilcox. University of Arizona Press, Tucson.

Parsons, J. J., and W. A. Bowen
1966 Ancient Ridged Fields of the San Jorge Floodplain, Colombia. *Geographic Review* 56:317–343.

Parsons, J. J., and W. M. Denevan
1967 Pre-Columbian Ridged Fields. *Scientific American* 217:93–100.

Pendergast, D. M.
1976 *Altun Ha: A Guidebook to the Ancient Maya Ruins.* University of Toronto Press, Toronto.
1979 *Excavations at Altun Ha, Belize 1964–1970, Volume 1.* Royal Ontario Museum Publications in Archaeology. Toronto.
1981 Lamanai, Belize: Summary of Excavation Results, 1974–1980. *Journal of Field Archaeology* 8(1): 29–53.

Phillips, D. A., Jr.
1979 *Material Culture and Trade of the Postclassic Maya.* Ph.D. dissertation, University of Arizona. University Microfilms, Ann Arbor.

Pohl, M. (editor)
1985 *Prehistoric Lowland Maya Environment and Subsistence Economy.* Papers of the Peabody Museum of Archaeology and Ethnology, Vol. 77. Harvard University, Cambridge.

Pollock, H. E. D.; R. L. Roys; T. Proskouriakoff; and A. L. Smith
1962 *Mayapán, Yucatán, Mexico.* Carnegie Institution, Publication 619.

Pope, K. O., and B. H. Dahlin
1989 Ancient Maya Wetland Agriculture: New Insights from Ecological and Remote Sensing Research. *Journal of Field Archaeology* 16(1):87–106.

Potter, D. F.
1977 *Maya Architecture of the Central Yucatán Peninsula, Mexico.* Middle American Research Institute, Tulane University, Publication 44.

Price, B.
1982 Cultural Materialism: A Theoretical Review. *American Antiquity* 47(4):709–741.

Pring, D.
1977a The Preclassic Ceramics of Northern Belize. Ph.D. dissertation, University of London.
1977b Influence or Intrusion? The "Protoclassic" in the Maya Lowlands. In *Social Process in Maya Prehistory,* edited by N. Hammond, pp. 135–165. Academic Press, New York.

Puleston, D. E.
1973 *Ancient Maya Settlement Patterns and Environment at Tikal, Guatemala: Implications for Subsistence Models.* Ph.D. dissertation, University of Pennsylvania. University Microfilms, Ann Arbor.
1974 Intersite Areas in the Vicinity of Tikal and Uaxactun. In *Mesoamerican Archaeology: New Approaches,* edited by N. Hammond, pp. 303–311. University of Texas Press, Austin.
1977a Ancient Maya Settlement Patterns in the Petén. Paper prepared for Lowland Settlement Patterns Seminar, School of American Research, Santa Fe.
1977b The Art and Archaeology of Hydraulic Agriculture in the Maya Lowlands. In *Social Process in Maya Prehistory,* edited by N. Hammond, pp. 449–467. Academic Press, New York.
1978 Terracing, Raised Fields, and Tree Cropping in the Maya Lowlands: A New Perspective on the Geography of Power. In *Pre-Hispanic Maya Agriculture,* edited by P. D. Harrison and B. L. Turner II, pp. 225–246. University of New Mexico Press, Albuquerque.
1983 *Tikal Report No. 13; The Settlement Survey of Tikal.* Museum Monographs, University Museum, University of Pennsylvania.

Puleston, D. E., and D. W. Callender, Jr.
1967 Defensive Earthworks at Tikal. *Expedition* 9:40–48.

Puleston, D. E., and O. S. Puleston
1971 An Ecological Approach to the Origins of Maya Civilization. *Archeology* 24:330–337.

Quiñónes, H., and R. Allende
1974 Formation of the Lithified Carapace of Calcareous Nature which covers most of the

Yucatán Peninsula and its Relation to the Soils and Geomorphology of the Region. *Tropical Agriculture* 51(2):94–101.

Quirarte, J.
1972 El Juego de pelota en Mesoamérica: su desarrollo arquitectonico. *Estudios de Cultura Maya* 8:83–96.

Raikes, R. L.
1984 *Water, Weather and Prehistory.* Humanities Press, New Jersey.

Rands, R. L.
1977 The Rise of Classic Maya Civilization in the Northwestern Zone: Isolation and Integration. In *The Origins of Maya Civilization,* edited by R. E. W. Adams, pp. 159–180. University of New Mexico Press, Albuquerque.

Rathje, W. L., and D. Phillips
1975 The Ruins of Buena Vista. In *Changing Pre-Columbian Commercial Systems,* edited by J. A. Sabloff, and W. L. Rathje. Monographs of the Peabody Museum, No. 3. Harvard University, Cambridge.

Redman, C. L.
1978 Multivariate Artifact Analysis: A Basis for Multidimensional Interpretation. In *Social Archaeology: Beyond Subsistence and Dating*, edited by C. L. Redman, M. J. Berman, E. V. Curtin, W. T. Langhorne, Jr., N. M. Versaggi, and J. C. Wanser, pp. 167–192. Academic Press, New York.

Reeves, C., Jr.
1970 Origin, Classification, and Geologic History of Caliche of the Southern High Plains, Texas, and Eastern New Mexico. *Journal of Geology* 78:352–362.

Reina, R. E., and R. M. Hill
1980 Lowland Maya Subsistence: Notes from Ethnohistory and Ethnography. *American Antiquity* 45:74–79.

Renfrew, C., and J. F. Cherry (editors)
1986 *Peer Polity Interaction and Socio-Political Change.* Cambridge University Press, Cambridge.

Rice, D. S.
1976 Middle Preclassic Settlement in the Central Maya Lowlands. *Journal of Field Archaeology* 3:425–445.

Rice, D. S., and D. E. Puleston
1981 Ancient Maya Settlement Patterns in the Petén, Guatemala. In *Lowland Maya Settlement Patterns*, edited by W. Ashmore, pp. 121–156. University of New Mexico Press, Albuquerque.

Rice, D. S., and P. M. Rice
1980 The Northeast Petén Revisited. *American Antiquity* 45:432–454.
1981 Muralla de León: A Lowland Maya Fortification. *Journal of Field Archaeology* 8(3):271–288.

Rice, D. S.; P. M. Rice; and E. S. Deevey
1985 Paradise Lost: Classic Maya Impact on a Lacustrine Environment. In *Prehistoric Lowland Maya Environment and Subsistence Economy,* edited by M. Pohl, pp. 91–106. Papers of the Peabody Museum of Archaeology and Ethnology, Vol. 77. Harvard University, Cambridge.

Ricketson, O. G.
1931 *Excavations at Baking Pot, British Honduras.* Carnegie Institution, Publication 403, Contribution No. 1.

Ricketson O. G., and E. B. Ricketson
1937 *Uaxactun, Guatemala, Group E—1926–1931.* Carnegie Institution, Publication 477.

Robertson [-Freidel], R. A.
1980 The Ceramics from Cerros: A Late Preclassic Site in Northern Belize. Ph.D. dissertation, Harvard University.
1983 Functional Analysis and Social Process in Ceramics: The Pottery from Cerros, Belize. In *Civilization in the Ancient Americas: Essays in Honor of Gordon R. Willey,* edited by R. M. Leventhal and A. L. Kolata, pp. 105–142. University of New Mexico Press, Albuquerque.
1986 The Ceramics. In *Archaeology at Cerros, Belize, Central America, Volume 1,* edited by R. A. Robertson, and D. A. Freidel, pp. 89–104. Southern Methodist University Press, Dallas.

Rovner, I.
1975 *Lithic Sequences of the Maya Lowlands.* Ph.D. dissertation, University of Wisconsin. University Microfilms, Ann Arbor.

Ruppert, K.
1952 Chichén Itzá: Architectural Notes and Plans. *Carnegie Institution,* Publication 595.

Russell, R. J.
1967 *River Plains and Sea Coasts.* University of California Press, Berkeley.

Sabloff, J. A., and W. L. Rathje
1975 The Rise of a Maya Merchant Class. *Scientific American* 233:72–82.
Sahlins, M. D.
1955 *Social Stratification in Polynesia.* University of Washington Press, Seattle.
1972 *Stone Age Economics.* Aldine Press, Chicago.
Sanchez, P. A., and S. W. Buol
1975 Soils of the Tropics and the World Food Crisis. *Science* 188:598–603.
Sanders, W. T.
1960 *Prehistoric Ceramics and Settlement Patterns in Quintana Roo, Mexico.* Carnegie Institution, Publication 606, Contribution to American Anthropology and History, No. 60.
1962 Cultural Ecology of the Maya Lowlands, Part 1. *Estudios de Cultura Maya* 2:79–121.
1963 Cultural Ecology of the Maya Lowlands, Part 2. *Estudios de Cultura Maya* 3:203–241.
1976 The Agricultural History of the Basin of Mexico. In *The Valley of Mexico: Studies in Pre-Hispanic Ecology and Society,* edited by E. Wolf, pp. 101–160. University of New Mexico Press, Albuquerque.
1977 Environmental Heterogeneity and the Evolution of Lowland Maya Civilization. In *The Origins of Maya Civilization,* edited by R. E. W. Adams, pp. 287–298. University of New Mexico Press, Albuquerque.
Sanders, W. T.; J. R. Parsons; and R. S. Santley
1979 *The Basin of Mexico.* Academic Press, New York.
Sanders, W. T., and R. S. Santley
1977 A Prehispanic Irrigation System near Santa Clara Xalostoc in the Basin of Mexico. *American Antiquity* 42:582–587.
1983 A Tale of Three Cities: Energetics and Urbanization in Prehispanic Mexico. In *Prehistoric Settlement Patterns,* edited by E. V. Vogt and R. Leventhal, pp. 243–292. University of New Mexico Press, Albuquerque.
Sanders, W. T., and D. Webster
1978 Unilinealism, Multilinealism and the Evolution of Complex Societies. In *Social Archaeology: Beyond Subsistence and Dating,* edited by C. L. Redman et al., pp. 249–302. Academic Press, New York.

Santley, R. S.
1979 Disembedded Capitals Reconstructed. *American Antiquity* 45:132–145.
1984 Book review of *Chalcatzingo: Excavations on the Olmec Frontier. Journal of Anthropological Research* 40(4):603–609.
Satterthwaite, L.
1933 *Piedras Negras Preliminary Papers 2: South Group Ball Court, and Preliminary Notes on the West Group Ball Court.* University of Pennsylvania, Philadelphia.
1944 *Piedras Negras Archaeology: Architecture, Part IV, Ball Courts.* University Museum, University of Pennsylvania.
Scarborough, V. L.
1978 Settlement Compaction among the Late Preclassic Lowland Maya of Northern Belize. Dissertation improvement grant proposal funded by the National Science Foundation. On file at Southern Methodist University, Dallas.
1983a A Preclassic Maya Water System. *American Antiquity* 48(4):720–744.
1983b Raised Field Detection at Cerros, Northern Belize. In *Drained Field Agriculture in Central and South America,* edited by J. P. Darch, pp. 123–136. British Archaeological Reports, International Series 189. Oxford.
1985a Late Preclassic Northern Belize: Context and Interpretation. In *Status, Structure and Stratification,* edited by M. Thompson, M. T. Garcia, and F. J. Kense, pp. 331–344. University of Calgary.
1985b Resourceful Landscaping: A Maya Lesson. *Archaeology* 38 (1):58–59, 72.
In press Courting in the Maya Lowlands: A Study in Prehispanic Ballgame Architecture. In *The Mesoamerican Ballgame,* edited by V. L. Scarborough and D. R. Wilcox. University of Arizona Press, Tucson.
Scarborough, V. L.; B. Mitchum; H. Carr; and D. A. Freidel
1982 Two Preclassic Maya Ballcourts at the Lowland Maya Center of Cerros, Northern Belize. *Journal of Field Archaeology.* 9:21–34.
Scarborough, V. L., and R. A. Robertson
1986 Civic and Residential Settlement at a Late Preclassic Maya Center. *Journal of Field Archaeology* 13:155–175.
Scarborough, V. L., and D. R. Wilcox (editors)

In press *The Mesoamerican Ballgame.* University of Arizona Press, Tucson.

Schele, L., and M. E. Miller
1986 *The Blood of Kings: Dynasty and Ritual in Maya Art.* Kimball Art Museum, Fort Worth.

Schuchert, C.
1935 *Historical Geology of the Antillean-Caribbean Region.* Wiley and Son, New York.

Serpenti, L. M.
1965 *Cultivators of the Swamps: Social Structure and Horticulture in a New Guinea Society.* Royal Van Gorlum, Assen.

Service, E. R.
1971 *Primitive Social Organization,* 2nd Ed. Random House, New York.
1975 *Origins of the State and Civilization: The Process of Cultural Evolution.* Norton, New York.

Shafer, H. J.
1982 Maya Lithic Craft Specialization in Northern Belize. In *Archaeology at Colha, Belize: The 1981 Interim Report,* edited by T. R. Hester, H. J. Shafer, and J. D. Eaton, pp. 31–38. Center for Archaeological Research, University of Texas at San Antonio.

Shafer, H. J., and T. R. Hester
1983 Ancient Maya Chert Workshops in Northern Belize, Central America. *American Antiquity* 48(3):519–543.

Sharer, R.
1974 The Prehistory of the Southeastern Maya Periphery. *Current Anthropology* 15:165–187.
1978 Archeology and History at Quirigua, Guatemala. *Journal of Field Archaeology* 5:51–70.

Sheets, P. D.
1979 Maya Recovery from Volcanic Disaster: Ilopango and Ceren. *Archaeology* 32:32–42.

Shook, E. M., and T. Proskouriakoff
1956 Settlement Patterns in Meso-America and the Sequence in the Guatemalan Highlands. In *Prehistoric Settlement Patterns in the New World,* edited by G. R. Willey. Viking Fund Publication in Anthropology 23:93–100.

Sidrys, R. V.
1976 *Mesoamerica: An Archaeological Analysis of a Low-Energy Civilization.* Ph.D. dissertation, University of California, Los Angeles. University Microfilms, Ann Arbor.

1983 *Archeological Excavations in Northern Belize, Central America.* Institute of Archaeology, Monograph 17. University of California, Los Angeles.

Siemens, A. H.
1976 Karstic Constraints on Prehispanic Land Use and Transportation in the Southern Maya Lowlands. Paper presented at the International Congress of Americanists, Paris.
1978 Karst and the Pre-Hispanic Maya in the Southern Lowlands. In *Pre-Hispanic Maya Agriculture,* edited by P. D. Harrison and B. L. Turner II, pp. 117–144. University of New Mexico Press, Albuquerque.
1982 Prehistoric Agricultural Use of the Wetlands of Northern Belize. In *Maya Subsistence: Studies in Memory of Dennis E. Puleston,* edited by K. V. Flannery, pp. 205–222. Academic Press, New York.
1983a Oriented Raised Fields in Central Veracruz. *American Antiquity* 48 (1):85–102.
1983b Modelling Pre-Hispanic Hydroagriculture on Levee Backslopes in Veracruz, Mexico. In *Drained Field Agriculture in Central and South America,* edited by J. P. Darch, pp. 27–54, British Archeological Reports, International Series 189, Oxford.

Siemens, A. H., and D. E. Puleston
1972 Ridged Fields and Associated Features in Southern Campeche: New Pespectives on the Lowland Maya. *American Antiquity* 37:228–239.

Simmons, C. S.; J. M. Tarano; and J. H. Pinto
1959 *Clasificacion de reconocimento de los suelos de la República de Guatemala.* Ministerio de Agricultura, Instituto Agropecuario Nacional, Servicio Cooperativo Inter-Americano de Agricultura. Guatemala City.

Simmons, E. G.
1957 An Ecological Survey of the Upper Laguna Madre of Texas. *Institute of Marine Science* 4 (2):156–200.

Smith, A. L.
1962 Residential and Associated Structures at Mayapan. *Carnegie Institution,* Publication 619, pp. 165–320.
1972 *Excavations at Altar de Sacrificios: Architecture, Settlement, Burials and Caches.* Papers of the Peabody Museum of Archaeology

and Ethnology, Vol. 62, No. 2. Harvard University, Cambridge.

1982 *Excavations at Seibal: Major Architecture and Caches.* Memoirs of the Peabody Museum of Archaeology and Ethnology, Vol. 15, No. 1. Harvard University, Cambridge.

Smith, C. (editor)
1976 *Regional Analysis* (2 vols.). Academic Press, New York.

Smith, C. T.; W. M. Denevan; and P. Hamilton
1968 Ancient Ridged Fields in the Region of Lake Titicaca. *Geographical Journal* 134:353–367.

Smith, R.
1937 *A Study of Structure A-1 Complex at Uaxactun, Petén, Guatemala.* Carnegie Institution, Publication 456, Contribution 19.

Soils Science Department
1978 *Agronomic-Economic Research on Soils of the Tropics, Annual Report for 1976–1977.* North Carolina State University, Raleigh.

Spooner, B. (editor)
1972 *Population Growth: Anthropological Implications.* M. I. T. Press, Cambridge.

Standley, P. C., and S. J. Record
1936 *The Forests and Flora of British Honduras.* Field Museum of Natural History, Chicago, Publication 350, Botanical Series, Vol. 12.

Steggerda, M.
1941 *Maya Indians of Yucatán.* Carnegie Institution, Publication 531.

Stephens, J. L.
1843 *Incidents of Travel in Yucatán* (2 vols.). Harper, New York. 1963 reprint, Dover.

Stern, T.
1949 *The Rubber-Ball Game of the Americas.* Monographs of the American Ethnological Society, No. 17. Seattle.

Stevens, R. L.
1964 The Soils of Middle America and their Relation to Indian Peoples and Cultures. In *Natural Environment and Early Cultures. Handbook of Middle American Indians,* edited by R. C. West, Vol. 1, pp. 265–315. University of Texas Press, Austin.

Stoltman, J. B.
1978 *Lithic Artifacts from a Complex Society.* Middle American Research Institute, Tulane University, Occasional Paper No. 2.

Stromsvik, G.
1952 *The Ballcourts at Copán with Notes on Courts at La Unión, Quirigua, San Pedro Pinula and Asunción Mita.* Carnegie Institution, Publication 596, Contribution 55.

Stuart, G. E.; J. C. Scheffler; E. B. Kurjack; and J. W. Cottier
1979 *Map of the Ruins of Dzibilchaltún, Yucatán, Mexico.* Middle American Research Institute, Tulane University, Publication 47.

Sweeting, M. M.
1973 *Karst Landforms.* Columbia University Press, New York.

Tamayo, J. L., and R. C. West
1964 The Hydrography of Middle America. In *Natural Environment and Early Cultures. Handbook of Middle American Indians,* edited by R. C. West, Vol. 1, pp. 84–121. University of Texas Press, Austin.

Thomas, P. M.
1974 Prehistoric Settlement at Becán: A Preliminary Report. In *Preliminary Reports on Archaeological Investigations in the Rio Bec Area, Campeche, Mexico.* Middle American Research Institute, Tulane University, Publication 31.

1981 *Prehistoric Maya Settlement Pattern at Becán, Campeche, Mexico.* Middle American Research Institute, Tulane University, Publication 45.

Thompson, J. E. S.
1931 *Archaeological Investigations in the Southern Cayo District, British Honduras.* Field Museum of Natural History, Chicago. Publication 301.

1936 Explorations in Campeche and Quintana Roo and Excavations at San José, British Honduras. *Carnegie Institution of Washington Yearbook* 35:125–128.

1940 *Late Ceramic Horizons at Benque Viejo, British Honduras.* Carnegie Institution, Publication 528, Contribution 35.

1971 Estimates of Maya Populations: Deranging Factors. *American Antiquity* 36:214–216.

1974 "Canals" of the Río Candelaria Basin, Campeche, Mexico. In *Mesoamerican Archaeology: New Approaches,* edited by N. Hammond, pp. 297–302. University of Texas Press, Austin.

1977   A Proposal for Constituting a Maya Sub-group, Cultural and Linguistic, in the Petén and Adjacent Regions. In *Anthropology and History in Yucatán,* edited by G. D. Jones, pp. 3–42. University of Texas Press, Austin.

Tosi, J. A., Jr.
1964   Climatic Control of Terrestrial Ecosystems: A Report on the Holdridge Model. *Economic Geography* 40:173–181, 189–295.

Tourtellot, G.
1970   The Peripheries of Seibal: An Interim Report. In *Monographs and Papers in Maya Archaeology,* edited by W. R. Bullard, pp. 405–420. Papers of the Peabody Museum of Archaeology and Ethnology, Vol. 6l. Harvard University, Cambridge.
1976   Patterns of Domestic Architecture at a Maya Garden City: Seibal. Paper presented at the Meetings of the Society for American Archaeology, St. Louis.

Turner, B. L., II
1974   Prehistoric Intensive Agriculture in the Maya Lowlands. *Science* 185:118–124.
1983   Comparison of Agrotechnologies in the Basin of Mexico and Central Maya Lowlands: Formative to Classic Maya Collapse. In *Highland-Lowland Interaction in Mesoamerica: Interdisciplinary Approaches,* edited by A. G. Miller, pp. 13–48. Dumbarton Oaks, Washington, D. C.

Turner, B. L., II, and P. D. Harrison
1978   Implications from Agriculture for Maya Prehistory. In *Pre-Hispanic Maya Agriculture,* edited by P. D. Harrison and B. L. Turner II, pp. 337–374. University of New Mexico Press, Albuquerque.
1981   Prehistoric Raised-Field Agriculture in the Maya Lowlands. *Science* 213:399–405.

United States Department of Agriculture
1962   *Soils Survey Manual.* Handbook 18. Washington, D.C.
1975   *Soil Taxonomy: A Basic System of Soil Classification for Making and Interpreting Soil Surveys.* Handbook 436. Washington, D. C.

Urrutia, V. M.
1967   Corn Production and Soil Fertility Changes under Shifting Cultivation in Uaxactun, Guatemala. M.A. thesis, University of Florida.

Vlcek, D. T.; S. Garza; and E. B. Kurjack
1978   Contemporary Farming and Ancient Maya Settlement: Some Disconcerting Evidence. In *Pre-Hispanic Maya Agriculture,* edited by P. D. Harrison and B. L. Turner II, pp. 211–224. University of New Mexico, Albuquerque.

Vogt, E. Z.
1961   Some Aspects of Zinacantan Settlement Patterns and Ceremonial Organization. *Estudios de Cultura Maya* l:i31–145.

Voorhies, B.
1982   An Ecological Model of the Early Maya of the Central Lowlands. In *Maya Subsistence: Studies in Memory of Dennis E. Puleston,* edited by K. V. Flannery, pp. 65–98. Academic Press, New York.

Waddell, E.
1972   *The Mound Builders: Agricultural Practices, Environment, and Society in the Central Highlands of New Guinea.* University of Washington Press, Seattle.

Wagner, P. L.
1964   Natural Vegetation of Middle America. In *Natural Environment and Early Cultures. Handbook of Middle American Indians,* edited by R. C. West, Vol. 1, pp. 216–265. University of Texas Press, Austin.

Wauchope, R.
1938   *Modern Maya Houses.* Carnegie Institution, Publication 502.

Webster, D.
1976   *Defensive Earthworks at Becán, Campeche, Mexico: Implications for Maya Warfare.* Middle American Research Institute, Tulane University, Publication 41.
1977   Warfare and the Evolution of Maya Civilization. In *The Origins of Maya Civilization,* edited by R. E. W. Adams, pp. 335–372. University of New Mexico Press, Albuquerque.
1985   Surplus, Labor, and Stress in Late Classic Maya Society. *Journal of Anthropological Research* 41:375–399.

Webster, D. (editor)
1988   *Household of the Bacabs, Copán: A Study of the Iconography, Epigraphy, and Social Context of a Maya Elite Structure.* Dumbarton Oaks, Washington.

West, R. C.
> 1964 Surface Configuration and Associated Geology of Middle America. In *Natural Environment and Early Cultures. Handbook of Middle American Indians,* edited by R. C. West, Vol. 1, pp. 33–83. University of Texas Press, Austin.

Wilk, R. R.
> 1975a Operation 303B. In *Archeology in Northern Belize: 1974–75 Interim Report of the British Museum-Cambridge University Corozal Project,* edited by N. Hammond, pp. 75–81. Centre of Latin American Studies, Cambridge.
> 1975b Superficial Examination of Structure 100, Colha. In *Archaeology in Northern Belize: 1974–75 Interim Report of the British Museum Cambridge University Corozal Project,* edited by N. Hammond, pp. 152–173. Centre of Latin American Studies, Cambridge.
> 1985 Dry Season Agriculture among the Kekchi Maya and its Implications for Prehistory. In *Prehistoric Lowland Maya Environment and Subsistence Economy,* edited by M. Pohl, pp. 47–58. Papers of the Peabody Museum of Archaeology and Ethnology, Vol. 77. Harvard University, Cambridge.

Wilk, R., and H. Wilhite
> 1982 Patterns of Household and Settlement Change at Cuello. Ms. on file, Department of Sociology and Anthropology, University of Texas at El Paso.

Wilken, G. C.
> 1969 Drained-Field Agriculture: An Intensive Farming System in Tlaxcala, Mexico. *Geographical Review* 59:215–241.
> 1972 Microclimate Management by Traditional Farmers. *Geographical Review* 62:544–560.
> 1976 Management of Productive Space in Traditional Farming. Actes du XLII Congres International des Americanistes, Paris.
> 1987 *Good Farmers.* University of California Press, London.

Willey, G. R.
> 1956 Problems Concerning Prehistoric Settlement Patterns in the Maya Lowlands. In *Prehistoric Settlement Patterns in the New World,* edited by G. R. Willey. Viking

Fund Publication in Anthropology 23: 107–114. New York.
> 1973 *The Altar de Sacrificios Excavations: General Summary and Conclusions.* Papers of the Peabody Museum of Archaeology and Ethnology, Vol. 64, No. 3. Harvard University, Cambridge.
> 1977 The Rise of Classic Maya Civilization: A Pasión Perspective. In *The Origins of Maya Civilization,* edited by R. E. W. Adams, pp. 133–158, University of New Mexico Press, Albuquerque.
> 1979 The Concept of the "Disembedded Capital" in Comparative Perspective. *Journal of Anthropological Research* 35:123–137.

Willey, G. R., and W. R. Bullard, Jr.
> 1965 Prehistoric Settlement Patterns in the Maya Lowlands. In *Handbook of Middle American Indians,* edited by R. Wauchope and G. R. Willey, Vol. 2, pp. 360–377. University of Texas Press, Austin.

Willey, R. G.; W. R. Bullard; J. B. Glass; and J. C. Gifford
> 1965 *Prehistoric Maya Settlement in the Belize Valley.* Papers of the Peabody Museum of Archaeology and Ethnology, Vol. 54. Harvard University, Cambridge.

Willey, G. R., and R. M. Leventhal
> 1979 Prehistoric Settlement at Copán. In *Maya Archaeology and Ethnohistory,* edited by N. Hammond and G. R. Willey, pp. 75–103. University of Texas Press, Austin.

Willey, G. R., and D. B. Shimkin
> 1973 The Maya Collapse: A Summary View. *The Classic Maya Collapse,* edited by T. P. Culbert, pp. 475–501. University of New Mexico Press, Albuquerque.

Willey, G. R., and A. L. Smith
> 1969 *The Ruins of Altar de Sacrificios, Department of Petén, Guatemala: An Introduction.* Papers of the Peabody Museum of Archaeology and Ethnology, Vol. 62, No. 1. Harvard University, Cambridge.

Willey, G. R.; A. L. Smith; G. Tourtellot III; and I. Graham
> 1975 *Excavations at Seibal.* Memoirs of the Peabody Museum of Archaeology and Ethnology, Vol. 14, No. 1. Harvard University, Cambridge.

Winters, H. D.
    1969   *The Riverton Culture.* Illinois Archaeological Survey, Monograph 1. Springfield.
Wiseman, F. M.
    1978   Agricultural and Historic Ecology of the Maya Lowlands. In *Pre-Hispanic Maya Agriculture,* edited by P. D. Harrison and B. L. Turner II, pp. 63–116. University of New Mexico Press, Albuquerque.
Wolf, E.
    1966   *Peasants.* Prentice-Hall, Englewood Cliffs.
Woodbury, R. B., and J. A. Neely
    1972   Water Control Systems of the Tehuacán Valley. In *The Prehistory of the Tehuacán Valley,* edited by F. Johnson, Vol. 4, pp. 81–153. University of Texas Press, Austin.
Wright, A. C. S.; D. H. Romney; R. H. Arbuckle; and V. E. Vial
    1959   *Land in British Honduras: Report of the British Honduras Land Use Survey Team.* Her Majesty's Stationery Office, London.
Wyshak, L. W.; R. Berger; J. A. Graham; and R. F. Heizer
    1971   Possible Ball Court at La Venta, Mexico. *Nature* 232:650–651.

INDEX

Note: Page numbers in bold indicate a figure; relevant text may also be on these same pages.

A

Abandonment, and sea level change, 171
Agriculture
  intensive, Late Preclassic Period, 187–88, 191–92, 194
  raised-field, 4, **17**, 18, 21, 128–29, 131, 162
    Albion Island, 20–21
    association with canals, 128–29, **138**, **139**
    construction, 149, 151, 154–55
    difficulty in finding, 168
    excavation, **148**, 149–50
    fertilization, 38, 155
    habitation loci on, 38–39
    location, 40
    managerial residences for, 106
    pot irrigation, 38
    Pulltrouser Swamp, 21
    sedimentation of canals from, 144
  surplus, 192
Aguada 1, 90, 168
Aguada 2, 29, **30**, 32
Aguada 3, 163
Albion Island, 20–21
Altar de Sacrificios, 176, 179
Altun Ha, 185, 189
Anchor weight, limestone, 102
Architecture. *See* Ball court; Mound; Structure
Aventura, 160, 184, 189

B

Ball court, 124–25
  spatial relationships, 34, **35**
  Structure 50, **113**, **115–16**, **118**, **120**, **122–25**, 166
    apron molding, 114
    bench, 114, 117–18
    construction sequence, 119, 121–23
    intrusive feature, 119, 121
    marker, 119
    plan, 116
    plaster
      floor, 114, 118, 123
      painted and molded, 114
    platform, 117
    playing alley, 114, 118, 119
    posthole, stone-lined, 123
    staircase, 117, 121, **122**
    wall
      construction pen, 122
      masonry, 117
      playing, 114, 117
      terrace, 117
  Structure 61, **108–9**, **111**, 124, 166
    bench, 108–9, 110, 112
      posthole, 110
      ritual defacement of, 112
    construction sequence, 110, 112, 114
    end zone, 109, 110
    marker, stone, 110
    pit, 110
    plaster
      floor, 107, 109, 110
      painted, 109
    playing alley, 107, **109**, 110, 112
    stairway, 110
    wall
      construction pen, 112, 114
      masonry, 108
      playing, 109–10
Ball game, significance of, 124
Barton Ramie, 177, 179
Becán, 176–77, 179
Benque Viejo, 184
Bomba North, 185
Burials and human bone, 49–50, 98, 102
  Late Postclassic Period, 68
  Late Preclassic Period, 49

C

Caledonia, 184, 189
Canal
  associated fields and features, excavation of, **148–49**, **150**–51
  basin, **146–48**, 149–50, **152**
    buttress stones, **147**, 149
    causeway (*sacbe*), **150**, 151
    soil analysis, 213
  function, 37–38, 151, 152
  lateral, 128, **144**, **145**, 147
    excavation, 144–45
    sedimentation, 154